I0138115

England's Jews

THE MIDDLE AGES SERIES

Ruth Mazo Karras, Series Editor
Edward Peters, Founding Editor

A complete list of books in the series is available from the publisher.

England's Jews

Finance, Violence, and the Crown in the Thirteenth Century

John Tolan

PENN

UNIVERSITY OF PENNSYLVANIA PRESS

PHILADELPHIA

Copyright © 2023 University of Pennsylvania Press

All rights reserved. Except for brief quotations used for
purposes of review or scholarly citation, none of this book may
be reproduced in any form by any means without written
permission from the publisher.

Published by
University of Pennsylvania Press
Philadelphia, Pennsylvania 19104-4112
www.upenn.edu/pennpress

Printed in the United States of America on acid-free paper
10 9 8 7 6 5 4 3 2 1

Hardcover ISBN: 978-1-5128-2389-9
eBook ISBN: 978-1-5128-2400-1

A catalogue record for this book is available from the
Library of Congress.

CONTENTS

Acknowledgments   vii

Introduction   1

Chapter 1. Isaac of Norwich and the Rebuilding of the
King's Jewry (1217–1222)   18

Chapter 2. Of Badges and Wet-Nurses: English Bishops Attempt to
Limit Contact Between Jews and Christians   40

Chapter 3. Simon de Montfort and the King's Jews   64

Chapter 4. Oxford Jews and Christian Hebraism   83

Chapter 5. From the Statutes of the Jewry to Little Hugh of
Lincoln (1253–1255)   116

Chapter 6. Baronial Revolts and Anti-Jewish Violence (1258–1267)   139

Chapter 7. A Curse upon Edom   160

Conclusion   187

Notes   193

Bibliography   225

Index   245

ACKNOWLEDGMENTS

This book grows out of more than three decades of research in the relations between Jews, Christians, and Muslims in the Middle Ages. In particular, an advanced grant from the European Research Council financed from 2010 to 2015 my research project RELMIN "The Legal Status of Religious Minorities in the Euro-Mediterranean World (5th–15th centuries)" (Under the European Union's Seventh Framework Progamme (FP7/2007–2013)/ERC grant agreement n°249416). The project examined the legal status of religious minorities through a comparative study of legal texts written in Latin, Hebrew, Arabic, Greek, and various European vernaculars. In the course of this project, I became particularly interested in the abundant documentation concerning Jews in England in the thirteenth century. A fellowship from the Herbert Katz Center for Advanced Judaic Studies at the University of Pennsylvania in 2013, on the annual theme "Institutionalization, Innovation, and Conflict in 13th-Century Judaism: A Comparative View," allowed me to study the topic in greater detail and launched me on the current project. My special thanks to the fellows and director of the Katz Center for their feedback at the beginning stages of this work, in particular Piero Capelli, Rita Copeland, Kati Inhat, Ephraim Kanarfogel, Sarah Pearce, Marina Rustow, Uri Shachar, and Rebecca Winer.

A number of invitations to discuss my work have provided invaluable occasions to get help and feedback from colleagues. I have presented parts of this research to conferences and seminars at the Institute of Advanced Studies, Jerusalem; Cambridge University; the Arye Maimon-Institut für Geschichte der Juden, Universität Trier (where I had the pleasure of being received by the late Alfred Haverkamp, scion of the study of European Jewry in the Middle Ages); the Medieval Seminar of the University of St. Andrews; the Hochschule für Jüdische Studien, Universität Heidelberg; Nouvelle Gallia Judaica, Montpelier; the Chicago Medieval Studies Workshop; the Institut de Recerca en Identitats i Societats, Universitat de Lleida; Ben-Gurion University of the Negev; University of Leeds; Université de Strasbourg; University of Pennsylvania; the Centro

Inderdisciplinar de História, Culturas e Sociedades da Universidade de Évora; the Château de la Bretesche, Missillac; the Österreichische Akademie der Wissenschaften; and the Center for Medieval Studies at Exeter University. My thanks to those who participated in these events and whose questions and reactions were extremely helpful, in particular to those who invited me: Elisheva Baumgarten, Judah Galinsky, Anna Abulafia, Nora Berend, Robert Bartlett, Johannes Heil, Christoph Cluse, Danièle Iancu, David Nirenberg, Flocel Sabaté, Chaim Hames, Axel Müller, Lionel Obadia, Anne-Laure Zwilling, Talya Fishman, Clara Almagro, Jenn Jahner, Warren Brown, Claudia Rapp, and Helen Birkett.

I conducted research for this project in libraries in France and the UK. Special thanks to the staff of the Bibliothèque Jacques Berque, the Bibliothèque universitaire de l'Université de Nantes, the Bibliothèque Nationale de France, the British Library, and the Bodleian Library. In Oxford, my discussions with Paul Brand and Guy Stroumsa helped me greatly in formulating my project. Thanks to the RELMIN project and the Institut du Pluralisme Religieux et de l'Athéisme, which financed these research trips. In 2016, I benefitted from a fellowship at the Kulturwissenschaftliche Kolleg in Konstanz, as part of a program devoted to religious minorities. Special thanks to Dorothea Weltecke for the invitation, and to my fellow residents, in particular Clara Almagro, Judith Beyer, Stefanie Diekmann, Ana Echevarria, Jean-Paul Ghobrial, Benjamin Scheller, Michelle Szkilnik, and Jack Tannous.

Thanks to Loren Fogle and Philippa Hoskin for sharing their work with me. Thanks to Heather Blurton and Amy Remensnyder for valuable feedback. Thanks to David MacMillan for bringing to my attention the folk song on "Little Sir Hugh." Special thanks to those who read a draft of my book and who offered valuable corrections and advice: R. I. Moore, Jen Jahner, David Carpenter, Emily Rose, and Miri Rubin. Thanks also to Jerry Singerman, Ruth Karras, and Jenny Tan for their energy and enthusiasm in making this publication possible, and to the two anonymous readers for University of Pennsylvania Press.

INTRODUCTION

In 2004, workers in Norwich made a macabre discovery: seventeen skeletons in a well shaft. Forensic analysis showed that the bodies, six adults and eleven children aged between two and fifteen, dated from the twelfth or thirteenth century. The adults had been thrown down head first, and the children after them. It is unclear whether they were dead or alive when they were tossed into the well. DNA sequencing suggested that a number of the persons were closely related to each other, and that some elements in their DNA were close to those of Ashkenazi Jews. While there is still uncertainty as to the identity of these people and the circumstances of their death, it seems that these were local Norwich Jews whose bodies were summarily disposed of by their Christian persecutors. The team of forensic pathologists and archaeologists who worked on the case and an episode devoted to it on BBC's *History Cold Case* brought it to the awareness of a broad public in Norwich and throughout the United Kingdom.[1]

Norwich citizens interviewed in the BBC program expressed shock that their city had been the theatre of anti-Jewish violence. Few were aware of the presence of Jews in thirteenth-century Norwich and the key role they played in the economy of what was then England's second largest city, a thriving port and trading center. Nor were they aware of the sporadic hostility and violence Norwich Jews faced. It is in Norwich, in 1144, that Jews were first accused of murdering a Christian child, a charge subsequently used to justify extortion and violence against Jews in England and throughout Europe. I will often evoke Norwich in the pages of this book, both as the site of a flourishing Jewish community and as a locus of anti-Jewish violence. Jews, though numerically a small part of the population, played a big role in the history of twelfth- and thirteenth-century Norwich.[2] Yet visitors to the local historical museum do not find a single mention of their presence.[3]

Whatever the truth may be behind the Norwich skeletons, their discovery and subsequent publicity shed light on the extent to which the English (like many others) are blind to their own history. Over the past several decades, historians of England and other European colonial powers have emphasized the extent to which the money and labor of slaves and colonial subjects helped drive economic growth and finance the building of key European institutions. Imperial capitals like eighteenth- to nineteenth-century London or Paris were built on the profits of empire: their universities formed colonial elites and their museums showcased colonial booty. Yet nationalist historiographies of the nineteenth and early twentieth centuries rarely acknowledged these facts, preferring narratives celebrating the achievements of the nation and downplaying the importance of slavery and imperialism. Historians who did take an interest in slavery often denounced it as an aberration and celebrated the enlightened Englishmen who fought to abolish it, minimizing the role of slaves and former slaves in the fight against slavery.

An analogous case could be made for Jews in medieval England. They were key actors in financing the crown and certain monasteries; their monies were crucial to the emergence of the university of Oxford; they participated in the transfer of land from lower gentry to the greater barons and to monasteries; and, as we will see, they played a largely unwitting role in provoking the crisis that led to baronial rebellion. This role, largely downplayed by previous generations of historians, is now widely accepted and documented by historians of twelfth- and thirteenth-century England. Various historians have written books about Jews in medieval England, often with an eye on explaining why King Edward I expelled them in 1290. This has led to a tendency to see over two centuries of English Jewish history as a prelude to expulsion. While I too will offer (in Chapter 7) my take on why Edward decided on expulsion, I have chosen to focus principally on the reign of Henry III, which paradoxically represents both the high-water mark in Jewish integration into medieval English society and the beginning of a precipitous decline.

Beyond Norwich, Jews were important actors in the financial, institutional, and political history of England in the thirteenth century. There were few if any Jews in England during the Anglo-Saxon period. Jews from Rouen arrived in the aftermath of the 1066 Norman conquest, establishing themselves in London. From the very beginning, Jews were closely associated with the crown, dependent on the king's protection and favor. They played a key role in financing trade between England and the continent, and they generated taxable income. By the reign of King Stephen (1135–1154), Jews had settled in towns throughout the kingdom. They became important agents, both in collaboration and in rivalry with monasteries, in providing finance for business endeavors and building projects. Whereas prior to Stephen's reign moneylending had been in the hands of monasteries and of Anglo-Saxon merchants and bankers in the principal towns, in the second half of the twelfth century Stephen and his successors Henry II and Richard I took measures favoring the Jews as their preferred moneylenders and facilitated their settlement in towns across England.[4]

The activity of Jewish financiers grew during the twelfth and thirteenth centuries as the English economy expanded. Demographically, Jews were few in number. In Norwich around 1200, there were probably about 200 Jews, 2 percent of a total population of about 10,000.[5] In 1240, there were perhaps 4,000–5,000 Jews in England, out of total population of about 5 million, roughly 0.1 percent of the population of the kingdom. Yet they had considerable assets obtained through lending, assets that consisted of coin, of items left as security, and of mortgaged land. The crown obtained significant revenue through fees on loans and through periodic taxes or "tallages."[6] To this could be added considerable sums such as fines for offenses (real or imaginary) committed against the king or other Christians, or "relief," an inheritance tax: on the death of a Jew, his heirs had to pay one-third of his wealth in order to inherit the remaining two-thirds. No wonder that historian Cecil Roth declared that England's Jews were "the royal milch cow."[7]

Heavy as these financial burdens were to England's Jews, they did not prevent a number of moneylenders from accumulating considerable wealth. Yet in the 1240s, this situation began to change. King Henry III, deep in debt and mired in failed military adventures, sought to raise money wherever he could, and in particular from his Jews who, unlike his other lay and clerical subjects, did not need to consent to new taxes. Between 1240 and 1258, about half of English Jews' wealth was transferred into the royal coffers via "tallages," a term designating a variety of taxes levied by the crown, but in this case referring to exceptional taxes that the king levied on Jews.[8] In this period, revenue from English Jews allowed him to increase overall royal revenue by about one-third.[9] Henry's excessive taxation was starving the "royal milch cow," which became increasingly unable to provide financial services or pay new taxes to the crown. At the end of Henry's reign and during the reign of his son and successor, Edward I, the crown had to turn to foreign (mostly Italian) moneylenders. England's Jews were dispensable, it seems, for Edward expelled them from the kingdom in 1290.

A toxic mix of financial debt, religious hostility, and wild conspiracy theories fueled resentment, persecution, and violence against Jews, in England as elsewhere in Europe. Royal and ecclesiastical legislation played a deeply ambiguous role in this. England's Jews were "the king's Jews" and as such were in theory protected by the king and subject solely to royal justice, not to baronial or ecclesiastical courts. Yet both royal and ecclesiastical legislators took measures to keep

Jews and Christians apart to avoid close contact and prohibit sexual relations between them. The fourth Lateran council in 1215 declared that Jews should wear distinctive clothing, so that they could be recognized and Christians could shun sexual relations with them. In 1218, England became the first European kingdom to turn that measure into law: a royal mandate ordered Jews to wear a distinctive badge on their clothing. While the king frequently instructed his sheriffs and other royal officials to protect Jews and to punish their aggressors, on occasion he himself lent credence to the most vicious anti-Jewish legends: in Lincoln in 1255, he became the first European monarch to convict Jews of ritually murdering a Christian child.

King Henry, his barons, and his Jews had close links to France and for the most part spoke better French than English. Henry often forged his policies in emulation of or in opposition to those of King Louis IX of France (1226–1270, the future Saint Louis). Indeed, the fates of the two kingdoms had been inextricably linked since 1066, when William the Conqueror, Duke of Normandy and vassal of the king of France, conquered England. Many of William's vassals subsequently held lands on both sides of the English Channel. William's great-grandson, Henry II (1154–1189), built up what historians have referred to as an "Angevin Empire." Henry II inherited England and Normandy through his mother, Matilda, and from his father, Geoffrey V Plantagenet, received the counties of Anjou, Touraine, and Maine. In 1152, he married Eleanor, Duchess of Aquitaine: the couple dominated a huge swath of territory stretching from the Pyrenees to the Scottish highlands, dwarfing the modest domains controlled by the French kings, largely confined to the Île de France.

Yet the French kings were at least in theory the suzerains of the continental part of these territories, and they fought to maintain and expand their privileges, none more ferociously or successfully than Philip II Augustus (1180–1223). In 1182, Philip became the first European king to expel the Jews from his realm (he readmitted them in 1198). Philip struggled, politically and militarily, against Henry II and his sons, Richard I "the Lionheart" (1189–1199) and John (1199–1216), finally conquering Normandy in 1204. John forged an alliance of Philip's enemies in an attempt to reconquer Normandy but suffered defeat in Anjou at the hands of Philip's son, Prince Louis (the future King Louis VIII, 1223–1226), and Philip's army then routed John's allies at the Battle of Bouvines in 1214. John's humiliating and expensive defeat dashed any hopes of the reconquest of Normandy and resulted in the loss of most of Anjou. It was in the wake of this defeat that a number of John's English barons rebelled against their king and called on Prince Louis, to whom they promised the English throne. During his struggle against the rebels, John contracted dysentery, which proved fatal: he died on 19 October 1216, leaving his nine-year-old son Henry III as heir. The royalist forces scored two key victories in 1217; the rebels surrendered and Louis returned to France.

During Henry's minority a regency council ruled the kingdom in his name. In January 1227, at the age of nineteen, he assumed control over his government. The previous year, his erstwhile rival Louis VIII had died of dysentery at the age of thirty-nine, leaving as heir his twelve-year-old son, Louis IX. The occasion was perfect for Henry to encourage the rebels who contested the rule of the boy king and the Queen mother and regent, Blanche of Castile. Henry saw an opportunity to strengthen his hand in Aquitaine and Poitou and to perhaps even reconquer Anjou and Normandy. Yet the result was the first of two key defeats against his younger rival, in 1230 and 1242, interspersed with truces and periods of rapprochement. The rapprochement was effected in large part by their queens, the sisters Marguerite of Provence (who married Louis in 1234) and Eleanor of Provence (who married Henry in 1236), daughters of Count Ramon Berenguer IV of Provence and Beatrice of Savoy. It is to Louis and Marguerite that Henry and Eleanor would turn in the 1260s, when they faced rebellion from English barons (as we will see in Chapter 6).

Louis IX was, in most respects, a far more successful king than Henry III. Temperamentally very different from his grandfather Philip II, in his own way he strengthened the monarchy, affirming royal power over justice and administration. As historian Jacques Le Goff wrote, with Louis "The state advances masked, under the mask of sanctity."[10] His biographer Jean de Joinville depicts him sitting under an oak tree dispensing justice to his subjects, listening to all, rich and poor.[11] His ostentatious piety, his patronage of monastic orders and in particular of the mendicants, Dominicans and Franciscans, lent an aura of sanctity to his royal authority. His two crusades, to Egypt in 1248 and to Tunis 1270, were military disasters, the first leading to his captivity and the second to his death, yet they only reinforced his reputation. He brought back with him from his first crusade Muslim converts to Christianity, whom he settled throughout France, providing them with regular stipends from the royal coffers.[12]

A telling aspect of his sanctity, for some of his contemporaries, was his hatred of Jews. Chronicler Guillaume de Chartres wrote: "As for the Jews, hateful to God and to men, he [Louis] felt such abomination for them that he could scarcely look at them."[13] Joinville says that Louis had told him of a "great disputation of clergy and Jews in the monastery of Cluny." A knight asked an eminent Jewish rabbi if he believed that the Virgin Mary was the mother of God; the rabbi replied that he did not. The knight said that the rabbi was a fool to come to her house to dishonor her; he then beat the rabbi senseless. When the abbot reproached him for his "foolish" behavior, the knight retorted that the abbot was more foolish still in letting Jews question the Christian faith in the presence of lay believers, whose faith might be weakened by hearing their blasphemy. Louis praises the knight's actions, and says that while a cleric may patiently debate with Jews in order to bring them to the true faith, "a layman, if he hears the Christian law defamed, should undertake its defense with the sword alone, and he should run it straight through the belly as far in as it will go!"[14] Both Jean de Joinville and Guillaume de Chartres were writing after Louis's death, when he was remembered as a saintly king. For both of them, hatred of Jews was an integral element of his piety, and part of his concern for justice involved protecting his subjects from being exploited, insulted, or injured by Jews.

Joinville makes clear that any disputation with Jews had to be conducted in very limited and controlled circumstances. In Paris in the 1240s, as we shall see, at the request of Pope Gregory IX, Louis put the Talmud on trial, and ultimately had it burned on account of its "blasphemies" against Christ and the Virgin. Throughout his reign, Louis took measures to restrict Jewish lending activities and to reduce royal involvement in them, in stark contrast to Henry's fiscal exploitation of Jewish lending. For English Jews, even at the worst moments of exploitation and persecution in the 1250s and 1260s, Louis IX's France would scarcely appear as a palatable alternative.

We begin this story in 1217, with the victory of the English crown's forces against the rebellious barons and the reaffirmation of royal power. In Chapter 1, we follow the life and career of one prominent and particularly well-documented man, Isaac of Norwich. Isaac was probably a teenager when, in 1189 and 1190, a wave of anti-Jewish violence swept across England, as Christians murdered Jews in London, York, and other towns, including Norwich, where Isaac and his family took refuge in the royal castle. Isaac went on to become one of the richest and most successful moneylenders in England. In 1210, King John imposed a heavy tallage of £40,000 on England's Jews, and, when payment was not forthcoming, imprisoned a number of prominent Jews, including Isaac, who spent the next seven years in captivity. In 1217, the council ruling in the name of the boy king reasserted control over the kingdom and freed Isaac and other Jews, issuing orders to royal officials to assure their protection and to allow them to resume business. Fiscal and judicial documents show Isaac's considerable lending activity over the following years. He developed close and friendly working relations with royal officials, particularly Peter des Roches, bishop of Winchester and close advisor to the king. He also paid large amounts into the royal coffers.

English bishops, abbots, and other church officials often worked closely with Jews, from whom they borrowed considerable sums of money. They also fretted about overly friendly relations between their Christian flock and Jews. Chapter 2 focuses on Stephen Langton, Archbishop of Canterbury (1207–1228) and the council of English bishops over which he presided in Oxford in 1222. Langton had taught theology in Paris and had written about the theological relationship between Judaism and Christianity and the legal and practical consequences concerning the place of Jews in Christian society. We have seen that a royal mandate of 1218 ordered Jews to wear a distinctive badge on their clothing. Yet the order was not enforced: indeed, fiscal records from 1221 and 1222 show that many Jews paid fees to the crown in order to be exempt from wearing badges. Langton and the assembled bishops fulminated against such laxness and reissued conciliar canons obliging Jews to wear their badges and prohibiting them from employing Christian servants in their homes. In order to enforce these prohibitions, they ordered that no Christian should sell food or other goods to Jews until they complied with these restrictions; Jews complained directly to the king, who countermanded the bishops' orders. Henry would brook no infringement on his exclusive dominion over "his" Jews.

Yet the situation changed after his failed military expedition to France in 1230, as we will see in Chapter 3. In 1231, a young knight named Simon de Montfort arrived from France to make homage to Henry and claim his inheritance as lord of Leicester; one of his first acts upon arrival was to expel the Jews from that town. He claimed the expulsion as motivated by spiritual concerns and as a concession to the town's burghers, the Jews' competitors in business. This expulsion is unprecedented, even more so since Simon, a vassal of the king who had only recently received his inheritance, does not mention the king in his edict: there is no evidence that Simon ever sought out Henry's approval for this measure. Nor is there any direct evidence concerning Henry's reaction to this vassal's singular act. Yet in the following year, the king established in London a house for converts from Judaism, an establishment where converts were modestly housed and fed. In 1233, Henry issued a Statute of the Jews, in which he emphatically reaffirmed the royal monopoly of control over "his" Jews.

Robert Grosseteste (c.1175–1253), friend, correspondent and advisor to Simon de Montfort, was chancellor of Oxford and subsequently bishop of Lincoln. As a theologian, university administrator and bishop, Grosseteste reflected on the role of Jews in Christian society. In Chapter 4, we will look at the place of Jews and Judaism in Oxford, before and during Grosseteste's tenure as chancellor and bishop. Oxford was home to a thriving Jewish community whose members were closely involved in the birth and development of the university, as they provided loans to students and teachers, rented out housing to them, and helped finance the acquisition of lands by scholarly patrons such as Walter de Merton, close advisor to King Henry and founder of Merton College. At the same time, Oxford dons wrote theological works concerning the relations between Judaism and Christianity. Grosseteste was a polymath: scientist, philosopher, and theologian. He learned Hebrew late in his life and translated and wrote several works on Jews and Judaism. In these works, he concluded that Jewish sages had known that Christ was their Messiah but kept the knowledge hidden out of spite.

Grosseteste fiercely defended the prerogatives of the English Church and its bishops, a defense that led him at times to frontal opposition to the archbishop of Canterbury, the pope, and King Henry. As we will see in Chapter 5, he was the spokesman for the English bishops who in 1253 submitted a list of grievances to the king, complaining of his interference in church governance and of his excessive taxation of the Church. Henry sought the bishops' approval for a new crusading tax on church revenues, and in order to mollify them, it seems, issued a new statute on the Jewry, in which he granted major concessions to the Church: Jews were to wear the badge and were forbidden to have Christian servants in their homes; they were to pay tithes to the Church. Two years later, in Lincoln, a young boy named Hugh was found dead. Jews were accused of having murdered Hugh in a ritual reenactment of Christ's passion. Henry's involvement in this trial, and his precipitous embrace of the prosecution, was at odds with his previous self-interested protection of the rights of "his" Jews; this was not to bode well for the future of England's Jewish community.

In the following decade, as we will see in Chapter 6, England foundered into civil war, and Jews became victims of renewed violence. Rebellious barons sought to attack royal power and privilege, and the king's Jews made an easy and tempting target. All the more so as many of the rebels were in debt to Jews, and some of them had lost their lands through this debt: not to the Jews themselves, but to monastic institutions and to a clique of nobles that enjoyed the king's favor. The rebels, led by Simon de Montfort, attacked Jews across England, destroying the documentation of their own debt, pillaging and killing. In London in April 1264, rebels massacred hundreds of Jews, as others managed to take refuge in the Tower of London. Simon forgave debts of his followers to Jews. Royal forces routed the rebels and killed Simon at the battle of Evesham in 1265, but it took two more years to quell the revolt.

The respite that followed the barons' revolt was short-lived for English Jews, as we will see in Chapter 7. Henry issued new mandates ordering his officials to protect his Jews and to allow them to pursue their debtors based on whatever documentation they were able to provide, in cases where the official documents had been lost or destroyed. London Jews moved out of the Tower of London and were able to take possession of their former homes, or what was left of them. Yet Edward's plan for a crusade led to fresh taxes on England's subjects, including its Jews, who had reason to fear fresh violence against them. Henry imposed new restrictions on Jews' financial activities in 1269 and 1271, abolishing the practice of perpetual fee debts and prohibiting Jews from renting land or housing to Christians. Henry died in 1272, and his son, Edward I, in 1275 prohibited Jews from lending money at interest. Fifteen years later, in 1290, Edward pronounced their expulsion, in exchange for a new major tax. As Robert Stacey has remarked, "The willingness of Christian taxpayers of England in 1290 to pay the king a tax of £116 000 to secure the expulsion of 2000 Jews from England cannot be explained on strictly economic grounds."[15] I will try to elucidate both the economic grounds of persecution and expulsion of English Jews as well as other ideas and sensibilities that contributed to these policies.

This book seeks both to highlight the important roles Jews played in thirteenth-century English society and to explain how and why they faced increasing persecution and ultimately expulsion. It is not a comprehensive survey or internal history of Jewish lived experiences, but rather an account of the role that Jews played in medieval English society, and particularly their relations with the crown. We will see that large sections of English society participated in acts of violence against Jews, but that the brunt of the killing was conducted by armed soldiers (crusaders in 1118–1190, rebel knights in 1262–1267) or by agents of royal authority (in the executions ordered in the murder trial of Little Hugh of Lincoln in 1255, or in various trials for coin clipping). We will also see that Christians of all social levels took risks to succor Jews: in the midst of the worst violence, Jews found refuge in the houses of their Christian neighbors, in churches and episcopal palaces, and in royal castles. William Jordan has looked at how Christian and Jewish butchers in Béziers worked together, notably allowing Christians to sell excess meat from Jewish butchers. Innocent III had railed against such practices, and various measures taken by church and secular officials attempted to put an end to them were largely ineffectual. Jordan concludes:

> despite misgivings about butchers as an occupational group and Jews as religious antagonists, the Church was as yet unable to impose the deadening hand of medieval anti-Semitism on mutually beneficial community activity particularly where it was fostered or at least tolerated

by a powerful local boss. Only with the support of kings and princes did the ecclesiastical prohibitions gather force and, by constant repetition, spur on the development of popular anti-Semitism as well. At least, the case of Béziers suggests that this aspect of medieval religious hatred like so many others was an elitist imposition on popular culture.[16]

This "elitist" imposition was the work of popes, bishops, and other churchmen who sought to restrict contact between Jews and Christians and to convince or cajole secular rulers to help them impose these restrictions. In England, from the twelfth century to just before the 1290 expulsion, ecclesiastical legislation attempted to limit or prohibit Jews and Christians from working together, living together, sharing meals or festivities, or having sexual relations.

This story is moving and compelling because it seems to offer a mirror to concerns of our own: the demonization of minority groups in society, the manipulation of religious or ethnic hostilities by corrupt and cynical leaders. Today, too, we debate about whether such prejudice has roots in popular culture or whether, on the contrary, it is imposed by "elites." Such concerns probably explain part of why I felt compelled to write this book and no doubt provide motivation for many of its readers. Yet this also is a reason to tread cautiously, to avoid the temptation to make quick and easy links between past and present.

In many ways, the dynamic described in the following pages corresponds to what R. I. Moore, writing about twelfth-century Europe, called the formation of a persecuting society.[17] Moore describes how, during the eleventh and twelfth centuries, a clerical elite, trained in schools in Bologna, Paris, and elsewhere, asserted its control over the Church and society, restructuring church government (in what has been called the "Gregorian reform" movement), reforming monastic life (in the Cluniac and Cistercian reform movements, and subsequently by the mendicant orders in the thirteenth century), reinvigorating the study of law, launching crusades, and manning the burgeoning bureaucracies in the entourage of popes, bishops, kings, and princes. Simultaneous to these developments (and integral to them, Moore argues) is the definition of a strict orthodoxy and orthopraxy and the social and legal marginalization of those who do not adhere to that orthodoxy: Jews, Muslims, heretics, lepers, homosexuals, prostitutes. As Moore summarizes: "It is the argument of this book that however that tremendous extension of the power and influence of the literate is described, the development of persecution in all its forms was part of it, and therefore inseparable from the great and positive achievements with which it is associated."[18] Members of this educated clerical elite penned stories of Jewish perfidy, painting Jews as tricksters and sorcerers, allies of Satan, implacable enemies of Jesus, Mary, and of Christians. While Jews were a tiny part of the population of England or other European kingdoms, they were also among the most educated men and women. As one of Peter Abelard's pupils noted in the twelfth century: "If the Christians educate their sons, they do so not for God, but for gain, in order that the one brother, if he be a clerk, may help his father and his mother and his other brothers . . . But the Jews, out of zeal for God and love of the law, put as many sons as they have to letters, that each may understand God's law . . . A Jew, however poor, if he had ten sons would put them all to letters, not for gain, as the Christians do, but for the understanding of God's law, and not only his sons, but his daughters."[19] European Jews were a small group of well-educated, literate men and women, linked together in an international network of trade and scholarship, closely associated with and protected by kings and princes (and in many cases, popes and bishops). No wonder that the emerging clerical elites saw them as potential rivals and did their best to marginalize them: repeatedly attempting to prohibit princes from employing them and Christians from fraternizing with them, justifying their exclusion through lurid conspiracy theories, in which the Jews became poisoners, sorcerers, murderers of innocent Christian children, and devotees of Satan himself.

Over the last several decades, there has been much discussion and debate about how to characterize medieval Christian attitudes toward Jews: anti-Judaism? anti-Semitism? racism? Each of these terms has its advantages and pitfalls. Hannah Arendt affirmed that modern anti-Semitism was very different from medieval Europe's attitudes about Judaism and violence against Jews: she places the birth of anti-Semitism in the early nineteenth century.[20] Yet in fact there are many troubling continuities and similarities between medieval Christians' anti-Jewish attitudes and the anti-Semitism (and, more generally, racism) of the nineteenth, twentieth, and twenty-first centuries. But of course she is right that in other respects the medieval attitudes are quite different from modern anti-Semitism and other forms of racism.

In recent years, particularly in the United States, scholars have debated the appropriateness of the terms "race" and "racism" to the study of the European Middle Ages. Geraldine Heng has argued that medieval European attitudes toward groups defined as "racially" other, from Mongols to Gypsies to black Africans, form a key part of the story of the development of racism in Europe. Heng devotes a chapter "A Case Study of the Racial State: Jews as Internal Minority in England." Cord Whitaker has examined medieval European representations of blacks and blackness and concluded that "racial ideologies and its hierarchies are based in the dynamics of a rhetorical mirage."[21] This means not only that medieval ideas on blackness predated and shaped real European encounters with Africans, but that modern (nineteenth- and twenty-first-century) European racist ideologies invoke a mythified pure, innocent, "white" medieval Europe contrasted with a decadent and strife-ridden racially mixed societies of modernity. This use and abuse of the Middle Ages is prominent among white supremacists, who portray themselves as innocent victims of unjust accusations by minorities. They often invoke the rhetoric of militancy and "crusade" to defend their status, affirming that their medieval forbears had to fight against enemies abroad (Muslims) and at home (Jews). "The white supremacist victimization complex itself has roots in the Middle Ages," Whitaker affirms, citing work on "anti-Semitic scapegoating" by Miri Rubin and R. I. Moore.[22] Indeed, as we will see in the conclusion to this book, modern anti-Semites from the nineteenth century to the twenty-first dredge up medieval anti-Jewish legends to justify their ideology.

Some scholars distinguish between "anti-Judaism" and "anti-Semitism." Christian anti-Judaism is directed against Jewish religion: Jews are condemned for not recognizing Christ as their Messiah, for obstinately clinging to the Old Law instead of embracing the New. Anti-Semitism sees Jews as an ethnic or racial group hostile to European Christians. As Gavin Langmuir defines the distinction: "anti-Judaism is a nonrational reaction to overcome nonrational doubts, while antisemitism is an irrational reaction to repressed rational doubts."[23] In other words, Christians' religious hostility to (for example) Jewish rejection of Jesus as Messiah is "anti-Jewish," whereas belief that Jews torture Eucharist wafers until they bleed is "anti-Semitic," an irrational reaction to repressed Christian doubt concerning the doctrine of transubstantiation. Scholars debate how, why, and when we see the transition from anti-Judaism to anti-Semitism, or whether the distinction in fact sheds much light on prejudice against Jews.

François Soyer perceives a gradual shift over the course of the Middle Ages from what he (like others before him) has described as the "Augustinian" model of limited toleration of the Jews to an increasingly hostile view of Jews as implacable enemies of Christians and Christianity.[24] For Augustine, Jews unwittingly killed the Messiah whom they failed to recognize; in punishment, God destroyed their temple and imposed on them a painful exile. They preserve, in Hebrew, the books of the Torah and the prophets. They are destined to convert to Christianity at the end of time, but in the meantime should be allowed to live among Christians in peace, but "humiliated" by an inferior social status.[25] Yet European Jews became increasingly victims of violence and hostility over the course of the

Middle Ages: the tipping point has variously been seen to be the attacks on Jews in 1096 during the First Crusade (for Bernard Blumenkranz),[26] the emergence of a "persecuting society" in the twelfth century (for R. I. Moore), or the aggressive missionary efforts of the Dominicans and Franciscans in the thirteenth (for Jeremy Cohen).[27] Soyer sees the thirteenth-century attack on the Talmud as a key element in the emerging perception of Jews as enemies seeking to harm Christians. More generally, a range of thirteenth-century sources including those from England (Matthew Paris, Robert Grosseteste, and others we will encounter in the following pages) testify to this growing perception of Jews as an enemy presence in Christian England.

Another important concept, highlighted in the work of Ana Abulafia and Lindsay Kaplan, is *servitus Iudeorum,* a key and problematic concept variously translated as Jewish "service," "servitude," "serfdom" or "slavery."[28] Kaplan explains how this *servitus* becomes a key theological and legal definition of Jewish inferiority within Christian society. Various Christian writers use biblical models to prefigure inferior Jewish status: the firstborn sons Ishmael and Esau, who both lost their inheritance to their younger brothers (Isaac and Jacob); Ham, who mocked his father's nakedness and hence was cursed by him to have his descendants become slaves; and worst of all, Cain, who killed his brother Abel and whom God punished with eternal exile. The anti-Jewish reading of these figures is already present in Paul's epistles; thirteenth-century popes such as Innocent III, as we shall see, used them to argue for strict enforcement of the separation and subordination of Jews within Christian society. It is also in the thirteenth century that various authors developed a physiological interpretation of the "mark" God imposed on Cain, and subsequently on the Jews: Jewish men menstruate, according to these authors, as a humiliating bloody punishment for their killing of Christ; this menstruation suggests that these Jews are not "real" men. In the thirteenth century, as well, textual and visual portrayals of the trial and passion of Christ increasingly depict Jews, not Romans, as responsible for the death of Jesus. The Jewish torturers and executioners are portrayed as evil, sadistic, ugly, and deformed, and in a number of manuscripts from England, as black. Together, for Kaplan, these elements constitute a "racist" view of Jews as ineluctably different from and inferior to Christians. We will put the emergence of this anti-Jewish iconography into the context of worsening Jewish-Christian relations in mid-thirteenth-century England, and into the vision of the place of Jews in Christian history in the writings of scholars such as Robert Grosseteste.

The thirteenth-century sources for this history are particularly rich for England. England's administration produced prolific documentation, principally in Latin: charter rolls recorded grants or privileges issued by the king to groups or individuals; close rolls recorded private letters sent by the king; patent rolls preserved open letters or proclamations by the king; fine rolls documented concessions granted by the king for payment; and receipt rolls registered monies received by royal officials.[29] Thousands of entries for the reign of Henry III allow us to trace the monarch's movements (they carry date and place of issue) and his changing entourage (the names of the documents' witnesses and beneficiaries) and to examine the financial, political, and military activities of his administration. Indeed, one of the reasons for focusing on the reign of Henry III is the sheer wealth of documentation. The production of royal chancery documents exploded during his reign: the number of documents was multiplied almost by nine between 1226 and 1271.[30] As we will see, Jews appear in many of these documents: as beneficiaries of gifts, privileges, or protection; as creditors seeking payment of debts due to them; as plaintiffs demanding redress; and as culprits upon whom the king imposes fines or punishment. As Jonathan Ray observes, "the medieval charters granted to Jews reflect a relatively high degree of Jewish power while simultaneously demonstrating an equally high level of social and political integration into Christian society."[31]

The plea rolls of the exchequer of the Jews are another major source of information about thirteenth-century English Jews. The crown created the position of exchequer of the Jews in the late twelfth century to monitor the financial activities of England's Jews and to exercise justice in the king's name over his Jewish subjects. The plea rolls record the proceedings of the justices: most of the cases involve Jewish lenders seeking to make Christian debtors pay their debts.[32] The exchequer of the Jews also coordinated the network of chirographers, who in each of the towns where Jews lived kept an *archa* (loan chest) containing the contracts of loans made by Jews to Christians: in general in Latin, sometimes with Hebrew annotations and signatures. While many of these documents have been lost or destroyed, a number are extant in various archives across England, notably in Westminster Abbey.[33] Hundreds of account rolls of the wardens of the *Domus conversorum,* a London institution that Henry III created to house and provide for converts from Judaism, have been kept in the chancery in leather pouches since the Middle Ages.[34] To these rich archival sources can be added the large number of chronicles written in Latin (and occasionally in French), which in many cases provide detailed descriptions of events involving English Jews. Particularly important is the work of Matthew Paris, monk of St. Albans, a royal abbey thirty kilometers northwest of London. Matthew reworked the *Flores historiarum* of his predecessor Roger of Wendover and then added his own detailed narrations of events from 1234 to 1259. Matthew spoke with the king during the frequent royal visits to the monastery; he saw him at Westminster Abbey, where he was even invited into the king's chamber to copy a world map painted on the wall. Matthew is a perceptive and opinionated observer, sometimes praising the king's actions, often issuing sharp criticisms. He also makes frequent reference to the kingdom's Jews, at times to commiserate with the unfair treatment they receive from the king, at times on the contrary to accuse them of plotting against Christians.[35]

The voices of Jews are all but absent from this rich array of sources. No Hebrew chronicler describes in any detail the life and activities of English Jews or the persecutions they faced. We do have writings by English Jews, but they say very little about their life in England. A number of bilingual Latin/Hebrew texts document loans, purchases of lands, and other transactions. There is rich and varied intellectual activity among English Jews, who produced treatises of grammar, theology, Jewish law, and other texts.[36] A number of *responsa* (in Hebrew, *she'elot u-teshuvot*, "questions and answers") by English rabbis advise English Jews on a wide range of legal issues: marriage and divorce, inheritance, and other concerns of daily life. Some of them affirm the legality, for example, of buying and consuming foodstuffs produced and sold by non-Jews: cheese, bread, fruit, cider, beer.[37] A few Hebrew poems evoke the tribulations faced by English Jews, for example Meir ben Elijah of Norwich's "Put a Curse on My Enemy," discussed at the end of Chapter 7. The poet laments that English Jews have been insulted, humiliated, and attacked, yet he presents their tribulations in a transcendent, universalized manner, so that it is impossible to know exactly to which incidents he is reacting. No Hebrew author offers descriptions of the trial of the Jews of Lincoln in 1255, of the massacre in London in 1264, or of the 1290 expulsion. "How could a great Jewish community—great in size and in cultural achievement—disappear without leaving some record of its journey into exile?" asks Susan Einbinder about the Jews of France, expelled by Philip IV in 1306.[38] We can ask the same question about England's Jews, and the answer will be similar: as Einbinder did for the Jews of France, we can find mentions of the tribulations of English Jews sublimated into liturgical poetry.[39] The ways of remembering of medieval Jews are not, it seems, the same as of medieval Christians. Fresh persecution is lived and remembered as the continuation of a long history of tribulation of God's people in exile.[40] Hebrew sources will provide important perspectives in the pages that follow, but they cannot provide the narrative backbone of the book.

The lives of Jews in thirteenth-century England were not simply a somber succession of humiliations and violence. Jewish communities thrived, intellectually, culturally and financially, and Jews developed cordial and friendly relations with their Christian neighbors. Salo Baron's massive eighteen-volume *Social and Religious History of the Jews* sought to show the richness and complexity of European Jewish history.[41] "All my life," he wrote in 1963, "I have been struggling against the hitherto dominant 'lachrymose conception of Jewish history'—a term which I have been using for more than forty years—because I have felt that an overemphasis on Jewish sufferings distorted the total picture of the Jewish historic evolution, and at the same time it served badly a generation that had become impatient with the 'nightmare' of endless persecutions and massacres."[42]

In the late twentieth and twenty-first centuries, a number of historians have continued in Baron's wake to explore the history of European Jews not as merely a marginalized minority and object of persecution, but as a vital part of European society. Elisheva Baumgarten, in her study of Jewish family life in medieval France and Germany, finds in rabbinical sources testimony to close and often friendly relations between Jewish and Christian neighbors. Jews hired Christian women to care for their children, sometimes lodging them in their homes, sometimes sending the children to the Christians' homes. This provided daily occasions for Christian and Jewish mothers and children to see each other's homes and lives. There are no "ghettos" or exclusively Jewish neighborhoods in these towns (or in English towns): houses of Jews were intermixed with those of Christians. Baumgarten gives a small but telling example of a Christian woman who saw that her Jewish neighbor's candles had been blown out by the wind on the Sabbath; knowing that Jewish law prevented her neighbor from relighting them, she went over to light them for her.[43] While there are few equivalent sources from English Jewish communities, these *responsa* allow us to hear Jewish voices from European Jews who had similar lives and concerns to those of English Jews.[44]

In England as elsewhere in Europe, Jews and Christians interacted daily, buying and selling, borrowing and lending, watching their children play together, sharing meals or stories, working together, coming together at weddings or other celebrations, or making love. Historians have paid less attention to such day-by-day neighborly interactions than to conflict and violence because the evidence for these interactions, as for much of daily life of the great majority of Europeans in the Middle Ages, is scarce, and in this case largely negative: we know about them because religious leaders frowned on them or tried to prohibit them. We have to read between the lines of rabbinic *responsa* or synodal canons to see that these activities that were repeatedly and futilely prohibited must have been part of the daily life of English Jews and Christians. A twelfth-century French rabbi, for example, said that he had heard from a traveler that English Jews drank with

Christians, which was prohibited because it might lead to sexual union and marriage. But perhaps, the rabbi opines, they should be forgiven, for if they refused they might provoke the animosity of their Christian neighbors.[45] Lurid stories of Jewish plots to kill Christians often begin with innocent and unsuspecting Christian children playing with Jewish children, who lure them into their homes where they meet their fate. These stories aim among other things to dissuade Christian parents from letting their children play with Jewish children.[46]

England's Jews are, perhaps more than anywhere else in Europe, the king's Jews. In royal charters and letters, Henry regularly refers to Jews, individually or collectively, as "our Jews." As we will see, he regularly reasserted his exclusive dominion over England's Jews by warding off attempts by secular lords and church officials to tax Jews, judge them, or interfere in their lives and livelihoods. In times of trouble or violence, he instructed his officials to protect Jews, and to let them take refuge in royal castles. He also used this exclusive dominion to impose arbitrary and increasingly exorbitant tallages on them. This dependence on the crown was a two-edged sword for England's Jews, who during baronial revolts against the king became easy targets. This was already clear to Isaac of Norwich, imprisoned by King John in 1210, who was safe in his cell in the Tower of London when rebels sacked the London Jewry in 1215, and was set free by the regency acting in the name of the boy king Henry III in 1217.

CHAPTER I

Isaac of Norwich and the Rebuilding
of the King's Jewry (1217–1222)

In 1217, Isaac of Norwich walked free from the Tower of London after being held as prisoner since 1210. In that year, King John had imposed a tallage of 60,000 marks on England's Jews and imprisoned a number of rich Jews, including Isaac. In 1211, Isaac was fined 10,000 marks, at the rate of one mark per day; in 1213, he was transferred from Bristol to the Tower of London. He remained in prison during the civil war (or "first Barons' war") of 1215–1217, a rebellion against King John. The conflict was finally resolved (after John's death in 1216) by the treaty of Lambeth in September 1217, in which the rebellious barons recognized John's son, ten-year-old Henry III, as king. The council of regency freed Isaac and other Jews, restored to them the documents concerning the loans they had made to Christians, and affirmed their rights to protection, to conduct business, and to collect loans due to them. This was part of a wider attempt to reassert the crown's control over royal lands (demesne lands and royal forest), royal castles, and other crown prerogatives, including the control of the "king's Jews."

This chapter examines the precariousness of the Jews' position during the reign of King John and the conditions that allowed them to recreate communal life and economic activity in the early years of the reign of Henry III. We will focus on Isaac of Norwich, one of the most active and best-documented Jewish moneylenders of the early thirteenth century, and place him in the context of the broader upheavals that affected England and particularly its Jewish communities. We will first look at the violence against English Jews during Isaac's youth, in the reigns of Richard and John. We will then show how, throughout the years following the civil war of 1215–1217, the crown attempted to reaffirm royal power over its castles, its lands, and its Jews. Finally, we will focus on Isaac's lending activities, which will provide a good example of how Jewish lending worked in thirteenth-century England, and the opportunities and dangers it presented to Isaac and others.

Isaac of Norwich, from Royal Protégé to Royal Prisoner (1190–1217)

Isaac of Norwich was released from captivity in October 1217. Like so many other incidents in the history of English Jews, we know this not from anything Isaac himself wrote, but through documents from the royal chancery, in this case a mandate sent to the constable of Norwich. After seven years of imprisonment, Isaac could walk free, receive royal protection, and try to collect the debts that had been long due to him. Yet this newfound freedom and royal favor, welcome though it must have been to Isaac, presumably did not dispel fears about his precarious standing as a Jew.

Isaac would have been a teenage boy when he received his first vivid lesson in the danger of being a Jew in England. In 1189 and 1190, a wave of anti-Jewish violence swept across the kingdom, in the wake of the coronation of King Richard I "the Lionheart" and his departure on a crusade. The last years of Henry II's reign had been marked by a bitter struggle with his son Richard, the latter aided by King Philip II of France. Philip and Henry had both shown they knew how to extort money from their Jewish subjects, but they did it in quite different ways. In 1182, shortly after his accession, Philip expelled the Jews from the royal domains (essentially the Île de France), seizing their possessions: he enriched himself considerably while at the same time giving himself a reputation for both piety and decisive action.[1] English gentry were also building up debts to Jews: Henry II's *Assize of Arms* (1181) prohibited Jews from holding, as pawn, mail shirts or hauberks, which suggests that some knights had previously used such items as collateral for their loans. In 1186, at the death of Aaron of Lincoln, a Jewish moneylender who was perhaps the richest man in England, Henry seized his estate, including all outstanding debts to him (estimated at £50,000), and had his officials vigorously pursue the collection of those debts, causing considerable resentment against the king and his officials. A special commission, the exchequer of Aaron (*scaccarium Aaron*) was established to collect those debts. Hence at Henry's death many, in particular those who had borrowed money from Aaron, hoped that his son and heir Richard would rectify the situation, that he would forgive or at least lessen their debt, perhaps even that he would follow Philip's lead and expel the Jews.[2]

Two years earlier, on 2 October 1187, the Ayyubid Sultan Salah ad-Din (or Saladin) had captured Jerusalem, capital of the crusader kingdom since the troops of the First Crusade had taken it in July 1099. Richard was in Tours, in November 1187, when he learned of the fall of the holy city. He almost immediately took the cross, vowing to take the city back for Christendom.[3] There is no evidence that he had any thoughts of the consequences of the crusade for Jews in England or elsewhere in Europe. In 1096, during the First Crusade, knights setting off for the holy land had attacked and plundered Jewish communities throughout the Rhineland and in Rouen, killing thousands and forcing others to accept baptism. During the Second Crusade (1147–1150), there were new outbreaks of anti-Jewish violence, though efforts of Church and lay officials to protect Jewish communities limited the damage to them. Jewish communities in England had escaped crusader violence before the reign of Richard; they would feel the full brunt of it now.

Richard's coronation took place at the royal abbey of Westminster on 3 September, 1189. Richard had prohibited women and Jews from attending the ceremony. For Roger of Wendover, the prohibition was to prevent Jews and women from casting spells on the new king.[4] Perhaps Richard wished to send a message to his new subjects that his Jewish policy would be different from that of his father. A song composed for his coronation presented Richard as a restorer of justice, a champion of the poor against the rich:

> The Golden age returns
> the world is reborn,
> the rich man now suppressed
> and the pauper is exalted.[5]

A delegation of Jews presented fealty and gifts to the new king: since they could not attend the ceremony in the abbey, they sought entrance to the banquet that followed in the royal hall. Yet here they were pushed away, and some were beaten by the royal guards, who (rightly or wrongly) thought that the prohibition of the Jews applied to the banquet as well as the ceremony in the abbey.[6] Members of the crowd outside the hall joined in to attack the Jews. Chronicler Roger of Howden says that the Jews had provoked the ire of the "people" (*plebs*), who "with scornful eye and insatiable heart, rushed upon the Jews and stripped them, and then scourging them, cast them forth out of the king's hall."[7] He says that when the people of London heard this, they attacked the city's Jews, burned their homes and killed them: "a few nevertheless escaped thanks to their Christian friends." Another chronicler, Ralph of Diceto, describes how he had just been consecrated dean of St. Paul's cathedral when "the peace of the Jews, which they had always obtained in ancient times," was broken by "foreigners."[8] He discreetly avoids making any association between Richard's coronation and this violence. Hebrew chronicler Ephraim of Bonn says that thirty Jews were killed.[9]

What was the new king's reaction to this wave of anti-Jewish violence on the evening of his coronation? It was "interestingly ambivalent," as Robert Stacey says.[10] The next day, Richard sent orders throughout his kingdom that Jews should be left in peace. Yet he did little to punish the perpetrators: three men were hanged, one of them for killing a Christian and two for setting fires that spread to Christians' houses. No one was punished for killing Jews or for destroying or stealing their property. Ephraim of Bonn says that Richard had his gatekeeper killed for failing to warn him of the violence, but no other source corroborates this.[11] Perhaps the new king feared that harsher measures might alienate Londoners at a time when he needed to assert his authority and prepare for his departure for the crusade. This ambivalent message was unlikely to satisfy those who wished to expel the Jews or who were in debt to Jewish moneylenders; and it could not have given English Jews much faith in the king's protection.

The crusader king left England for the continent in December 1189; the English army that was to accompany him would join him in Sicily. With the king gone and crusader armies mustering, a succession of massacres of Jews took place in towns throughout England. As Diceto relates:

Many in England, hurrying off towards Jerusalem, decided to first attack the Jews before invading the Saracens. Hence on the eighth day of the ides of February (6 February) all the Jews that were found in their own houses in Norwich were killed; others took refuge in the Castle. On the nones of March (7 March), at the time of the [Lent] fair in Stamford, many were killed. On the seventh day of the Calends of April in York, according to what is said, almost five hundred were put to death, attacking and killing each other. For they preferred to be struck down by their own rather than perish at the hands of the uncircumcised. On the 15th of the Calends of April (18 March), which is to say on Palm Sunday,[12] as it is related, 57 Jews were slaughtered in Bury St. Edmunds. Wherever they were found, Jews were struck by the hands of the pilgrims [i.e., crusaders], except those protected by municipal officials.[13]

Ralph Diceto describes a massacre of those Jews of Norwich who had not found refuge in the castle on 6 February. Yet royal records suggest that the number of Jews killed was smaller than elsewhere in 1190: the total value of their chattels was subsequently assessed at less than a pound and a half.[14] Among the Jews who escaped to the castle, twelve heads of household can be identified in the records of payment made by Norwich Jews in 1194: among them is Isaac's father, Jurnet, and his uncle, Benedict.[15] No doubt Isaac, probably a teenage boy, fled along with the other members of his family to find safety in the castle.

The Jews of York suffered worst of all. Roger of Howden relates how, fearing violence from Christians, they took refuge in the castle, with the permission of the castellan and the sheriff. Yet when the sheriff subsequently sought admission to the castle, the Jews, fearing treachery, refused, and this provoked the ire of the sheriff and an attack on the tower in which both local Christians and crusaders took part. When the Jews attempted to negotiate their departure and were refused, they decided to take their own lives. Subsequently the Jewish houses of York were pillaged and burned—in particular, Roger notes, the pillagers burned the records of their debts to Jews.[16] Ralph of Coggeshall relates the massacres of Jews in London and York and concludes that since Jews had spread throughout England in the reign of Henry II and had become opulent and arrogant, what they suffered was not unmerited.[17]

The York massacre was the bloodiest and it received most attention from the chroniclers, as well as from modern historians.[18] We have seen that Diceto blames the crusaders for the massacres, in York as elsewhere. William of Newburgh also associates some of these massacres with *perigrini* (crusaders), in particular at King's Lynn. The ringleader of the killers, Richard Malebysse is particularly well-named, says Newburgh, calling him "Mala Bestia"; he had been deeply in debt to York's Jews (notably to Aaron of Lincoln in the 1180s). He succeeded in wiping out his debt but subsequently had to pay a thirty-mark fine for his part in the violence. A number of the chroniclers condemn the massacres, and none more strongly than Newburgh, who describes them in great detail: for him they are the damnable product of greed, not zeal for Christianity. In his commentary on the Song of Songs, he saw the Synagogue as mother of the Church just as Mary is the mother of Christ. Through deicide and rejection of their Messiah, the Jews lost their inheritance as God's people and must now be in servitude to Christians. Mary prays daily for their conversion, Newburgh insists, which will come at the end of time.[19] He presents the plight of York's Jews as similar to the Jews historic tribulations in Egypt and Masada, perhaps suggesting that their destiny was expulsion or exile from England.[20] It seems that both Jews and Christians of England read these tragic events through the lens of Josephus, or rather from their distinct partisan versions of Josephus, the Hebrew *Yosippon* and the Latin *Hegesippus,* both of which describe the mass suicide of Masada's Jews as the ultimate act of resistance to Roman hegemony.[21] For Christian readers of *Hegesippus,* such as Peter of Blois, Roman emperors Titus and Vespasian prefigured the crusaders, as they captured Jerusalem from rebellious Jews and punished them for killing Christ.

Yom Tov of Joigny, poet and biblical scholar, had written a poem in commemoration of Jews killed in Blois in 1171; in 1190 he was in York, and it was he, according to various sources, who urged the Jews besieged in the castle to kill each other rather than submit to their enemies. The tragic fate of York's Jews would subsequently be commemorated in England and across Europe in poems and liturgy. As Joseph of Chartres lamented:

> Instead of their herds, they sacrificed their children.
>   They slaughtered their firstborn before their eyes
> These saints did not withhold their only children from You,
>   for they held onto the deeds of their ancestors.[22]

Twelfth-century English Jewish scholar Berekhia ha-Naqdan on the contrary blamed English Jews, saying that they brought ills upon themselves through their greed: the massacre at York was a divine punishment.[23]

Many Yorkshire gentry were deeply in debt, in what Hugh Thomas has called the "crisis of the gentry."[24] Henry II had actively sought, in York as elsewhere, to expand his powers to judge and to tax: between 1155 and 1169 the city had to pay increasing amounts to the crown in rents, aids, and fines. In addition to these sums demanded of the town, further levies were made on various individuals and groups. In York as elsewhere, townsmen were increasingly subjected to royal justice, which meant in many instances hefty fines paid to the crown, in some cases creating debt that was passed on to their heirs. Resentment against this situation is no doubt part of the reason that when a major revolt against Henry II broke out in 1173–1174, led by the king's son ("young king Henry"), a number of prominent York citizens allied themselves with the rebels—and incurred substantial fines when the revolt was quelled. It is in the wake of the 1174 crisis that Jews first settled in York (probably from Lincoln): much of the moneylending activity of the "king's Jews" in York financed the considerable debt that York citizens had accumulated to the crown. While in other towns, most Jews escaped death by taking refuge in royal castles, the York mob was more organized and

mercilessly led by prominent leaders intent on killing their creditors and burning the records of their debt.

In Bury St. Edmunds, according to Diceto, fifty-seven Jews were killed; he
is the only chronicler to mention the massacre at Bury, though later royal documents attest to the value of the goods of slain Jews (£1 8s. 2d.; a rather small
amount if fifty-seven Jews had indeed been killed) and the fines levied on one
Thomas de Burgo for his role in the violence.[25] At Bury, the fate of the Jews was
intricately bound up with the financial and political conflicts involving the abbey, the archbishop of Canterbury, and the king. Jocelin of Brakelond, a monk
of Bury St. Edmunds, wrote a chronicle, which relates the history of the abbey
from 1173 to 1202.[26] He opens his chronicle with a long, detailed description of
the financial crisis of the monastery in the last years of Abbot Hugh (1157–1180).
The monastery and a number of its officials had built up significant debts to both
Christian and Jewish lenders, including two prominent Jews of Norwich, Jurnet
(Isaac's father) and Jurnet's brother Benedict. Jocelin relates how Archbishop Richard of Canterbury (in his capacity of papal legate) and officers of King Henry II
made inquiries into the situation and received assurances from the prior and
abbot. Clearly, the abbey's debt had placed it in a delicate situation in relation
both to Rome and to the crown. Dobson relates that "when the monk obendi-
entiaries of Bury St. Edmunds fell into serious debt in the 1170s, their single largest loan was apparently raised not from Isaac son of Rabi Josce of London or
Benedict of Norwich but from William fitz Isabelle, sheriff of London."[27] As
Dobson notes, it seems to be around 1164 that Henry II decided to turn from
Christian to Jewish moneylenders, leading to the gradual cessation of Christian
moneylending and to the expansion of Jewish settlement in England.[28]

The debt to Jews irks Jocelin. Later, in describing the rivalry, after Hugh's
death, between the future abbot Samson and the sacrist William, he paints the
latter as a friend of the Jews: "The sacrist was referred to as the father and Patron
of the Jews, for they enjoyed his protection. They had free entrance and exit, and
went everywhere throughout the monastery, wandering by the altars and round
the shrine while mass was being celebrated. Their money was deposited in our
treasury, in the sacrist's custody. Even more incongruous, during the troubles,
their wives and children were sheltered in our pittancery."[29] There is no doubt
an element of exaggeration in this passage. To discredit William, Jocelin paints
him as a friend and patron of the Jews, a classic trope of medieval invective. Jews
wandering behind the altar during the mass become a symbol of a world upside
down, a catastrophic situation that the good Abbot Samson would remedy. Yet,
beyond the hyperbole, several things here may point to important links and close

cooperation between Jews and the abbey. This is not the only text from twelfth- and thirteenth-century England that mentions Jews entering churches and keeping their valuables in church treasuries. Several church councils prohibited just such practices, which suggests that they were relatively common.[30] Prior to the 1190 massacre, York Jews apparently kept loan records in the cathedral treasury.[31] After all, the church sacristy was often one of the safest places to keep valuables, certainly safer than in the Jews' own homes.[32] This hints at a familiarity between Jews and the Christian monks; perhaps it was at this time that the abbey obtained Hebrew manuscripts, including a Hebrew Psalter now in the Bodleian Library in Oxford.[33] The "troubles" (*werre,* war) Jocelin mentions probably refer once again to the revolt 1173–1174, when Flemish and English forces of the Young Henry, in rebellion against his father Henry II, occupied Bury. Bury's Jews, this passage suggests, found refuge in the abbey. They may have not unreasonably feared that troops in rebellion against the king might attack them. Yet Jocelyn portrays Jews as dangerous to Christians: he claims that in 1181 a boy named Robert was martyred by Jews, buried in the abbey, and duly produced miracles.[34] For Jocelyn, granting Jews refuge is *absurdius,* "most incongruous." If his beloved Abbot Samson thought so too and refused to give refuge to Bury's Jews in 1190, this may explain why many of them died.

Jocelyn does not mention the massacre of Jews. He does discuss the expulsion of the Jews of Bury, seven months later, in October 1190. This expulsion does not seem to be either a logical sequel to the violence or a sign of any particularly virulent Jew-hatred on the part of the townsmen or the abbot. Were that the case, one would expect Bury's Jews to be driven away within days or weeks of the violence, not months later. Jocelyn describes Abbot Samson's 1190 expulsion of the Jews from Bury as a "sign of his great goodness": "The abbot asked the king for written permission to expel the Jews from St. Edmund's town, on the grounds that everything in the town and within its district [*banleuca*] belonged by right to St. Edmund: therefore, either the Jews should be St. Edmund's men or they should be banished from the town. Accordingly, he was given permission to turn them out, but they were to retain their movable possessions and also the value of their houses and lands."[35] The anti-Jewish violence, which Jocelyn does not mention, plays no role in his version of this expulsion. On the contrary, the issue seems to be the status of Bury's Jews: if they are to stay in town they, like everything and everyone else in town, must be subject to the abbey. If the king insists that they are "his Jews," they should leave. Richard accepts this, and the Jews leave Bury with their possessions.[36]

The next town mentioned in Diceto's catalogue of massacres is Lincoln. Legend has it that there disaster was averted for the Jews through the vigorous intervention of Bishop Hugh, though the text cited as evidence for this, a hagiographical text by Adam of Eynsham, speaks of Hugh's courage in facing down an angry armed mob, but does not give a date and does not say that he was protecting Jews. Adam mentions another incident where Hugh apparently quashed an incipient cult of a Christian who had plundered Jews, had been murdered and robbed by one of his accomplices, and was subsequently venerated as a martyr by the "vulgus." It may then be more than hagiographical *topos* when the author of *The Life of St. Hugh of Lincoln* affirms that Jews wept as his funeral, lamenting the loss of one devoted to the one true God.[37] While crusaders may have played a role in the attack, the ninety-four fines recorded for the incident point rather to local city merchants.[38]

Richard was away on crusade in 1190; he would not return to England until 1194. But clearly such a direct affront to royal finances and to royal prerogatives over the "king's Jews" could not be left unpunished. The royal administration and royal justice reacted to the massacres, reaffirming the Jews' right to protection and punishing those guilty of violence, or at least those whom the crown chose to associate with the violence. For York, Lincoln, Bury, and other towns we have lists of the men fined and the amounts they were to pay to the crown. In the aftermath of 1190, the crown established a royal administration devoted to Jewish affairs. Richard founded in 1194 a special Jewish exchequer, a much-expanded version of the earlier exchequer of Aaron, to oversee all loans made by Jews and all royal revenues to be tallaged from Jews. Under the exchequer for the Jews, royal justices of the Jews were to judge any cases involving the Jews, including those pertaining to Christians' debts to Jewish lenders. *Archae* (chests) in each of the towns with Jewish communities were put into place. Each loan was to be recorded by a pair of cyrographers, one Christian and one Jewish, on a document cut into three parts: one for the debtor, one for the creditor, and one placed into the *archa*. This system has been seen as an effort to avoid the destruction of debt documents such as that that took place in York, though it is no doubt also meant to avoid fraud by either party. It also developed into a formidable tool to monitor and tax the activities of the king's Jews, an "economic panopticon" in the words of Geraldine Heng.[39]

After the storm of 1189–1190, a relative calm returned for English Jews. Jurnet continued his lending activities, and in 1194 we first find Isaac mentioned in a loan document as a partner with his father and mother. In 1197, he paid the crown 1,000 marks for the right to inherit the debts owed to his father.[40] When,

at the death of Richard I in 1199, his brother John took the throne, the coronation was marred by none of the anti-Jewish violence seen in 1189–1190. John issued in 1201 a charter guaranteeing protection and privileges to England's Jews
(a charter for which they reportedly paid 4,000 marks). It guaranteed that Jews
would enjoy the privileges they held under Henry II, in particular to be tried before royal officials, to travel freely without paying tolls, and to inherit from their
fathers.[41] When London Jews complained of attacks by Londoners, John issued
a stiff rebuke to the mayor and barons of the city: "If we have given our peace
even to a dog it shall be inviolably preserved."[42] Moreover, John helped Jewish
lenders collect their debts by issuing letters to his sheriffs ordering them to enforce payment: the lenders got their money, and John received a fee for this service equivalent to about 10 percent of the money collected. Yet at other times,
John simply annulled debts or interest on loans to Jews, an easy and cheap way
for him to accord favor to those of his entourage who had accumulated debt.[43]

Yet the relative peace and prosperity that Isaac and fellow Jews may have enjoyed was not to last long, and would not survive the turmoil of John's hapless
reign. Here is not the place to attempt to relate the history of the baronial revolt
against John. The loss of Normandy to Philip II in 1204 caused widespread contempt and resentment, particularly from barons who had held land in both Normandy and England and who in most cases were now obliged to choose between
their Norman and English holdings. John was increasingly strapped for cash and,
as we will see in the next chapter, often in conflict with bishops and Pope Innocent III, a conflict that culminated in his excommunication. One of the causes
of resentment by both barons and churchmen was the king's practice of imposing taxes (or simple seizure of property) without precedent or recourse to due
process.

John had Jews throughout England arrested shortly before Easter, in
April 1210. Various monastic chronicles mention his spoliation of the Jews, their
imprisonment, and the death of some of them.[44] These chroniclers present the
Jews alongside other victims of John's extortionary policies, such as Cistercian
monks. John imposed on the Jews a tallage, reportedly 60,000 or 66,000 marks,
though this figure may be exaggerated. The pipe rolls record that on 1 November 1210, John levied at Bristol an extraordinary tallage on England's Jews, but
do not give the amount.[45] For Roger of Wendover, it was shortly after Christmas 1210 that on John's orders all the Jews in his kingdom, men and women, were
"seized, imprisoned, and tortured severely, in order to do the king's will with their
money; some of them then after being tortured gave up all they had and promised more, that they might escape." One of these Jews, at Bristol, had seven teeth

removed, one each day; finally, on the eighth day, he agreed to pay the king 10,000 marks.[46] Could this unfortunate fellow be our Isaac? He was probably the richest Jew in John's kingdom, and we know that he did agree to a 10,000 mark fine. Roger (and subsequently Matthew Paris) are the only ones to mention this incident, which may be apocryphal, but given John's reputation is plausible. If true, the gaping hole that once held seven molars was for the rest of Isaac's life a bitter reminder of the precariousness of his place in English society. And other Jews were less fortunate: some died under torture; Isaac of Canterbury was hanged.[47] According to Matthew Paris, "Many of the Jews fled the kingdom, on account of the great affliction they suffered."[48]

We have seen that in 1211 Isaac was fined 10,000 marks, payable at one mark per day. As he languished in prison, royal officials seized his property in Norwich to pay for his fine: bonds, house, and chattels were confiscated, yielding £140.[49] Isaac stayed in captivity in Bristol until 26 July 1213, when the king wrote to the constable of Bristol, ordering him to have Isaac transferred to Tower of London.[50] On September 1, the king granted a house seized from Isaac to papal nuncio Ralph of Carlisle; significantly, none of the witnesses to the transaction is Jewish.[51] John had seized the Jews' wealth, much of which was in the form of loans to Christians: hence those who had loaned money from Jews now found themselves in debt to the king, who had much more coercive power to collect the money owed him.[52]

King John's plans to retake Normandy through an alliance with Emperor Otto IV were crushed by Philip II's victory at Bouvines on 27 July 1214. This debacle, coupled with the resentment against his treatment of his vassals and his extortionary fiscal policy, provoked the revolt of a number of his barons. Isaac perhaps would have found reason to be thankful to be safely imprisoned in the Tower of London on 17 May 1215, when rebel barons entered London and, according to chronicler Ralph of Coggeshall, "broke into the houses of the Jews, rifling store-houses and strong boxes, and having spent much time in this holy work, abundantly restuffed their own empty purses. Robert fitz Walter, Marshal of the Army of God and Holy Church, and Geoffrey de Mandeville, earl of Essex and Gloucester, vigilantly and daily reinforced the city walls with stones taken from the houses of the Jews."[53] London's Jews were an easy and lucrative target. Rebels also attacked the Winchester Jewry.[54]

On 4 March 1215, John took a crusading vow and William, bishop of London, gave him and his men white crosses, like the ones his brother Richard and his troops had worn. He sought no doubt more to protect himself with the status of *crucesignatus* in the face of baronial revolt than to bring succor to the holy land.[55] With his barons in open revolt and London occupied, John was forced to negotiate, with Archbishop Stephen Langton as mediator between John and the rebels. At Runnymede on 15 June 1215, the king and the rebel barons sealed an agreement, now known as Magna Carta. It granted important freedoms to the English Church, guaranteed rights to free heirs and widows, limited different sorts of fees and taxes that the king could demand of his subjects, upheld the traditional right to self-government of London and other towns, and limited the powers of royal officials. It established the principle of justice by peers and a baronial "royal council," which needed to ratify any new taxes proposed by the king.

Three of the sixty-three clauses involve debt, two specifically mentioning debt to Jews. In clause 9, John agrees that neither he nor his royal officials will seize debtors' land if the debtors' other resources suffice for repaying the debt. Clauses 10–11 read:

> 10. If anyone has taken a loan from Jews, great or small, and dies before the debt is paid, the debt is not to incur interest for as long as the heir is under age, whoever he may hold from. And if the debt comes into our hands, we will take only the principal recorded in the charter.
>
> 11. And if anyone dies, and owes a debt to Jews, his wife is to have her dower and pay nothing towards that debt. And if there are surviving children of the deceased who are under age, their needs are to be provided for them in proportion to the dead man's tenement, and the debt is to be paid from the residue, saving the service owed to the lords. Debts owed to others besides Jews are to be dealt with in like manner.[56]

These clauses suggest that inherited debt was causing financial hardships for debtors' heirs and widows. In particular, the barons sought to protect landowners: while clause 9 does not prohibit seizure of land for debts, it attempts to limit it, making it a last resort. Clauses 9–10 limit the impact of inherited debt, without annulling it. A widow does not inherit her late husband's debt, and her dower is excluded from the resources that creditors can claim. Heirs are obliged to pay the debts of their fathers, but interest is not to accrue while they are minors. This indeed had been the policy under Richard.[57] Sufficient resources are to be allocated for the upkeep of the household. Tellingly, the final sentence of clause 11 seems almost an afterthought: "debts owed to others besides Jews are to be dealt with in like manner." This suggests that Jews were already perceived as lenders *par excellence*.[58]

Yet John had little intention of respecting his agreement; he quickly sent a delegation to Rome, and Pope Innocent III duly annulled Magna Carta on 24

August. Already in July 1215, the pope had affirmed that the rebels were worse than Saracens because they opposed their crusader king (*rex crucesignatus*).[59] By then, war had erupted between the king and the rebels, who invited Philip II's son Louis (future king Louis VIII) to come lead the rebel force and to become king of England. Prince Louis disembarked on the coast of Kent in May 1216 and arrived triumphant in London. Each side tried to present itself as divinely guided: Geoffrey de Vinsauf presented John as "the soldier of the cross and of Christ, and sword of the entire church," and papal legate Guala Bicchieri excommunicated the rebels, while the rebel knights donned crusader crosses.[60] Robert Fitz Walter, leader of the baronial opposition to the king, styled himself as "Marshal of God's Army."[61] The exchequer ceased functioning in 1215 and, according to Roger of Wendover, "nobody would make payments to the king or obey him in anything."[62]

The Crown Struggles to Gain Control of Castles, Forests, and Jews (1217–1221)

John died of dysentery in Newark Castle on 19 October 1216. Nine days later, on 28 October, in Gloucester, his nine-year-old son was crowned King Henry III. John had sent Henry for safekeeping and education to his close advisor and bishop of Winchester, Peter des Roches. A regency council was established, consisting of three of John's close collaborators and advisors: Papal Legal Guala Bicchieri, Earl William Marshal, and Peter des Roches.[63] Guala had the boy king take the cross, as a way to reinforce the tie between the papacy and the new king, and to cast the fight against the rebels as a crusade. Several contemporary chroniclers relate that many of Henry's men took the cross in order to expel Louis and the French from England.[64] The royal forces managed to gain the upper hand in the struggle against the rebels, notably through a major victory in Lincoln in May 1217, followed by a naval victory over a French fleet in August: in both battles, royal forces wore white crosses. Prince Louis and the rebellious barons subsequently sealed the treaty of Lambeth in September 1217, recognizing Henry as king. The regency council now had the difficult job of reestablishing both peace and royal authority in England. In what David Carpenter qualifies as "a political masterstroke," in 1216 the regency reissued Magna Carta in the name of Henry III, "ripping the carpet from underneath the rebels' feet, although the controversial 'security clause' [authorizing rebellion by the barons if the king failed to respect the charter] was quietly omitted."[65] Since 1215, only a small trickle of revenue had been arriving in the royal coffers; some royal demesne lands, forests, and castles had fallen into rebel hands, and even those that had remained in loyalist hands did not necessarily produce revenue for the crown, as those who held them claimed (often with some justification) that they used them to support the king's cause. The great task before the regency council in 1217, that would occupy them for over five years, was the restoration of royal authority and taxation: reaffirmation of the king's rights over his castles, his lands, his revenues—and his Jews.

The regency council was aware that in his brutal treatment of his richest Jewish subjects in 1210, as in much else, John had done a disservice to the interests of the crown. Jewish lending was an important element in the English economy and an important source of royal funding. It was thus in the interest of the crown to free those Jews who were still imprisoned, to allow them to resume their lending activities, and to offer them assurances of protection.

No time was wasted. On 23 September 1217, a royal mandate ordered William de Beaumont to hand over to "Earl William Marshal, our rector and regent, all letters and cyrographs which he has from Isaac of Norwich and other Jews." The mandate, issued in the king's name, was witnessed by William Marshal, at Lambeth. On the same day, the very next entry ordered that Isaac of Norwich be given letters of safe conduct permitting him to travel everywhere in the kingdom.[66] Hence the marshal freed Isaac from prison and ordered those who had (legally or illegally) taken the documents concerning his loans to restore them to him. He apparently was still in London on 2 October, when he obtained the following writ from William Marshal:

> The king to the constable of Norwich, greetings. Know that we have taken under our protection and defense Isaac, our Jew of Norwich, and all his dependents and all his possessions and all of our other Jews of Norwich. And therefore we command you that you protect this Isaac and his people and his possessions and all the other Jews of Norwich and to not allow any harm to befall them. And if any offense should be committed against them, make amends to him without delay, because we wish and order that they themselves and all their possessions be protected and maintained, as if they pertained to our fisc. And you shall receive this same Isaac with his dependents and his possessions in our castle. And in this matter witness the Earl [William Marshal] in the same place [Lambeth palace, London] in the same year [2 October 1217].[67]

Isaac was clearly planning to return to Norwich. While in theory the two brief texts issued on 23 September would have sufficed to allow him to return to

Norwich and take up his business there, Isaac was taking no chances and had the marshal address to the constable a quite specific mandate guaranteeing the safety and freedom of Isaac, his family and associates, and all the other Jews of Norwich, as well as their property. These Jews were to be granted refuge in the royal castle at Norwich if necessary. In the mandate, William, speaking for the king, refers to these Jews as "our Jews"; they and their property are considered "tanquam dominica nostra" ("as our dominion"). The word "dominica" indicates the exclusive domain of royal power. This shows both a desire to assert recovery of royal prerogatives usurped by the barons in revolt against King John at the end of his reign (here dominion over the Jews) and to reassure Jews such as Isaac that they would henceforth suffer neither from excessive arbitrary taxation or imprisonments or the exactions of the barons. Just like the castles, lands, and royal revenues usurped by the barons, the Jews must return to the royal fold.

Another royal mandate (issued in London, with, again, William Marshal as witness) on 26 October ordered the prior of Norwich to hand over immediately to Isaac or his representative the letters and chirographs, which he had received by royal mandate. It seems that Isaac, already in Norwich, had met resistance in his attempts to obtain these documents and pursue these debts, unless he was still in London on 26 October and was merely gathering all the documentation possible to enable him to obtain these documents. On 6 November, a royal mandate ordered the sheriff of Norwich to assist Isaac in collecting the debts incurred to him during the reign of King John.[68] This policy would soon bear fruit, both for Isaac and for the royal coffers: on 13 November, William Marshal and Peter des Roches witnessed a royal mandate acknowledging the receipt of one mark of silver from Isaac "by the hand of our venerable father Peter Bishop of Winchester . . . for the one mark per day which he is to render for the fine of ten thousand marks which he enacted with lord John the King, our father."[69] The same day, on the next entry in the patent rolls, the king bade the authorities of England's ports to allow Jews to enter the kingdom freely, but not to leave without explicit royal permission.[70] The regency council sought to encourage Jews to come (or return) to England—and to prevent them from leaving. The crown deftly exploited debt to Jews to fill its own coffers: on 31 May 1218, it had the executors of the will of the late Thomas de Neville pay eighty marks to the crown in repayment of a loan made by Isaac.[71]

While Isaac and other English Jews were enjoying freedom and resuming their business endeavors, troops were mustering across Europe for a new crusade (known to historians as the Fifth Crusade). Many of the knights who had taken the cross during the civil war honored their crusading vow by participating in the expedition. Some of the rebels had taken crusading vows as part of their reconciliation with the king.[72] Hence a number of English knights participated in the expedition, which captured the Egyptian port of Damietta in 1219, though subsequently Egyptian sultan al-Malik al-Kamil routed the crusader forces at al-Mansura and forced them to surrender Damietta. Peter des Roches took the cross on this occasion and was reportedly elected, in absentia, bishop of Damietta.[73] Jews throughout Europe must have looked on with apprehension as clerics preached to recruit soldiers and as recruits donned the crosses that sanctified their vows. In England, Jews may well have feared a repeat of the killings of 1190; they probably solicited measures of protection from the crown. On 7 March 1218, in Gloucester, William Marshall, in the name of the king, established a committee of twenty-four prominent citizens of Gloucester who he charged with protecting the Jews, lest they "be vexed by crusaders or others."[74] Similar councils of citizens charged with protecting Jews from crusaders are established in Lincoln (30 March), then in Oxford and Bristol (27 April).[75] Henry, we have seen, had hastily been crowned shortly after the death of his father in 1216. At the age of twelve, on 17 May 1220, he had a proper coronation ceremony in Westminster Abbey. But beforehand, London's Jews were locked up in the Tower of London, no doubt to avoid a repeat of the massacres of 1189.[76]

On 19 June 1218, a royal mandate was sent to the sheriffs of Hereford, Worcester, York, Lincoln, Stamford, Bristol, Gloucester, Northampton, Southampton, and Winchester in order to assure that they offered their protection to their respective Jewish communities. The register of patent rolls has preserved the mandate sent to Hereford with (as is standard) a list at the end of the other recipients of the same mandate. The king accorded to the Jews the right to live in Hereford and to have a commune (*communa*), presumably granting them autonomy in managing and judging communal affairs,[77] "as they used to in the time of Lord John, our father." He furthermore instructed the sheriff, Walter de Lacy, to "guard, maintain and protect" these Jews. He told him to proclaim everywhere in his shire the peace of the Jews "notwithstanding any prohibition concerning this established by the bishop of Hereford, since nothing concerning our Jews pertains to him." This suggests that there was some clerical resistance to the reestablishment at Jews, either specifically from the bishop of Hereford or more generally (it is not clear whether this same clause was included in the copies of this mandate sent to other shires). Finally, the king affirmed their direct dependence on royal justice, specifically on the judges to the Jewry: the sheriff himself could not arrest or punish them, nor could they be taken before a Christian court concerning their lending practices.[78]

Joe Hillaby has closely studied Hereford, where Sheriff Walter de Lacy played an active role in resettling Jews in the town and assuring them his protection. He was to become the best customer of Hamo, the most prominent member of Hereford's renewed Jewish community. Walter, who at the turn of the thirteenth century benefitted from extensive land holdings in Normandy, England, and Ireland, came up against significant financial difficulties, prompted first by the loss of Normandy by John in 1204, then troubles in Ireland, which cost him dearly in lost income and in military expenses. And he had to answer to Kings John and Henry for his Irish vassals, and was on three occasions fined for their rebelliousness, in 1198, 1215, and 1225, for a total of £7,000. It was no wonder he came to depend on the services of Hamo and other Jewish lenders, and at his death was indebted to them for over £955.[79]

Prominent Jews like Hamo and Isaac flourished in their role as moneylenders to the landed nobility and financiers to the royal coffers. The early years of Henry III's reign brought freedom of movement and renewed prosperity. In London, for example, where Jews had lost land and houses through the attacks of 1189 and perhaps even more so through the expropriations by King John in his efforts to collect the Bristol tallage, Jews were able to buy land and build houses.[80] Henry's government encouraged their enrichment and avoided the harsh treatment doled out by John. But it did not rescind the Bristol tallage: on the contrary, various documents over the following years show that royal officials continued to keep careful track of what individual Jews owed and to obtain payment from them.[81]

Isaac, Moneylender and Royal Agent

Royal documents—fiscal receipts, court records, and loan contracts—allow us to follow Isaac's career from his release from the Tower of London in 1217 until shortly before his death in 1235 or 1236. We also have an exceptional document, the so-called Norwich Day Book: four parchment rolls now in Westminster Abbey that record a series of loan transactions involving Norwich lenders between 1225 and 1227. Of the 365 transactions, Isaac is involved in 87; the total value of his bonds is £1,647.[82] Together, these documents paint a portrait of an active, aggressive businessman who travels ceaselessly and often appears in court, as either defendant or accuser in trials involving his loans.

Isaac was at work by 1218 pursuing his debtors or acknowledging receipt of debts. Sometime after 24 June, he issued a quitclaim (receipt of payment) for debts of William de Walsham, prior of Norwich. Nine men, six Christians and three Jews, were witnesses to this quitclaim, preserved in Norwich Cathedral.[83] The most important source of information on the legal dealings of Isaac and other Jews comes from the plea rolls of the exchequer of the Jews, which document the litigations brought before the exchequer, most of which deal with debtors who have defaulted.[84]

At Michaelmas term 1218 (the session of the court of the exchequer of the Jews that met in the days following the feast of St. Michael, 29 September), the exchequer of the Jews heard a number of cases involving Isaac. In one, Isaac had sued a woman named Alice for a debt made by her husband Ralph. Alice appointed a certain Robert de Cokfeld as her attorney in the matter. The court instructed the sheriff of Norfolk to leave her in peace until the day after Martinmas (11 November), so that the king's rolls could be consulted to see whether the debt was due to Isaac or to the king—in other words, if John's agents had taken over this debt as part of Isaac's payment of his debt incurred in the Bristol tallage or not. Isaac, meanwhile, was to appear before the sheriff's court in Norwich and produce the chirograph documenting this debt.[85] Later records allow us to trace the development of this case: Alice was subsequently ordered to appear before the court within fifteen days following St. Hilary's day (13 January 1219).[86] In November 1219, she was again summoned to appear before court in January 1220.[87] This is the last mention we have of the case: as often, we do not know how it was resolved. Alice is one case among many that Isaac pursued: sometimes his debtors are ordered to appear in court to answer charges; sometimes Isaac is summoned to present documentation for his claims.

Among Isaac's prominent clients are not only noblemen but also ecclesiastical institutions, including the cathedral of Norwich (as we saw above) and Westminster Abbey. The abbot and monks of Westminster complained to the papal legate Pandulf that Isaac was regularly pestering the monks, before the justices of the Jews, concerning their debts to him. Pandulf in turn wrote to Peter des Roches and Hubert de Burgh, asking them to intervene.[88] For Pandulf, Isaac's actions were a clear breach of Lateran IV's prohibition of excessive usury (*graves et immoderatas usuras*); Christian debtors oppressed by these practices can scarcely breathe, he affirms. He urges Peter and Hubert to bring a quick end to this practice, which is the cause of scandal. It should be noted that Pandulf does not argue that all interest-based moneylending is illegitimate: he instead reiterates Lateran IV's injunction against excessive usury. The definition of what corresponded to "gravis et inmoderata" was of course debatable. We do not know what Peter and Hubert's response to this letter may have been, nor how the issue of Westminster's debt may have been settled. But this clearly shows that even one of the most central and powerful religious institutions of the kingdom could get into serious financial troubles through debt to Jewish lenders and be compelled to answer before the justices of the Jews. The abbot and monks attempted to use their connections with Pandulf to avoid paying their debts (or at least the interest on them). Whether or not Isaac actually received the payment that was due to him, he clearly was not prevented from aggressively pursuing other debtors over the course of the following years.

In the cat and mouse game that Isaac pursued with his debtors, the latter often sought subterfuges to avoid payment. We see this in the records of the exchequer for Hilary term (January) 1220. In one case, Isaac came to court with a chirograph recording Walter of Thorpe's loan of £14, contracted sometime before 1210, which in the over ten years had accumulated an unspecified amount of interest.[89] Walter had apparently died in the meantime, so Isaac demanded payment from his son and heir, Gilbert. Gilbert appeared in court and claimed that while his father was indeed named Walter of Thorpe, Isaac's debtor was a *different* Walter of Thorpe. Isaac retorted that when he was imprisoned in the Tower of London (between 1213 and 1217), royal justices came to him inquiring about the identity of Walter and whether he was indeed the father of Gilbert. In other words, King John had not only imprisoned Isaac and other Jewish lenders, he and his officers attempted directly to collect the monies due to the Jews, and at times demanded help and information from their despoiled Jewish prisoners. Gilbert had apparently already told the royal officials that it was a different Walter of Thorpe who had taken loans from Isaac; this trick had allowed him to avoid payment for several years, although interest continued to accumulate. Now the debt had been restored to Isaac, who was pursuing it in court. The court summoned both Isaac and Gilbert to appear in court a month after Easter. And indeed, on the fourth day of the Easter session, Isaac was there, but not Gilbert. Isaac demanded seisin of the gage—in other words the right to occupy (or more likely, to rent out) Gilbert's land until payment was made. The court ordered that Gilbert be summoned before the justices at Westminster on the quindene of the Trinity to hear his judgment.[90] We have no record of what happened at Westminster that day or if Gilbert appeared, but clearly the court was not well disposed to him and did not appreciate his attempts to shirk responsibility for this debt.

Isaac and others tried to recover long-standing debts in cases where their debtors were often dead and the heirs could contest the validity of the contract or deny that they were in fact the heirs of the debtors. A certain Adam of Illeg, son of Adam of Illeg, complained to the court that Isaac was unjustly pursuing him for a loan—there were a number of men named Adam in the town of Illeg, he explained: the debt must have been contracted by someone other than his father.[91]

In the case of Gilbert, the judges seem to have ruled in Isaac's favor, and he was probably granted seisin of Gilbert's lands. Yet the process was costly and time-consuming. On at least one other occasion, Isaac took matters into his own hands and forcibly occupied the lands gaged to him. In January 1219, at the Hilary term session of the exchequer of the Jews, one of Isaac's debtors, Peter of Nereford, appeared in court with twelve witnesses, complaining that Isaac and his men had disseized him of his land of Panneworth (Norfolk) before the feast of St. Michael. He named Isaac's associates (twenty-one Christians and one Jew), who, he said, attacked and ransacked his estate. They damaged several houses and beat some of Peter's men, inflicting serious financial and physical harm. The judges instructed the sheriff of Norwich to summon both Peter and Isaac to court for quindene of the Holy Trinity.[92] Once again, we do not have the final outcome of this case; we only have Peter of Nereford's deposition and have no way of judging whether he was accurately reporting what had happened. If there is anything to his accusation, it could show that Isaac was not beyond employing aggressive extralegal pressure on his debtors. This is not the only entry in which Isaac was accused of violence. Nor was he the only Jewish lender to employ such tactics: Elias, son of Aaron of Lincoln (who also cultivated friendly relations with Peter des Roches), in 1220 sent twenty-six men to break into the estate of one of his debtors, to carry off anything of value, and to uproot his trees.[93] Elsewhere in the plea rolls, we see Isaac presenting to the exchequer court the documents concerning debtors who had defaulted on their loans. In the Easter term session of 1220, for example, Isaac's name appears in ten different cases.[94] Over the following years, the plea rolls frequently mention Isaac. For many English Jewish lenders, these traces of litigation are all the record we have of their lending activities, unless the debtors or third parties (notably monastic institutions) preserved their copies of the loan documents.[95] In the case of Isaac and his Norwich associates, we also have the daybook, containing dozens of records of payments large and small made to Isaac by various debtors.[96]

Isaac owned houses in Norwich and London. In 1225 he purchased a license to expand his house and an adjacent quay on the banks of the Wensum river in Norwich: the impressive stone house, with vaulted storerooms opening onto the quay, is still standing.[97] Isaac appears to have played a prominent role in England's Jewish community, as we see in his involvement in the case of Comitissa. Comitissa is a Jewish woman who appears before the exchequer of the Jews at the

St. John's session (June–July) 1220, accusing Abraham Gabbay of the murder of her husband, Solomon Turbe.[98] In Easter term of 1220, Abraham accused Solomon of "maliciously wounding" him.[99] Solomon was put in jail in Gloucester. According to Comitissa, Abraham then paid ten marks to five men who killed Solomon by pushing him off a tower of Gloucester Castle. Abraham denied the charges before the judge of the exchequer of the Jews and affirmed that he was in Hereford on the day Solomon fell from the tower. The judge ordered to have the five men arrested and to have them appear before the court in Westminster. Comitissa also said that Abraham, while he was recovering from his wounds, made false accusations against her, causing her to be put in prison where she was "so starved she despaired of her life." There she had heard Abraham plotting her husband's death with the prison guards, so as soon as she was freed she rushed to London and exposed the plot to Alexander de Dorset, Isaac of Norwich, and Hel' Martin.[100] Why did Comitissa go to London to expose her case? It is not clear, but it seems that these three men are prominent Jews who possibly serve as judges in a Jewish court, or *bet din*, which in general consisted of three judges.

Isaac also was employed by the royal administration to assess and levy tallages on England's Jews. In a mandate dated 11 November 1224, the king instructed the Jewish and Christian chirographers to assist Isaac, Elias of Lincoln, Joceo le Prestre, and their associates in assessing a tallage to be paid to the crown by the Jews of England.[101] Presumably Isaac and his colleagues travelled to the towns with Jewish populations and examined the loan documents in the *archae* to appraise the wealth of these Jewish communities and establish the level of taxation for each of them.[102]

Isaac also cultivated friendship among Henry's influential advisors, in particular Peter des Roches, bishop of Winchester. Peter, as we have seen, was one of the three men comprising the regency council of the young king. He collected the payments, one mark per day, that Isaac owed to the crown. In September 1220, Isaac paid £604, supposedly to cover his one-mark-per-day fine from St. John's Day (21 June) 1218 to Easter (18 April) 1221, although he in fact seems to have enjoyed a discount, as the payment is 126 marks less than what he should have paid.[103] On 8 December 1221, the king, through the good graces of Peter des Roches, reduced Isaac's annual payment from 365 marks to 250 marks.[104] Various royal records over the following years acknowledge Isaac's payment of this debt.[105] Isaac gratified Peter des Roches with gifts: he had 58,000 herrings delivered to Peter's manor of Southwark, which the bishop then distributed among the religious of the diocese.[106] Over subsequent years, Isaac's special tallage was reduced first to 200 marks per year, then to £100 in 1225.[107] We will look more closely at Peter de Roches and his relation to Isaac in the 1230s in Chapter 3. Isaac continued to be one of England's most successful Jewish lenders until his death around 1235.[108]

We have followed here the career of Isaac, one of the richest, most prominent, and best-documented Jews of England during the early part of Henry III's reign. Isaac was by no means typical, yet we can learn a great deal from his life. We have seen Hamo forge a close relation with Walter de Lacey, sheriff of Hereford, who provided him with lucrative loan contracts. If Isaac and Hamo are perhaps the best-documented English Jews of their generation, a handful of others probably also enjoyed prominence and perhaps several hundred others were involved in loans on a smaller scale. While most of the lenders that appear in the documents are men, women played a key role as well, often identified as the "widows," suggesting that they were partners with their husbands in lending, and that they often continued the family business after their husbands' deaths. We see this network of Jewish men and women making loans small and large in all the towns that held *archae* and often well beyond into the countryside.[109] These Jews had daily contact with Christians as clients and trading partners. They also knew them as neighbors, since even the so-called Jewish districts of cities like Norwich, London, or Oxford were not wholly Jewish, but had mixed populations of Jews and Christians. Some well-off Jews hired Christian servants to work in their homes. From the point of view of a number of churchmen, in England and beyond, this kind of close daily contact could lead to a dangerous fraternization.

CHAPTER 2

Of Badges and Wet-Nurses

English Bishops Attempt to Limit Contact
Between Jews and Christians

.

In April 1222, Stephen Langton, archbishop of Canterbury, brought together English bishops at the Council of Oxford. The council pronounced a series of fifty resolutions, or "canons." Under the authority of the archbishop, the council sought to apply a reformist agenda, inspired in good part by the Fourth Lateran Council (1215), on the English church. The great majority of the canons regulate the behavior of bishops, priests, monks, and other churchmen: their ordination, their dress, their financial activities, their respect of canonical rules, and their sexual proclivities. The council also weighed in against improper relations between Christians and Jews. Jews were not to have Christian servants in their homes; they were to wear distinctive badges on their outer garments to distinguish them from Christians. Since the Church had no direct authority over Jews, the archbishop and several bishops subsequently ordered Christians to stop selling food to Jews until they complied. The Jews of Lincoln complained to the king (or rather to the regency ruling in his name), who ordered that Christians sell to Jews as usual or face imprisonment. This conflict between the English Church and the crown shows how jealously the crown protected its legal monopoly over "the king's" Jews and how some bishops saw danger in daily Jewish-Christian contact. The 1222 Oxford Council reiterates concerns about Jewish-Christian relations that had long preoccupied the church hierarchy. These are part of a larger concern in England and in France that fraternization between Christians and Jews, in particular Christians working and living in Jewish homes, could lead to sexual relations or, worse, apostasy.[1]

Dangers of Cohabitation?
Jews and the Church in England Before 1222

Pope Alexander III (1159–1181) sent a bull to the bishop of London in which he wrote that he had heard that English Jews controlled church lands and revenues and obtained oaths of fealty from Christians.[2] This was contrary to the "institutions of the Christian faith," he affirmed. He asked the bishop to enroll the aid of King Henry II to enforce these prohibitions. Normally, the pope would write to the archbishop of Canterbury rather than to his subordinate bishop of London: the fact that he wrote to the latter suggests that he was writing either between 18 April 1161 and 3 June 1162 (when the archbishopric was vacant), during Thomas Becket's exile in France, or during the vacancy that followed Becket's murder. This would indicate that even in a time of tension between Rome and the English king, the pope sought the aid of his "dearest son in Christ" to protect the interests of the Church.

This bull is one of a number of texts from this period that prohibits use of church property as pawn or surety for loans made by Jews: often it is ecclesiastical books, vestments, and liturgical objects that are prohibited; here it is land and revenue from land. The principle, reiterated frequently in papal bulls and conciliar canons, is that "infidels" should not exercise power over Church properties or over Christians. Hence the association of a second issue, here, prohibiting Christians from making oaths of fealty or homage to Jews. This letter, written fifty or sixty years before the Oxford Council, contains *in nuce* a number of issues that would continue, throughout the reign of Henry III, to cause contention between crown and Church over the proper relations between Jews and Christians.

In 1175, Archbishop Richard of Canterbury presided over the Council of Westminster in the presence of King Henry II. Thirty-seven canons were proposed to the council, which finally adopted twenty-two of them.[3] Two of the rejected canons concerned Jews: the first prohibits Jews from receiving oaths of fealty from Christians and prohibits Christians from making such oaths; the second prohibits them from occupying church lands and taking revenue from churches. Both initiatives correspond to papal policy of prohibiting Jews from exercising authority or dominion over Christians or over church property.

As we have seen, the two issues addressed in these canons had been raised in the letter addressed by Pope Alexander III to the Bishop of London; there is clearly an attempt to enforce papal restrictions on Jewish-Christian interaction.

Yet here that attempt failed: the council did not adopt the proposed canons. Why? Jews were in theory direct dependents of the king, and perhaps Henry II did not want the church to impose restrictions on them, particularly in matters (such as entering into feudal relations with Christians) that he may have considered beyond the Church's jurisdiction. Perhaps Jews had convinced the king or the archbishop not to pass these restrictions. In any case, this clearly shows that prelates were often unable to affirm, much less enforce, papal restrictions on Jewish-Christian contact. Mary Cheney has shown that in several cases, Alexander III sent decretals to English prelates after the Westminster Council, demonstrating that he still sought to enforce them in spite of the failure to have them adopted by the council.[4]

Popes, bishops, and councils were attempting to restrict and regulate relations between Jews and Christians in England. Jews were to be kept in a position of social inferiority to Christians: they should not enter into feudal relationships with them nor should they have Christian servants; and they should certainly not be able to obtain control or ownership of church property (land, buildings, vestments, or sacred objects). These restrictive measures against Jews were part of a wider movement of church reform, which sought to wrest control of the Church away from laymen.

The papacy was a driving force, in England as elsewhere in Europe, in attempts to regulate and limit interaction between Jews and Christians and to protect Jews from violent attack by Christians (in particular crusaders). Pope Calixtus II (1119–1124) issued a bull *Sicut Judaeis*, which prohibited Christians from forcing Jews to convert. It further barred Christians from injuring Jews or taking money from them, disrupting Jewish festivals, exacting additional services, or desecrating Jewish cemeteries to extort money. Those who would violate this decree were to be excommunicated or to lose their office. Issued between the First and Second Crusades, probably at the request of Jewish communities, it sought to protect their place in Christian society.[5] The same bull was reissued by Calixtus's successors, Eugenius III (1145–1153), Alexander III (1159–1181), Clement III (1187–1191), and Celestine III (1191–1198).

Pope Alexander III issued a number of bulls dealing with relations between Jews and Christians. He instructed the bishop of Marseille to prohibit Christians from working for Jews, lest they "convert to the perfidy of Judaism"; Jews were to pay tithes to the Church on any property they own; and they were to keep their doors and windows shut on Good Friday.[6] He wrote to the bishop of Bourges that Jews were not to have Christian servants and were not to build new synagogues.[7] In 1179, Alexander presided over the Third Lateran Council. Most of the council's twenty-seven canons concern papal and episcopal elections, ecclesiastical reform, and repression of heresy. Canon 26 reads: "Jews or Saracens should not have Christian servants. They should accept judicial testimonies of Christians. Apostates from Judaism should not be stripped of their possessions."[8] Granted, such conciliar canons and papal bulls lacked teeth: Alexander's letter to the bishop of Bourges shows his frustration that King Louis VII of France paid little heed to canon law restrictions on Jews building new synagogues and employing Christian servants.

Innocent III ascended the throne of St. Peter in 1198: his papacy (1198–1216) is often seen as the high-water mark of medieval papal power. Innocent launched three crusades, played a decisive role in the political fates of European monarchs (notably King John), aggressively pushed a reform movement that affirmed strong papal control over the Church, and convened the Fourth Lateran Council in 1215. He has also been blamed for the worsening of relations between the Church and Jews.[9] He indeed managed to confirm traditional papal policy toward Jews while simultaneously affirming a harder anti-Jewish line and stepping up anti-Jewish rhetoric. His promulgation of the *Constitutio pro Judeis* is highly instructive. The *Constitutio* is a reissue of the *Sicut Iudeis*, the traditional text guaranteeing papal protection for Jews, specifically assuring that they may practice their religious rites, be free from undue pressure to convert, and have synagogues and cemeteries; violence against their persons and property was punished by excommunication. While Innocent cited his five predecessors who had issued the same privileges, he added two brief paragraphs that changed the tone considerably: first, an introduction in which he provides a theological justification for the limited and conditional tolerance offered to Jews: "Although in many ways the disbelief of the Jews must be reproved, since nevertheless through them our own faith is truly proved, they must not be oppressed grievously by the faithful."[10] And at the end of his *Constitution* he adds a sentence that makes these traditional guarantees precariously conditional: "We desire, however, that only those be fortified by the guard of this protection who shall have presumed no plotting for the subversion of the Christian faith."[11] The implication is that some Jews plot against Christianity, and for them there is no papal protection against violence.

On 16 January 1205, Innocent sent a letter to King Philip II Augustus of France. In this bull, *Etsi non displiceat Domino,* the pope complained of the privileged status that the king accorded to Jews, which unconscionably placed them above Christians.[12] The Jews of the French kingdom had become "insolent," claimed the pope. He attacked in particular the practice of moneylending, which inverted the normal power relationships between Christians and Jews: Jews absconded with the property of Christians and of the Church. Particularly unacceptable, for the pope, was the trampling of traditional jurisprudence based on oral testimony (in which Christian witnesses were accorded more authority than Jews). Here, on the contrary, more credence was given to signed documents (loan contracts in the Jews' possession), upturning traditional hierarchies. The letter is a bitter (if implicit) criticism of the aid and abetment that the king and his officers granted to Jewish lenders, to the detriment of Christian debtors. Beyond the question of usury, the pope lambasted what for him were other examples of Jewish "insolence": they constructed new synagogues (one of which was taller than a neighboring church); they had Christian servants, in clear violation of church law; they openly mocked Christians and made jest of veneration of the cross during Holy Week. Jewish butchers sold the meat they considered not good enough for themselves to Christian butchers, who resold it to Christians: this practice is indeed well attested throughout Europe, including in Norwich and probably in other English towns.[13] The pope accused the Jews of being accomplices to thieves and even of killing Christians, giving the example of a student found dead in a latrine. The final lines of this bull are a barely veiled warning to the king and an exhortation to restrain the Jews and to punish their "blasphemies." Innocent pursues these issues in other bulls: *Etsi Iudeos*, sent to the archbishop of Sens and the bishop of Paris on 15 July 1205,[14] and *Ut esset Cain*, to Count Hervé IV de Donzy of Nevers on 17 January 1208.[15]

While Innocent reworked well-worn themes, commonly found in anti-Jewish polemics, the bulls present an uncommonly clear and uncompromising legal argument founding Jewish social inferiority on theological principles. In the three bulls, Innocent presents his action as a defense of divinely ordained hierarchies merited by Jewish sins. In the opening words of *Ut esset Cain*, he compares the Jews to Cain. Just as Cain was a murderer and an untouchable, despised and rejected by humanity because he killed his brother Abel, the Jews, guilty of murdering their Lord, are vagabonds on the face of the earth; their perpetual exile punishes and recalls their crime. But just as the sign of God prevented Cain from being killed, so we must let Jews live among us. The Jews are the enemies of Christ and utter blasphemies against his name. They should be tolerated but must be kept in a position of social inferiority; they must be prevented from exercising power over Christians. Innocent affirms that they have been reduced to slavery as punishment for the crime of having killed their Lord who had come to free them. In *Etsi non displiceat Domino*, he develops another biblical prefiguration: the story in Genesis of the two sons of Abraham: Isaac, "the son of the free woman" (Sarah), who prefigures the Christians, and Ishmael, the "son of a servant" (Hagar), who represents the Jews, whose destiny is eternal servitude. Moreover, the Jews themselves implicitly accepted their status as slaves: when Pontius Pilate washed his hands of his responsibility for the death of Jesus, Jerusalem's Jews cried out, according to Matthew: "His blood is on us and on our children!" (Mt. 27:25, cited in two of the three bulls). The Son's blood still cries out to the ears of the Father, says Innocent in *Etsi non displiceat Domino,* echoing Genesis where Abel's blood cried out to God: thus any prince who fears divine wrath must make sure that the Jews remain subservient to Christians. This continuity of punishment is natural because of a continuity of guilt: Jews are and remain agitated by their rabid hatred of their Christian benefactors, and they delight when their affairs cause divisions and conflicts among Christians, the pope affirms in *Ut esset Cain.*

Nothing in Innocent's theology of Judaism is particularly new, except for the sharpness of its anti-Jewish rhetoric. Indeed, Augustine had made the parallel between the Jews and Cain, both punished by God for murder, cursed to wander the world but protected from being killed.[16] The idea was much discussed in the Parisian school of Peter the Chanter, where Innocent had studied alongside Stephen Langton.[17] In this as in many things, Innocent pursued his policy with energy and aggressiveness. He did not hesitate to favor vicious rumors in order to drive home his point. In *Etsi Iudeos* he denounced what he presented as a common practice: Jews obliged their Christian wet-nurses to discharge milk into the latrines for three days after they have taken communion.[18] Innocent used this vicious rumor to prohibit the common practice of Christian women working as wet-nurses in Jewish homes, to little avail, as we can see from the repetition of such prohibitions in the following centuries and in rabbinical sources that mention the practice as common and widely accepted.[19] Yet Innocent was skillful at finding subordinates to turn his initiatives into policy, men like Stephen of Langton, whom he elevated to the archbishopric of Canterbury in 1206.

Stephen Langton, Scholar and Archbishop

By 1222, Stephen Langton had been archbishop of Canterbury for sixteen years, yet calling of the Council of Oxford was perhaps the first instance of his exercising any real authority over the English Church.[20] Like many other prominent English churchmen of his generation, he was educated in Paris. He arrived there about 1170, which probably means that he was born c. 1150–1155, at Langton by

Wragby in Lincolnshire. Paris was to be his home for the better part of thirty-six years: first as a student, then as a teacher in the schools that would become in the early thirteenth century the University of Paris. Here he joined the circle of Peter the Chanter, in which the intellectual, spiritual, and political dimensions of reform were a constant subject of preoccupation. As John Baldwin has noted, Stephen was one of the most prolific theologians of the Paris schools in his day: he composed over seventy biblical commentaries, more than two hundred disputations and at least five hundred sermons.[21] One subject of constant debate was the relationship between *regnum* and *sacerdotium* and the need for the liberty of the Church to function free of lay intrusion. As Stephen explained in his commentary on Joel 2:31, ecclesiastical power was the sun to the moon of princely power (*principatus*): just as the light of the moon is reflected from that of the sun, princes' legitimacy comes from the authority of the Church. One of the great heroes of this struggle was the twelfth-century archbishop of Canterbury, Thomas Becket, whose fierce defense of the rights of the English Church against the despotic king Henry II culminated in martyrdom in 1170. This at least is how Thomas appeared to Peter the Chanter and his students, a lesson not lost on Stephen, nor on a fellow student, Lotario dei Conti di Segni, the future Pope Innocent III.

Stephen was a prolific scholar during his Paris years, and his work gives us a glimpse of how he perceived Jews and their place in sacred history. He is the author of treatise on the interpretation of Hebrew words, which reflects no direct knowledge of Hebrew on his part, since it seems entirely derived from the work of earlier Latin writers (principally Jerome).[22] There is no evidence that his desire to understand the meaning of these biblical Hebrew words ever led him to discuss the topic with Parisian Jews (as had Andrew of St. Victor a half century earlier).[23] Stephen used Andrew's work to understand and present (in neutral, nonpolemical terms, for the most part) Jewish interpretations of scripture. There are many passages in his numerous biblical commentaries that shed light on his understanding of the place of Jews in Christian society.

Let us look at one, namely his presentation as Hagar as a figure of the Jewish people. According to Genesis, Sarah was barren, so it was her slave Hagar who bore Abraham's first son, Ishmael. Sarah accuses Hagar of insolence and punishes her: "Then Sarai mistreated Hagar; so she fled from her. The angel of the Lord found Hagar near a spring in the desert; it was the spring that is beside the road to Shur. And he said, 'Hagar, slave of Sarai, where have you come from, and where are you going?' 'I'm running away from my mistress Sarai,' she answered (Gen. 16:6–8). Here is how Langton glosses this passage:

Then Sarai mistreated Hagar: because the Jews have been afflicted in many ways concerning the death of Christ: the temple has been destroyed, their priesthood destroyed. *So she fled from her*: because the haughtiness of the Jews did not want to submit to grace, they fled from it; hence they are dispersed throughout the world. *The angel of the Lord found Hagar*: the words of the prophets that seek them out and warn them to return to our faith.

Near a spring: And the Jew clings to his law like Tantalus who is surrounded by water but cannot drink, and who sits hungry at a table laid with different dishes. He is like the *boy with five small barley loaves* (John 6:9) who does not eat them. The Jews are like the servant of Abraham waiting with the donkey (Gen 22:5), which is to say they are stupid. *The well is deep* (John 4:11): the well or spring is deep with the doctrine of the Law, which they follow, but they do not know how to tap from it the spiritual meaning, and they die of thirst beside the fountain. The prophet Haggai (1:5–6) says: *Give careful thought to your ways. You have planted much, but harvested little. You eat, but never have enough. You drink, but never get drunk. You put on clothes, but are not warm.* The Jews have drink but do not know how to get drunk, but we drink and get drunk. For it is said to us in the Song of Songs (5:1): *Eat, friends, and drink.* The bread to be broken must be understood spiritually. The boy does not break the bread, but the Lord breaks it for him and feeds him . . .

These Jews are *in the desert, by the spring on the road to Shur.* Shur means "distress." They are placed by God's grace in the desert and inhabited by distress. They have abandoned their rites and ceased to respect their laws. *Where have you come from, and where are you going?* (Gen. 16:8, the Angel speaking to Hagar), as if to say, you have come from God. For these Jews come from God, who gave them their Law. And you wander in a land of misery and darkness: this could be said of any sinner. *I'm running away from my mistress* (Gen. 16:8, Hagar's response to the Angel): in this way the Jews flee from the face of God. Indeed, many of them do this against their conscience, knowing full well that our faith is better than theirs, and that the Lord was incarnated and died, yet nevertheless they wish to follow their fathers.[24]

Jews (and subsequently Christians and Muslims) identify Hagar and her son Ishmael as ancestors of the Arabs, while from Sarah and her son Isaac come the Jews, who benefit from God's covenant. Yet a Christian allegorical interpretation, found in

Paul's Letter to the Galatians (4:22–31), symbolically identifies the two brides of Abraham with the two covenants: the slave Hagar represents the Old Covenant, given on Mount Sinai, while the free woman Sarah is the New Covenant, granted by Christ. Stephen, in this tradition, sees the rejection and punishment of Hagar as allegories for the tribulations suffered by the Jews who have run away from their mistress, the Church. They are paying for their faithlessness in this life: their temple destroyed, they are unable to fulfill their own laws; they wander in hunger and thirst. They have the scriptures and the prophets, but do not understand them or benefit from them: they drink from them but do not get drunk; they perish from thirst beside the spring. Not only are the Jews in error, Langton affirms, but many of them know it: they choose to follow the ways of their forefathers even though they know Christ was their promised Messiah.

In his exegesis of Genesis, Langton also develops the identification between the Jews and Cain: both guilty of murder, both cursed to wander the world. In Genesis (4:10–12), when Cain kills Abel, God reprimands him and pronounces his punishment: "What have you done? Listen! Your brother's blood cries out to me from the ground. Now you are under a curse and driven from the ground, which opened its mouth to receive your brother's blood from your hand. When you work the ground, it will no longer yield its crops for you. You will be a restless wanderer on the earth." Cain says that he is afraid that he will be killed, but "the Lord put a mark on Cain so that no one who found him would kill him." In one part of Langton's long exegesis of the story of Cain and Abel, he offers this allegorical interpretation:

> The reason that Jews are not killed by Christians. *God placed a mark on Cain.* Allegorically, Cain designates the Jews, wandering and dispersed. *Scatter them O Lord by thy Power* (Psalms 58:12). The Lord has put a mark on them. Their practice of circumcision and literal observance of the law constitutes the mark preserving them from being killed, so therefore they are spared. Or the Lord has marked them with our faith, because through that we discern the passion of the Lord and call it to mind; thus they are witnesses of the Lord's passion. Or the mark denotes the fulfillment of what has been foretold by the prophets; by the reality of their dispersion, predicted so long beforehand, it has been proved that the other prophecies will be fulfilled.[25]

The "mark of Cain" is both a protection and a curse. Circumcision visually sets Jewish men apart from Christians, marking them as inferior but protected. The

Jews are keepers of the Old Law and witnesses to their own crime of killing Christ. They are not to be killed: this is more than an academic concern in an age when throughout northern Europe Jews were increasingly objects of violence, in particular (but not solely) on the part of crusaders. Yet their punishment, through exile and humiliation, is just and should be maintained. Hence Peter the Chanter, Langton's and Lotario's teacher, affirmed that "the Jews are the porters of our book bags, bearers of our books, witnesses to the passion of the Lord, sweepers of our streets. They should not be allowed to become rich."[26] Here in a nutshell, is the program for Jewish-Christian relations that Lotario and Stephen learned in Paris (and that Stephen subsequently taught)—and that the two of them, pope and archbishop of Canterbury, would attempt to enforce.

Innocent was elevated to the papacy in 1198. In 1206, he made Stephen cardinal. The new cardinal was still in Rome later the same year when a group of Canterbury monks arrived. They complained to Innocent that King John wished to force them to elect as archbishop his candidate, John de Gray, whom these monks opposed. Innocent proposed Stephen as his choice; the monks quickly elected him. The pope wrote to John to inform him of the election and then, in June 1207, in Viterbo, consecrated Stephen archbishop. John would have nothing of this papal candidate whom he did not know; several prominent English bishops, including Peter de Roches of Winchester, opposed Stephen's nomination. For Stephen, and perhaps for Innocent, this was a reenactment of the drama between Henry II and Beckett, with Henry's son John refusing to recognize the authority of Thomas's successor Stephen. There ensued a long struggle: in March 1208, Innocent imposed an interdict on England; in November 1209, he excommunicated John. He subsequently threatened to authorize French King Philip II to invade England and depose John. Finally, royal and papal negotiators reached an agreement: John, facing a revolt of his barons and fearing an invasion by Philip, gave over his kingdom to Innocent, who granted it back to John as a papal fief. John recognized Stephen as archbishop and sent a delegation to fetch him. One of the members of the delegation was Peter of Cornwall, Augustinian prior of Holy Trinity in Aldgate, London. It may be on this occasion that Peter offered to Stephen the treatise that he had composed during the interdict and that he dedicated to his archbishop: the *Disputation Against Symon the Jew*.[27] Peter explains in the preface to the treatise that he had met a very clever Jew named Symon and had debated with him for three years before convincing him to convert to the true faith. His text purports to be the record of his exchange, and perhaps he meant it as a blueprint for the conversion of England's Jews, for which Langton would be the architect.

Stephen returned to England on 9 July 1213. Having spent most of the previous forty years in the schools of Paris, he was ill-prepared to assert any real control over the Church. Not only did he face continued (though now less open) resistance from royal officials, he was also sidelined by a series of papal legates who exercised greater power over the English Church and had more influence over the crown than he did: Nicholas of Tusculum (1213–1214), Pandulf Verraccio (1213–1216 and again 1218–1221), and Guala Bicchieri (1214–1218). John continued to be embroiled in conflict with his barons and in war with Philip. In 1214, John invaded the Poitou; in a coordinated maneuver, his ally, Emperor Otto IV, attacked from the north, only to be routed by Philip's forces at the Battle of Bouvines in August 1214. As we saw in Chapter 1, this led to a general rout of the English forces and strengthened baronial opposition to the king. Langton appears to have stepped forward to attempt to negotiate a peace settlement between the barons and the king, in particular helping forge the agreement in Runnymede in June 1215 to what is now known as Magna Carta.[28] If we are to believe Roger of Wendover, Langton upon his arrival had John swear that he would love and protect the Church and respect the ancient laws of his predecessors. Langton had discovered the coronation charter of Henry I, which he brandished before the barons: this became the basis for Magna Carta, by which the barons were simply reaffirming their rights of old, acknowledged by John's great-grandfather.[29] The story is probably apocryphal, but it reflects the strategy on both sides to invoke the precedent of a largely mythical past. Langton himself looked back to Thomas Becket as a model and justification for his powers over the English Church; the barons evoked privileges given by former kings.

Yet when John failed to uphold his agreement and the peace settlement collapsed during the summer of 1215, both sides blamed Langton. John appealed to Innocent, who annulled Magna Carta and had the barons excommunicated. Stephen refused to publish the excommunication, leading Peter des Roches and Pandulf, acting under the pope's orders, to suspend Langton, who went to Rome to plead his case. His suspension was confirmed in November at the Fourth Lateran Council (at which Stephen was present).[30] Stephen, still titular archbishop of Canterbury but prevented from exercising his office, spent most of the next five years in Rome in obscurity (he seems to have played no significant role in the Fourth Lateran Council and was little consulted as cardinal).

Innocent III summoned the Fourth Lateran Council on 19 April 1213 for November 1215. The council's purpose, as Innocent explained it, was to reform the Church and Christian society, to eradicate heresy, and to assist the Crusader Kingdoms. It was attended by 404 bishops, numerous other prelates and secular authorities, one patriarch of the Eastern Church, and one patriarch's legate. The English delegation included both archbishops (Langton, archbishop of Canterbury, and Walter de Gray, archbishop of York) and the bishops of Rochester, Lincoln, Coventry, Exeter, and Chichester. Peter des Roches, bishop of Winchester, was notably absent.[31] The council met in three sessions, on the 11th, the 20th, and the 30th of November. It approved seventy canons concerning ecclesiastical discipline and reform, heresy, episcopal elections and benefices, taxes, marriage, tithes, and Christians' relations with Jews and Muslims. The final canon called for another crusade to meet in Sicily in June 1217. One of the canons sought to limit the interest that Jews could charge on loans:

> The more the Christian religion is restrained from exacting interest, the more burdensome the perfidy of the Jews grows over Christians, so that their means are soon exhausted. Therefore, desiring to protect Christians in this matter lest they be unduly burdened by the Jews, we prescribe in this synodal decree that henceforth if the Jews extort burdensome and excessive interest, the society of Christians ought to be taken from them, until they have properly made satisfaction for the excessive burden. If needed, let Christians be compelled through ecclesiastical censure to refrain from doing business with them.[32]

This is not a prohibition of Jewish lending, but simply of "burdensome and excessive" interest (*graues et immoderatas usuras*). The assembled prelates had no authority over Jews, since they were outside the Church. So the council proposed to prohibit Christians from doing business with Jews who charged excessive interest.

Another canon imposed distinctive dress on Jews:

> In some provinces, differences in dress distinguish the Jews and Saracens from Christians, but in others some confusion has arisen as no difference is discernible. Whence it sometimes happens that by mistake Christians join with the women of Jews and Saracens, or Jews and Saracens join with the women of Christians. Therefore, lest this transgression of damnable mixing spread further under the cover of such an error, we decree that such people of both sexes be distinguished from other people publicly by the manner of their dress in all Christians' provinces and all of the time; as indeed we read that they are enjoined to do by Moses.[33]

This was the first text of canon law that required Jews and Muslims to be visibly distinguishable from Christians.[34] Throughout Europe papal legates and provincial synods sought to apply the reform program of Lateran IV; Innocent and his successors wrote letters to various European kings in order to have them implement the council's rulings and punish those who resisted. It is hence no surprise that England, a papal fief with a papal legate serving on the regency council for a child king, should be the first European kingdom to translate the Lateran Council's injunction into royal law.

The Royal Badge Mandate

On 20 March 1218, a mandate was issued in the name of King Henry III (who was at the time eleven years old) ordering that all Jews wear, on their outer garments, a badge in the form of two white tablets. The boy king thus gained the dubious distinction of being the first European monarch to require Jews to wear a badge:

> The king to the Sheriff of Worcestershire, greetings. We order that you have announced and observed in all your jurisdiction that all Jews, wherever they walk or ride, in or outside the town, should wear on their chest, on their outer garments, two emblems in the form of white tablets made of linen cloth or parchment, so that in this way Jews may be clearly distinguished from Christians. Attested by the Earl [the regent William Marshal] at Oxford 20 March 1218. The same was sent to the sheriffs of Gloucestershire, Warwickshire, Lincolnshire, Oxfordshire and Northamptonshire, and to the mayor and sheriffs of London.[35]

The mandate is clear about the color and shape of the twin *tabulae*, "tablets," which were no doubt meant to represent the tablets of the law that Moses received on Mount Sinai. The mandate was sent to the royal officials of Worcester, Gloucester, Warwick, Lincoln, Oxford, Northampton, and London: in other words, to several of principal towns where Jews resided, though it is not clear why there is no mention here of other shires with important Jewish communities (Yorkshire, Cambridgeshire, Norfolk, Kent, and others).

This mandate was not the initiative of the boy king, but rather that of his council of regency. As we have seen, one of the three members of the regency was

Guala Bicchieri, papal legate.[36] Guala, a native of the Piedmont, studied law in Bologna and rose in the ranks of the ecclesiastical hierarchy; Pope Innocent III made him cardinal in 1205. Guala participated in the Fourth Lateran Council in November 1215. Two months later, in January 1216, Innocent named Guala papal legate to England, replacing Pandulf Verraccio. Guala paid a key role in dele-gitimizing the rebels, excommunicating Prince Louis and the rebellious English barons and making the royalist cause a quasi crusade. At his coronation ceremony, Henry did homage to the papacy, represented by Guala, making the boy king the Pope's "vassal and ward."[37] A representative of Pope Innocent III (and, from July 1216, of the new pope Honorius III), Guala helped legitimate Henry's au-thority and assert his rights. It seems very likely that Guala was behind the man-date imposing the badge on English Jews.[38] If so, the papal legate was seeking to implement, in a kingdom that was after all a papal fief, a stipulation of one of the canons of the Fourth Lateran Council.

The royal mandate dispenses with all justification and asserts that the goal is to distinguish Jews from Christians "with a clear sign." Rather than a vague injunction to dress differently from Christians of Lateran IV, canon 68, the man-date has Jews wear "two white tablets" on their outer dress, both in town and while traveling, on horse or on foot. The color (white) and material (linen or parchment) of these "tablets" is clearly indicated, though not their size. Guala translated the Lateran directives into clear and applicable legislation, and con-vinced the other members of the regency council to agree to this mandate, is-sued in the king's name and sent to the royal officials of some of the major towns where Jews resided. So while Guala's actions and motives seem clear, it is much less clear how much he and the other members of the regency meant for the mea-sure to be enforced.

Issues of the proper place of Jews in English Christian society were raised the following year, in 1219, when Bishop William de Blois of Worcester presided over an episcopal synod. The synod issued thirteen statutes: the first four involve proper respect of funeral and burial rites and of the rules of inheritance, the fifth prohibited Church lands from being alienated to laymen, the seventh and eighth prohibited laymen from seizing or judging clerics, and canons 9–13 involved other issues of ecclesiastical procedure. It is the sixth canon that interests us: it sought to restrict what it judged abusive practices associated with Jewish loans.[39] It pro-hibited Jews from receiving church vestments, books, or other consecrated items as security for loans or for any other reason. If they refused to comply, they were to be cut off from all contact with Christians (a penalty that had been inflicted by canon

67 of Lateran IV, on Jews who charged excessive interest). Christians were prohibited from taking Jewish money for deposit in churches for safekeeping. Finally, Christians could not enter into loan partnerships with Jews in order to
profit from the Jews' authorization to charge interest. The synod also reiterated
the common prohibition of Christian servants working in Jewish homes, here
specifically targeting women who spent the night in Jewish houses and threat-
ening them with anathema. Four years after Lateran IV and three years before
the Council of Oxford, this text provides important evidence that some English
churchmen were both seeking to enforce restrictions on Jewish lending activity
pronounced by Lateran IV and also going further in attempting to tackle what
they see as particular local problems. We know that papal legates Guala and Pandulf, in alliance with some of the English bishops, were making other efforts to
apply reform: ban tournaments and *scotales* (raucous drinking parties associated with religious holidays), curb lay control of church offices and lands, and
promote crusade.[40]

Stephen was probably in Rome in 1216 when Honorius III succeeded Innocent III. Only well after the settlement of the civil war, in May 1218, did Stephen
return to England and begin his struggle to gain control over the English Church,
a struggle not against the boy king Henry III, but principally against the papal
legates: Guala, who resigned in November 1218, and then Pandulf. Two years
later, Stephen finally obtained two important symbolic victories in his efforts
to appear as the head of the English Church: in May 1220, he presided over the
second coronation of Henry at Westminster; then, on 7 July 1220 he celebrated the jubilee of St. Thomas Becket and presided over the translation of
the saint's relics, allowing him once again to highlight his role as successor to
the martyred archbishop.[41] In the fall of 1220, Stephen went to Rome to con-
sult with Pope Honorius. His primary aim, it seems, was to convince the pope
to recall his legate Pandulf, leaving Stephen free reign as primate of the English
Church.[42]

During his absence, at Easter 1221, the English crown received significant
revenues from Jews who paid in order not to wear their badges. These revenues
are recorded in the royal receipt rolls.[43] Receipt rolls are registers of the royal exchequer that record payments from individuals to the agents of the royal treasury. The rolls are organized by shire. In general, there is one line for each
payment, listing the payer, the amount paid, and usually a brief mention of the
reason for payment: debt, fine, or tax. For some years, including 1221, a separate
roll contains the revenue received from Jews. Here, too, each entry is usually accompanied with a brief explanation of the reason for the payment. A number of

the Jews recorded in the Easter 1221 roll, for example, made payments toward the Bristol tallage, the extraordinary tax that, as we have seen, King John had imposed on his Jewish subjects in 1210—and that was still being paid by a significant number of Jews in 1221 (entries for payments toward the Bristol tallage are also found in the receipt rolls for 1220, 1222, and 1224).

Thirty-five entries from the Easter 1221 receipt rolls involve payments by Jews, for exemption from wearing the badge or *tabulae*. The total of the payments is £28 8 s. 6 d., a non-negligible contribution to the royal coffers. Jews from thirteen different shires are listed here: sums vary from a mere 5 shillings collected in Northamptonshire to £7 18 s. for Lincolnshire. These sums seem not to correspond to the relative size and wealth of the Jewish communities of the different shires: London was the largest Jewish community, yet its Jews paid a mere 13s. for the right not to wear the badge. Individual payments vary widely as well: from 10p. for Manasser, son of Abraham (entry number 2639) to a whopping £4 for Moses, son of Abraham in Norfolk/Suffolk (2761). We lack the context that would explain these variations. Most of the payments seem to be made by individuals for the individual privilege of not wearing the badge, though a number of them are followed with the term "cum duplo," literally with a "double" or "copy." It is unclear whether this means that a certificate attesting their exemption was issued to them or if the "duplum" refers to an extended permission (there is no mention of how long this permission is meant to last, or if it is perpetual) or perhaps to permission granted for two people. Several entries mention that the payment is made for a man and his wife (or in one case, his daughter). Finally, four entries involve communal payments: it seems that they obtain the exemption for the entire Jewish communities of Canterbury, Oxford, Stanford, and London, although in the case of Oxford there are individuals who pay for this exemption in addition to the payment for the general exemption.

The sums in the Easter 1221 rolls catalogue payments made to royal officials between Michaelmas 1220 and Easter 1221, which seems to have been an exceptional period for the collection of these fees. There is no mention of fees collected for the right not to wear badges in the 1220 or 1222 receipt rolls. The receipt roll for the seventh year of Henry's reign (for Michaelmas 1224) has only two such entries, for a total of five shillings and nine pence (entries 1959 and 4158). Henry Richardson mentions similar records from the (as yet unedited) rolls of 1226 and 1227, but nothing on the scale of 1221.[44] Here again, we lack the context to explain why the crown was able to put sufficient pressure on English Jews in 1221 to make them pay considerable sums to avoid wearing the badge, and why it never did so again to the same scale. This may suggest that the grants were permanent.

There has been some debate among historians over the enforcement of the badge. For some, Henry's 1218 law was a significant change in Jewish policy. Cecil Roth pictures Jews winding their way through the streets of medieval Oxford marked by the tablets, a humiliating distinction suffered by English Jews.[45] Yet we may doubt whether these measures were enforced or ever intended to be enforced: was the 1218 mandate simply a pious gesture, little more than a sop to ecclesiastical opinion, a measure that the king and his regency had little will to enforce and that quickly became a dead letter? These records from receipt rolls give us pause. They show that numerous Jews in England were ready to pay significant amounts of money in order not to wear the badge. Clearly, if there were no threat of enforcement, these people would not willingly pay such sums. Conversely, were the law enforced strictly, one would presumably not be able to buy exemptions from it. What this shows is that Henry's regency saw this legal obligation as a means both to assert royal jurisdiction over the king's Jews and to extract money from them. As often in medieval Europe, justice is among other things a means of obtaining income. Guala had returned to Italy in 1219; it is significantly only after his departure that the crown sees fit to sell exemptions from wearing the *tabulae*; it was also, as we have seen, during the absence of Archbishop Stephen Langton, who was in Rome.

Stephen returned to England in July 1221. He did not waste any time: shortly after his return Pandulf resigned (on 26 July 1221): the archbishop must have brought instructions from the pope to this effect. Upon his return, he also brought the following letter from Pope Honorius III, addressed to Stephen as archbishop of Canterbury and dated 6 July 1221:

> Honorius bishop, servant of the servants of God, to venerable brother archbishop of Canterbury, cardinal of the holy Roman church, greetings and apostolic blessing. Since the general council, whose complete statutes we wish to serve, upon careful deliberation decreed that in every land Jews should be distinguished from Christians by different clothing, lest some Christian men should have intercourse with Jews' women or Jewish men with Christians' women; and since the Jews of your diocese do not observe this (as we have learned from you), on account of which the crime of damnable commerce could be subsumed under the veil of error, by Apostolic mandate we order your fraternity to compel Jews to distinguish themselves from Christians in their dress by removing them from contact with the faithful. Given at the Lateran on the second day of the Nones of July in the sixth year of our pontificate (6 July 1221).[46]

Langton no doubt solicited this letter from the pope, in order to obtain a clear mandate to impose these measures on the English church.[47]

The issue was important to Honorius, who sent similar letters to other European prelates as part of an attempt to enforce conciliar regulations that aimed to limit contacts between Jews and Christians. The pope refers to "the general council," meaning the Fourth Lateran Council of 1215. Honorius reiterates the language of canon 68, in particular concerning the goal of avoiding sexual mixing, and the general, unspecific requirement of distinctive dress. He does not mention the royal mandate of 1218 or the specific requirement to wear *tabulae*, although he (through Stephen) is no doubt aware of both. Nor does he mention the exemptions sold to Jews recorded in the Easter 1221 receipt rolls, of which he may well have been unaware (since Stephen had been away from England since 1220). While Honorius's letter closely follows canon 68, there is one very important difference. Canon 68 had no teeth: there was no mention of how it might be enforced. Stephen provided the answer, and this will lead him into direct conflict with King Henry III.

The Council of Oxford

Armed with papal letters and rid of papal legates, Stephen was poised to affirm his control over the English Church. As Stephen and the bishops were preparing the council, an incident in Stamford may have hardened their resolve to restrict the place of Jews in English society. In March 1222 some Jews of Stamford were arrested for having undertaken a "ludum" (play or taunt) insulting the Christian faith. They were to appear before the royal court for judgment in Westminster within fifteen days after Easter.[48] It is not clear exactly what these Jews had done: perhaps mocked Christianity as part of a celebration of Purim. In any case, it was deemed important enough for royal officials to arrest them and for Hubert de Burgh to summon them to London.

The provincial Council of Oxford took place on Sunday, 17 April 1222 in the monastery of Osney, just outside of Oxford.[49] According to various thirteenth-century English chroniclers, the first business of the council was to pass judgment against several individuals. First there was a deacon who, for love of a Jewess, had apostatized and was circumcised "according to the Jewish rite." As John of Basingstoke, archdeacon of London, related the story to Matthew Paris:

An English deacon loved a Jewess with unlawful love, and ardently desired her embraces. "I will do what you ask," said she, "if you will turn
apostate, be circumcised, and hold fast the Jewish faith." When he had
done what she bade him, he gained her unlawful love. But this could
not long be concealed and was reported to [Archbishop] Stephen [Langton] of Canterbury. Before him the deacon was accused . . . he was convicted and then confessed all these matters, and that he had taken part
in a sacrifice which the Jews made of a crucified boy. And when it was
seen that the deacon was circumcised, and that no argument would bring
him to his senses, he solemnly apostatized before the archbishop and the
assembled prelates in this manner: a cross with the Crucified was
brought before him and he urinated on the cross, saying: "I renounce
the new-fangled law and the comments of Jesus the false prophet," and
he reviled and slandered Mary the mother of Jesus and made against her
a charge not to be repeated. Thereupon the archbishop, weeping bitterly
at hearing such blasphemies, deprived him of his orders.[50]

He was defrocked by the council and handed over to the lay authorities for
execution, although the chroniclers do not agree if he was beheaded, hanged, or
burned. Another man had tried to crucify himself, affirming that he was the redeemer of the world; he was imprisoned for life on a diet of bread and water.
The canons of the council mention nothing of either of these cases.[51] Whatever
the truth behind the tale of the apostate deacon, Matthew's lurid version, in
which he crucifies a Christian child, blasphemes the Virgin, and urinates on a cross,
is meant to show how dangerous fraternization with Jews can be. The fate of the late
deacon may well have been on the minds of the assembled bishops.

The bishops pronounced a series of fifty canons. Twelve of the bishops present, including Langton, had attended the Fourth Lateran Council; they now
sought to apply that council's reformist agenda on the English Church.[52] Thus
the great majority of the canons regulated the behavior of bishops, priests, monks,
and other churchmen: their ordination, their dress, their financial activities, their
respect of canonical rules, and their sexual transgressions (they were prohibited
from keeping concubines). A number of the canons curbed lay power over the
Church and in particular the alienation of Church property to laymen. Two of
the canons (46 and 47) dealt with Jews. The case of apostasy, connected as it was
with a sexual liaison between a Christian deacon and a Jewish woman, may in
part explain the concern with the use of badges to distinguish Jews, explicitly

presented as a means to avoid sexual union between Jews and Christians (canon 47). Both of these texts are fundamental for understanding Langton's conception of the proper place of Jews in Christian English society and merit close attention. Here is the text of canon 46:

> Since it is absurd that the children of a free woman should be slaves to the children of a bondswoman, and since no little scandal regularly arises in the Church of God from Jews and Christians living under the same roof, we decree that in the future Jews shall not possess Christian servants. For the observance of this injunction we wish the servants to be effectively constrained by ecclesiastical censure, and the Jews by regular punishment or such extraordinary punishment as may be devised by the diocesan official; and since beyond the decrees of the law we need show them no favor, and inasmuch as, by the many enormities which they have committed at this time, they have been proved to be most ungrateful, we forbid them to construct synagogues in the future, but we enjoin that they shall be held bound to the churches, in whose parishes they dwell, in respect to tithes and contributions out of their usury.[53]

This canon is one of a long series of laws, originating in fourth-century Roman law, prohibiting Jewish ownership of Christian slaves. The goal in this case is explicitly to prevent Christians and Jews from living together in the same household. While in the thirteenth-century Jews in England would not have owned Christian slaves, some did have Christian servants who lived in their homes. This is no doubt what the council means by *mancipia*: Innocent III had similarly prohibited Jews from having Christian servants in their homes, at times using *mancipia*, at times the more correct *servientes*. No doubt the scandal of sex between a Christian deacon and a Jewess was on the council's mind, but more generally we see the hand of Stephen Langton, who used the council to disseminate reform decisions made in Rome, in particular those of the Fourth Lateran Council. The other two subjects of the canon are the prohibition to build new synagogues and the requirement to continue to pay tithes due to the churches for lands they held, whether they had bought them or whether they simply held them temporarily in mortgage for unpaid loans, in order to prevent the loss of Church revenue.

Canon 47 also addresses issues raised by Lateran IV:

Since in these parts such confusion has arisen between Christians and Jews that they are barely distinguishable, and as a result it sometimes happens that Christians unite with Jewesses or vice versa, we decree by the authority of the present general Council, that each and every Jew, whether male or female, shall wear clearly exposed on the outer garments, on the chest, woolen tablets of a different color from that of his garment, so that each patch shall measure two fingers in width and four in length; and that they shall be compelled, by ecclesiastical censure, to observe this regulation. They shall moreover not presume to enter churches in the future. And lest they have occasion to enter, we strictly forbid them to deposit and keep their property in churches; and if anyone dare act to the contrary, he shall be corrected by the local bishop.[54]

This canon goes beyond what the Lateran Council had proclaimed in canon 68: that Jews (and Saracens) were to dress in a distinctive and recognizable manner, in order to avoid unintentional sexual mixing. Here we have not a general (and rather vague) rule on distinctive dress, but a quite specific regulation, in accordance with the royal mandate of 1218, requiring every Jew, male and female, to wear a badge on his or her outer clothing. Compared to the royal mandate, there are a few important differences. The 1218 text imposed "two white tablets made of linen cloth or parchment" (*duas tabulas albas . . . factas de lineo panno vel de parcameno*), whereas here it is "woolen tablets of a different color from that of his garment" (*tabulas laneas alterius coloris quam vestis*), in order to assure that the tablets be clearly visible. For the same reason, the canon specifies the minimum size of the tablets (which had not been mentioned in the 1218 mandate): two fingers in width and four in length: in fact a fairly small badge.[55]

The other measure taken in this canon is the prohibition of Jews entering churches and in particular keeping their property there: probably, as we have seen, a reference to the practice of Jewish lenders using church treasuries as places of safekeeping for their money and for goods received as pawn or surety. We have seen that this seems to have been a common practice, though it is mentioned only by ecclesiastical authors who purport to be scandalized by it or who attempt to prohibit it. It also evokes an easy, cordial fraternization between Christian clergy and Jews that the canon attempted to abolish.

The canon also proscribes the means to enforce this measure: *censura ecclesiastica*, Church censure. Clearly what Stephen and the council have in mind is the sort of indirect punishment explicitly authorized by Pope Honorius III in the previous year: cutting Jews off from contact with Christians and hence depriving them of their livelihood and means of subsistence. This is exactly what Stephen and some of his bishops will do in the following months, and in so doing will provoke a strong reaction from the crown.

The year 1222 saw important successes in the reaffirmation of royal power: the resumption of the royal demesne and the growing royal control over shires. This is seen in the Michaelmas exchequer of 1222, which marked significant advances in royal revenues and royal power. The young king, who turned fifteen on October 1, was playing an increasingly active role. Langton was crucial, alongside justiciar Hubert de Burgh, in helping the crown reaffirm its prerogatives. The archbishop mediated between the crown and the barons, as is seen the following year (in January 1223), when at his urging the king issued a confirmation of Magna Carta.[56]

Yet the resurgent power of the crown affirms itself not only against baronial usurpers of royal demesnes and shires, but also against Langton's attempts to limit Jewish-Christian contact. On 10 November 1222, the following mandate was issued in the king's name:

> The king to the sheriff and to the Mayor of Canterbury, greetings. Our Jews of Lincoln showed us that, on account of a precept issued by the venerable fathers the Archbishop of Canterbury and the bishop of Lincoln, it was prohibited for anyone to sell them food or to engage in commerce with them. They were indeed unable to find anyone who would sell them anything. Therefore we order you that, once you have seen these letters, you order and proclaim on our behalf, in your territories, that food and other necessities be sold to them. And if you find someone who refuses to sell them food and other necessities in the city of Lincoln or elsewhere, seize him and keep his body securely, until we send you a mandate concerning him. Witness H. [Hubert de Burgh], etc., at Westminster, November 10th. Similar letters were sent to the mayor and provost of Oxford concerning the Jews of Oxford and to the bailiff of Norwich concerning the Jews of Norwich.[57]

Clearly, some Jews had complained to the king that the archbishop of Canterbury and the bishop of Lincoln had prohibited Christians from selling food to Jews. The text does not say why this ban had been proclaimed, but as we have seen, Honorius and Langton had already envisioned this measure in order to compel the Jews to wear the badge and to cease to employ Christian servants in their homes. Prohibiting Christians from selling to Jews would force the Jews to comply. But Jews obtained the annulment of the ban by the king, without having to make any concessions to the clergy. The mandate was addressed to an unspecified sheriff (perhaps of Kent?) and to the mayor of Canterbury; it was also sent to royal officials in Norwich and in Oxford (which was under the ecclesiastical jurisdiction of the bishop of Lincoln). This suggests that there were attempts to enforce the decrees of the Oxford Council in the dioceses of Canterbury, Lincoln, Oxford, and perhaps Norwich. In reaction, Henry strongly reaffirms his monopoly of power over "his" Jews, who are under his protection. There is no evidence that Langton further pursued this issue or tried to enforce the wearing of the badge.

Yet documents from 1229 and 1245 show that Jewish-Christian relations, and in particular the issue of wearing badges and that of Jews employing Christian servants in their homes, continue to provoke clerical concern. On 26 November 1229, Pope Gregory IX addressed a letter to Richard Grant, Stephen's successor as archbishop of Canterbury. Gregory says that William de Blois, bishop of Worcester, informed him that Jews were not wearing their badges and that they continued to employ Christian servants in their homes: "As a result of this, a thousand abuses occur, putting souls in grave danger."[58] Hence the pope writes to the archbishop, demanding that he see that these regulations are enforced. Yet the letter proposes little in the way of means of coercion: whereas Honorius in 1221 had enjoined Stephen Langton to prohibit Christians from commerce with Jews, Gregory does not attempt to use these means, perhaps aware that Langton's actions had been overruled by the king. There is no evidence that this letter had any impact in England.

The next text we have concerning this issue is a royal mandate from December 1245: "For the Jews. It is mandated to the sheriffs of London that, not withstanding any prohibition which the Bishop of London or any ordinary may have made in the City of London, prohibiting that food be sold to the king's Jews, food shall be sold all over the above-mentioned city to those same Jews who have business there, as has been done previously. Witness the king at Westminster on the 17th day of December [1245]."[59] It seems that Fulk Basset, bishop of London, had tried to prohibit Christians from selling food to Jews in London, just as Stephen Langton and his bishops had done in 1222.[60] Henry reacts in the same way, ordering that food be sold to Jews as usual. As in 1222, the royal mandate does not mention the reasons behind the bishop's prohibition, but it seems very likely that at issue here, as earlier, were what were seen as improper relations between Christians and Jews, as represented in particular by the issues of servants and badges. What is clear is that in 1245 bishops still resent the refusal of Jews to recognize restrictions on their status and that Henry is willing to override bishops in order to defend "the king's Jews." Indeed, this was to remain a preoccupation, not to say an obsession, for at least some prominent English bishops until the eve of the 1290 expulsion. These churchmen sought at all costs to avoid regular friendly relations between Jews and Christians, for fear that this subvert the proper hierarchies implied by Jews' servile status, in particular that they might lead to sexual relations between Jews and Christians or to apostasy. We have seen that Pope Innocent III went so far as to proffer lurid stories illustrating the hostility of Jews to Christians: Jewish employers making their wet-nurses dispose of their milk in the latrines after taking communion; Jews secretly plotting to kill Christians. Such accusations would multiply, in England as elsewhere in Europe, in the coming decades.

CHAPTER 3

Simon de Montfort and the King's Jews

In August 1231 Simon of Montfort expelled the Jews from the town of Leicester. He presents the expulsion as motivated both by spiritual concerns and as a concession to the town's burghers, which suggests some of them may have felt disadvantaged by the commercial or financial activities of the town's Jews. This expulsion is unprecedented, all the more so in that Simon, a vassal of the king who had only recently received Leicester from Henry, does not mention the king in his edict: it does not seem that Simon ever sought out Henry's approval for this measure.

There is no direct evidence concerning Henry's reaction to this expulsion, which seems a breach of his authority by an important vassal. Yet two royal initiatives in the following years (1232 and 1233) may be seen to some extent as responses both to Simon's expulsion and to Capetian anti-Jewish legislation. In 1232, Henry established in London a *Domus conversorum*, a house in which converted Jews could live in a quasi-monastic setting. In 1233, the king issued the *Statute of the Jews*, in which he emphatically reaffirms the royal monopoly of control over "his" Jews and proclaims that any Jew who does not provide service to the king should leave the kingdom. The king asserts his lordship over the Jews and at the same time limits their presence, probably in response to the anti-Jewish measures taken by both ecclesiastical councils and by Simon de Montfort.

These events need to be understood against the background of the rivalry between Henry, who assumed formal control over the crown in January 1227 at the age of nineteen, and King Louis IX of France, who acceded to the throne at the age of twelve, upon the death of his father Louis VIII in November 1226. The Queen Mother Blanche de Castile was ruling France in the name of her son and faced rebellion from some of the crown's principal vassals. Henry saw an opportunity to reclaim the lands his father had lost to Philip II. All the more so as some of the French rebels asked Henry to join forces with them. Duke Peter of Brittany, who had fought alongside Louis VIII, first in England against King John in 1216 and then in the Albigensian crusade, joined the rebel forces. He came to Portsmouth to do homage to Henry in October 1229. Henry needed to raise money quickly in order to unite forces with the French rebels and reclaim his heritage. According to Roger of Wendover, "on the demand of the king, the archbishops, bishops, abbots, and priors throughout all England gave to the king a large sum of money to enable him to recover the provinces on the continent which had been taken from his father. The citizens of London too were compelled to redeem themselves by the payment of a heavy amount for the same purpose; and the Jews, whether they would or not, were compelled to give up a third of all their property."[1] Wendover's claim of a *captio* of one-third of the property in not confirmed by fiscal records, which on the contrary record tallages of 8,000 marks over three years from 1229 to 1231.[2] The citizens of London would come to resent the financial hardship imposed by Henry's military fiascos, Wendover suggests. And the bishops and other Church prelates who contributed to his coffers would pressure him to respect and to support their reforming agenda, which as we have seen included restrictions on the kingdom's Jews.

Henry crossed over to Saint Malo in May 1230, where he met up with Peter; he then made his way to Nantes. Louis raised an army and marched to Angers, then west to the town of Oudon on the Loire, where he blocked Henry's advance. Henry chose to avoid direct confrontation with French forces and decided against invading Normandy, instead going south to the Poitou, where he received homage from his principal vassals. He returned to England in October, having accomplished little in what proved to be an expensive expedition. Louis succeeded in forcing the rebels into submission over the following years: Peter of Brittany submitted unconditionally to the French king in 1234. The rest of Henry's reign would be marked by rivalry with Louis and by a series of expensive military failures against him.

Simon de Montfort's Expulsion of the Jews of Leicester

The idea of banning Jews from Christian communities was not novel. As we saw in Chapter 1, Abbot Samson of Bury St. Edmonds expelled the Jews from the monastic town in 1190. We also saw that French King Philip II banished the Jews from his royal domains in 1182. As William Jordan has shown, this expulsion was among other things a way for the young king to show his strong will and his piety, boldly moving against those who could be portrayed as enemies of the Christians and from whom one had little cause to fear retaliation.[3] Similar motives may have been at play when Simon de Montfort, new Lord of Leicester, expelled the Jews from the city.

Simon de Montfort will loom large throughout this study: vassal and confidant of the king, he married the king's youngest sister and became Earl of Leicester.[4] Estranged several times from the king and subsequently restored to his good grace and confidence, Simon would finally become the leader of the baronial opposition to Henry's rule, rout the king at the battle of Lewes and keep him hostage for over a year (1264–1265). Simon's troops, like those of so many antiroyal rebellions before, would engage in anti-Jewish violence and pillaging; indeed theirs would be the bloodiest anti-Jewish massacres since those of 1189–1190, as we will see in Chapter 6.

Yet all of this was far in the future in 1231, when Simon, new Lord of Leicester who had recently arrived for the first time in England, decreed the expulsion of the Jews from the city of Leicester. Simon's father, also known as Simon de Montfort, led the "Albigensian" crusade against alleged heresy in the lands of the Count of Toulouse. The young Simon was ten years old when, in June 1218, his crusader father met his death while laying siege to Toulouse, his head smashed by a rock hurled from a mangonel fired by one of the city's defenders. The elder Simon had been both Earl of Leicester and Lord of Montfort-l'Amaury (about fifty kilometers west-southwest of Paris). Like many aristocrats of his generation, he had lands on both sides of the English Channel. And like many of them, he had to choose sides in the conflict between King Philip II of France and the kings of England, Richard and John. He fought beside Philip against Richard in Normandy.[5] John seized his lands in Leicester in 1207 and subsequently (in 1215) granted them to Ranulf de Blundeville, Earl of Chester.

Young Simon was only nine years old when in 1217 his mother, Alice (or Alix) de Montmorency, attempted to oblige Toulouse's Jews to convert to Christianity, according to a Hebrew text probably composed in the late thirteenth century. Alice was ruling the city for her husband, who had obtained Toulouse's submission the previous year. The Hebrew text reports that Alice had all Jews, men, women, children and the elderly, taken captive. Children under six years of age were handed over to the clergy for baptism and adoption. The rest were imprisoned and told that they would have to choose between baptism and death. Fifty-seven of them accepted baptism. It is unclear from this narrative if any others had indeed been put to death, but on 7 July 1217 an order arrived from Count Simon that the Jews should be freed and their possessions returned to them, that such had been the order of the papal legate.[6] It is hard to assess the

accuracy of this Hebrew narrative, probably written well after the fact and preserved only in a sixteenth-century chronicle. But there is nothing implausible
about it. Alice was a countess ruling a city marked by resistance to the Church:
no doubt forcing conversion of the Jews would send a strong signal to others,
within and outside Toulouse. Alice was the wife and daughter of crusaders: her
father, Bouchard V de Montmorency, was a vassal of Philip II who took a vow of
crusade, but who died in 1189 shortly before Philip set off.[7] Alice's attempt to convert the Jews by force was far harsher than what Philip II had done or than what
her son Simon would do, and it was clearly against church law, as the cardinal
legate ruled. A clumsy attempt, perhaps, by a northern French countess to impose her will on a subjected southern city. Toulouse would soon throw off Simon's and Alice's yoke, and it was while trying to take back the city, as we have
seen, that the elder Simon lost his life the following year.

Young Simon was the youngest of his parents' four sons. His eldest brother,
Amaury, inherited their father's French lands and titles and in 1230 became grand
constable of France. Simon decided to lay his claims to the family lands and titles
in England, at Leicester. Robert de Beaumont IV, Earl of Leicester, had died in
1204, without an heir, splitting his inheritance between his sisters. The elder
sister, Amice, had married our Simon's grandfather (also known as Simon de
Montfort): it is through her that Simon's father had obtained the title of earl and
half the lands of Leicester. Robert de Beaumont's younger daughter, Margaret,
inherited the other half of her father's lands; she subsequently married Saer de
Quincy, Earl of Winchester, who died in 1219.

Hence Simon had a good claim to the title and lands that had belonged to
his father, all the more so as his elder brother Amaury renounced them in his
favor. Simon managed to win over to his side Ranulf de Blundeville and to be
received by King Henry, to whom Simon made homage in August 1231. Henry
recognized Simon's claims to the family lands at Leicester (though not yet to the
title of earl, which he would bestow seven years later). Simon arrived in Leicester in late 1231 or early 1232. It seems that he wanted to affirm his power, especially since half the Leicester lands were in the hands of his great-aunt, Margaret,
now Countess of Winchester by marriage. And what better way than to take a
page from his father's lord, Philip II, who had similarly marked his advent by expelling Jews. It is in this context that Simon issued the following order:

> Simon de Montfort, son of Earl Simon de Montfort, Lord of Leicester,
> to all the faithful in Christ, who may see and hear the present page,
> health in the Lord. Know all of you that I, for the good of my soul, and

the souls of my ancestors and successors, have granted, and by this my
present charter have confirmed, on behalf of me and my heirs forever, to
my burgesses of Leicester and their heirs, that no Jew or Jewess, in my
time or in the time of any of my heirs to the end of the world, shall within
the liberty of the town of Leicester, inhabit or remain or obtain a residence. I also wish and command that my heirs after me observe and war-
rant forever that liberty entire and inviolate to the aforesaid burgesses.[8]

With this edict, Simon expelled the Jews from Leicester, or rather, from the
half the town that he controlled. He presents the expulsion as motivated both
by spiritual concerns (the benefit of Simon's soul and those of his ancestors) and
as a concession to the town's burgers. This suggests that at least some of them
derived profit from eliminating the competition that the commercial or financial activities of the town's Jews entailed. This expulsion is the first recorded act
of Simon as Lord of Leicester, issued within months after his assumption of power
in August 1231.

Jews had been present in Leicester since 1185, but the town was not mentioned among the seventeen recognized Jewish communities of 1218 and made
no contributions to the royal tallages of 1221, 1223, or 1226.[9] Perhaps Ranulf considered that the town's Jews were his, and not the king's: on 23 June 1226, the
crown issued a concession to Ranulf that "the Jews now present in Leicester and
Coventry may reside and stay there." The king instructs the sheriffs of Leicester
and Warwick to allow these Jews to remain there "without impediment or ha-
rassment."[10] In other words, Leicester's Jews depended directly on their lord, and
royal officials could neither tax them nor harass them. They were a seigneurial
community, like that of Bury St. Edmonds before their expulsion in 1190, an
anomaly already in England in 1190 and all the more so forty-one years later, when
the majority of communities were "the king's Jews." Hence Simon judged that
they were his Jews to expel as he saw fit. But contrary to the abbot of Bury, there
is no evidence that he sought the king's approval for this expulsion.

Another source that mentions Simon's expulsion of the Jews from Leicester
is a letter that Robert Grosseteste, then archdeacon of Leicester, sent, sometime
between August 1231 and November 1232, to Margaret de Quincy.[11] Grosseteste
wrote that he heard the countess had "decided to welcome unto your land the
Jews whom the lord of Leicester expelled from his town to prevent their further
pitiless exploitation from usury of the Christians who live there." Historians have
cited this letter either as proof that Grosseteste encouraged Simon to expel Leicester's Jews, or that he tried to dissuade him from doing so, but in fact it says nei-

ther.[12] Grosseteste neither condemns nor praises Simon's action, though he does suggest that Jews' abusive practice of usury could justify such action. There is no evidence that Simon consulted him or associated him with the expulsion: he is not named as one of the witnesses to the order. Moreover, the archdeacon neither praises nor condemns Margaret's decision to welcome these Jews. He explains to her, in terms that echo the language of bulls of Innocent III, that Jews are punished by God for the sin of murdering Jesus, that they are to live in punishment and captivity. Thus Christian rulers are obliged to protect Jews, while at the same time preventing them from oppressing Christians—in particular through usury. Here Grosseteste advises the countess not to let the Jews she has taken in practice oppressive usury, but rather to have them make their living through working the land. God will punish Jews who oppress Christians and will also punish, he warns, Christian princes who permit this or, worse, who profit from it. The implications of Grosseteste's letter is that all Jewish lending, a royally controlled monopoly providing significant income to the crown and playing a key role in the English economy, should be brought to a halt. Yet there is no evidence that he ever suggested such a radical policy change to King Henry, or that he ever opposed the practice of Jewish lending when he later became chancellor of Oxford and bishop of Lincoln.

Simon may have been inspired by Capetian legislation. Already in 1223, Louis VIII, along with the principal barons who ruled over Jewish communities, pronounced a *stabilimentum,* an agreement according to which they would no longer enforce Jewish loans.[13] In early 1227, during the regency of Blanche de Castille (Louis VIII's widow and Louis IX's mother), another ordinance reiterated that usury was not to be levied on debts to Jews incurred after 1223.[14] Churchmen in France also railed against what they portrayed as the hostility of Jews to Christ and Christians. Sometime between 1227 and 1230, Guillaume de Beaumont, bishop of Angers, wrote a series of propositions to the archbishop of Tours in preparation for the 1231 Council of Château Gontier. He complained that Jews live everywhere among the Christians and that their impiety and mocking risk corrupting the faith of the simple. They "detest the articles of the faith," insinuate that it is impossible for a virgin to conceive or give birth or for the bread of the Eucharist to be transformed into the body of the Lord. Christian women go into the homes of Jews to borrow money: there Jewish men impregnate them. Jews blaspheme against God, composing songs in Hebrew mocking Christianity and teaching them to their children. The 1231 Council of Château Gontier prohibited Jewish blasphemy and affirmed that Jews should not be able to bear witness in court against Christians.[15]

In December 1230, Louis IX issued the ordinance of Melun, instructing Christians to pay their debts to Jews, but not to pay usury, which is defined as *"quidquid ultra sortem"* (anything beyond the principal). Debts are to be paid back in installments over the next three years. Moreover, the ordinance ruled that every Jew had one lord, and that that lord had exclusive domain over him, that the Jew was "like his serf" (*tanquam proprium servum*).[16] Whereas French Jews were dependent on their local lords, England's Jews were "the king's Jews," and their lending activity, and the interest charged, were closely monitored and controlled by the crown. In 1230 the French king told his Christian subjects not to pay interest to Jews and recognized his vassals' right to dominium over their Jews. Simon's brother, Amaury V, Lord of Montfort and grand constable of France, witnessed the ordinance of Melun and attached his seal to it (along with those of the king and other barons).

Simon subsequently, it seems, overstepped his rights and attempted to seize some of his great-aunt's lands. At issue was whether Simon or Margaret had jurisdiction over the eastern suburb of Leicester, the town's communal bread-ovens (probably those outside the gates), the manors of Belgrave and Glenfield, and rents in the estates Desford and Whetstone, southwest of the town. In January 1232, the king told the sheriff of Leicester that Montfort's claims to the lands and title of his father gave him no rights over Margaret's lands. The dispute continued unsettled until September. Aggressively asserting his authority over the territory by expelling the Jews and seizing the lands of his rival and great-aunt, Simon already showed signs of the ruthlessness and audacity that would mark his career.[17] He made these moves without the king's approval and earned the crown's reprimand for his seizure of Margaret's lands (though not, it seems, for expelling Leicester's Jews).

By expelling the Jews from Leicester, Simon made a bold assertion of his authority and independence as Lord of Leicester. Framing the expulsion as an act of piety and a favor to the town's burgesses, he affirmed his legitimacy over Margaret. Unlike Abbot Samson, who in 1190 had requested permission of King Richard I to expel the Jews from the town of Bury St. Edmonds, Simon makes no mention of King Henry. His authority, it seems, came not from the king to whom he recently made homage, but from his father the Earl of Leicester, from God, and from the burgesses of Leicester. To those who might contest this bold move, Simon could retort that he was acting in accordance with the authority granted to him by his father, by his respect for the will of the town's burgesses, and by his love for God. This is the first such expulsion from an English town since that of Bury in 1190, and the fact that it was issued by a major baron (to become briefly de facto ruler of

England) and potentially sanctioned by Robert Grosseteste could make it a model for future expulsions. Simon shows himself at age twenty-three, freshly arrived in England, already a force to be reckoned with. We have no record of reactions to this measure by the Jews who were expelled. But they, and other Jews of England, learned that Simon was no friend. This would not prevent Simon from contracting a loan for £110 from Jewish lender David of Oxford in 1243.[18]

In a context where English bishops criticized the king for being insufficiently zealous in his enforcement of conciliar measures concerning Jews' obligations to wear badges or the prohibition to employ Christian servants, Simon's expulsion was potentially embarrassing to King Henry. And that a newly arrived vassal would take such an initiative without the slightest bow to the king's supposedly exclusive dominion over English Jews posed a challenge. Simon's move may have been on the king's mind the following year, when he founded a house for converts, and in 1233, when he issued a new statute for the English Jewish community.

The Foundation of the *Domus conversorum*, London 1232

On 16 January 1232, Henry issued a charter founding the *Domus conversorum,* or house for converts, in honor of the Virgin Mary, on Newstreet (now Chancery Lane), in London. He accorded seven hundred marks to the new institution in order to pay for the expenses of the converts and to build a church for their use.[19] Converts residing in the *Domus conversorum* were to live a quasi-monastic life, in this convent devoted to the Virgin Mary, with a modest subsistence furnished by the king, though there is no mention of vows to be taken and provisions were made for families of converts. The importance of this foundation is underlined by the prominence of the witnesses summoned by the king to Lambeth Palace to sign the charter: the royal justiciar Hubert de Burgh; Peter des Roches, bishop of Winchester; Walter Mauclerck, royal treasurer and soon to become the first warden of the *Domus conversorum*. Peter des Roches, as we have seen, had close relations with Isaac of Norwich and with other Jewish lenders; he had also been a key administrator of kings John and Henry until his estrangement with King Henry in 1223. He had left the kingdom and made pilgrimage to Jerusalem and Rome from 1227 to 1231. In July 1231, he returned to England and resumed his close relations with Jewish lenders and his patronage of local monasteries. He also found his way back into the king's good graces: Henry and Eleanor spent Christmas 1231 at his episcopal palace at Winchester. It is possible that the *domus* was his brainchild.

On 9 March 1232, Henry sent a mandate to Walter Mauclerck, ordering that out of the seven hundred marks per year assigned by the king for the sustenance of the *fratrum conversorum*, he provide two chaplains in food, clothing, and other things necessary for the celebration of the divine office in the chapel that the king has had built for the converts.[20] Later the same year, in another mandate to Walter Mauclerck, the king ordered that the convert Roger de Parten be received in the *domus* and to be given the necessaries just like the other converts in the *domus* ("sicut alios conversos eiusdem domus"). Documents attest to the admission in 1233 of two men and one woman into the *domus*; seven men, eight women, and four children in 1234.[21] A steady but modest trickle of converts entered the *domus*. The king made grants of lands and goods he had seized from criminals sentenced to death or exile: he gave to the converts in 1235 some lands and houses in London that had belonged to John Herlicun, who had been convicted of murder.[22] Constantine Fitz Aluf was hanged in 1247: Henry granted his lands in London to the *domus*.[23] David of Oxford, a prominent Oxford Jew whom we will discuss in Chapter 4, died in 1244. According to law, one-third of his property was inherited by the king, who granted some of his lands and houses in Oxford to the *domus*.[24] A legacy of £100 from Peter des Roches was also devoted to the endowment of the house.[25] On various occasions, the king granted tunics to the converts: on 6 May 1257, the king and queen ordered that tailors make 164 tunics made for poor converts for Pentecost (though probably they did not all reside in the *domus*).[26]

The *domus* was only one of a number of religious institutions that benefited from the king's largesse.[27] The motivation for this foundation, according to Henry's 1232 charter, is divine inspiration and the concern for the salvation of his own soul and those of his ancestors. This language is echoed in the description that chronicler Matthew Paris gives of the foundation:

> Henry III built a decent church, fit for a conventual congregation, with other buildings adjoining, at his own expense, in the place where he had established a House of Converts, for the ransom of his soul and that of his father, King John, and all their ancestors, in the 17th year of his reign, that is to say, in London, not far from the Old Temple, To this house converted Jews retired, leaving their Jewish blindness, and had a home and a safe refuge for their whole lives, living under an honourable rule, with sufficient sustenance without servile work or the profits of usury. So it happened that in a short time a large number were collected there.

And now, being baptised and instructed in the Christian law, they live a praiseworthy life under a Governor specially appointed.[28]

In the margin of the manuscript, Matthew provides a drawing of the church,

The *Domus conversorum* is unique in thirteenth-century Europe: a royally-funded institution devoted wholly to converts from Judaism, providing sustenance for them in a quasi-monastic environment. It is perhaps no wonder that various historians have seen this as proof of Henry's zeal for the conversion of Jews. Yet it is not clear how effective it was. Various documents give the names of the wardens of the *domus*. The first, as we have seen, is Walter Mauclerck, royal treasurer and bishop of Carlisle. This choice of a prominent member of his entourage no doubt shows that Henry wished to entrust the new institution to someone with power, influence, and access to crown revenues; but it also meant that the new warden probably spent little time at the *domus,* occupied as he was with other charges. Occupied, too, with political conflict and intrigue, as in the 1230s he experienced exile, excommunication, and finally reconciliation with the English church and crown.[29] Walter is indeed mentioned in subsequent documents from 1234 and 1240.[30] Moreover, the *domus* was chronically underfunded:

Figure 1. Matthew Paris, drawing of *Domus Conversorum,*
British Library MS Royal 14 C VII, f. 121r.

it rarely received the full seven hundred marks per year that Henry had promised at its foundation, and the various grants of land and money mentioned above did not suffice for the upkeep of the church and lodgings and the living expenses of converts and personnel. Its most recent and thoroughest historian, Lauren Fogle, concludes that its funding was "convoluted."[31] Granted, these converts were not the only objects of royal neglect: the king, known for his extravagant spending and costly (and unsuccessful) European military adventures, often failed to respect his financial engagements. Indeed, an inquiry made at Henry's demand toward the end of his reign indicated that the *domus* was in a precarious state.[32] In view of the limited capacity of the *domus* to house and feed converts, Henry also wrote to monasteries to ask them to receive converts and provide for them. In 1247, he made such arrangements with 13 convents for 17 converts; in 1254–1255, he wrote to 40 convents for the housing of some 160 converts.[33] But this, as we will see, was in a context very different from that of 1232.

The only substantial relief to the financial troubles of the *domus conversorum* came much later, on 26 May 1280, through a mandate by Henry's son and successor Edward I. Edward ordered various reforms to improve the situation of the *domus* and its residents: designating clergy to cater to the spiritual needs of the converts, encouraging the converts to learn trades. Edward took measures to ensure the financial solvency of the institution and a decent allowance for its inmates: these include the assignment to the *domus* of various revenues, in particular from the chevage, or poll tax, levied on Jews.[34] But no doubt the most significant measure was the abolition of the previous royal practice of seizing the possessions of Jews who converted to Christianity: henceforth converts would be able to keep half their goods: the other half would go to the crown but would specifically be used to for the maintenance of converts and the upkeep of the *domus*. In contrast, King Jaume I of Aragon in 1243 assured that converts from Judaism or Islam would be able to keep *all* of their goods.[35] Almost forty years later, Edward conceded only half their property to converts, something his father Henry had never done. Indeed, if Henry's foundation of the *domus* can be said to represent a modest attempt to encourage conversion of Jews to Christianity, it must be weighed in the balance against royal fiscal policy. The practice of seizing 100 percent of the property of converts was a mighty disincentive to conversion, and indeed the fisc had little reason to wish that prominent, rich Jewish moneylenders cease their activity, which was very lucrative for the crown, and convert to Christianity. This royal policy was a clear violation of canon law, as the Third Lateran Council in 1179 had ruled that no one should dispossess converts.[36]

Occasional documents show Jews resisting the pressures to convert and attempting to prevent children from following their parents into the Christian fold. On 12 May 1236, Henry issued a mandate ordering the custodians of the *domus* to accept two new converts: Fermin of Amiens and his wife. On 3 June, Henry says Firmin had informed him that while he was a still a Jew in Northampton, but presumably already considering converting, some of his Jewish neighbors took his children away from him and would not let him see them. The king orders the constable of Norwich to have the Jews hand over the children to him, so that they may be presented to their father and may tell him whether they want to follow him (and accept baptism) or to "remain in their error."[37] Other Jews in the 1230s are accused of kidnapping or forcibly circumcising children: these incidents are probably to be understood as (largely futile) attempts to prevent or nullify conversions from Judaism to Christianity.[38]

Repeated heavy and arbitrary taxation of Jews (in the form of tallages) led a number of Jews to financial ruin, and in some cases landed them in prison. Add to this the sporadic outbreaks of anti-Jewish violence and increasing pressures from the church to limit Jewish-Christian contact and to proselytize among Jews. Those Jews who were bankrupt and faced imprisonment, as well as those whose families had been decimated through violence, might indeed find a peaceful and modest life in the *domus* to be an attractive (or at least palatable) option. But this hardly makes Henry into someone who took conversion seriously or who held it "closest to his heart," as Robert Stacey claimed.[39] On the contrary, he was unlikely to do anything to endanger the Jews' role as prominent contributors to the royal coffers.[40] Yet in the face of episcopal pressure to limit Jewish-Christian interaction, Louis IX's restriction on Jewish usury through the *Ordonnances de Melun* and Simon's expulsion of the Jews of Leicester, Henry perhaps wished through the foundation of the *domus* to show that he was indeed interested in bringing Jews into the Christian fold.

1233 Statute of the Jewry
and the Hardening of Royal Policy

On 4 April 1233, at Canterbury, Henry issued the following statute:

In the seventeenth year of the reign of Henry, son of King John, on the fourth day of April, the day after Easter, it was established by the same king, in Canterbury, that no loan should be made by tally but by chirograph, one part of which the Jew is to have, with the seal of the Christian of the contracting Christian hanging from it, while the contracting Christian has the other part. The third part, which is called *pes* [foot], should be kept safe in the *archa* [chest], which is guarded by both the Christian and Jewish chirographers. And a chirograph whose *pes* is not found in the *archa*, as prescribed above, has no validity.

No Jew shall grant a loan with penalties, but for a pound shall take two pennies per week and no more, so that he shall have no benefit shall be posited in the loan except the initial interest.

No Jew shall remain in our kingdom unless he is in a position to serve the king and to provide proper gages of his fidelity. Other Jews, who are not able to serve the king, should leave the kingdom before Michaelmas [29 September] of the above-mentioned seventeenth year of the reign of the above-mentioned king [1233]. If they stay beyond that date, they shall be detained in prison and shall not be liberated without a special mandate from the king.

Furthermore, no Jew shall contract a loan on church vessels, or clothing that is blood-stained, wet, or torn.[41]

The first part of the text specifies the terms of the loans made by the Jews, a system already in place. The goal was to ensure that any loan made passes through this controlled and auditable system. This was meant to prevent abuse and to allow royal officers to know the details of the loans and then, if necessary, to tax the Jews and, in the case of the sale of bonds to a third party to enable the purchaser of the debt to pursue its debtors. Instead of the old system of wooden tally sticks, chirographers were to draw up for each loan a chirograph, a document in three parts, giving one part to the lender, one to the debtor, and retaining the third part in the chest (*archa*).[42] The last sentence in the mandate has restrictions (already standard) on the objects that can be received in pledge, prohibiting liturgical objects (because it was considered sacrilegious to leave these items in the hands of Jews) and clothes stained with blood or torn (to prevent concealment of clothing of murder victims) or wet. Interest charged is to be limited to two pennies per pound per week (an annual rate of 43.3 percent, which was to become standard[43]), with no compounded interest (i.e., interest is to be calculated only on the principal, not on accumulated interest).

This restriction on English Jews may have been the brainchild of Peter des Roches and his nephew Peter de Rivallis. Des Roches, as we have seen, returned from crusade in 1231 and soon found his way back into royal favor, obtaining considerable benefits for himself and de Rivallis. He succeeded in turning Henry against royal justiciar Hubert de Burgh, who was stripped of honors and lands and imprisoned.[44] The meteoric rise of the two Peters created considerable resentment and animosity, all the more so as they were seen as foreigners who took advantage of a young, weak king to enrich themselves at England's expense. Part of their strategy of defense, Nicholas Vincent suggests, was to target England's Jews as a more foreign, more despised minority. Taking inspiration from Capetian legislation and perhaps responding to Simon de Montfort's expulsion of the Jews of Leicester, they urged the king to restrict and better control Jews' lending activities.[45] We have seen that in 1230, Louis IX, in the *Ordonnances de Melun*, had ruled that Christians should not pay any interest on loans. Henry's milder restrictions were perhaps meant to show that he also was concerned with the issue. It is likely that he saw these measures as a concession to English bishops in return for support for his candidate (John Blund, close to the two Peters) for the see of Canterbury. If so, the ploy worked: the monks of Canterbury, duly cowed, elected John Blund as archbishop, though Pope Gregory IX refused the election and appointed his own candidate, Edmund of Abingdon.[46]

The third paragraph of this statute is most novel. The very presence of Jews is permitted only if they are "useful" to the king; the others must leave or be jailed. This is both a strong affirmation of the power of the king over "his" Jews and unprecedented restriction on their right to reside in the kingdom. This affirmation of the royal monopoly over Jews is all the more remarkable in that he had delegated his power over them the previous year: among his many grants to Peter de Rivallis, Henry granted him custody for life over the English Jewry on 28 June 1232 and over the Jewish community of Ireland on 28 July 1232.[47] This suggests all the more strongly that the two Peters are behind this legislation, which is simultaneously a sop to English bishops, a move to restrict and marginalize Jews, and an affirmation that no interference will be broached with the exclusive power over England's Jews exercised by the king—or rather, by Peter de Rivallis in the king's name.

We have no evidence that this edict was followed by an exodus of Jews from England or by imprisonment of those deemed to be "useless." Moreover, as noted by Gerald Richardson, this law was never "enrolled" (i.e., copied on the rolls of chancery), suggesting that it had a limited scope. This reinforces the idea that it was a declaration for show rather than a serious piece of legislation, and that the fall from power of the two Peters the following year made it a dead letter. Peter des Roches and Peter de Rivallis, in promoting this new, more restrictive policy toward Jews, no doubt sought to deflect criticism of their own dealings with Jewish financiers. A satirical poet had affirmed that Peter des Roches was "energetic at reckoning and lazy at the Gospel"; for him "lucre overcomes Luke, and he weighs a mark heavier than Mark."[48] We have seen that des Roches had close dealings with Isaac of Norwich, now in his sixties, who remained one of the most prominent and favored of England's Jews. In 1231, Isaac gave ten palfreys to the king and forgave a debt of £100 due by Hugh de Vivonne, Seneschal of Poitou and Gascony, prominent vassal of the king. In return, Henry reduced Isaac's annual payment to one hundred marks (£66). On 3 December 1231, Henry granted Isaac freedom from tallage for the rest of his life, except in the case of special levies.[49] On 10 February 1234, his annual payment was reduced to sixty marks (£40).[50] On 25 July 1234, Henry instructed the justices for the Jews that Isaac should not be required to travel to London to make his payments.[51]

Isaac's close relations with the crown, and in particular with the increasingly unpopular Peter des Roches and Peter de Rivallis, created resentment and hostility. We see this in what seems to be a sort of political cartoon sketched in the upper margin of an exchequer receipt roll from 1233, in which Isaac figures prominently. The caricature is complex and difficult to interpret but has benefitted from an excellent recent study by Sarah Lipton.[52] On each side is a crenellated wall of a building, with a tower prominent in the right center; in the center is what looks like a platform or stage surrounded by curtains. It may represent (as Lipton suggests) the offices of the exchequer at Westminster. The central bearded figure, labeled "Isaac de Norwich," has three faces and wears a crown. On the left, wearing a pointed helmet, is "Mosse Mokke" (i.e. Moses ben Abraham), another prominent Norwich Jew and a close associate of Isaac. Mosse in 1221 had paid a substantial sum of £4 in order not to wear the badge[53]; he subsequently was one of those accused of the circumcision of a Christian boy Edward—a crime that he would finally be hanged for in 1240.[54] Across from Mosse is a woman, Avegaye (otherwise unattested). A creature, perhaps a demon, with a long snout and horns reaches out to touch Mosse's and Avegaye's noses with his fingers. Several other demons are placed on the castle battlements: one blows a horn; others carry what seem to be pitchforks. On the far left, a hooded man holds a scale filled with what seem to be coins while he (as Lipton argues) at the same time makes a lewd gesture toward the other three figures.

What are we to make of this strange cartoon? Isaac, the central figure, is associated with Antichrist: three-faced figures had become common in medieval depictions of Antichrist.[55] Hence the demon in the tower is named "Dagon," a Phoenician deity reviled in the Bible and associated with Antichrist.[56] Isaac wears a crown, which is consistent with depictions of Antichrist but which also, particularly in the context of a royal exchequer roll, suggests association with King

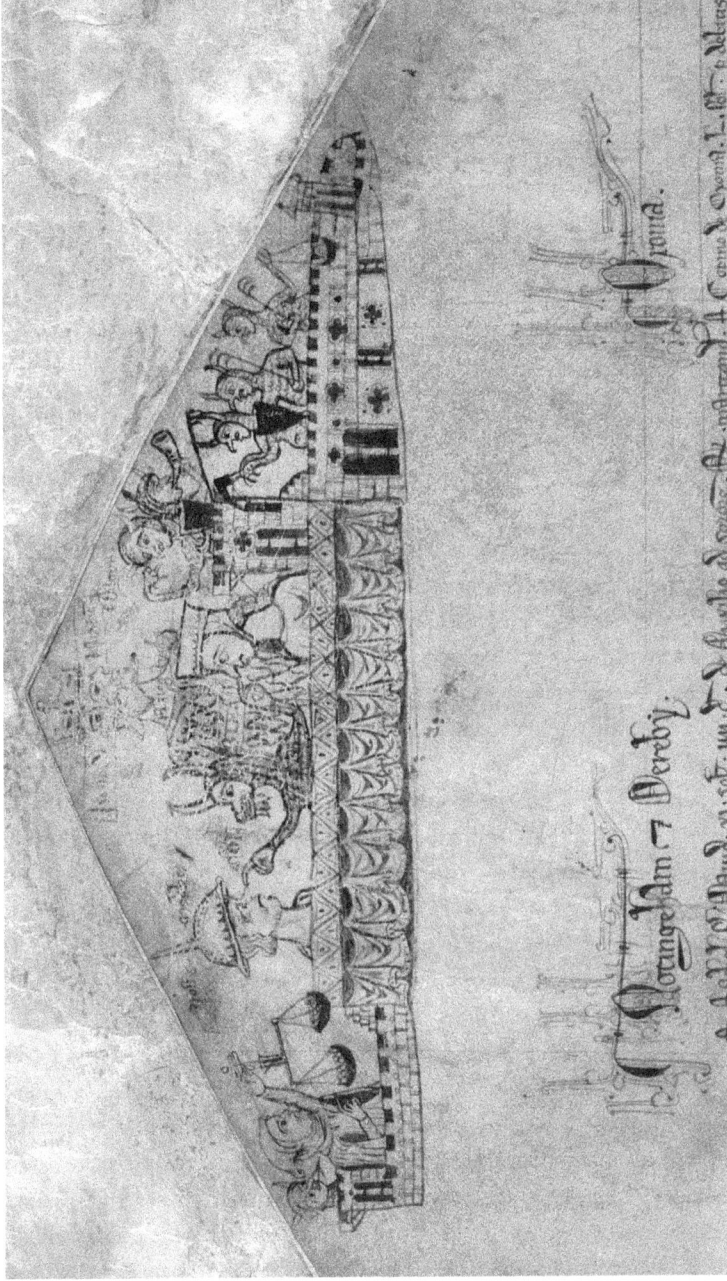

Figure 2. Exchequer Receipt Roll, Hilary and Easter terms, 1233. Image courtesy of the National Archives, Kew, E 401/1565 M1.

Henry III. Is Isaac accused of usurping the king's crown, as well as the coins being proffered to him? Or is the real object of the parody the two Peters, foreigners who have usurped royal power and demeaned the crown by associating with Jewish moneylenders?

Peter des Roches dominated the royal administration between 1232 and 1234. His fall from grace in the summer of 1234 brought a respite for London Jews. Three officials close to des Roches, Robert Passelewe, Peter de Rivallis, and Peter Grimbaud, were accused of taking bribes from Jews and of extortion in their attempts to raise money from London Jewry. A new group of bishops replaced the disgraced administration; they encouraged London Jews to air their grievances.[57] Among other things, these London Jews accused Robert Passelewe of taking the *archa* containing loan contracts, having it opened and removing some of the documents: all this was a clear breach of the system set up by royal authority to document Jewish lending. They also charged that Robert had imprisoned Jews without due cause, simply to extort money from them. Henry made a point of righting the wrongs committed by his erstwhile courtiers to his subjects, including Jews.

In the wake of the Leicester expulsion, other towns sought and obtained royal writs expelling their Jews or prohibiting Jews from taken up residence.[58] On 4 July 1234, the king wrote to the sheriff of Northumberland, informing him that he concedes to "our respected men" of Newcastle on Tyne and to their heirs that they have "this liberty": that "no Jew, during our reign or that of our heirs may remain or reside in that town."[59] On 11 September, Henry sent a mandate to the sheriff of Warwick, instructing him that Jews of the town were to be banned from living in the city. They were to acquit their tallages as required by Michaelmas (29 September), at which time they would have one month to depart.[60] On 28 November, the king issued a similar mandate to the sheriff of Buckinghamshire, decreeing the banning of Jews from High Wycombe.[61]

At the same time, the crown stepped up efforts to win over the bishops by enforcing canon law restrictions on Jews. On 20 November 1234, Henry wrote from Westminster to Thomas de Heningham, sheriff of Norfolk and Suffolk, instructing him to prohibit Christian women from serving in Jewish homes in Norwich and in other towns, either as nurses for their children or in other capacities.[62] He probably issued this mandate at the request of Thomas Blunville, Bishop of Norwich, who was with the king at Westminster. The previous day, Blunville had complained to the king that Heningham had judged and released excommunicate prisoners in the royal prison of Norfolk before they could be tried before the bishop's court.[63] The king ordered the sheriff henceforth not to free excommunicate prisoners until they "had satisfied the Holy Church." Here we see a conflict between royal and ecclesiastical jurisdictions, in which the king sides with the bishop against his own sheriff. This means that the bishop's excommunication carried considerable clout, accompanied with the threat of prison. This also means that the writ he obtained the following day, prohibiting Christians from working as servants in Jewish homes, could be backed up with the threat of excommunication and imprisonment.

Two days later, on 22 November, the king ordered Heningham to send to London some Norwich Jews who had been accused of seizing a Christian boy and circumcising him.[64] While it is not clear what was behind these accusations, it may well be, as Paola Tartakoff suggests, that the boy, known by the Jewish name Jurnepin and the Christian name Edward, was the son of a Jewish mother and a Christian father. This would explain the alleged circumcision in 1230 and the trial of the accused Jews, thirteen of whom were imprisoned, which dragged on for a decade. These allegations may explain the attacks on the Jewish community of Norwich in 1235: several Jews were beaten by Christians and two of their houses were set on fire. Henry passed through the city on 11 March 1235 and heard complaints by Norwich Jews concerning these attacks and the sheriff's failure to address them. Henry fined the citizens of Norwich for their role in the disturbances.[65] Roger of Wendover and Matthew Paris give a lurid account of the affair, affirming that Jews had "stolen" the boy, circumcised him, and planned on crucifying him.[66]

The king was again eager to exploit whatever income he could get his hands on, all the more as he would marry off his sister Isabella to Emperor Frederick II in June 1235. This provided him with a key European alliance, but it came at a cost, as he had promised the emperor £20,000 in dowry.[67] Isaac of Norwich disappears from the records in 1235; he probably died in 1235 or 1236. In October 1238, his heirs paid two hundred marks to inherit his estate and in 1242 they were still paying Isaac's share of the Bristol tallage to the crown.[68]

English Jews in the 1230s had reason to be concerned about the growing fiscal burden placed upon them and the violence and hostility of some of their Christian neighbors. Yet their correligionaries across the channel fared no better. Some French Jews, it seems, wrote to Pope Gregory IX describing the persecution they faced at the hands of the French authorities, who responded on 6 April 1233, by issuing his bull *Etsi Judeorum* to the bishops and archbishops of France.[69] He reminds them that the Jews have a legitimate and useful place in Christian society. He regrets that "certain Christians" in the kingdom mistreat Jews, torturing or imprisoning them. "Certain ones of these lords rage among these Jews with such cruelty, that unless they pay them what they ask, they tear their finger-nails and extract their teeth, and inflict upon them other kinds of inhuman torments." He asks the prelates to prevent Christians from mistreating Jews and to oblige them to respect their contracts with Jews—but not to permit Jews to practice usury. The pope reissues the bull in 1235.[70]

On 14 January 1236, in Canterbury Cathedral, King Henry married Eleanor of Provence, daughter of Count Raymond Berenger of Provence and Beatrice of Savoy and sister of Queen Margaret of France. The couple then traveled to Westminster where Eleanor was crowned queen. Taking no chances, Henry had London Jews locked in the Tower of London during the ceremony.[71] In spring 1236, crusaders mustering for what historians call the "barons' crusade" massacred Jews across the archdiocese of Tours (much of what now is western France, including Brittany, Anjou, and the Poitou). A provincial council in Tours in June "strictly forbids crusaders or other Christians from presuming to kill or to beat Jews, to steal their possessions or carry them off, or to impose any threat or injury on them."[72] In September, Gregory addressed a letter to French prelates concerning the massacres. The origin of the pope's information, as he says, was a "tearful and pitiful complaint from the Jews who live in the Kingdom of France." They had told of the brutal massacre of 2,500 men, women, and children at the hands of the crusaders. The descriptions suggest that at least some of these Jews had been offered a choice between baptism and death. Gregory denounces this cruelty and barbarity and accuses the crusaders of hiding their greed and brutality under the veil of piety. He reminds the bishops that baptism is to be voluntary. He commands them to curtail the violence, to bring the perpetrators to justice, and to compensate the surviving Jews for their material losses.[73] Hebrew poet Solomon ben Joseph laments, "The blood flowed like water on the day of the murder . . . The blossoms of my youngsters were dedicated to you as a gift, O God!" and prays to God, "Raise the head of the children of Israel!"[74] In the following years, Louis IX would have inquests made to find and punish those responsible for the violence. John the Red, Duke of Brittany, on the contrary expelled the remaining Jews in 1240 from his duchy and cancelled all debts owed to them.[75]

The news was chilling to England's Jews. Matthew Paris describes their reaction: "At this time a great slaughter of the Jews took place on the continent, especially in Spain; and those on this side of the sea, fearing that they would suffer in the same way, made the king a present of money, on which he caused a proclamation to be made by the crier, that no one was to do any injury or cause any annoyance to any of the Jews."[76] Where Pope Gregory had expressed his pity for the plight of the Jews and denounced the "unheard of and unprecedented outburst of cruelty" of their oppressors, for King Henry, it seems, it simply provided another opportunity to extract money from his Jews.

CHAPTER 4

Oxford Jews and Christian Hebraism

In the early 1230s, Robert Grosseteste, Franciscan lector at Oxford, bishop of Lincoln, and one of the intellectual giants of thirteenth-century England, penned his *De cessatione legalium*, in which he sets out to show that continuing observance of the Mosaic law by Christians is heretical. Grosseteste also wrote the preface to a bilingual Hebrew-Latin psalter, one of about a dozen Hebrew manuscripts from a group of thirteenth-century English Hebraists. Oxford was the home to a thriving Jewish community, economically prosperous and intellectually active. While historical records indicate tensions and occasional violence between Christians and Jews, these manuscripts testify to intellectual exchanges and collaboration.

In his pioneering *Jews of Medieval Oxford* (1951), Cecil Roth painted a bleak portrait of Jewish-Christian relations in the town. He describes a town with filthy streets and a chaotic jumble of shops.

> From time to time an exotic, bearded figure, marked off all the more clearly by the coloured badge in the traditional form of the ten commandments which he was forced to wear over his heart, would thread his way nervously through the throng on his way to the Synagogue or House of Study, or the womenfolk would go from stall to stall buying choice delicacies in honour of the Sabbath, seemingly indifferent to the jeering of the mob. But they stirred out of doors as little as possible. Oblivious to the shouting and chaffering outside, they sat in their houses conning the traditional literature and awaiting their clients; and the traditional sing-song of the Talmudical students would sometimes blend with the chanting of a religious procession as it passed between the kneeling townspeople on its way to the Shrine of St. Frideswide.[1]

Roth paints a vivid image both of medieval piety (the blending of the chants of
Christian pilgrims and Talmudic students) and of the unbending hostility of
Christians to Jews. Yet this portrait is based on little real evidence, and several
elements are false. In 1221, as we have seen, Oxford's Jews paid the modest sum
of 4s. 6 p. to the crown in order to be exempt from wearing the badge. So Roth's
"exotic, bearded figure" was very unlikely to be wearing a badge. Or for that
matter a beard: as Roth notes elsewhere, several Jews are indeed given the epi-
thet "Lumbard" (Long-beard), presumably because their sporting a long beard
marked them off from other Jews.[2] And while there are certainly incidents of
Christian hostility and violence against Jews, nothing permits us to imagine that
a Jew going out into the street in front of his house was invariably met by a jeer-
ing, hostile mob.[3]

In this chapter, we will examine the development of Christian Hebraism—
that is, the study of Hebrew and of Jewish texts by Christians—in England in
the twelfth and thirteenth centuries. We will then look at the Oxford Jewish
community and its ties to the Christian town and in particular to the schools
that emerge as the University of Oxford in the early thirteenth century. Then
we will bring these two strands together by focusing on the figure of Robert Grosseteste, who as theologian, chancellor of the university, and bishop of Lincoln,
was implicated both in defining the theological correlation between Judaism and
Christianity and in shaping the relations between Oxford scholars and the local
Jewish community.

English Christian Hebraism:
From Andrew of St. Victor to Grosseteste

When Robert Grosseteste undertakes the study of Hebrew and the commentary
of the Psalms, he takes his place in a century-long tradition of Christian Hebraism in England. The first prominent figure in this movement is Andrew of St. Victor, who was probably a native of England and who went to Paris to study at the
Augustinian Abbey of St. Victor in the 1120s or 1130s.[4] There he studied under
Hugh of St. Victor (1096–1141), one of the prominent teachers and scholars of
twelfth-century Paris and author of texts of didactics, theology, and exegesis.
Hugh and other canons of the Abbey of St. Victor (or Victorines, as they are
known) showed a particular interest in exegesis. The Victorines placed the Bible
at the center of both their contemplative life and of their educational program,

and for them the understanding of the Bible needed to be grounded in the literal meaning of the text. It was Andrew, in particular, who devoted his scholarly career to exposing the literal meaning of the Hebrew Bible through a series
of commentaries on most of the books of the Old Testament (he wrote no commentaries on the New Testament). While much of his exegesis is quite traditional
(he incorporates passages from Jerome and from the standard biblical glosses),
he does include material from eleventh- and twelfth-century Jewish exegetes, in
particular from Rashi (1040–1105). But his immediate sources were probably Parisian Jews, as it seems unlikely that his Hebrew was good enough to read Rashi on
his own. His goal of seeking the literal or historical meaning (*simplicitas*) may have
corresponded to the notion of *peshat* among contemporary Jewish exegetes.[5]

Andrew's student Herbert of Bosham became much more proficient in Hebrew than his teacher.[6] Herbert studied in Paris, probably with Andrew and with
Peter Lombard. In 1162, he became a close advisor to the new archbishop of Canterbury, Thomas Becket, whom he served until Thomas's murder in 1170; Herbert wrote a life of Thomas in 1184–1186. Herbert remained in exile following
Thomas's death, finally returning in the late 1180s to England, where he obtained
the patronage of William de Longchamp, bishop of Ely. In the early 1190s, he
produced his *Psalterium cum commento*, a new Latin translation of the Psalms
with his own commentary, one of the most remarkable works of Christian Hebraist scholarship in the Middle Ages.[7] Herbert provided a literal, word-for-word
translation of the Psalms, giving more importance to the consistency of translation (always the same Latin word for one Hebrew word, always a noun to translate a noun, a verb a verb, etc.), than for Latin syntax or general sense. His
comments contained discussion of specific Hebrew terms (in transliteration), and
of the meaning of different passages and the history of their interpretation. He
used the work of earlier exegetes, principally Jerome and Rashi: his access to other
postbiblical Jewish traditions seems to pass primarily through Rashi. He also
seems to have used a Hebrew-Latin glossary, which may be an earlier version of
a glossary now extant in one thirteenth-century manuscript.[8] He also mentions
loquax meus and *litterator meus*, which seem to refer to his teacher (or teachers)
of Hebrew.

There is some evidence also of English Jews reading the Latin works of Christian authors and responding to them. Berekhia ha-Nakdan, who probably lived
in England in the late twelfth century,[9] had read the works of Petrus Alfonsi, an
Andalusian Jew converted to Christianity who had moved to England during
the reign of Henry I (1100–1135). Through word play based on Alfonsi's own texts,

Berekhia affirms that his apostasy proved him to be a mule; it would have been better for him to have been stillborn than to exchange his previous glorious name (Moses) for that of Petrus. Berkhia is writing in Hebrew for a Jewish audience and hence feels free to indulge in ridicule. He provides a good example of how Jewish authors could react to Christian polemics and attempt to reassure their Jewish readers of their intellectual and cultural superiority over the *goyim*.

While Herbert of Bosham stands head and shoulders above contemporary English Christian Hebraists, he is the representative (and perhaps the initiator) of a movement that lasts well into the thirteenth century, and that continues to focus on the text of the Psalms. Among the Hebrew manuscripts in thirteenth-century England, Gilbert Dahan has identified two Psalters that clearly served as teaching tools for Christian students of Hebrew.[10] It is not surprising that the Psalms would be popular for use for the teaching of Hebrew: they were well known to both Jews and Christians of the Middle Ages and figured prominently in the liturgy of both. Individual Psalms provided short texts more convenient for teaching than sections of other books of the Hebrew Bible. The Hebrew text of one of the Psalters was copied toward the end of the twelfth century. In the margins of the manuscript are notes and bits of translation, in Latin and in French (probably written between 1230 and 1250), which, Dahan convincingly argues, were penned by Christian students as they listened, in French, to Hebrew lessons given by a Jewish teacher. The teacher uses the text of the Psalms to illustrate lessons in Hebrew grammar and syntax, word roots, and semantics. Another manuscript tells the same story: it contains the Hebrew text of the Psalms (copied in the first half of the thirteenth century) and similar marginal notes in Latin and French.[11] Nothing in either of these manuscripts indicates where these lessons took place, nor the identities of the Jewish teachers or their Christian students.

One of the most remarkable testimonies to the activity of Christian Hebraists in England is a dictionary of biblical Hebrew probably composed at the East Anglian Benedictine monastery of Ramsey in the mid-thirteenth century, though based on earlier sources.[12] It is a hefty book: 115 folios, composed right to left, in two columns: Hebrew terms (generally biblical vocabulary) and corresponding Latin transliterations and definitions, with frequent recourse to the vernacular (over one thousand occurrences of words in Anglo-Norman French and three in Middle English). The sources used include Talmud, Rashi, and the twelfth-century Hebrew lexicon by Ibn Parhon: these probably indicate that the dictionary was a collaborative effort between Jews and Christians, which would also explain the large number of French terms, since the principal language of communication between these English Jews and Christians was probably French. As

Judith Olszowy-Schlanger has shown, the same scribe who copied this dictionary had written marginal notations, glosses, and interlinear translations on six
other Hebrew manuscripts over the preceding several decades. The dictionary
seems to be in some ways the continuation, perhaps the culmination, of the study
of biblical Hebrew initiated by Herbert of Bosham and continued by the various commentators and glossators of Hebrew manuscripts (notably of the Psalms).
The compiler of the dictionary uses these earlier manuscripts, it seems, as his
principle sources.[13] The same manuscript contains a unique treatise on Hebrew
grammar.[14] Ramsey Abbey seems to have been an important center for Hebrew
studies in the thirteenth century; as we will see, Bishop Robert Grosseteste of
Lincoln subsequently visited the abbey in the 1230s and 1240s.

While the numbers of English Christians who had any knowledge of Hebrew remained small, it is clear that over the course of the twelfth and thirteenth
centuries Jews taught biblical Hebrew to Christians, and Jews and Christians
collaborated in producing scholarly tools for the use of Christians who wished
to learn Hebrew and to study the Hebrew scriptures. Throughout these works,
there is little evidence of anti-Jewish polemics or of attempts to proselytize Jews.
Differences in Jewish and Christian interpretations of scriptural passages are often noted, but seldom are the object of apologetics or polemics. It will take the
concerted action of the Dominican and Franciscan friars, with the support of
Pope Gregory IX, to change that.

In June 1239, Gregory wrote to Henry III, saying that if what he had heard
about the Jews in England was true, no punishment was sufficient for them. It
has been alleged, he says, that the Jews, not content with the Old Law given by
God to Moses, now followed another law, called Talmud, which they falsely
claimed that God revealed orally to Moses. Much later, certain men they called
sages or scribes wrote the Talmud down, a book that was bigger than the Bible.
It contains, he says, "so many offensive things that they are a source of shame to
those who repeat them and a horror to those who hear them." Moreover, the Talmud "is said to be the main reason that keeps the Jews stubborn in their perfidy."[15] Gregory's source of information was apparently Nicholas Donin, a Parisian
Jew converted to Christianity, who went to Rome to denounce the Talmud to
the pope. Gregory here was affirming three things about the Talmud. First, that
it represented a new scripture and hence a new religion (which could imply that
one of the main reasons traditionally given for tolerating Jews in Christian society, that they remained faithful to the Old Law given to them by Moses, no longer applied). Second, that it contained "offensive" material (as we will see,
particularly negative statements about Mary and Jesus seen as blasphemous).

Third, that the Talmud was the principal obstacle to their conversion to the true faith.

The pope asked Henry to have all books belonging to Jews books seized on "the first Sabbath of next Lent (17 March 1240), in the morning when the Jews assemble in their synagogues" and handed over to Dominican and Franciscan friars who were to examine them. The pope sent similar letters to the kings of Aragon, Portugal, Navarre, Castile, and France.[16] It is unclear why the pope addressed those specific kings: no doubt because they all had significant Jewish communities; also perhaps because he thought there were in those kingdoms friars sufficiently well versed in Hebrew to examine the books. (Unsurprisingly, he did not write to Emperor Frederick II, whom he had excommunicated.) Gregory also wrote similar letters to the archbishops of these kingdoms. There is no evidence that Henry replied or reacted to the pope's letter. Nor, apparently, did any of the other monarchs he addressed, except one: Louis IX of France.

Jewish tradition distinguishes the "written Torah" or Pentateuch (the first five books of what Christians call the Old Testament) from the "oral Torah," a collection of laws, stories and rabbinical discussions transmitted orally and put down in writing between the third and sixth centuries CE, first as the Jerusalem Talmud and then the Babylonian Talmud. The Talmud became a central part of Jewish life in northern Europe over the course of the ninth to early twelfth centuries: a source of law and rabbinical traditions and the object of study and commentary.[17] Rashi of Troyes wrote the first comprehensive commentary of the Talmud; his work was continued and completed over the following two centuries by rabbinical scholars across northern Europe known as the Tosafists, because they compiled *tosafot*, "additions" to Rashi's fundamental work. English Jewry, closely linked with Jewish communities in France, also produced significant scholarship based on the Talmud. In 1110, Petrus Alfonsi penned his *Dialogues Against the Jews,* in which he ridiculed passages from the Talmud. Originally from the Iberian Peninsula, Alfonsi lived and taught in England and northern France, and his anti-Talmudic polemics influenced other Christian writers, including Peter of Cluny, who attacked the Talmud in his venomous tract, *Against the Inveterate Obduracy of the Jews.*[18] But there is little widespread awareness of the Talmud in Christian Europe until Nicholas of Donin denounced it to Gregory IX.

Louis IX ordered the seizure of large numbers of books belonging principally to Parisian Jews. The examination of these books took the form of an oral dispute (often referred to as a "trial" by historians) in 1240 between Christians, led by Nicholas Donin, and two Parisian rabbis, Yehiel ben Joseph and Judah ben David, in the presence of the Queen Mother Blanche de Castile. Both Latin and Hebrew accounts survive, and give very different assessments of the procedure, but largely agree on the arguments made on each side.[19] Donin made thirty-five accusations against the Talmud, rejecting Jewish claims about the origins and authority of the Talmud and affirming that it contains silly and blasphemous assertions about God and various holy figures. In particular, it blasphemes against Jesus (said to be punished in hell in a pit of boiling excrement) and Mary (who conceived in adultery). Moreover, Donin claims, the Talmud authorizes and encourages dishonest and hostile behavior toward *goyim* (which Donin takes to mean Christians); it even, he claims, encourages Jews to kill Christians. The Parisian rabbis replied (reasonably) that the rules about *goyim* applied to pagans of the Talmudic age and (disingenuously) that the Mary and Jesus referred to in the Talmud were not the Mary and Jesus of the Christians. At one point, Donin, in order to prove that the Jews' current sufferings show that God has abandoned them, taunts: "Did not many thousands of you fall by the sword in Brittany and Anjou and Poitou? If you are a treasured people, as you have said, where are the signs and wonders which your God performed for you?"[20]

The result, after some hesitation by Christian authorities, was the order to burn the Talmud: hundreds of Hebrew manuscripts were consigned to the flames in Paris. This was chilling to Jews throughout Europe, who suddenly realized that Christian scrutiny of their Hebrew manuscripts could be dangerous. In 1244, the new pope, Innocent IV, wrote to Louis IX alleging that French Jews continued to blaspheme against Christ and that he should continue to track down and burn their books. Yet some French Jews appealed to Innocent, insisting on the centrality of the Talmud for their comprehension of the Bible and for the practice of their rites. Innocent had a change of heart and wrote to Louis IX in 1247, affirming that rather than burn the Talmud, commissions of friars were to examine it carefully, expunge from it any anti-Christian blasphemies, and then return it to the Jews. He also wrote in a similar vein to Odo of Chateauroux, who as papal legate had played a key role in the 1240 proceedings, and who was clearly hostile to backtracking. He reported to the pope that he had reopened an inquiry that confirmed the earlier judgment that the Talmud was heretical. The books seized should not be returned to the Jews, but should be burned. Thus the condemnation of the Talmud was upheld in Paris, against the pope's wishes and orders, but was not put into effect elsewhere.

Pope Gregory IX instigated this assault on the Talmud, but the Dominicans and Franciscans turned it into reality. It is they who were charged with the study of the Hebrew manuscripts and with them lay the responsibility of identifying passages that could (in 1241 or 1242) consign them to the flames or (after 1247) lead to their partial censorship. The disputation of Barcelona in 1263 pitted Pablo Cristia, a Dominican friar and convert from Judaism, against Rabbi Nachmanides of Gerona, but involved no threat of book burning. Fourteenth-century Dominican Theobald of Saxony composed a virulent *Quiver of the Faith Against the Talmud of the Jews*, but his attack remained rhetorical.[21] This increasing knowledge of the Talmud by Christians, with a focus on the (few and minor) passages referring to Jesus and his mother, could only reinforce the idea of Jewish hostility toward Christians. Bonfires of Hebrew books could suggest to Christians that these books were full of blasphemy and hostility. To Jews, they were a tragic loss of precious and sacred texts. Meir of Rothenburg, who had come to Paris to study the Talmud with Yehiel, looked on helplessly in 1242 as the Talmud burned:

> O You who are burned in fire, ask how your mourners fare
> They who yearn to dwell in the court of your dwelling place
> They who gasp in the dust of the earth and who feel pain
> They who are stunned by the blaze of your parchment . . .
> How could she who was given by the flaming God be consumed by
>   the fire
> Of mortals, while the foes were not scorched by your embers?[22]

This is all very far from the tranquil study of the Psalms with English Jews teaching Hebrew to Christians. In Oxford in the twelfth and thirteenth centuries the Jewish community played a key role as financiers and landlords to the emerging university. In future decades, Franciscans at Oxford took up the study of Hebrew, but there is no evidence that they turned their attention to the denunciation of the Talmud. Yet the idea that the Talmud inculcated in Jews the hate of Christians and Christianity, and that it authorized or even encouraged Jews to kill Christians, marked an important break with the Augustinian schema of Jews as living letters of the law bode ill for Jews in England as elsewhere in Europe.[23]

Town and Gown:
The Oxford Jewry and the Rise of the University

The Oxford Jewish community, one of the largest in England, was already well established by 1141.[24] In that year, in the midst of the civil war with his cousin Matilda, King Stephen set fire to the house of Aaron ben Isaac and threatened

to burn down the rest of the Oxford Jewry if the Jews did not pay him considerable sums of money to pursue his war. Over the course of the late eleventh and
twelfth centuries, Jews settled in Oxford; their houses were scattered throughout the town and in the outlying areas, but were particularly concentrated around
Fish Street (now St. Aldate's St.) near the south gate and St. Frideswide's priory
(in the area where today are Pembroke and Christ Church colleges). In 1177, a
group of Jews bought a tract of land outside the city walls, along the Cherwell
River, to establish a cemetery; in 1231, the Hospital of St. John requested this land
from Henry III, who granted it, obliging the hospital to accord the Jews a separate tract of land for the cemetery. Although Oxford Jews owned significant
amounts of land within and outside the town, their debts, and indeed the Jews
themselves, were the property of the king, for him to dispose with as he saw fit.

Over the course of the twelfth century, Oxford also became an important
center of learning.[25] No English town could rival the great European centers of
study, Bologna and Paris. But in the early twelfth century, several new monastic
communities were founded, including convents for Augustinian canons at Osney
and St. Frideswide. Henry I established a new royal residence just north of the
town in 1133. The first mention of a schoolmaster in Oxford is in 1090, although
as Richard Southern notes the evidence for teaching activity for the half century
between 1135 and 1185 is "exasperatingly blank."[26] Its first well-known master of
theology, Alexander Neckam, taught there beginning in about 1190.

Gerald of Wales, royal clerk and chaplain to King Henry II, gave a public
lecture of his *Topographica Hibernica* (Topography of Ireland) in Oxford in 1187
or 1188. He chose Oxford because it was the town in which "the clergy of England
are in greatest strength and repute."[27] While in Oxford he no doubt visited the
sanctuary of St. Frideswide, for several years later, when he wrote his *Gemma
ecclesiastica* (*Jewel of the Church*) in Lincoln, in the midst of a series of stories on
how God wreaks vengeance on blasphemers, he tells the story of a Jewish boy in
Oxford.[28] Philip, prior of St. Frideswide, relates the same story in greater detail
in his collection of miracles of the patron saint of his abbey. He says that a certain Jewish boy, called Deus-eum-crescat (Deulecresse), son of Moses of Wallingford (who was "less detestable than many other Jews," Philip says), "agitated
by an evil spirit," ridiculed the Christians' devotion to Frideswide.[29] He pretended to be crippled and then to be cured by the saint, whom he then mocked.
Both Jews and Christians chided him for his behavior, his father in particular.
In the evening, his father urged him to dine with him, but the boy went up to
his room and hanged himself. The father, who discovered the body the next
morning, attempted to keep his death secret (just as the Jews had attempted to

suppress the news of Christ's resurrection, Philip adds). Yet the news spread quickly through the town, "bringing joy to the faithful and confusion to the infidels." Philip then describes, with some relish, how the body was taken to London for burial (Oxford did not yet have a Jewish cemetery), where it was joined by a pack of howling dogs "giving suitable setting to a blasphemer's funeral." As a final mark of St. Frideswide's vengeance, the body fell from its cart, breaking the neck through which the blasphemous words had passed.

It is impossible to know how much of this is true. Yet Philip wrote within twenty years or so of the alleged blasphemy, so it seems unlikely that he fabricated the story. Moses of Wallingford is indeed attested in Oxford, where he died on or before 1190; his house on Fish Street was around the corner from St. Frideswide's (about one hundred meters).[30] Philip's assertion that he was "less detestable than many other Jews" attests perhaps to polite if not warm contacts. We know that some of Philip's successors at St. Frideswide borrowed money from Oxford Jews; the same may be true of Philip himself.[31] The scene he describes is plausible: Christian worshippers showed public devotion for a saint whose relics had been recently translated to her new shrine and who (according to Philip) was duly performing thaumaturgical miracles. Indeed, the translation, and the consecration of the new church, had been performed with a good deal of pomp: Archbishop Richard of Canterbury himself presided over the ceremony in 1180.[32] Yet if this incident took place after the establishment of the Oxford Jewish cemetery in 1177, the boy's body would not have been taken to London for burial. In any case, this story has a Jewish teenager openly mocking the saint's devotees for their credulity. His mockery brought down on him fierce verbal rebuke from Christians, but no physical violence. Jews (particularly his father) also chided him: indeed, his behavior threatened the delicate entente between them and their Christian neighbors.

How are we to explain Deulecresse's suicide? Did he fear the consequences of his mockery? Ephraim Shoham-Steiner suggests that he may have been attracted to Christianity and to the cult of St. Frideswide, only to then reject it and choose the path of resistance, mockery, and death as a martyr for Judaism. The story provides evidence both for the fairly relaxed neighborly relations between Jews and Christians of the town and for the fragility of those relations. For Philip, of course, the moral of the story is clear: those who mock St. Frideswide are duly punished for their blasphemy. "In a wonderful way," says Philip, "miracles encourage the believer and confound the unbeliever."[33] The intended audience of his story, Oxford's Christians, are enjoined to show proper reverence to the saint lest they incur her wrath. They should side with the saint's devotees, not with the Jewish blasphemer. Gerald of Wales draws the same lesson, more broadly, about the dangers of blasphemy. The figure of a Jewish blasphemer often appears in hagiography, openly doubting the power of the saint only to be persuaded by the show of miracles—or to incur the saint's righteous wrath.

The Jews had a powerful ally, for Gerald: Satan himself. In his *Speculum ecclesie,* he tells of two Cistercian monks whom the devil inspired to renounce their faith and their monastic calling, "flee to the synagogue of Satan," and have themselves circumcised, subjecting themselves to "the torments of Gehenna." God himself punished them for the crime of apostasy, Gerald relates, by striking them with epilepsy: writhing on the ground, grinding their teeth, spewing saliva, they served as a lesson for all in the perils of frequenting Satan and his Jewish allies. Again, it is impossible to know what truth (if any) lies behind this story; clearly for Gerald it served among other things to sully the reputation of the Cistercian order.[34] Gerald also relates, in his *De instructione principis*, that Robert de Cricklade, prior of St. Frideswide's immediately before Philip (1141–1180), knew Hebrew. He had manuscripts of Josephus gathered from towns in England where Jews lived. In two of them, he found a testimony of Christ written at great length, but recently scratched out; in the others they had been removed long before, so there was no evidence that these passages had ever been there. "And when this was shown to the Jews of Oxford summoned for that purpose, they were convicted and confused at this fraudulent malice and bad faith towards Christ."[35] For Gerald, this is just the latest example of Jewish duplicity and malice: from the beginning of Christian times, the Jews had been removing passages referring to Christ from their books; as a result, the books of the Greeks and Latins were much more reliable than those of the Hebrews.[36]

The idea that Jews were hostile to Christ and his mother was well established in twelfth-century Oxford (as elsewhere in England and Europe). As Kati Ihnat has shown, the Jew often served as foil in the miracle stories of the Virgin Mary, expressing doubt about her powers or hostility to her cult: she chastised hostile Jews through miracles, which led to their punishment or to their conversion to the true faith.[37] These stories remained popular in the thirteenth century, as we see in the Book of Hours that William de Brailes composed in Oxford in about 1240 for a patroness named Susanna, consisting particularly of the Hours of the Virgin.[38] William lived on Catte Street, a stone's throw from the Jewish neighborhood, and was a devotee of St. Frideswide, whom he frequently invokes. Various apocryphal stories extant in twelfth- and thirteenth-century texts relate that after the Virgin died, as the apostles carried her through the streets of Jerusalem, a Jew named Jephonias (or in some versions, two Jews) tried to overturn her bier: his hands miraculously withered (or in some versions, an angel chopped them off with a sword). The apostles urged him to humbly ask forgiveness from the Virgin, which he did and was swiftly cured, leading to his conversion and that of other Jews who witnessed the miracle. William de Brailes inserts the legend into the text for compline (night prayer), accompanying the text of Psalm 42, and illustrates it by showing two Jews, with distorted, grimacing faces, touching the Virgin's bier borne by two haloed apostles.

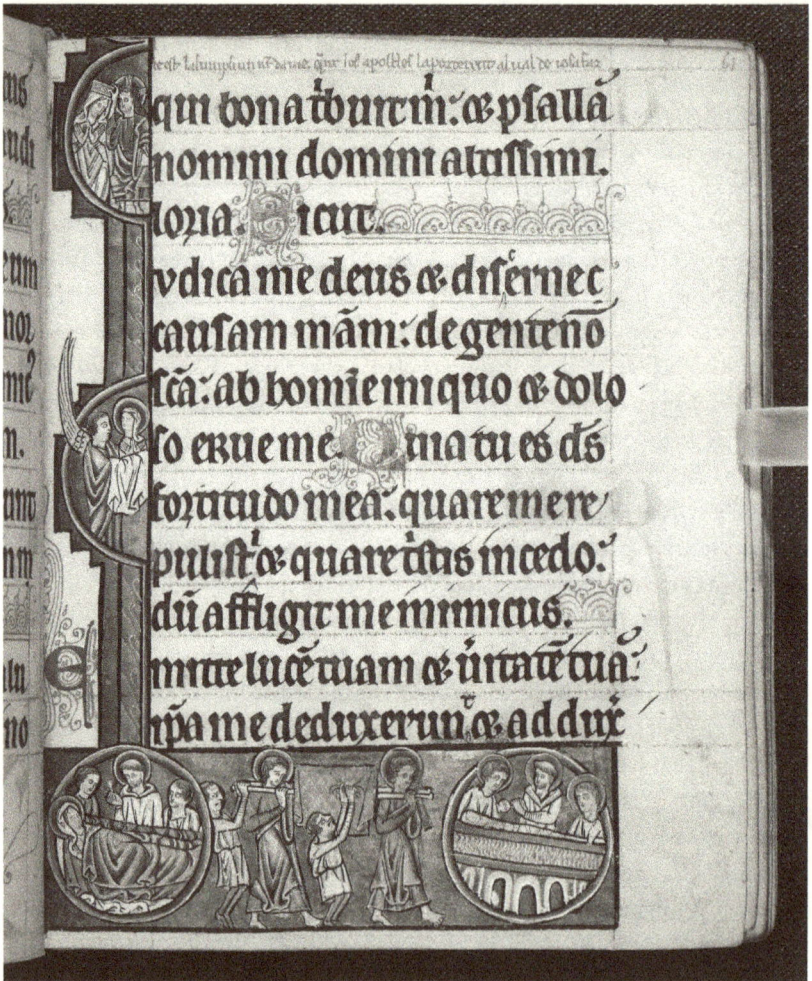

Figure 3. Two Jews attack Mary's funeral procession, miniature from the de Brailes Hours, British Library Additional Manuscript 49999, folio 61r.

Nine Jews were struck blind: William depicts them, eyes closed and looking down, with the French caption "les giues aveoglerent," "the Jews are blinded." Of those nine Jews, seven are depicted with dark skin, two with light skin.

The next text in the Book of Hours is Psalm 130, which concludes with the verse "Let Israel hope in the Lord: from henceforth now and forever." In the initial to the Psalm, one of the blinded Jews kneels in prayer before St. Peter. The caption explains that he asked Peter for mercy, and Peter asked him if he believed

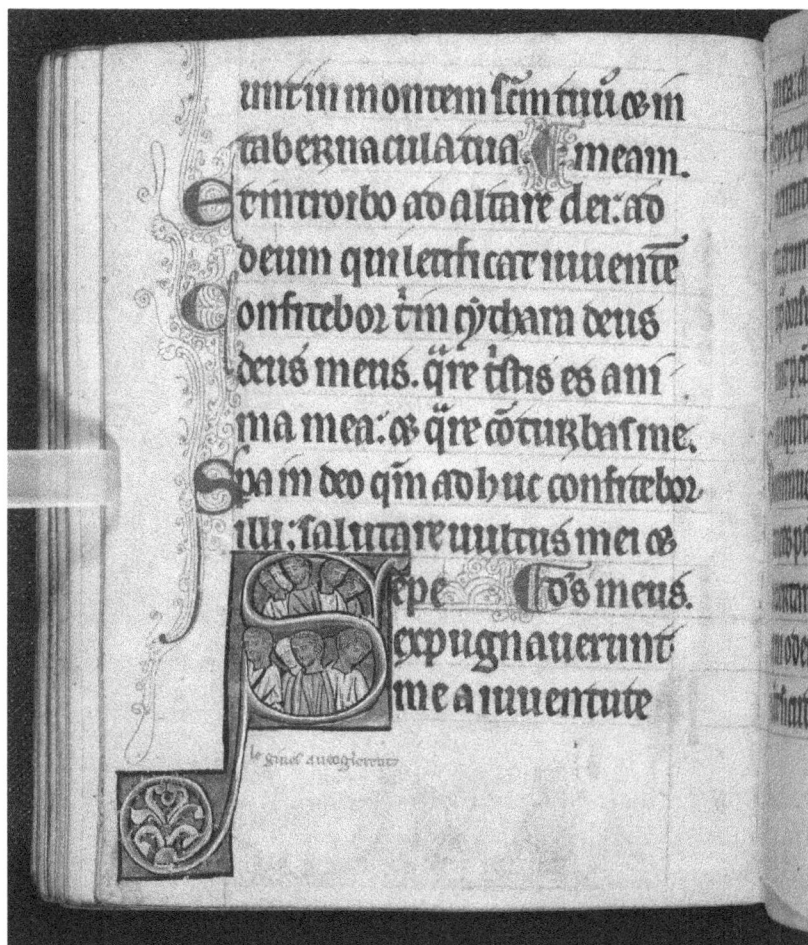

Figure 4. *Les giues aveoglerent*, miniature from the de Brailes Hours, British Library Additional Manuscript 49999, folio 61v.

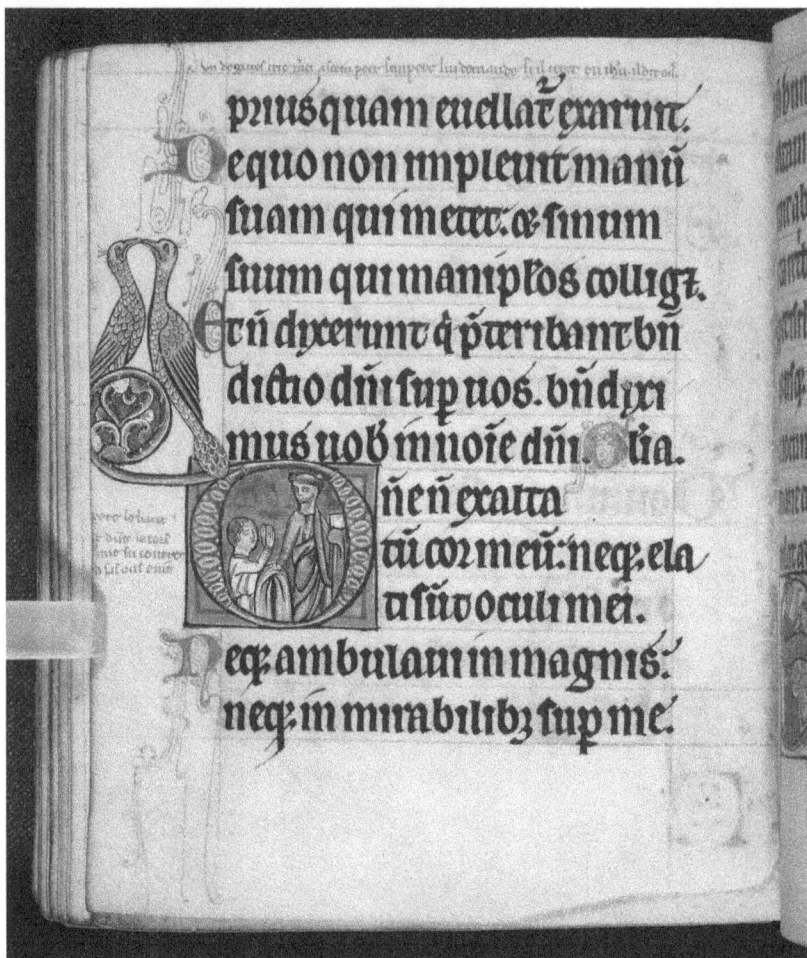

Figure 5. Conversion of believing Jew, miniature from the de Brailes Hours,
British Library Additional Manuscript 49999, folio 62v.

in Jesus. When the Jew replied yes, Peter wiped his eyes with the shroud that had
covered Mary's body, and the Jew recovered his sight.

Those Jews who had refused to believe, who had mocked the Virgin and attacked her funeral procession, could be cured through faith. Yet not all Jews
chose to believe: a final initial shows one blind Jew turning away from the shroud
that could have restored his sight. The caption explains: "Qui ne veut croire re-
meint avegle," "She or he who does not wish to believe stays blind." Those Jews

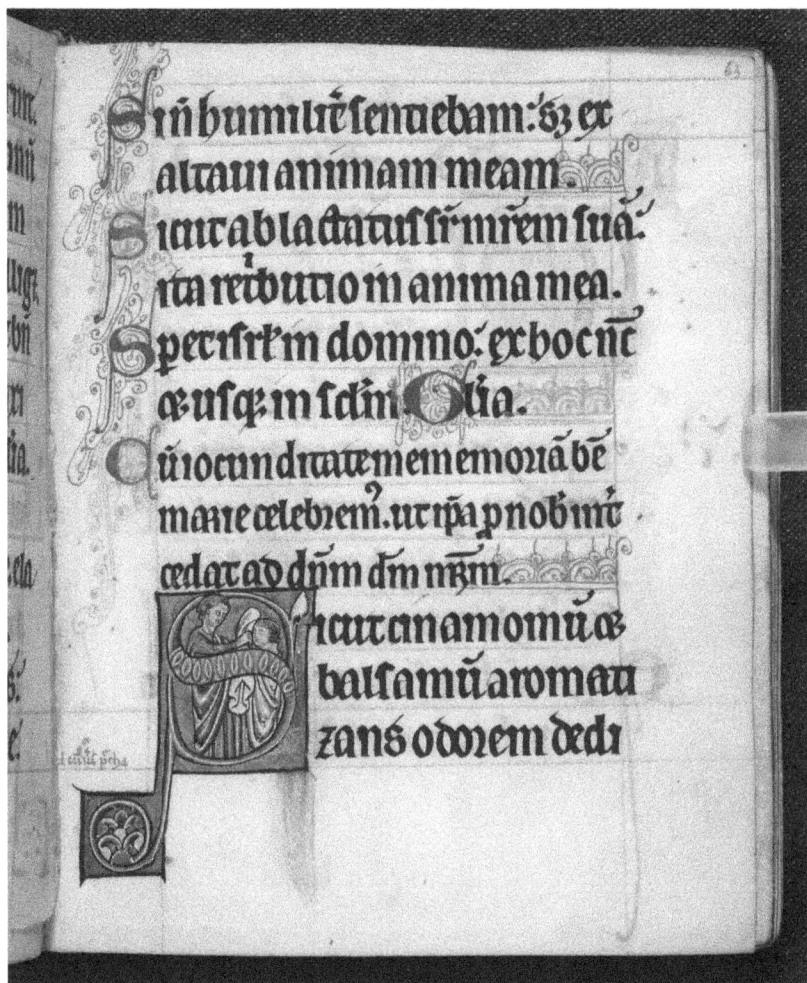

Figure 6. Miracle of cure of blind Jew, miniature from the de Brailes Hours,
British Library Additional Manuscript 49999, folio 63r.

who refused the miraculous grace of the Virgin, during her life or after her death,
including those Jews that William saw in the street on his way to pray at St. Frideswide, had chosen to remain blind. The Jew who accepted the Christian truth is
portrayed as light-skinned, whereas the one who chooses blindness is dark-
skinned.[39] Whereas here only the skin tone distinguishes the "good" Jews from
the permanently blind ones, two Psalters produced in Oxford at about the same

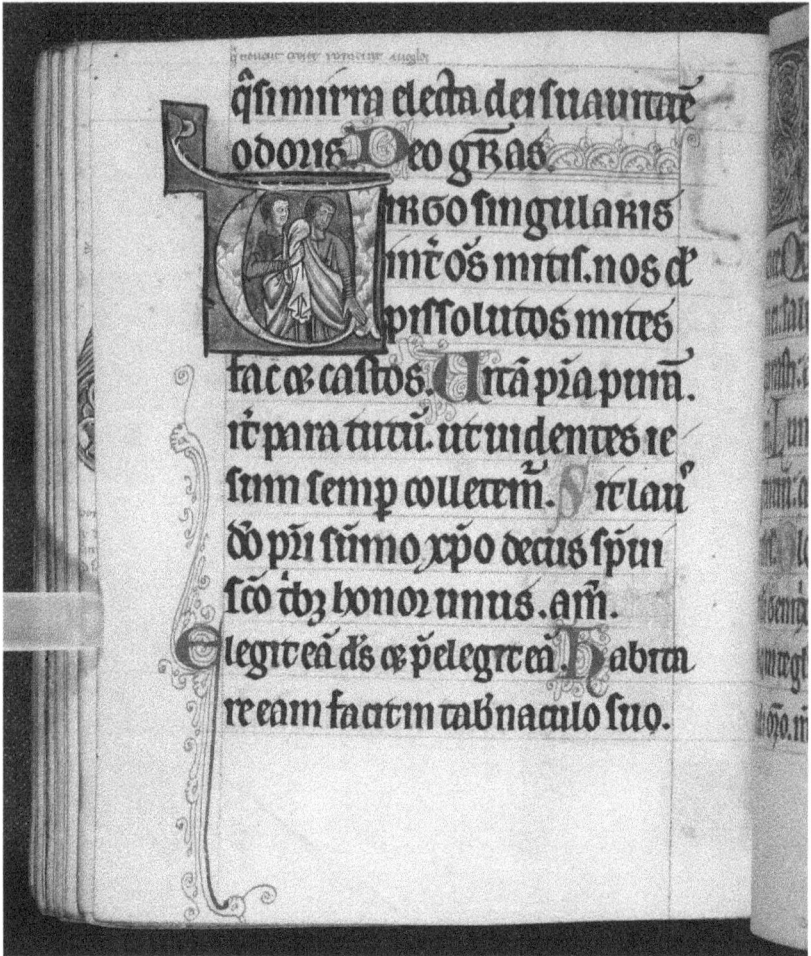

Figure 7. "Those who do not believe stay blind," miniature from the de Brailes Hours, British Library Additional Manuscript 49999, folio 63v.

time have illuminations showing Jesus' Jewish persecutors as black, with deformed features.[40]

Oxford's Jewry and the schools grew side by side. Over the course of the twelfth and thirteenth centuries, Oxford Jews bought up a number of houses in town and in the hinterland. Urban real estate was one of the few means of livelihood open to English Jews, other than moneylending, and it offered regular income in the form of rents with less risk than lending.[41] Hence many students and teachers rented their lodgings from Jews. Many of them also had recourse to loans from Oxford Jews to help finance their studies. This led to a close relationship between Oxford's Jews and its scholars: a relationship that was advantageous to both but could also erupt in conflict.[42]

The years 1208–1217 brought crisis to Oxford, both to its scholars and to its Jews. As we have seen, in March 1208, Pope Innocent III imposed an interdict on England; in November 1209 he excommunicated King John. This put clerics in England (including Oxford scholars) in a difficult position; some of them left for the Continent (especially Paris). Moreover, in December 1209, a student killed his mistress and then fled; the town authorities arrested the murderer's two roommates and had them hanged.[43] This was an affront to the clerical immunity of the scholars and led many masters to leave Oxford in protest: the continued interdict and the civil war prevented any settlement (and incidentally favored the rise of Cambridge). In 1213, as we have seen, John accepted Stephen Langton as archbishop of Canterbury, and papal legate Nicholas of Tusculum came to England to receive John's submission. Nicholas traveled to Oxford in November 1213 and again in May 1214; on 20 June 1214, he published the terms of the settlement of the Oxford conflict, which reconciled townsmen and scholars. In addition to establishing ways to regulate disputes between students and townsmen, the charter had the townsmen promise to reduce rents (a commission of four townsmen and four masters of the university was established to review rents) and to sell food and other necessities at reasonable rates. A chancellor was established, to be named by the bishop of Lincoln.[44]

There is no mention of Jews in this document; while some Jews had probably served as landlords before 1209, by 1214 many of them had been expropriated. Oxford's Jews had been particularly hard hit by the Bristol tallage of 1210.[45] Some were imprisoned, others fled. John's officials seized many of the Oxford Jews' properties in lieu of payment of the tallage. Oxford had over the course of the twelfth century grown into an important center of learning and a major Jewish settlement: by 1210, both the Jewry and the schools seemed in danger of disappearing. By 1214, the future of the new university seemed assured, but the Jewry was decimated. Oxford Jews, as those elsewhere in the kingdom, benefitted from protective measures in the first years of Henry III's reign. On 27 April 1218, the regent William Marshal was in Oxford and issued in the king's name a mandate establishing a local council of twenty-four burghers to protect Jews from violence (in particular that perpetrated by crusaders).[46]

The newly established mendicant orders arrived at Oxford in the 1220s, as they were doing at the same time in so many other European university towns.

In Oxford they seemed not to have provoked the hostility from secular masters that they faced in Paris and elsewhere.[47] According to chronicler Nicholas de Triveti, the first Dominicans came to England in 1221. Thirteen of them arrived in Canterbury, accompanied by Peter des Roches, who was returning from a pilgrimage. Archbishop Stephen Langton showered favors on the friars. They went to London on the feast of St. Laurence, and then to Oxford on the feast of the Assumption of the Virgin (15 August), in whose honor they built an oratory; they established "those schools which are now called Saint Edward."[48] Introduced into England by a bishop who was close to the king, and with the encouragement and approval of the archbishop of Canterbury, the Dominicans first established themselves not in London or Canterbury, but in Oxford, the intellectual capital of the kingdom. Their convent was established on Fish Street, in the heart of the Jewish neighborhood.[49] This is perhaps no accident: as often in medieval cities, Dominican and Franciscan convents were established in or near Jewish quarters. In the 1233, they moved to a larger site just outside the south gate, which became Blackfriars. The Franciscans arrived in 1224 and gradually obtained patronage and land, enabling them to establish a convent near the castle. This convent, which would gradually grow over the course of the thirteenth century, was probably where Robert Grosseteste taught the friars.[50]

The 1220s witnessed the gradual recovery of the Oxford Jewry as some Jews managed to get out of debt and to purchase property once again. In 1228, one of the town's prominent Jews, Copin, obtained land from St. Frideswide's on Fish Street, where he built a synagogue.[51] As we have seen (Chapter 2), in 1221 Oxford's Jews paid a lump sum of 4s. 6d. for exemption from wearing the badge: a rather modest amount, which perhaps suggests limited means. Two persons paid separate, individual fees: Sara, sister of Mulin paid 26d. and David of Lincoln made two payments amounting to £1 14 s. 10d., more than the rest of the Oxfordshire Jews combined, which suggests his considerable wealth. In the same year, he paid over £14 as tallage to the king, again over half of Oxford's contribution; the same was true in 1223. David of Lincoln, subsequently known as David of Oxford, as we already have seen (in Chapter 3) counted among his clients Simon de Montfort.[52]

David was able to use his influence with the court to compel some of his debtors to pay. St. Frideswide's abbey had built up a debt of £10 to David and £33 to Copin. Walter Mauclerk, bishop of Carlisle, royal treasurer, and keeper of the London *domus conversorum*, issued (on 28 November 1234), in the king's name, a mandate to the prior of St. Frideswide, instructing him to pay one third

of his debt during the current year, another third the following year, and the final third the year after that. In return, no further interest would be levied on
this capital.[53] The following year (18 May 1235), Pope Gregory IX wrote to the
archbishop of Canterbury saying that two brothers, the knights Thomas and William of Warblington, had complained that David and other Jews were extorting
immoderate usury from them; Gregory ordered the archbishop to compel them
to refrain from this by withdrawing from them the communion of the faithful
(i.e., by prohibiting Christians from doing business with them, a strategy that,
we have seen, had failed in 1222).[54] The king was unlikely to bother David on this
matter: David had, on 10 April of the same year, sent him a gift of £100.[55] As the
richest Jew in Oxford and one of the wealthiest in the kingdom, David made frequent and considerable contributions to the royal treasury, in the form of tallages, fees, fines, and "gifts." Indeed, the three richest Jews in England, David,
Aaron of York, and Leo of York, between them paid over half of the 1241–1242
tallage.[56] In 1236, the king ordered the justices of the Jews to not assess him ex-
cessively. On several occasions, David was appointed to help levy tallages on the
Jewish community or to help royal investigations into allegations of coin clipping in 1238.

The pressure to convert to Christianity at times caused tension and conflict,
often involving youths. Several entries in the Close Rolls for 1236 address the case
of a Jewish boy (*puer*) who had been baptized and who was subsequently kid-
napped by a group of Oxford Jews. The king ordered that the Jews in question
be judged by the constable of Oxford and that the boy himself be handed over
to the custody of Dominican friar Robert Bacon.[57] It is difficult to know how
old this "puer" was, nor do we know the circumstances of his conversion to Christianity. He was old enough, it seems, to take the initiative for his conversion (or
to allow a Christian, perhaps Robert Bacon himself or a fellow Dominican, to
convince him), but young enough, apparently, so that a group of Jewish men felt
that they could intervene to take him into their custody to prevent this conversion from being effective. Perhaps Robert saw in this boy the first fruits of his
efforts to evangelize his neighbors in the Oxford Jewry; perhaps the Jews involved
in this case felt a sense of betrayal. In any case, the ruling was, unsurprisingly, in
favor of Robert, confirming the conversion of the baptized boy and assigning him
to the care of his new spiritual father. It also seems that there was a will to pacify
the situation and to allow the Jews who in their anger had captured the boy and
tried to prevent (or reverse) his conversion to be released and escape further punishment. The same Robert Bacon obtained a royal mandate in 1245 to imprison

a convert from Judaism to Christianity who had returned to Judaism.[58] Within Jewish communities in England and elsewhere, many feared losing their children to conversion.[59]

Conflicts between Jews were usually negotiated within the community, but sometimes one of the parties would appeal to royal justice if he were not satisfied with the decisions of the Jewish authorities. Around 1240, David filed for divorce and obtained a *get* (certificate of divorce) from the local Jewish community. His wife, Muriel, was childless, and David wished to remarry and father children. But Muriel refused to consent to the divorce. The case was sent before a *bet din* (rabbinical court) consisting of rabbis from Oxford, London, and Canterbury. The rabbis of the *bet din* wrote to French rabbis for advice as to how to judge the case. We do not have the decision of the French rabbis, but David, either because they decided against him or because the procedure was taking too long, appealed directly to the royal court, which ruled in David's favor. King Henry III (or his officers) upbraided those who had appealed to French rabbis and forbade English Jews from appealing to foreign Jews. David got his divorce and was able to marry another woman, Licoricia, who duly provided him a son and heir.[60]

In 1244, not long after his second marriage, David died, and the crown took a close and active interest in his estate. On 15 March, the king wrote to the sheriff of Oxford and ordered him to have the sealed chests and boxes of the late David sent to Windsor, along with all those Jews involved in his estate.[61] Licoricia was kept in the Tower of London, apparently to ensure that the crown got its share of the estate. On 26 June 1244, we find the following entry in the fine rolls:

> For Licorice the Jewess. Order to the barons of the Exchequer and the justices assigned to the custody of the Jews that, having accepted all manner of security which can be provided, both by themselves and by eight of the more wealthy and more discreet Jews of London, or that which shall have been provided by Licorice the Jewess, who was the wife of David, Jew of Oxford, for paying 5000 m. to the king at the terms assigned for paying the tallage of the Jews, by which [sum] the same Licorice has made fine with the king for having the debts and chattels of the aforesaid David, her husband, then they are to cause those chattels to be delivered to her together with the books that are in the king's custody, which the king shall cause to be delivered to her, saving to the king a certain Bible, a glossed psalter and certain decretals, and saving remittances made by the king before that fine for those debts, so that she pays 500 m., allowing therein the 300 m. which they received by the

hand of the sheriffs, by her hand or by the hand of the sheriffs before St. Peter in Chains in the twenty-eighth year, and they are to cause it to be investigated whether any book can be found which is against the law of the Christians or Jews, and if such is found, it is to be condemned, and they are to cause the body of the aforesaid Licorice to be delivered from the king's prison.[62]

Licoricia pays a substantial sum, 5,000 marks, to recover her inheritance from David (including the unpaid loans due to him); she is to be released from the tower; if David's estate was assessed at the traditional rate of one-third, that makes it 15,000 marks total (£10,000), a substantial fortune. Among the items seized by the royal officials were books, most of which were returned to Licoricia, apart from those the king has retained for their artistic or monetary value, and those the justices kept to examine for blasphemy. No doubt the Paris Talmud burnings were fresh in the king's mind. As we have seen, Henry made no direct response to Gregory's letter of 1239 asking him to seize Jewish books and hand them over to Dominican and Franciscan friars for examination. He perhaps saw this as an infringement on the royal monopoly over Jews and a breach of trust toward his Jews. But here the library of one of his richest Jewish subjects was available for inspection. He confided the task of examining these books not to friars (who in other European kingdoms would be most competent) but to the justices of the Jews (who both in terms of jurisdiction and probably in knowledge of Hebrew were the best-qualified persons in England).

David seems to have built up a considerable library of books in Hebrew and Latin (and perhaps French). Some of those manuscripts he no doubt purchased, while others were probably left in pawn by scholars for their debts. Books were prominent among those items that Oxford students and professors used as collateral for their loans, and various documents testify to this practice over the course of the thirteenth century.[63] Many of the Jewish lenders were also scholars, and in some cases they read some of the manuscripts left in their care. Some Jews seem to have taken an interest in Latin learning, though they have left us few written accounts of these activities or their reaction to what they read.

David's wealth was to help finance the *Domus conversorum*: on 30 April 1245, Henry donated part of David's Oxford properties (lands and houses) to the *domus*.[64] As the thirteenth century wore on, Jewish lenders played a key role in helping Oxford ecclesiastical institutions, many of them precursors of the colleges, to obtain land. In 1231, Henry established a hospital in Oxford on land appropriated from Jews.[65] A Hebrew quitclaim (a document that acknowledges payment of a debt) dated 26 March 1251 released a certain William de la Barre from his debts to Abraham Crespin. Osney Abbey had helped William repay these debts and had received lands from him as mortgage.[66] Similar documents show how ecclesiastical institutions in Oxford bailed out Christian debtors, paying their debts to Jews, and in turn received their mortgaged lands. We will see (in Chapter 6) how this system in 1258 provoked the ire of the smaller gentry who rallied around the antiroyal reform movement. It also played a key role in consolidating the land holdings of Oxford's colleges. Walter de Merton, close advisor to Henry III and chancellor of England from 1261 to 1263, bought up the debt of a number of Christian debtors between 1245 and 1272. These lands (along with others, notably taken from the allies of Simon de Montfort after his defeat in 1265) would constitute the patrimony of Merton College.[67]

Grosseteste and the Containment of Judaism

Robert Grosseteste was a prolific scholar of science and biblical exegesis, professor of theology at Oxford, and chancellor of the university before becoming the bishop of Lincoln. As an impassioned advocate of reform, he did not hesitate to speak his mind to all, including Henry III and a succession of popes. His attitudes toward Jews and Judaism have been the object of widely varying assessments among scholars. He has been variously portrayed as philosemitic, as brutally anti-Jewish, and as "not very interested in Jews or Jewish learning."[68] We have seen that in his letter to Margaret of Winchester in 1231 or 1232, he gave a vigorous argument against allowing Jews to practice usury. Yet as chancellor of the University of Oxford, he recognized that loans from Jews played an important role in financing studies and he sought to limit the rate of interest, not to prohibit loans. Theologically, he showed a consistent interest in the relationship between the Old Law and the New, and toward the end of his life, he translated several works that suggested that the Jews had long known that Christ was their Messiah and willfully kept this knowledge hidden from Christians.

Grosseteste was born c. 1170 in Suffolk into a family of modest means.[69] He probably pursued his studies in England. In 1190 he was in the entourage of Bishop Hugh of Lincoln. In Lincoln, Grosseteste met Gerald of Wales, who several years later (probably in 1194–1195) wrote a warm and enthusiastic letter of recommendation for him to William de Vere, bishop of Hereford. In 1196, Grosseteste began working for Bishop William and then (after the bishop's death) for Hugh of Foliot, archdeacon of Shropshire and then bishop of Hereford. Dur-

ing his Hereford years (1196–1220), Grosseteste produced a large and original
corpus of scientific works: on astronomy, acoustics, and optics. He wrote the first
Latin commentary of Aristotle's *Posterior Analytics*, which shows both a vivid
engagement with Aristotle's thought and an independent spirit of inquiry, as he
does not hesitate to disagree with the philosopher and to propose his own theories that differ from those of Aristotle on, for example, the composition of com-
ets or the twinkling of stars.[70] During the interdict (1209–1213) he seems, like
many other English churchmen, to have spent some time in exile in France. In
1225 he became rector of Abbotsley, about one hundred kilometers northeast of
Oxford, in the diocese of Lincoln. This is his first benefice, which means he had
a regular income and could now devote himself to study and teaching. It is perhaps at this time that he began teaching regularly in Oxford, lecturing on (among
other things) the Psalms.

Active teacher and prolific scholar, Grosseteste was also engaged in his pastoral duties. In 1229 he was appointed archdeacon of Leicester. It may be at about
this time that he served as chancellor of the university. In 1231, he abruptly quit
his benefices and his university responsibilities to devote himself to teaching the
Franciscans in Oxford; in 1232, he resigned his post of archdeacon of Leicester.
In letters to his sister and to Adam Marsh in 1232, he explained that he had decided during an illness, which he saw as divine punishment for pluralism (holding multiple benefices), for failure to practice the Franciscan simplicity and
poverty he purported to admire. So he gave up these positions, except for one, as
canon of the cathedral of Lincoln, which no doubt offered him sufficient income
to pursue his activities as a scholar and teacher. He tells Adam March that some
of his friends thought he had acted rashly.[71] Yet clearly he remained a prominent
and respected member of the Oxford community. When, in 1234, Henry III
sought to enforce his ban on prostitutes in the town, he asked Grosseteste and
Dominican Robert Bacon to assist the chancellor in driving them out.[72] During these years (1231–1235) he produced a number of works of exegesis: commentaries on the Hexaemeron (the description of the six days of creation in Genesis),
the Ten Commandments, and on Paul's letter to the Galatians. In 1235, Grosseteste was elected bishop of Lincoln, the largest diocese in England; he remained
an active scholar and remained closely involved in the university, since, as bishop
of Lincoln, Oxford was under his jurisdiction.

As a master of theology, Grosseteste gave lectures, participated in disputations, and preached sermons. The Bible was central to teaching in the medieval
schools: exegetical works by Grosseteste and other twelfth- and thirteenth-
century authors were teaching tools: the commentary elucidates issues that the

teacher/exegete raises with his students in studying the biblical text. Grosseteste's notion of teaching theology is very different from the practice of the Parisian schools; he never lectured, it seems, on Peter Lombard's *Sentences*. The biblical texts remained at the center of his theological reflections. Let us examine two examples, both of which touch on Grosseteste's understanding of Jews and their relationship with Christianity: one from his commentary on the Psalms and another from his commentary on Paul's letter to the Galatians.

First, we will look at what Grosseteste has to say about Psalm 101:1, "Misericordiam et iudicium cantabo tibi Domine" ("I will sing of mercy and judgment: unto thee, O Lord, will I sing").[73] In his commentary to the opening line of this Psalm, Grosseteste launches into a long reflection on the genealogy of Mary and Jesus, insisting on their humility. In the gospel (Mt. 1:5) we learn that one of Mary's forbearers is Rahab, a Canaanite prostitute who helped Joshua's army capture Jericho and who was subsequently accepted into Israel (Jos. 2:6). A harlot and an idolater who enters into God's service and becomes an ancestor of Jesus Christ: her story exemplifies, for Grosseteste, God's mercy. And her story bears a moral lesson, which Grosseteste exposes with an excerpt from John Chrysostom's *Homilies on Matthew*:

> For such a man, though he have an alien for his ancestor, though he have a mother who is a prostitute, or what you will, can take no hurt thereby. For if the whoremonger himself, being changed, is nothing disgraced by his former life, much more will the wickedness of his ancestry have no power to bring to shame him that is sprung of a harlot or an adulteress, if he be virtuous. But He [God] did these things not only to instruct us, but also to bring down the haughtiness of the Jews. For since they, negligent about virtue in their own souls, were parading the name of Abraham, thinking they had for a plea their forefathers' virtue; he shows from the very beginning that it is not in these things men ought to glory, but in their own good deeds.[74]

Grosseteste, like Chrysostom, deemed the Jews proud of their lineage rather than striving for moral righteousness. They were wedded to the past rather than concerned about the present and the future, stuck in the Old Covenant rather than embracing the New.

This is but one passage, taken out of context, from a long and rambling commentary. What is perhaps most striking about his commentaries on the Psalms and on the Hexaemeron is that there is, at this point in his career, no evidence that he took any particular interest in Jews, no knowledge of Hebrew, and no evidence of discussion with Oxford Jews on anything theological: unlike the Victorines or Herbert of Bosham, he does not seem to imagine that the Jews who live just down the street from him might have anything interesting to teach him about the Psalms. What could at first glance seem like criticism of the attitude of contemporary Jews is in fact a passage from Chrysostom, written eight centuries earlier, yet assumed to still hold true for Jews of the thirteenth century. The same could be said for his other exegetical works. The third commandment is "remember the Sabbath day, to keep it holy." In his treatise on the Ten Commandments, Grosseteste argues that Christians, not Jews, properly keep the Sabbath. Here he based his argument principally on lengthy quotations of Augustine. Augustine, he says, denounces the Jews for spending the Sabbath indulging in trifles and lust. They would be better off spending their Sabbaths working in the fields than lolling in the theatres; their women should rather spin yarn than dance lasciviously.[75] Presumably Grosseteste did not see many Oxford Jews lolling in theatres or dancing lasciviously.

In his commentary to Paul's letter to the Galatians, Grosseteste addressed the question of the relation between the Old Law and the New, to which he later (c. 1230–1235) devoted a treatise, the *De cessatione legalium*. Paul raises the question of the value of continued observance of the law (notably through circumcision) and affirms that "those who rely on faith are blessed along with Abraham, the man of faith," while "all who rely on the works of the law are under a curse" (Gal. 3:9–10). The choice of Galatians for teaching and commentary perhaps reflects a particular interest in the question of the abrogation of the covenant between God and his chosen people, though little or nothing in his treatment of the question betrays any specific interest in contemporary Jews. In Galatians 2, Paul criticizes the circumcised who separated themselves from the Gentiles, while Peter sees merit in the Jews' continued observance of their law. For Paul, this divides the Christian community by maintaining a distinction between Christian Jews and Christian Gentiles. In his commentary on this text, Grosseteste discusses patristic arguments concerning the supercession of the Jewish law in Christianity. In particular, he cites the exchange of letters between Jerome and Augustine over the interpretation of this passage, Jerome affirming that Christ had abolished the law while Augustine felt that continued Jewish observance of the law was licit in the first years of the Church. While he shows a preference for Augustine's position over Jerome's, he concludes that the issue should rather be resolved in a disputation. *De cessatione*, then, represents his response to this issue. In other words, Grosseteste's teaching of scripture (in this case Paul's letter to the Galatians) led him to explain patristic notions of the relationship between the Old Law and the New, and subsequently spurred him to compose a theological treatise on the question. There is no reason to think that he composed *De cessatione* with contemporary Jews in mind, much less that he meant it to be a tract for missionary activity, as Samuel Pegge suggested in 1793.[76] Grosseteste directs his argument to Christian theologians to show that the continued observance of the ceremonial precepts of the Jewish law is heretical. In the first part of the treatise, Grosseteste demonstrates that the idea that law of Moses should continue to be observed by Christians derives from erroneous readings of scripture. In the second part, (called "cur Deus homo" by later hands in one manuscript), he affirms that the life, death, and resurrection of Jesus fulfill messianic prophecies and that the Incarnation hence cancels and invalidates the Mosaic *legalia*, rendering their observance both heretical and blasphemous. Moreover, he affirms in part three, to continue to observe the *legalia* is to deny the Church its key place, and (in the fourth and final part) continued observance of *legalia* denies the evangelical activity of the Holy Spirit.

Here is how Grosseteste presents the objective of his *De cessatione*:

> There were many in the primitive Church who asserted that the rituals of the Old Law together with those of the New Law must be observed and that there could be no salvation without observing them. Their opinion was rejected by the decree of the Apostles written in the Acts of the same Apostles and repudiated most effectively by blessed Paul in his letters to the Romans and the Galatians. Because, therefore, they were able to support the error of their position with authorities as well as with fallacious arguments—and by these arguments and authorities even now the faith could waver in the minds of the weak—I will set out the points that seem to confirm their position as they occur to me, though my ability and memory are small and little. After these arguments are set out in my own way and refuted in their turn, I will also make the arguments that disprove this error and establish that the Law was made void by the grace of Christ.[77]

De cessatione is concerned above all with a theological problem: explaining why the continued observance of Mosaic law is not merely superfluous, but heretical. The fact that this problem preoccupies Grosseteste, that he dealt with it first in his commentary to Galatians and subsequently at greater length in *De cessatione*, reflects, once again, the centrality of the biblical texts to his theology:

the presence of the numerous laws of the Pentateuch must be explained as divinely ordained laws that were "made void" through Christ's incarnation. The continued presence in Christian society of Jews, who purported to respect the Old Law and who refused the New Covenant, may also be a contributing factor, though nothing in this treatise shows any specific concern for the Jews of the thirteenth century. When he uses the present tense to talk about Jews, he says things that could have been written (and sometimes were) by Patristic theologians. The "Laws, in which the synagogue glories, ought to cease."[78] He cites at length Jerome's letters to Augustine: "I proclaim that the ceremonies of the Jews are dangerous and deadly for Christians, and whoever observes them, whether he be a Jew or a Gentile, falls headlong into the Lower World of the Devil."[79] The law is dead, and the Jews should give it its final honors and bury it; "to keep, then, after Christ the Law as Law . . . is altogether wicked, because this is to deny Christ and to preach another still to come, just as at present the unfaithful Jews do."[80] To crown his argument, he affirms (again citing Jerome by name) that the Jews "keep neither the corporal Law—for it is impossible—nor the spiritual Law, which they do not understand."[81]

What relationship, if any, is there between Grosseteste's theological assessment of Judaism and the Jewish law and his pastoral and legal positions on the place of Jews in English society? We have seen that in 1231 or 1232 he wrote a letter to Margaret of Quincy, Countess of Winchester, in which he affirmed that Christian rulers should protect Jews but at the same time prevent them from oppressing Christians through usury. In this letter, Grosseteste expounds clearly and forcefully the theology of Jewish captivity and punishment based on Augustine, which had been the object of a number of papal bulls by Innocent III. Jews are guilty for the murder of Christ, yet like Cain who slayed Abel they should not be killed, but should live in exile and punishment as a reminder of their sin. While Richard Southern calls Grosseteste's attitude "brutal" and characterizing his "peasant's violence and passion," it is in fact no harsher than the writings of Innocent.[82] The letter is indeed uncompromising: "as long as they persist in their unbelief, blaspheme Christ, the Savior of the world, and mock his passion, they will be held captive under the princes of the world as a just punishment for their sin."[83] This means that they should continue to live under the curse of punishment, and that Christian princes should both protect and punish them. "The Jews should not, then, be indulged by Christian rulers so that they may oppress Christians with usury and from that usury live in luxury and labor." Those Christian princes who aid Jews in oppressing Christians will share their punishment in the next life, he warns the countess. They should rather make the Jews toil the land. Grosseteste then moves on to what may be the real occasion for writing the letter: one of Margaret's officers had deprived Grosseteste of some funds due to him as tithes.

While in his letter to Margaret, Grosseteste develops a clear argument against permitting Jews to make loans for interest, there is nothing to suggest that he attempted to impose such bans either in Oxford or in the diocese of Lincoln. On the contrary, only on rare occasions does he show any interest or concern for Jews and their dealings with Christians, indeed less than his contemporary and close associate Walter de Cantilupe, bishop of Worcester, whose synodal statutes of 1240 prohibit Christian women from serving as wet-nurses for Jews or staying overnight in their houses, and prohibits Jews from depositing pawned items in churches.[84] Grosseteste's statutes for the diocese of Lincoln (probably dated to 1239) contain not a single mention of Jews.[85] Sometime in 1243 or 1244, he sent a circular to his archdeacons, complaining of a number of irregularities in the diocese. He had heard that some priests were not saying mass, or were doing so improperly. They kept concubines, though they did their best to hide them (and perjure themselves) when their bishop came visiting. They performed or participated in miracle plays and other May Day and harvest day festivities, including drinking parties ("scot ales"), which Grosseteste had earlier prohibited. Some of these clerics not only refused to listen to the sermons of the Franciscan and Dominican friars, they tried to prevent their parishioners from doing so. He bade his archdeacons to eliminate these practices, telling them, "You are Judas Maccabaeus, duty bound to purge the Lord's temple of every impurity." He continued his admonition with strict orders for proper observance in each of the cases mentioned. After this, at the very end of his letter, he adds, "And you are to do all you possibly can to put a stop to the practice of Christians living with Jews."[86] This admonition, rather an afterthought, is very much in accord, as we have seen, with the repeated prohibitions of Christians working and living in Jewish households, pronounced notably by the Council of Oxford in 1222. There as here, it is one element among many, in an effort to reform the mores of clergy and laity.

On Annunciation Day, 25 March 1244, the first day of Passover, a group of students invaded the Oxford Jewry and sacked the Jews' homes.[87] The sheriff intervened, and forty-five students were imprisoned. Grosseteste, as bishop of Lincoln with jurisdiction over clerics in his diocese (including students of Oxford), protested at this breach of justice. On 2 May, the king ordered that the imprisoned students be handed over to Grosseteste so that they could be submitted to ecclesiastical justice.[88] It appears that the sheriff, whose duty was to protect

the king's interest, and in this case his Jews, intervened to defend Oxford's Jews
and to punish the offenders. Yet for Grosseteste, he alone as bishop could judge
these students. It is not that the bishop did not see the necessity of protecting
Oxford's Jews and punishing the students who robbed them. While here the conflict involved Jews, at other times, the conflict was between Christian townsmen and the students: this was true in 1209, as we have seen; it was also true in
spring 1248. On 8 May 1248, Grosseteste wrote to Adam Marsh, saying that the
chancellor had written telling him that several townsmen had murdered a scholar
and that the town bailiffs had let the murderers go unpunished, provoking a
strike by Oxford's masters, who had threatened to leave the town. He ordered
Adam to go to Oxford and to solemnly proclaim the excommunication of those
guilty of the murder.[89]

The situation was serious enough that the king intervened. On 14 May,
Henry was at the royal palace in Woodstock, fifteen kilometers north of Oxford.[90] Between 20 and 23 May, Henry fined the burgesses of Oxford eighty
marks for the murder of this clerk, Gilbert of Dunfermline. Clearly he received
in Oxford representatives of the townsmen and the university, as over the next
few days he granted a series of concessions to the university,[91] which were subsequently issued as a charter of privileges on 29 May.[92] The first and primary concern was to regulate future conflicts between town and gown: in case of injury
done to scholars, the university could conduct inquiries not only in Oxford, but
also in surrounding towns. If those guilty of violence toward scholars were not
brought to justice, the entire town was liable. The mayors and bailiffs of Oxford
had to swear to respect the privileges of the university. The charter also addressed
financial issues: prices of bread and ale were controlled. Jews were limited to
charging an interest rate of two pence per pound per week (43.5 percent annually, the maximum amount, as we have seen, already theoretically imposed on
all Jews in England in 1233).

The measures taken in 1248 sought to curb abuses in the practice of loaning
money for interest, not to eliminate it. If we are to believe Matthew Paris, on his
deathbed Grosseteste expounded on the ills of this world and notably the cor-
ruption that infested the papal court. He complained in particular of the rapa-
cious practices of the pope's moneylenders, compared to whom London's Jews
practiced compassion and magnanimity.[93] In 1240, Grosseteste established St
Frideswide's loan chest in order to provide interest-free loans, from annual fees
paid by the town burgesses to the university, to students with modest income. The
institution was to be a model for the Franciscan Mounts of Piety founded throughout Europe in the later Middle Ages. Grosseteste also fostered the foundation of

scholarships for penurious students.[94] These elements help us put his letter to Margaret of Winchester in perspective. On principle, he did not approve of anyone, including Jews, practicing usury. But he was also aware that Jewish loans were an integral element of the English economy and in particular of the financing of an Oxford education. He therefore took measures to alleviate the financial pressures on the poorer students at Oxford and to limit the rates of interest charged by Jewish lenders.

At the height of his career as a bishop, when he was probably in his sixties, Grosseteste set out to learn Greek, in which he became proficient, and possibly Hebrew, though he probably never developed real proficiency. While his translations from Greek included works of Aristotle, they were above all theological. Several of them show his continued interest in the question of the guilt of Jews in the killing of Christ. Sometime before 1242 Grosseteste translated from the Greek seventy-one entries from the *Suda*, an encyclopedia of learning composed around the tenth century, including the entry for Jesus.[95] It relates a purported conversation of two friends, a Christian and a Jew, during the reign of Justinian (527–565). The Jew confided to the Christian that Jesus had been named one of the twenty-two priests of the temple of Jerusalem, and that in order to name him the priests needed to ascertain the identity of his father and mother. They interviewed Mary, who said she was Jesus's mother and that he had no earthly father; she related the story of the Annunciation. The priests were skeptical: they had midwives verify that Mary was a virgin and they brought in witnesses who had seen Mary give birth to Jesus. They then named Jesus priest and inscribed in the register of the temple that his mother was Mary and his father was God. Yet subsequent Jews kept this secret. It is unnecessary to insist on the apocryphal nature of this text. Yet Grosseteste must have seen it as authentic, as did his readers. Indeed his translation was well appreciated: the chapter was the most recopied of all his entries from the *Suda*. Here, again, we find the idea that Jewish texts can provide evidence both of the truth of Christianity and of the duplicity of contemporary Jews.

In 1242, Grosseteste translated from Greek into Latin the *Testaments of the Twelve Patriarchs*.[96] Grosseteste may have learned Greek from John of Basingstoke, archdeacon of Leicester, who had lived and studied in Athens; it may be John who brought the existence of the *Testaments* to Grosseteste's attention. Matthew Paris writes that the bishop sent a messenger to Athens to obtain the text and then translated it with the help of a certain Nicholas Graecus (this is confirmed in the colophon of the manuscript).[97]

The text may have been composed in Hebrew in the second century CE.[98] It purports to represent the dying words of the twelve sons of Jacob, in which (among other things) they utter prophecies concerning the coming of Christ as Messiah. The translation proved to be the most widely read of Grosseteste's works: it is extant in fifteen thirteenth-century manuscripts and is cited by Vincent de Beauvais, Bonaventure, and Roger Bacon. For Grosseteste and his readers, the *Testaments* proved that the Jewish patriarchs had clearly foretold the coming of Christ and that their prophecies had been written down for all Jews to see. Matthew Paris explains that Jews, out of envy, had hidden the text from Christians, but that it had been translated from Hebrew to Greek and now the good bishop rendered it into Latin "for the greater confusion of the Jews."[99] In other words, the Jews *knew* that Jesus was their Messiah but kept the knowledge hidden out of spite.

These two translations show us that in his seventies, Robert Grosseteste, one of the most powerful and influential men in the English church and one of the outstanding scholars in Latin Europe, had come to the conclusion that his Jewish contemporaries were aware that Jesus Christ was their Messiah but they were malevolently keeping this secret. It may be at the same time that he was translating these works that he embarked on the study of Hebrew. The case for his knowledge of Hebrew comes from several later authors: chronicler Nicholas de Triveti says that he was erudite in three languages (Latin, Greek, and Hebrew), and that he "gleaned many things from the glosses of the Jews"; Roger Bacon, fulsome in his praise of his former teacher, nevertheless says that he was not proficient enough in either Greek or Hebrew to translate by himself, but that he had "many helpers."[100]

The other piece of evidence of his involvement in Hebrew scholarship is a series of manuscripts containing the text of the Psalms in three columns: the Hebrew on the right, and two Latin translations, including the Gallican or Vulgate (translated from the Greek text of the Septuagint) and the Hebraica (translated by Jerome from the Hebrew). The Hebrew text is annotated with Latin terms in superscript: the Latin equivalent for each Hebrew word is written above the word. We have already seen the centrality of the Psalms in the study of Hebrew in twelfth- and thirteenth-century England. Here, if we are to believe fourteenth-century Hebraist Henry of Cossey, it is Grosseteste himself who had this superscript composed.[101]

While none of the extant manuscripts are in the hand of Grosseteste, Beryl Smalley argues that several of them are copies, which show various stages of later corrections, and the closest is Oxford, Corpus Christi MS 10, which contains a preface that bears Grosseteste's imprint. In this preface we read: "In order to quiet the collision and conflict of these two [Jews and Christians] in their mother's womb, it profits us something, as we think, to bring the nations together into the unity of faith under the guidance of Christ, by reconciling their differences through a knowledge of both tongues and both Scriptures, and to set them side by side, lest because they differ they should forever fight. The zeal of God's house incites me to edit the Hebrew Scripture that it may confirm the faithful and convert the infidel."[102] Grosseteste sees his intellectual activity and his pastoral duties as a whole, and part of his mission is in both cases to "confirm the faithful and convert the infidel."

In the 1240s and until his death in 1253, Grosseteste defended the rights of the English Church and bishops and did not hesitate to oppose the archbishop of Canterbury, King Henry, or the pope. In 1245, Grosseteste crossed to France as part of the English delegation to the First Council of Lyon, convened by Pope Innocent IV. One of the canons of the council ruled that in preparation for the coming crusade (to be led by Louis IX), all those who took crusader vows should be exempted from paying interest on loans, from the day of their vow to the day of their return.[103] In 1250, he returned to Lyon, accompanied by his dean, Richard de Gravesend, for an audience with Innocent IV. Boniface of Savoy, archbishop of Canterbury (and uncle of Queen Eleanor) planned to make visitations to the dioceses under his jurisdiction and to make the bishops provide him hospitality and pay his expenses. Grosseteste argued to the pope and his curia that it was against canon law and episcopal authority to make the bishops pay these expenses.[104] He seems to have been successful in this appeal. Grosseteste also opposed taxes on the English Church for Henry's project of a crusade. Here he was less successful. But we see him appealing directly to the pope in an attempt to curb the abuses of the archbishop of Canterbury and the king.

By the mid-thirteenth century, it seems, the "Augustinian" doctrine of toleration, based on the idea that Jews erroneously continued to be faithful to the Old Law of the Torah, which they preserved for the Christians, was seriously challenged by a new vision of Jews as inimical to Christians and Christianity. For Nicolas Donin and others, the Talmud encouraged Jews in their violent hostility toward Christians: for this, as well as for its blasphemy against Christ and the Virgin, it was burned in Paris in 1242. While there is no evidence that Robert Grosseteste thought that Jews were violently hostile toward Christianity, he clearly came to believe that they knew the truth of Christianity and refused to recognize it out of spite and pride.

In the later years of his life, Grosseteste became the chief spokesman for the bishops in their complaints against the king. On 13 January 1253, at a provincial synod called by Archbishop Boniface, Grosseteste presented, in the name of the English bishops, a series of complaints (*gravamina*) about Henry's failure to respect the prerogatives of the Church, in breach of natural and ecclesiastical law.[105] The confrontation between bishops and the crown became a major conflict and was to lead the king to make new restrictions on England's Jews, as we will see in the next chapter.

CHAPTER 5

From the Statutes of the Jewry
to Little Hugh of Lincoln (1253–1255)

In 1253, Henry issued a new statute on the Jewry, in which he again affirmed his authority over "his" Jews. Yet at the same time, he granted major concessions to the Church: Jews were to wear the badge and were forbidden to have Christian servants in their homes; they were to pay tithes to the Church. A politically and financially weakened king made concessions to his bishops (concerning Jews and other matters) in order to win their approval of new taxes on church property.

Two years later, in Lincoln, a young boy named Hugh was found dead. Local Jews were accused of having murdered Hugh in a ritual reenactment of Christ's passion. This was not the first accusation of ritual murder on English soil: similar stories had been told in particular about William of Norwich, who had died in 1144. But this is the first case in which a king took an active part in the prosecution: Henry went to Lincoln and presided over the trial himself. Eighteen Jews were proclaimed guilty and brought to London, where some of them were subsequently hanged. Thanks in part to the intervention of Franciscans who helped them plead their innocence, the remaining Jewish prisoners were released. Henry's involvement in this trial, and his precipitous embrace of the prosecution, seems to be at odds with his previous self-interested protection of the rights of "his" Jews; this was not to bode well for the future of England's Jewish community.

The 1253 Statute of the Jews in Context

On 31 January 1253, Henry issued the following mandate:

> Mandate of the King to the Justices assigned to the custody of the Jews touching certain statutes relating to the Jews in England which are to be rigorously observed, the thirty-seventh year of King Henry, AD 1253.
>
> The king has provided and ordained that no Jew remain in England unless he do the king service, and that from the hour of birth every Jew, whether male or female, serve us in some way. And that there be no synagogues of the Jews in England save in those places in which such synagogues were in the time of King John, the King's father. And that in their synagogues the Jews, one and all, subdue their voices in performing their ritual offices, that Christians may not hear them. And that all Jews answer to the rector of the church of the parish in which they dwell touching all dues parochial relating to their houses. And that no Christian nurse in future suckle or nourish the male child of any Jew, nor any Christian man or woman serve any Jew or Jewess, or eat with them or tarry in their houses. And that no Jew or Jewess eat or buy meat during Lent. And that no Jew disparage the Christian Faith, or publicly dispute concerning the same. And that no Jew have secret familiar intercourse with any Christian woman, and no Christian man with a Jewess. And that every Jew wear his badge conspicuously on his breast. And that no Jew enter any church or chapel save for purpose of transit, or linger in them in dishonor of Christ. And that no Jew place any hindrance in the way of another Jew desirous of turning to the Christian Faith. And that no Jew be received in any town but by special license of the King, save only in those towns in which Jews have been wont to dwell.
>
> And the Justices assigned to the custody of the Jews are commanded that they cause these provisions to be carried into effect, and rigorously observed on pain of forfeiture of the chattels of the said Jews. Witness the King at Westminster, on the 31st day of January. By King and Council.[1]

In this mandate, which Henry sent to the judges exercising jurisdiction over Jews, the king affirms his authority over Jews while at the same time giving royal sanction to various measures concerning Jews taken by church councils in Rome (Lateran III, 1179, and Lateran IV, 1215) and in England (Oxford, 1222, among others). The king begins by affirming that no Jew, of whatever age or sex, may remain in England unless he provides service to the king. This is a strong statement of the direct dependency of Jews to the person of the king (and echoes the provisions of the 1233 statute). Yet other measures of a quite different nature are added, which reflect the persistent demands of English bishops and other churchmen to limit contacts between Jews and Christians: curbing expansion of Jewish settlement and prohibiting building of new synagogues. A series of stipulations echo measures taken at the Council of Oxford in 1222: Jews are prohibited from having Christian servants and from sexual relations with Christians; they are obliged to pay tithes on their lands and houses to the parish rector and to the wear a badge in the shape of "tablets." While many of the measures in this mandate had been the object of canons in previous church councils, here Henry III lends royal authority to these laws and specifically instructs his royal justiciars to enforce these laws, if necessary through the seizure of Jews' property.

Whereas the king had previously guarded his judicial and fiscal monopoly over "his" Jews and vigorously countered bishops who tried to impose limits on Jews, here Henry seems to cave in to episcopal demands. As we will see, this is in large part in order to convince the English Church to finance new military adventures—and pay debts incurred on previous ones. The mandate comes at the end of over a decade of increasing financial pressure on English Jews. To understand the 1253 mandate in context, we must return to 1239–1241, which Robert Stacey has defined as a "watershed" in English Jewish policy.

As Stacey has shown, in these years "royal policy towards Jewish taxation changed dramatically."[2] We saw in Chapter 1 how the Bristol tallage and the civil war had devastated English Jewry in the years 1210–1217, and how in the first years of Henry's rule, royal officials took pains to help Jews regain their place in English society, reclaim moneys due to them, and reestablish commercial activities. Between 1221 and 1239, the crown taxed Jews at about 2,000 to 3,000 marks per year, a rate that permitted significant contributions to the fisc without endangering the livelihood and the lending activity of Jews. This changed dramatically in 1239, when royal officials demanded a staggering one-third of the value of all Jews' goods and debts. Unsurprisingly, the crown was unable to collect such astronomic sums, and two years later, in 1241, assessed a new tax of 20,000 marks.[3] In the following years, a series of major tallages were assessed (and only partially collected): 60,000 marks in 1244, 10,000 in 1250, 4,500 in 1251, 4,500 again in 1252, 5,000 in 1253, 10,000 in 1254, and 2,000 in January 1255. That makes a total of over 100,000 marks between 1241 and 1255, over three times as much as what they had paid between 1221 and 1239. Royal records suggest that these amounts (or something close to them) were indeed paid to the fisc. In order to understand the events narrated in this chapter and the next, we will need to bear in mind the intense financial pressure and extreme hardship that this imposed on Jewish communities.

Why this change in policy? Henry was strapped for cash and frequently involved in costly (and almost invariably unsuccessful) military adventures. In 1242, Henry led his troops to the Poitou in support of Hugh of Lusignan, who was in rebellion against King Louis IX and his brother Alphonse of Poitiers, Count of Poitou. Yet Henry, indecisive, avoided direct engagement with Louis's much larger force that ravaged the territories of the rebellious barons and slowly enticed them to abandon Henry, who the following year asked Louis for a five-year truce.[4] One of his Poitevin vassals, troubadour Bernart de Rovenac, castigated him: "I beg the English king to listen to me, for he is now ruining his slight reputation through excessive fear, given that he is unwilling to defend his own people. Instead he is so limp and confused that he seems to be fast asleep, for the French king is entirely unopposed in robbing him of Tours and Angers, Normans and Bretons."[5] As David Carpenter has remarked, "Henry had no aptitude or interest in the business of war."[6] This disastrous Poitevin expedition cost him roughly £80,000.[7] He returned defeated to England in early 1243 and attempted to use ceremonial, largesse, and conspicuous piety to restore regal image. This of course did not help the crown's finances.[8]

In the following years, Henry imposed heavy levies on many of his subjects, including Jews. Matthew Paris describes how in August 1243, "the king extorted from the most unfortunate Jews a heavy ransom in gold and silver." He took gold from the hand of each Jew and Jewess in his realm, Matthew says, extorting in particular 4 marks of gold and 4,000 of silver from Aaron of York. At the same time, he demanded precious gifts from abbots and priors, and when not satisfied with what they gave him, demanded more: "he thus was made from a king into a tyrant."[9] Yet worse was to come for England's Jews the following year, in 1244: a 60,000 mark tallage. As Stacey explains, "The double blows of the 20 000 mark tallage of 1241-2 and the 60 000 mark tallage of 1244-50 ruined the Jewish magnates of England, and effectively decapitated the class structure of medieval Anglo-Jewry. By so doing, Henry broke the financial backbone of the English Jewish community, and permanently reduced its financial value to the crown."[10] At least two prominent Jews attempted to flee the tallage: Jacob of Exeter succeeded, probably taking exile in France, while Bonefey of Bristol was captured and imprisoned.[11] Matthew Paris says that the king extorted as much money as he could from prelates, monks, burghers, and Jews.[12]

Henry tried to assure that "his" Jews would not try to escape. He sent this mandate to the justiciars of the Jews:

> It is mandated to the justiciars charged with the custody of the Jews that, immediately upon reading these letters, they proclaim in all the counties of England where the king's Jews reside, that if any Jewess, wife of any Jew, or their children, should escape or flee, or hide in any way from the town where they had lived, on the feast of St. Andrew in the 29th year of the king's reign to the following year, in such a way that when summoned by the King or his bailiffs in whose bailiwicks they had been living they cannot be found that that same Jew and that same Jewess and all their children should be immediately outlawed and all of their lands, taxes and chattel shall be seized into the hand of the king and immediately sold for the crown, and they shall not return to the kingdom of England without special permission from the king.[13]

Henry here prohibited Jews and their families from leaving England without his permission. Those Jews who had fled England without the king's leave were to be outlawed and their goods seized by the crown. This mandate marks a key passage in the degradation of the status of English Jews. While they had always in theory been subject to the king's authority and (according to the 1233 Statute of the Jewry) were only allowed to stay in England as long as they were useful to the king, this is the first law that prohibits Jews from leaving the kingdom. Some Jews, unable to leave, converted to Christianity and sometimes regretted that decision and attempted to return to Judaism. In Oxford, Franciscan friar Robert Bacon signaled one culprit to the king, who on 6 April 1245 ordered his sheriff to have the apostate arrested and imprisoned. On 18 July 1247, the king sent a mandate to the sheriff of Wiltshire, ordering him to have an apostate named Solomon sent to London to be held in Newgate prison.[14]

While Jews had little ability to resist royal taxation and were now prevented from leaving the kingdom, other English subjects pushed back against this increasing fiscal pressure. In response to demands for new taxation, ostensibly to pay the debts for the Poitou campaign, a committee of four bishops (including Robert Grosseteste), four earls (including Simon de Montfort), two barons, and two abbots drew up a "paper constitution," which purportedly proposed to set up a commission to oversee royal finances. It is uncertain that this document was ever in fact given to the king, but the standoff reflects increasing frustration with the parlous state of royal finance and with exorbitant taxation.[15]

In 1247, according to Matthew Paris, Louis IX decreed that English coinage would no longer be accepted in France, since it had been compromised by coin clipping. Matthew claims that English Jews had resorted to clipping coins because they had been reduced to poverty by excessive tallages.[16] He later adds that these "detestable falsifiers" were, in addition to Jews, "Caursins" (Christian moneylenders from Cahors or elsewhere in Provence or Languedoc) and Flemish wool merchants.[17] In 1250, says Matthew, Henry, through his "avaricious thirst," pitilessly impoverishes the Jews further.[18] He tries to extort 14,000 marks from Aaron of York, who was, along with Elias Blund, arrested while trying to flee with their families.[19] By 1255, Aaron, formerly the richest Jew in England, had paid his entire fortune in taxes and was declared a pauper.[20]

The king's financial needs were linked to his ostentatious piety: he gave alms to thousands of paupers, showered gifts of clothing and jewels on monasteries, and rebuilt Westminster Abbey. In September 1247, Henry received a gift from the patriarch of Jerusalem: a phial said to contain the blood of Christ, collected by Joseph of Arimathea at the crucifixion.[21] The very blood of Christ, spilt by the Jews, a passion relic even greater than the cross of thorns that Louis IX had received from Latin Emperor Baldwin II of Constantinople in 1238. Louis was building the Sainte Chapelle in Paris to house the crown of thorns; Henry solemnly bore the vial from St. Paul's Cathedral to Westminster, where, he hoped, it would become a prized relic that would attract pilgrims. He had the bishop of Norwich preach a sermon on the merits of the Holy Blood and had Robert Grosseteste compose a treatise on it.[22] The crown of thorns and the blood of Christ were reminders of Christ's passion; their veneration could not be good news for Jews who were associated with that passion. And these ostentatious royal cults were closely linked with crusade: Louis left on his crusade to Egypt shortly after consecrating the Sainte Chapelle in 1248. In 1249, news arrived of Louis's success in capturing the Egyptian port of Damietta: Queen Mother Blanche of Castile wrote glowingly to Henry of the glorious victory God had bestowed on her son. Henry solemnly took the cross from Archbishop Boniface in Westminster on 6 March 1250, though by 1 August news arrived of Louis's defeat and capture.[23]

Crusading cost money. In April 1250, Pope Innocent IV granted Henry a crusading tenth: a tax of 10 percent of all revenues of the English Church for two years, in order to pay for his crusade. Robert Grosseteste stood before the pope in Lyon on 13 May 1250 and tried to convince him not to authorize this exceptional tax on the English Church, but to no avail.[24] The pope upheld the tax, which the English bishops then approved, though implementation was delayed until the king set a date for his departure.[25] Grosseteste reworked his plea to the pope into a treatise on tyranny, which he sent to Simon de Montfort.[26]

On 13 December 1250, Henry's brother-in-law, Emperor Frederick II, died. Innocent IV saw an opportunity to prevent the late emperor's Hohenstaufen heirs from ruling in Sicily: this goal soon became more urgent than the recovery of the Holy Land. The pope wrote to the English bishops, saying that the crusading tenth should be extended from two to three years, and that collection should be approved immediately. Though the pope's instruction seemingly left little choice to the English bishops, they were in no mood to comply, and refused during two church councils in April 1252, even though Henry promised that he would indeed conduct a crusade to the Holy Land, and that he would set out within four years. Just as Louis had finished the Sainte Chapelle before heading off on crusade in 1248, Henry wanted to consecrate the renovated Westminster Abbey before leaving.[27] In October 1252, to break the deadlock, Henry offered to set aside the papal order and instead to request a voluntary aid from the Church. Matthew Paris again paints a vivid picture of royal avarice: "The king, therefore, in order to comply with the pope's urgent desire, extorted from the Jews whatever visible property those wretched people possessed, not only, as it were, skinning them merely, but also plucking out their entrails. Thus this dropsical thirster after gold cheated Christians as well as Jews out of their money, food, and jewels, with such greediness that it seemed as if a new Crassus was arisen from the dead."[28]

On 13 January 1253, the bishops of the province of Canterbury met in London. Robert Grosseteste, at seventy-seven years old the *éminence grise* of the English church, had drawn up for the bishops a series of grievances (*gravamina*) that the king needed to address.[29] Grosseteste and the assembled bishops were willing to grant Henry his crusading tax, but they intended to take full advantage of the occasion to insist that in return the king respect the privileges of the Church. The seventeen grievances involve the king's disrespect of ecclesiastical jurisdiction and property: the king judges clerics in secular courts, he usurps church properties, and he demands hospitality in monasteries when he travels, among others. There is no mention of Jews in these seventeen articles of complaint.

Yet it may be in reaction to this clerical discontent that Henry issues just eighteen days later (31 January 1253), the new statute concerning the Jews. As we have seen, the mandate seems to concede to the English episcopate all they have been requesting concerning the Jews since the Council of Oxford in 1222: imposition of the badge, prohibition of Christians working or socializing in Jewish homes, requirement that Jews be respectful of Christianity and discreet in their religious observance, and payment of tithes on Jewish-controlled properties to the local churches.[30] While Henry never directly addressed the seventeen *gravamina* drawn up by Grosseteste and his colleagues, here he may be offering a concession to clerical demands: it is easier and less costly, no doubt, to yield to them concerning the status of the Jews than to renounce on royal prerogatives over the English Church. He also forgave Grosseteste a £100 fine that the bishop owed the crown.[31]

If this mandate was a sop to the English clergy, it may have had the desired effect. In April the bishops agreed to grant the king the tax. Henry did not directly address their complaints, although he did reissue Magna Carta, with a solemn excommunication of those who infringed it, during the parliament, or Great Council of the realm, at Westminster in May.[32] To what extent the king intended to respect his promises is another matter. In December 1253, Pope Innocent IV offered the throne of Sicily to Henry's nine-year-old son Edmund. To affirm his son's title to the crown, Henry would need to finance another expensive (and unwinnable) military campaign, which historians would dub "the Sicilian adventure."[33] Henry would continue to extract as much money as he could from whomever he could, without opposition from Robert Grosseteste, who died in Lincoln on 9 October 1253.

In 1253 not only was there no relief in sight for English Jews living under extreme fiscal pressure from the crown, but their scant hope of royal protection from ecclesiastical restriction on Jewish-Christian relations was evaporating. And while English Jews may have contemplated leaving the kingdom, it was not clear where their life would be better: Louis IX had, as we have seen, ordered the burning of the Talmud in 1241. In 1251, the Pastoureaux (or "Shepard's crusade"), whose recruits sought to rally Louis IX in the Holy Land and pursue the crusade, attacked Jewish communities in Bourges, Orléans, and elsewhere.[34] In 1253, according to Matthew Paris, Louis sent a mandate from the Holy Land prohibiting Jewish usury and expelling Jews who did not accept living by commerce or manual labor. Matthew said that he was prompted by comments by Saracens, who did not understand why he tolerated those who had slain Jesus. In any case, the following year, in December 1254, upon his return to France, Louis issued a *Grande Ordinance* for the reform of the kingdom. Article 32 of the ordinance orders that Jews cease "usury, blasphemy, and sorcery." The books containing their blasphemies, including the Talmud, are to be burned. Jews are to live by the labor of their hands, or through trade with no usury. Those who do not wish to comply are to be expelled.[35]

In 1254 Jews in England asked the king for permission to leave the kingdom: Matthew Paris relates a tearful speech to the king by Archpresbyter Elias of London: since your highness seems set on destroying us and favoring papal money-lenders, why not let us leave? The king refused.[36] In January 1255, when the king asked for a payment of 8,000 marks, the Jews responded, according to Matthew, "Your Majesty, we see that you spare neither Christians nor Jews, but make it your business on diverse pretexts to impoverish all: no hope remains to us of breathing freely; the pope's usurers have supplanted us; therefore permit us to depart from your kingdom under safe conduct, and we will seek another abode of some kind or other."[37] The king again refused, saying he needed money. Finally, realizing that the Jews could not give him the money he needed, he sold them to his brother Richard: "Becoming, then, a second Titus or Vespasian, he sold the Jews for some years to his brother Earl Richard, that the earl might disembowel those whom the king had skinned."[38] They were prohibited from leaving, but not necessarily authorized to stay. We have seen that the mandate of 31 January 1253 said that no Jew should stay in England unless he was useful to the king: impoverished by exorbitant taxation, harassed by clergy whose rights over them are now acknowledged by the king, then sold by the king to his brother, the situation of English Jews was grim indeed. It comes then as no surprise that 1255, a year in which Henry III massively taxed "his" Jews and had nineteen of them put to death for supposedly crucifying a Christian boy, represented for Sophia Menache "probably a peak year in the history of Anglo-Jewry's conversions."[39] Indeed, the *Domus conversorum,* a modest and poorly-funded establishment as we have seen, was not big enough to handle the Jews who sought refuge in conversion. Henry sent missives to 125 different religious houses, asking them to house 150 converts from Judaism.[40] Yet 4 October of the same year, their situation became suddenly bleaker.

Little Hugh of Lincoln

In the *Canterbury Tales,* Chaucer's prioress tells of a Christian boy who sang the praises of the Virgin Mary as he walked through the Jewish neighborhood of an Asian city. The Jews in spite cut his throat, but miraculously he kept singing. The civil authorities condemned the Jews to death and the boy was revered as a martyr. The prioress concludes her tale by evoking a saint closer to home:

O yonge Hugh of Lyncoln, slayn also
With cursed Jews, as it is notable,
For it is but a litel while ygo,
Pray eek for us, we synful folk unstable,
That of his mercy God so merciable
On us his grete mercy multiplie,
For reverence of his moder Marie. Amen.[41]

By the time Chaucer penned the *Canterbury Tales* in the 1390s, Little Hugh
of Lincoln was celebrated with a cult in Lincoln Cathedral.[42] A martyr who,
along with other youths supposedly slain by "cursed Jews," revealed the Jews' ad-
amant hostility to Christianity.

Hugh was a Christian boy of Lincoln who disappeared on 31 July 1255.[43] His
mother searched for him and, when she could not find him, accused local Jews
of being responsible for his death. The boy's body was finally discovered on 29
August. He was hailed as a martyr and, according to the later hagiographical accounts, quickly produced a miracle, restoring sight to a blind woman. Richard
de Gravesend, dean of Lincoln, and his canons bore the body to Lincoln cathedral in solemn procession with song and candles and buried Hugh as a martyr
alongside the tombs of bishops Robert Grosseteste and Hugh of Avalon. Meanwhile, the boy's mother had gone to Scotland to petition King Henry and beg
for justice. On his return trip to London, on 3 October, the king stopped in Lincoln. He listened to the accusations, which intimated a vast conspiracy of English Jews to kill Christian children. He took them seriously enough to send the
next day a mandate to the guardians of the English ports, ordering them to prevent Jews from leaving the country. He appointed his steward, the knight John
of Lexington, to lead the investigations. John interrogated Copin, the principal
Jewish suspect, who confessed to being the ringleader of the murder. Henry ordered that Copin be tied to the tail of a horse and dragged through the streets of
Lincoln: his battered and broken body was then hanged.

Henry was in a hurry to get back to London, so after this hasty act of justice
he left Lincoln on 6 October, just three days after he had arrived. He ordered
ninety-two Jews of Lincoln brought to London. They arrived on 22 November:
eighteen of them were executed; the other seventy-four were imprisoned in the
Tower of London to await their fate. At this point, Dominican and Franciscan
friars intervened and pleaded with the king, as did his brother Richard. A new
trial was ordered, for which there are no surviving records, but which probably
concluded that the remaining Jews were innocent. In any case, they were soon

set free; some sources suggest that they paid significant sums to Richard to help secure their release.

If the court in London indeed concluded that the Jews were innocent, it is no surprise that this decision was not communicated widely: to do so would highlight that Henry had committed a grave act of injustice in Lincoln. It would also compromise the cult of the young martyr. The author of the *Annals of Burton* (completed in 1263) harshly reprimands the Dominicans for their role in securing freedom for the Jews who had, he claims, crucified young Hugh. The annalist's version is similar to that given by two other sources, an anonymous hagiographical poem in French (composed between 1255 and 1272) and Matthew Paris's *Chronica majora*.[44] Here is part of Matthew's description:

> In this same year [1255], about the time of the festival of the apostles Peter and Paul [27 July], the Jews of Lincoln stole a boy of eight years of age, whose name was Hugh; and, having shut him up in a room quite out of the way, where they fed him on milk and other childish nourishment, they sent to almost all the cities of England where the Jews lived, and summoned some of their sect from each city to be present at a sacrifice to take place at Lincoln; for they had, as they stated, a boy hidden for the purpose of being crucified. In accordance with the summons, a great many of them came to Lincoln, and on assembling, they at once appointed a Jew of Lincoln as judge, to take the place of Pilate, by whose sentence, and with the concurrence of all, the boy was subjected to divers tortures. They beat him till blood flowed and he was quite livid, they crowned him with thorns, derided him, and spat upon him. Moreover, he was pierced by each of them with a wood knife, was made to drink gall, was overwhelmed with approaches and blasphemies, and was repeatedly called Jesus the false prophet by his tormentors, who surrounded him, grinding and gnashing their teeth. After tormenting him in divers ways, they crucified him, and pierced him to the heart with a lance. After the boy had expired, they took his body down from the cross and disemboweled it; for what reason we do not know, but it was asserted to be for the purpose of practicing magical operations.[45]

Jews were accused of the murder of young Hugh in a parody of the crucifixion. This reenactment of the passion reflects the Jews' hostility toward Christ and Christianity. Moreover, the guilt fell on the entire community of English Jews, since Lincoln's Jews had summoned their comrades from all over England to take part in this ghastly rite. Matthew accuses the Jews of magic, for which they extracted the boy's internal organs. What is most astounding in this story is that Henry III, protector of "his" Jews, was so quick to believe this horrific story and to summarily order the execution of nineteen people. If Lincoln's Christians and the king himself believed these accusations, it is because such tales of Jews ritually murdering Christian boys had been circulating in England (and elsewhere) for over a century.

In March 1144, in the woods near Norwich, the body of William, a young leather-worker's apprentice, was found. It is not clear how he died: accident, suicide, or murder. At least one of his family members accused Norwich Jews of his murder but produced no evidence; the boy's death, it seems, was largely forgotten. Its memory was revived five years later, in 1149, when Norfolk knight Simon de Novers was put on trial in London for the murder of Deulesalt, a Norwich Jew to whom he was deeply in debt. All the evidence pointed to his guilt, yet William Turbe, bishop of Norwich, came to the knight's defense by affirming that Deulesalt deserved to die, since he had been responsible for the death of the boy William five years earlier, as part of a communal ritual enactment of the killing of Christ. The ploy worked: the case was adjourned *sine die* and Simon walked free. For Emily Rose, "the accusation of ritual murder would appear to have originated as a clever legal tactic."[46] One of the monks of Norwich priory, Thomas Monmouth, gives an account of the trial in his *Life and Miracles of St. William of Norwich*. He affirms that the king and his counselors were so incensed that they thought the Jews should be punished for this horrible crime yet that the king deferred decision to "another season"; he insinuates that the Jews subsequently bribed King Stephen and his officials to avoid having the case brought to justice.[47] Jews of Norwich were never formally accused of William's murder, nor do they seem to have suffered any violence on account of the trumped-up accusations, to which King Stephen probably gave little credence. This, Europe's first documented case of an accusation of ritual murder, could have ended there.

But Bishop William Turbe and his cathedral priory were not finished with young William. The cathedral needed a new saint who could attract pilgrims, money, and patronage. At the behest of the chapter, Thomas of Monmouth became William's advocate, crafting a text that made him into an innocent young martyr cruelly murdered by Jews. Thomas fabricated testimonies from now-dead "witnesses," recounting successive translations of the boy's body into (and around) Norwich cathedral, relating miracles produced at his tomb. Yet despite Thomas's best efforts and the patronage of bishop and chapter, the cult never took off: William remained a minor local saint and the cult "went cold" in the late twelfth century.[48] There is no evidence of any direct impact of the cult on Norwich Jews or on Jewish-Christian relations in the town.

In the following decades, similar accusations were made against Jews in various towns in England and northern Europe: Würzburg (1147), Gloucester (1168), Blois (1171), Bury St. Edmunds (1181, mentioned in Chapter 1), Paris (undated, but mentioned by chronicler Rigord as a justification for Philip II's expulsion of Jews from French royal domains in 1182), and Mainz (1187).[49] In Gloucester, Richard de Clare used the threat of a ritual murder accusation to extort money from local Jews in order to finance his military expedition in Ireland. In Blois, Count Thibaut V burned Jews in punishment for their supposed role in a murder; he did so for his own financial gain and to enhance his power and prestige against his sovereign Louis VII. The abbey of Bury St. Edmunds used the accusation to justify the expulsion of Bury's Jews and the reaffirmation of abbatial jurisdiction over the town. Expelling Jews from the French royal domain gave Philip II a financial windfall and allowed him to rebuild much of Paris, incorporating lands seized from Jews. As Emily Rose has shown, these twelfth-century events are not the result of "popular" mass-movements, nor the reflection of deteriorating relations between Christians and Jews. They are not "irrational" charges showing intolerance of the "other." On the contrary, they are based on calculation: inventing and exploiting outrageous accusations against Jews brought financial and political profit to their authors, at little danger or political cost. The men who forged these false accusations were members of the clerical and political elite, neither ignorant nor naïve.[50]

Nor was Hugh the first case of such accusations in England during Henry's reign. In 1232, a twelve-month-old boy was found strangled in Winchester. The boy's mother had fled the town, yet suspicion fell on a local Jewish lender, Abraham Pinche, accused of having ritually murdered the child. The sheriff imprisoned the town's entire Jewish community, who were eventually released upon paying a fine of 20 marks: it was concluded that the boy's mother was guilty of his death.[51]

In December 1235, five Christian children were reported to have been killed in Fulda (in what is now Hesse, Germany). The *Chronicle of Fulda* reports that Jews had killed the five children in a mill, and that subsequently crusaders killed all the Jews of the town.[52] The case was brought before Emperor Frederick II. The Jews of Fulda were accused not only of having killed the five children, but having done so to procure their blood, which they placed in a sealed bag in order to use it for magical or medicinal purposes. This is the first recorded instance of the "blood libel," the accusation that Jews kill Christians in order to obtain their blood—a charge made against Jews in various parts of Europe until the twentieth century.[53] Frederick sent letters to various European sovereigns, including to his brother-in-law Henry III of England, asking that they send converted Jews to testify concerning the credibility of these accusations. On 24 February 1236, Henry wrote a reply to the emperor. He said that he had received his messenger, Henry of Aeps, who bore the news of "a case which was unheard of for us, which recently occurred in your territories." At the emperor's request, King Henry was sending two "neophytes," ready to carry out the emperor's orders.[54] Louis also sent converts, including Nicholas Donin, who would several years later, as we have seen, spearhead the attack against the Talmud.[55]

In July 1236, the emperor issued a privilege in favor of the empire's Jews.[56] He began by confirming the privileges that his grandfather, Frederick I Barbarossa, had issued to the Jews of the empire, protecting them from violence and oppression. He called the Jews *servi camera nostre* ("servants of our chamber"), who as such were directly dependent on imperial authority and protection. He then came to the matter at hand: the death of the children in Fulda, of which the town's Jews had been accused. Moreover, the entire German Jewish population was suspected of complicity in such acts. He explained that in order to find the truth behind these accusations, he had called together prominent lay and ecclesiastical authorities, and asked various European sovereigns to send converts from Judaism to Christianity to give testimony. These converts testified that nothing in the Bible or the Talmud could justify the consumption of human blood, that on the contrary even the blood of kosher animals is forbidden. As a result, Frederick pronounced the Jews of Fulda and of the rest of Germany "completely absolved of this imputed crime." He went on to prohibit any Christian from accusing Jews of this crime or for attacking them on account of this. This was a strong, solemn rebuke meant to lay the issue to rest. Frederick's brother-in-law Henry III contributed to this effort, but would play a very different role in the accusations against the Jews of Lincoln in 1255.

Jews were also at times accused of plotting to obtain the Eucharist—the body and blood of Christ—for use in their rituals or magical or medicinal practice. Alexander of Stainsby (or Stavensby), bishop of Coventry and Lichfield (1224–1238) issued statutes for his diocese. He presents the sacrament of the Eucharist as endangered by "wicked Christians and Jews":

> Since God left us for this purpose nothing more valuable upon earth after his ascension to heaven than the sacraments in the sight of which his memory is preserved, we ought to venerate them to such an extent

that no blasphemy ever exist against them or against their authority. Yet there are certain persons who, on account of their disdain of Christ, as for example skeptics or others who on account of their contempt, descend into the profound abyss, or others, as for example, wicked Christians and Jews, who, on account of their practice of magic, are accustomed to try with outrageous daring various shameful acts against the Eucharist and the holy oil. We therefore command that these objects shall be placed in separate vases, and kept under the most efficient lock.[57]

Matthew Paris relates, with little or no skepticism, the stories of other Christian children supposedly murdered by Jews. In 1244, "On the first of August, in this year, there was found, in the cemetery of St. Benedict, in the city of London, the unburied body of a boy, on whose legs and arms, and under the chest, was an inscription written regularly in Hebrew characters."[58] Matthew at times expresses sympathy for the travails of Jews groaning (like their Christian compatriots) under the yoke of royal oppression and extortion. Yet elsewhere he presents them as enemies of English Christians ready to kill their children. The supposed hostility to Christian symbols provoked, according to Matthew, a London Jew named Abraham of Berkhamsted puts an icon of the Virgin and child in his latrine, where he could defecate on it daily. His wife found this offensive, took the icon out and cleaned it. Abraham, furious, murdered her. Abraham was thrown into jail, and all wanted him to be put to death. But Richard of Cornwall intervened for him, and had him freed for a fee of 700 marks.[59] This story of blasphemy and murder suggests unbending hostility of Jews to Christians: indeed, stories of Jews insulting images of the Virgin, often by defecating on them, were standard fare in many miracle collections, where they invariably provoked miracles of vengeance or conversion.[60] As implausible as they seem to modern readers, they were meant to be credible and provided a ready store of "fake news" that those wishing to criticize the king or those close to him, in this case his brother Richard, could draw from to denounce their relationships with Jewish lenders.

The year 1240 corresponded to the year of creation 5000 in the Hebrew calendar, a year associated for some European Jews with the hopes of the coming of the Messiah: perhaps some of them saw the Mongol invasions as a hopeful sign of the end of times when God would succor and avenge his people.[61] Three hundred rabbis supposedly left France, via the port of Marseille, to emigrate to the Holy Land.[62] The number is no doubt exaggerated, and there is no evidence of

English Jews attempting to make the voyage. Matthew Paris insinuates that Europe's Jews were plotting with the Mongols for the destruction of Christendom. In entry for 1241 (the same year that a Mongol army scored a decisive victory over a Polish-Templar alliance at the Battle of Legnica), Matthew affirms that Jews saw the Tartars as God-sent allies who would liberate them from the yoke of slavery. Jews in Germany bought up weapons and hid them in casks, which they pretended were full of wine. They then told the Christians that since the Tartars were Jews who only drank wine produced by other Jews, they had prepared poisoned wine to kill them and eliminate this threat to Christendom. "The Christians therefore permitted these wicked Jews to make this wicked present to their wicked enemies." But a suspicious Christian bridge-keeper discovered their plot, broke open their casks of weapons, and cried out, "Oh, unheard of treachery, why do we allow such people to live among us?" These Jews were handed over to the authorities, "to be either consigned to perpetual imprisonment, or to be slain with their own swords."[63]

Antichrist had long been associated with Jews: for Jerome, he would be born of a Jewish virgin, in a parody of Christ's birth.[64] Antichrist was expected to arise in the final days, free the nations of Gog and Magog (sometimes portrayed as lost Jewish tribes) that Alexander the Great had imprisoned in the Caucasus, and wreak havoc before being defeated by Christ. We see this in the commentary to Revelation composed by Berengaudus, probably an English Benedictine monk writing in the late eleventh century, the *Expositio super septem visiones libri Apocalypsis*. A number of lavishly illustrated manuscripts of the text of Revelation along with Berengaudus's commentary were produced in England in the second half of the thirteenth century. An illustration from one of them, the "Gulbenkian Apocalypse" (c. 1265–1270), vividly portrays Jews as allies of Antichrist and enemies of Christianity.[65] One image portrays Synagoga (Synagogue) and Ecclesia (Church), represented allegorically as two women. On the right, Synagogue is placed on a mound of earth inside a low-domed structure. In her left hand she holds a broken lance with a drooping pennant, a symbol of her lost power. The tablets of the law, marking the Old Covenant (just as they continued to mark the clothing of English Jews), slip from her right hand. She is blindfolded and turns away from the Church and the other figures in the scene; her head is bowed in defeat. Ecclesia, by contrast, is seated on a throne (looking like a bishop's chair) in a high gothic chapel. In her right hand she holds a scepter topped with a pennant, and in her left a chalice, symbolizing the sacraments; the crown on her head emphasizes her power and grandeur. She sits upright and holds her head high. She directs her gaze to the center of the composition, taking in and dominating the scene. This is a standard representation of Church and Synagogue, frequently found in thirteenth-century sculpture and illuminations, particularly in France.[66] But here the theme is place in the context of Revelation 5, and several figures are placed between Church and Synagogue. The Lamb, mentioned in Revelation and here as often representing Christ and his sacrifice, is shown bleeding into the chalice held by the Church; he, like Ecclesia, holds a pennant. In the center are four men clearly presented as Jewish (two have pointed caps and one is veiled). They seem to be hesitating between the two figures of Church and Synagogue, and it is this hesitation that embodies (from the Christian viewpoint of the artist) the position of thirteenth-century Jews, forced to choose between joining the victorious Church or blindly persisting in following the defeated Synagogue. Of the four, one has clearly chosen the Church, as his right hand, already within the sanctuary, offers a book to the Church and to the Lamb/Christ. The man on the right holds tightly onto his book and seems to be walking toward Synagogue, though he turns back to look toward the Church. We have seen how William de Brailes presented Jews present at the death of the Virgin Mary, which is to say at the outset of the history of the Church, as divided between those who accepted the miracle of Christ—who chose to see—and the others who preferred to remain blind. Here in this Apocalypse commentary, this division is projected onto the final days: some Jews will at long last turn toward the Church, while others will persist in their blindness.

The canons and the larger Christian community of Lincoln had a visual reminder of Jewish hostility toward Christianity in their cathedral: a stained glass representation of the miracle of the Jewish boy of Bourges, probably produced in the 1220s or 1230s (before or during Robert Grosseteste's tenure as bishop).[67] The earliest surviving version of the story, in Greek, is found in the sixth-century *Ecclesiastical History* of Evagrius Scholasticus; there are subsequently various Latin versions: two of them, from twelfth-century England, place the story in Bourges.[68] The Lincoln artist may have known the legend from one of the Latin versions written in England or through the very popular French version in the *Miracles de Nostre Dame* by Gautier de Coincy (1177–1236).[69] Gautier assures his reader that he hates the Jews so much that if he were king he would have them all drowned or burned; in any case, he would not let a single one of them live.[70] He relates that in Bourges a Jewish glassmaker had a young son who accompanies his Christian friends to Mass, where he gazes at a statue of the Virgin and child and exclaims that he has never seen anything so beautiful. At this point, the statue ("ymage") comes down from the altar and gives com-

Figure 8. Commentary illustration for Revelation 5:2: Ecclesia and Lamb,
book with seals, and Synagoga. Gulbenkian Apocalypse, c.1265–1270.
Lisbon, Gulbenkian Museum, L. A. 139, fol. 4r.

munion to the boy. He returns home, glowing with joy, and tells his father he
has taken communion. Furious, his father throws him on the ground, beats him,
then drags him by the hair and throws him into his blazing glass-making furnace. The boy's mother cries out, and 10,000 townsmen flock to the scene. They
throw open the furnace and find the boy unharmed: not a single hair on his head
has burned. The townsmen beat the father and toss him into the furnace. The
boy says that the "bele ymage" that he had seen that morning came to him and
put her veil over him, and he went to sleep without feeling the heat of the flames.
Tears flow, prayers of thanks and praise are offered to the Virgin. Joyously, the
boy, his mother and many Jews of the town accept baptism. In the window in
Lincoln Cathedral, the drama is expressed in two scenes: on the right, the glassmaker, with his pointed Jewish cap, thrusts the boy into the flaming furnace. On
the left, he opens the furnace to discover his son safe amid the flames, as the haloed Virgin Mary stands watch.

Figure 9. Lincoln Cathedral, the Jewish boy of Bourges,
stained glass (c. 1220–1230).

These stories of Jewish hostility to Christians and of conspiracy to undermine Christendom circulated in England and elsewhere in Europe in the mid-
thirteenth century, and help to explain why Henry III, when he arrived in Lincoln
on 3 October, was ready to believe that Jews were responsible for the murder of
young Hugh. As Gavin Langmuir emphasizes, "By 4 October little Hugh's shrine
and the fantasy that justified it had had a month to take firm root."[71] None of
the sources speak of any formal accusation or any violent action taken against
Lincoln Jews before that date. Bishop Henry of Lexington, Dean Richard de Gravesend, and the cathedral canons had encouraged the development of the cult
of the young martyr. They do not seem to have sought the intervention of royal
justice; it was Hugh's mother who had pleaded with the king to punish those
who she believed were responsible for the murder of her son. King Henry, in a
hurry to return to London, delegated the investigation to John of Lexington, a

close advisor, well-versed in both canon and civil law—and the brother of Bishop Henry of Lexington. If John were to find the Jews innocent of the accusation, the basis of the young martyr's cult would be called into question, much to the chagrin, no doubt, of his brother the bishop and the cathedral canons. How different the outcome might have been if either Hugh of Avalon or Robert Grosseteste had still been bishop.

The belief that the Jews' maliciously sought to kill Christian children, even to reenact the crucifixion on them, was well enough established that when Hugh disappeared, his mother suspected local Jews of having killed him. The discovery of his body apparently heightened the suspicion, and the cathedral chapter was happy to exploit this in order to be able to grace the cathedral with a new saint. And they would know what to say about Hugh and how he died: little did it matter that they knew nothing about the real circumstances of his death, accidental or criminal. They had the hagiographical models at hand from earlier stories of ritual murder, and they could quickly and easily produce narratives that would have begun to circulate in the days following the discovery of the boy's body. It is this narrative that John of Lexington induced Copin to confirm.

In the Anglo-Norman poem, Hugh was captured and taken before a "great assembly of the richest Jews in England" (v. 69–70), led on a rope, like a sacrificial animal, by Jopin (i.e., Copin). They stripped him naked, "Just as the Jews had done to Jesus" (75). Jopin sold him for thirty silver pieces to another Jew, named Hagin, just as Judas had sold Jesus. The Jews then brought out a cross and nailed Hugh's feet and hands to it. Hagin pierced him in the side with a knife. At this point Hugh died, and his soul was taken to heaven by angels. The anonymous poet then narrates (in an account similar to that of Matthew Paris) how the Jews attempted in vain to dispose of his body: they dug a deep grave and buried Hugh in it, but in the morning found his body lying on top of the ground. They then took him and put him in a "stinking privy," yet the next morning the body was found outside of the latrine: "The Jews of Lincoln were filled with grief and dread when they could not at any time hide the body, night or day." One Jew found a solution: he had a "close friend," a Christian woman (or one who "was thought a Christian"), his former nurse. He paid her to bear Hugh's body by night out of the Jewish quarter and toss it in a well, where it was subsequently found by another Christian woman who went to find Hugh's stepfather to have him come see the body. The mother was away, seeking out King Henry; none of the three texts mentions Hugh's father. It is possible that his mother had remarried; but it is just as likely that the poet had not wanted to give a father to Hugh, who is a new Christ, but rather a stepfather like Joseph. He came to examine the body, and recognized it as Hugh. At this point, the dead boy performed his first miracle, restoring sight to a blind woman. The suspicion weighed on the Jews, a convert from Judaism (only in this version) came forward and urged that the body be washed to expose its wounds.

> No sooner was the body washed
> Than the convert understood what had happened;
> Then he revealed to them the treason
> That was done through the Jewish plot.
> The same wounds with which God was afflicted
> Were found on the child.
> Through the city of Lincoln
> The news went quickly. (260–67)

The clerks from the cathedral caught wind of the incident, forcibly carried away the boy's body and placed it in the cathedral. The Anglo-Norman poet says the Jews were "seized at once" and placed in "a strong prison," awaiting the arrival of the king.

The Anglo-Norman poet does not name John of Lexington, but merely says that a "wise man" spoke in the king's presence, promising to spare the life of whoever would reveal the truth to the king. Jopin steps forth and confesses, relating the crime in detail. The poet then says that the Jews took council among themselves and that it was they who sentenced Jopin to death as a traitor: he was turned over to the royal officials to be dragged through the city until he died and then to be hanged "as a traitor and thief" (358). The poem ends with a description of Jopin's punishment, and no mention of further actions taken against Jews of Lincoln.

The Anglo-Norman poem, for all its hostility to the Jews, testifies to the importance of liminal figures between the two religious groups. The Christian nurse, here an evil figure who is bribed to dispose of Hugh's corpse, is presented as a traitor. We have seen that Church councils, bishops, and popes repeatedly attempted, to little avail, to prevent Christians from working in Jewish homes, particular women who served as wet-nurses: this figure of treachery embodies the fears that such cohabitation could cause. The woman "passes" as Christian, but her faith has been corrupted by frequenting Jews and their money. The other liminal figure is the Jewish convert, who here confirms that the wounds on Hugh's body correspond to what he knows is the standard practice of Jewish crucifixion of Christian children. In other words, he gives the opposite testimony to that of the real historical English converts that Henry had sent to Frederick II, who discounted the charge of ritual murder.

Meanwhile, the trial of Lincoln's Jews continued in London and the king took an active interest in their possessions. On 26 November, he appointed John de Wincle and Simon Passelewe to appraise houses of all Lincoln Jews who had fled, were hanged, or were imprisoned. They were to inquire into the possessions of the Jews who had been executed and to seize them for the fisc: the goods had been granted to Richard, in payment of the king's debt to him, but priority was to be given to the queen for what Jews owed her.[72] On 7 December, the king issued a royal pardon to Benedict, son of Mosseus of London, who was declared not guilty of killing Hugh but only consenting to his death afterward. The pardon specifies that when Benedict appeared before the judges in Westminster, the boy's mother acknowledged that he was not guilty. This again shows the active role of the mother in the case, over six months after her son's death. The pardon insists that all Benedict's possessions seized by the crown are to be restored to him without delay.[73] On 7 January 1256, Henry wrote to the sheriff of Lincoln, asking him to send to Westminster by Candlemas (2 February) twenty-four "of the most loyal and discrete knights in your shire" (*legalioribus et discretioribus militibus de comitatu tuo*) in order to judge the Jews accused concerning the death of "Hugh the son of Beatrice" (again the name of the mother, and not the father, is mentioned).[74] Three days later (on January 10), Henry issues a pardon, at the instance of Dominican John of Darlington, confessor to the king, for John the convert, former Jew of Lincoln.[75] We do not know John's former Jewish name, nor the exact circumstances of his conversion. But he may well have been one of the Jews imprisoned in the Tower of London: conversion would have given him a path to safety and freedom; for this reason, perhaps, he put himself under John of Darlington's protection and took his Christian name. Meanwhile, royal investigations continued: on 27 March, the king commissioned Roger de Thirkelby and Nicholas de Turri to inquire into the "horrible crime" of the crucifixion of a Christian boy. In particular, they were to investigate the Lincoln "scola" (synagogue) of Peytevin the Great, who had fled. They were to convene in Lincoln on Tuesday before Palm Sunday, with the sheriff of Lincoln, twelve knights and twelve citizens to conduct the investigation: all Jews and Jewesses who had been present in Lincoln over the last two years were called to testify.[76] Five months later, on 20 August, the investigation seemed to be concluding, as the king appointed Simon Passelewe (justice of the Jewish exchequer) and William de Lergton (sheriff of Lincoln) to sell houses of Lincoln Jews who had been hanged and to inventory their possessions.[77] In June 1258, the king acknowledged receipt of seventy-two marks for the sale of these houses.[78]

Henry is not the first European ruler to profit from the accusation of ritual murder. Count Thibaut V of Blois used the charge in 1171 to justify the killing of thirty-two Jews and the seizure of their property. Rigord justified Philip II's 1182 expulsion of Jews from the French domains by such a charge: he claims that every year before Easter, Parisian Jews crept into tunnels that run under the city, where they sacrificed an innocent Christian boy, mentioning the case of a boy Richard, whom they martyred. But Henry is the first European king to take an active role in prosecuting and punishing Jews for this supposed offense, in marked contrast to his brother-in-law Frederick II. In 1255, Henry thus becomes the most important promoter of English anti-Semitism. As we saw in the introduction, for Gavin Langmuir defines the distinction: "anti-Judaism is a nonrational reaction to overcome nonrational doubts, while antisemitism is an irrational reaction to repressed rational doubts."[79] Key to this irrational reaction is belief in the trio of anti-Semitic myths that originated in the twelfth century and gained increasing popularity in the thirteenth: host desecration (Jews supposedly obtained consecrated Eucharistic bread and tortured it), blood libel (Jews killed Christian children to obtain their blood for medical, magical, or dietetic use), and ritual crucifixion (Jews annually re-enacted the crucifixion on an innocent Christian child).[80] In actively promoting the last of these three myths, Henry provided a facile justification of increased financial exploitation of Jews and of violence against them.

Henry had rashly believed the accusations against Lincoln's Jews, unjustly condemned nineteen of them to death, and had only spared the remaining Jews because his brother Richard and Franciscan and Dominican friars intervened in their behalf. Yet far from admitting his error or offering compensation to the surviving Lincoln Jews or the families of the victims, Henry had his agents calculate the value of the possessions of those he had put to death in a travesty of justice, whose property was his, since they after all had been his Jews. The accusation against Lincoln's Jews became another way to take money from them. As R. I. Moore writes, "one of the advantages of the circulation of anti-Semitic stories was that they were capable of providing a rare instance where royal avarice might be made to seem acceptable."[81] In 1272, the year of Henry's death, Pope Gregory X reissued *Sicut iudeis*, with explicit rejection of blood libel accusation.[82] Perhaps some European Jews took comfort in this papal protection, though it would do little to stem the tide of such accusations, and of course it was too late for Lincoln's Jews. For English Jews in 1255, the "protection" offered by their sovereign offered little comfort. In the following decade, they were to face even greater dangers from the king's enemies.

CHAPTER 6

Baronial Revolts and Anti-Jewish Violence (1258–1267)

In 1258 Henry III was deep in debt and faced the threat of excommunication by Pope Alexander IV if he were to default on his payments to Rome. He turned to his barons to obtain funds. A group of barons opposed to the Sicilian adventure and increasingly hostile to Henry's lavish gifts to his Poitevin half brothers (sons of his mother Isabelle of Angoulême and her second husband, Hugh X of Lusignan) opposed his demands. They managed to compel the king to call a parliament, which met in Oxford on 11 June 1258 and pronounced the Provisions of Oxford, in which the barons voiced their grievances. In preparation for the parliament, the barons produced a list of demands, the *Petitio Baronum* (petition of the barons). One of their complaints was that "magnates" and "powerful persons" were taking over the debts of the Jews and then seizing the lands pledged. Indeed, Jewish lenders often sold their debts to lay and ecclesiastical lords, in particular when they needed to raise cash quickly in order to pay a tallage to the king: inevitably, they sold these debts for much less than they were worth. Those who bought the debt often had at their disposal methods of coercion that Jewish lenders did not possess. Here it appears that at least some of those magnates involved abused their position by refusing to accept payment of capital in order to continue to receive lucrative interest payments and, after default, to be able to seize debtors' lands.

It was a vicious circle: landowners in debt to Jews, heavy taxes (or exceptional tallages) that the king imposed upon the Jews that required them to sell (at a loss) their debts to the great barons, and the tenacity with which the latter exploited this situation to enrich themselves and get new land. It is therefore not surprising that some of the indebted barons are the first to join the "baronial revolt" of

1263–1265. The rebels managed to seize power and to capture Henry. Rebel leader Simon de Montfort, ruling in the king's name, annulled debt to Jews, and Jews became frequent targets of violence and massacre: by attacking the king's Jews, rebels struck at a group closely associated with the crown's financial exploitation of its subjects, wiped out records of their own debts, and obtained booty. Jews were massacred in many towns, in particular London, in April 1264. Association with the king was a double-edged sword, as in times of rebellion Jews had no effective protector and became clear and visible targets.

Jewish Loans and the Transfer of Land
to Barons and Monastic Institutions

When Christians borrowed money from Jews, they had to offer security for their loans: sometimes jewelry, clothing, or books, and other times land. The Jewish lender could seize the collateral if the debtor defaulted on the loan. Loans were often renegotiated, which prevented the debtors from losing their land and which extended the period in which the lenders could profit from the transaction. Only rarely did Jews seize the debtors' land. Yet the increasing financial pressures placed by the crown on both Jewish lenders and Christian debtors changed this situation. Jews often did not have the cash to pay the exorbitant tallages exacted by the king. The only way to raise money quickly was to sell their debts at a discount. Those who bought up those debts were wealthy Christian barons or ecclesiastical institutions. We saw in Chapter 4 how the emerging Oxford colleges depended on this dynamic, as wealth and land were transferred from the lesser gentry through Jewish lenders to ecclesiastical institutions or to prominent officials like Walter de Merton, chancellor of England and founder of Merton College. Such practices were not new in 1258: in the twelfth century, Aaron of Lincoln had lent considerable funds to monasteries; a monastic chronicler said that Aaron boasted that his money had provided a glorious shrine for the martyr Alban, who would otherwise have been homeless.[1] We have seen that Peter des Roches, bishop of Winchester (1205–1238) and close advisor to Kings John and Henry, bought up lands mortgaged to Jews to give them to Premonstratensian and Cistercian monasteries.[2] Jewish lending was both complementary to, and in some cases in competition with, monastic financial activities, as monasteries in the eleventh and twelfth centuries were significant sources of finance in Normandy and England.[3]

Various documents, in Latin and in Hebrew, describe this situation throughout England starting in the 1230s. Judith Olszowy-Schlanger has recently produced an edition and translation of over three hundred Hebrew documents from medieval England. Many of them deal with loans, and a number with the purchasing of Jewish debt by Christians. There is, for example a letter from one Jewish lender, Lavan, to another, David, about a debt incurred by a certain Geoffrey. The latter appeared to owe a considerable amount of money to Lavan, for he made arrangements for the prior of Linton to buy his land so that he would be able to repay his debt in full by Michaelmas (29 September). The year is not given, though it is probably sometime in the 1230s or 1240s. This Hebrew document exemplifies the process of which the barons complained in 1258: a Christian landowner (perhaps pertaining to the small gentry), Geoffrey developed a significant debt to his Jewish lenders, which forced him to sell his land to a Church institution in order to pay off his debt.[4]

The abbots of the Premonstratensian convent of Newhouse (now Newsham, in Lincolnshire), were particularly adept at exploiting debts to Jews in order to obtain land. Quitclaims testify to at least eight transactions between 1220 and 1257, through which Newhouse obtained lands in the town of Lincoln and in areas near the abbey.[5] The final document in the series, from Valentine's Day 1257, is a quitclaim in Latin, with a Hebrew signature, acknowledging that Elias Kohen and Manser of Bradsworth had received payment from Newhouse Abbey for a loan undertaken by Johanna, widow of Radulph de Vermels, and by their son Philip. Just one year before the Parliament of Oxford, a widow and her son lost their mortgaged lands, and a rich abbey took possession of these lands they had used as security to Jewish lenders.

Elsewhere in England, other ecclesiastical institutions benefitted from landowners' inability to pay their debts (and Jewish lenders' inability to pay their tallages) to acquire more land. The bishop of London obtained land in this way in 1223,[6] as did the priory of the Holy Trinity, in London, in the 1230s,[7] St. Bartholomew's hospital in London in 1250,[8] and the cathedral chapter of St. Paul's, in London, in 1255.[9] Priories, convents, and other religious institutions enriched themselves through such means: the convent of Bullington,[10] the convent of Greenfield,[11] and Holy Trinity of Canterbury[12] all appear in quitclaims. Church institutions were adept at taking advantage of indebted lesser gentry and of Jews overburdened by tallages in order to buy up loans and expropriate small landowners.

Prominent English barons did the same. King Henry's brother, Richard of Cornwall, in 1255, took over debts owed to Abraham de Berkhampstead, amounting to £180; Richard seized 180 acres of land and ejected William de Beauchamp and his subordinates from the lands, putting some in prison, probably to be able to extract further payments from them.[13] William had taken advantage of his close relations with Worcester's Jewish lenders to take over the lands of his neighbors who were in their debt. While clearly in the 1255 case he lost out to Richard, this did not prevent him from continuing to profit from his exploitation of debt to Jews.[14] Among those who most profited from such practices were Henry's Poitevin half brothers.[15] The crown granted 500 marks of debt to Geoffrey de Lusignan. Guy de Lusignan received 550 marks worth of debt in 1256 and another 100 in 1257. It was the third brother, William of Valence, Earl of Pembroke, who most profited from this scheme, amassing income that by 1258 amounted to about 1,000 marks per year. William and his brothers' sudden wealth and prominence (of which the monies and lands obtained through Jewish debt were only one element) provoked anger and resentment, which in turn became, as we will see, one of the main motors of the baronial revolt.

Queen Eleanor enriched herself in the same manner. She shared with the king the revenues from tallages, bringing significant sums into her coffers.[16] A certain Barnabas de Stukeley had been lord of the manor of Wardon, which he had mortgaged to an unnamed Jewish lender. Eleanor had acquired the manor through wardship during the minority of the heir and to retain it had to pay off a debt of three hundred marks to Richard of Cornwall. On 20 April 1258 the queen confirmed the grant of the land to the convent of Wardon for a period of thirteen years, against a lease of three hundred marks, after which the land was to revert to the queen until Barnabas or his heir could pay off the debt. The king confirmed this arrangement in Oxford on 19 June, just eight days after the pronouncement of the Provisions of Oxford, probably seeking to reaffirm that in this it would be business as usual notwithstanding the proclamations of the barons.[17] This is just one of many cases where Eleanor deftly exploited the system of Jewish debt to receive payments from debtors and to seize their land.[18]

The abuses led to discontent, and it is in this context, for Cecil Roth, that we should understand the demand in 1244 that the council of the realm be allowed to nominate at least one of the justices of the Jews.[19] The barons were in essence contesting the king's monopoly over justice concerning the Jews. Similarly, English prelates affirmed that they should have a say concerning justice meted out to Jews in cases that touched the Church. Various bishops and synods reiterated the Jews' obligation to wear badges and the prohibition of Christians working as servants in Jewish homes. In 1257, Giles of Bridport, bishop of Salisbury, presided over a synod that affirmed that, while both the Fourth Lateran Council and the 1222 Oxford Council had prohibited Jews from having Christian servants, "many Jews in our diocese" continue to employ Christians as wet-nurses, midwives, and maids. This leads these Jews to great folly, the synod proclaims: to sexual relations between Jewish men and Christian women, both single and married. The women involved are to be excommunicated and the Jews denied all commerce with Christians.[20]

On 22 August 1257, Boniface of Savoy, archbishop of Canterbury, presided over a council of the province of Canterbury at London, in spite of Henry's instructions that they should not meet. The council issued canons that have been described as "the ecclesiastical equivalent of the Provisions of Oxford."[21] In the midst of a long list of complaints of clerics against the king, his officers, and other lay powers, there are several passages that concern the royal privileges accorded to Jews:

> 32. When a Jew commits an offense against a person of the Church or against Church property, or when he commits a sacrilege or an act of bodily violence against a cleric, or commits adultery with a Christian woman, and should be convened before an ecclesiastical judge, the judicial examination (*causae cognitio*) is impeded by royal prohibition, since it is alleged that they have their own judge, the sheriff of the territory, and their own officials, who neither can nor should inquire into such things. And they purge themselves by a simple negation of the accusation and by the simple testimony of another Jew and one Christian, without taking a formal oath, and in this way the proof of the accuser is thoroughly rejected.
>
> 33. Also, if the Church prohibits them from having contact with Christians because they do not wear their *tabulae,* or because they retain Christian nursemaids against the precepts of the Church, or they are excommunicated for other excesses, the royal bailiffs, on behalf of the lord king order that this not be respected and have them [the Jews] received and admitted to commerce.[22]

English bishops were reiterating the same complaints that we have seen since the Oxford Council of 1222, targeting in particular the failure to enforce the wearing of badges and the employment of Christian servants in Jewish homes. But the nature and tone of the complaints have changed: the bishops refuse to accept that the "king's Jews" should be exempt from episcopal justice and should in effect be immune from all punishment for not respecting restrictions that had not only been issued by church councils but sanctioned by royal mandate. Moreover, they raised the specter of sexual relations between Jewish men and Christian women to stress what was for them the intolerable nature of Christian-Jewish fraternization. The previous year, on 3 December 1256, King Henry had pardoned (for a fine) Abraham Russell, Jew of Wilton, for intercourse with Letitia de Cerfmenistre, a Christian.[23]

Bishops' complaints about the king's handling of Jews and his failure to respect his promises concerning the enforcement of restrictions on Jews were not isolated, but part of a litany of grievances about Henry's exploitation of the Church. Add to this the discontent among nobles and London burgesses concerning Henry's failed military adventures and excessive taxation, and disastrously poor harvests leading to famine in 1258, this created a crisis in the kingdom.[24]

1258: Episcopal Resistance and Baronial Rebellion

Henry faced increasing resistance from bishops and barons that was to culminate in 1258 with the Provisions of Oxford. Among the subjects that rankled, two were foremost: the Sicilian campaign, with the considerable financial burden it placed on the kingdom, and the favoritism that the king showed to his Lusignan half brothers. By 1258, they provoked open rebellion. We have seen throughout the 1250s, Henry heavily taxed Jews to pay for, among other things, his planned crusade, funds for which were subsequently diverted to the campaign to conquer Sicily for his son Edmund. Jews were not by any means the only victims of Henry's fiscal pressure: as we saw in Chapter 5, the English bishops in 1253 finally succumbed to royal pressure to grant Henry a crusader's tenth of church revenues. Henry at times seemed to maintain his intention to go to the Holy Land or to aid Alfonso X of Castile against Muslims in North Africa, at times to lend credence to accusations that he was using his crusading vow and crusading income to further his Sicilian plans. He handled the issue, as Christopher Tyerman has remarked, "with astonishing incompetence."[25]

Yet in October 1255, when it had become clear that the crusading tenth would now be employed to attempt to conquer Sicily with the pope's blessing, English bishops collectively refused to comply. As Matthew Paris tells it, the assembled bishops defiantly told the king and papal nuncio that they refused. Fulk Basset, bishop of London, declared that he would rather be decapitated than to consent to the Church suffering such "servitude, insult and intolerable oppression." At which Bishop Walter Cantilupe of Worcester went further, saying that he even preferred to be hanged: more drastic indeed, since beheading was a punishment reserved for noblemen while hanging was for common criminals. They all swore on the relics of Thomas Becket to defend the English Church.[26] Yet the shrill rhetoric invoking Becket was perhaps, in addition to a sign of frustration, something of a bargaining chip, as the bishops in spring 1257 approved a payment of 52,000 marks in support of the Sicilian expedition, on two conditions: there would be no further taxation on the Church to support the campaign and the king would cease his abuses of church liberties.[27] As we have seen, such "abuses" included failing to enforce restrictions against Jews. An anonymous poet complained: "The king and pope think of nothing but of how they can take gold and silver from clerics."[28]

The following spring baronial resentment erupted. Henry had called a parliament at Westminster, which opened on 7 April. The principal goal, from the king's point of view, was to assure financial and political support from his barons for the Sicilian expedition. Yet things did not go as planned. A few days before, on 1 April, a land dispute between John Fitz Geoffrey and the king's half brother Aymer of Lusignan, bishop elect of Winchester, had resulted in an attack by Aymer's men on John's servants in the disputed estate, leading to the death of one of them. John Fitz Geoffrey came before the king and barons to complain of the attack and demand justice. Henry refused to hear him out, showing his clear partisanship toward his half-brother. This led a group of barons, including Simon de Montfort, to swear allegiance to each other and to vow to expel the Lusignans from England. According to the *Tewksbury Annals*, these barons came armed to the royal palace on 30 April. They lay down their swords at the entrance to the chamber and went to the king, who asked them if he were now their captive. No, they protested, he was their lord and king, but he must force the Poitevins to leave the kingdom. They also said that he, along with his son Edward, should swear on the gospels to establish a council of twenty-four "prudent men" whose advice would be sought in governing, and without whose assent no new taxes would be levied. Henry had little choice but to submit, and he and Edward swore the oath the same day and confirmed it in writing on 2 May.[29] A parliament was convoked at Oxford in June.

As Sophie Ambler has shown, the bishops steered clear of the Parliament of Oxford, no doubt unwilling to sanction a revolt against royal power but reluctant as well to take the side of the king.[30] Boniface of Savoy, archbishop of Canterbury, the queen's uncle, had good reason to be satisfied with the diminution of the power of the Poitevin faction. Yet he prudently avoided taking sides in the conflict. Avoiding Oxford, he summoned a large number of prelates for a council, which assembled in Merton on 6 June, then apparently moved to Westminster on 8 June and drew up a list of articles calling for the protection of the Church's liberties against the encroachment of the crown and of other lay powers. The archbishop and assembled prelates reaffirmed the Church's rights and denounced abuses by laymen in a series of twenty-four canons. Among them was a reiteration of the 1257 canon calling for Jews to be judged by ecclesiastical judges in cases that involve the Church and for excommunication to be pronounced and enforced on Christians who do not respect prohibitions on contact with Jews (though without mentioning the issue of sexual relations between Jews and Christians).[31]

While Boniface was presiding the synod in Westminster, Henry and the barons met at the Parliament of Oxford, which opened on 11 June. The council of twenty-four bishops and barons consisted of twelve men named by the king and twelve by the barons. The baronial party had come fully armed: the threat of military conflict in the event of failure of the parliament was quite real. The barons drew up a list of grievances, the *Petitio baronum:* they complained of abuses of power by royal officials, of punitive taxing imposed by the crown. While the barons were clearly defending their own interests, they took pains to address the concerns of less fortunate subjects, subject to arbitrary and excessive fines levied by sheriffs and other royal officials who were pressured by the crown to raise as much money as possible.[32]

One of the articles in the *Petitio baronum* involves Jewish lenders:

Further, they [the barons] seek a remedy in this: that Jews sometimes transfer their debts, and the lands pledged to them, to magnates and other persons powerful in the kingdom, who on this pretext enter the lands of minors, and although those who owe the debt are ready to pay it, with the interest, the magnates put off the matter, in order that by hook or by crook the lands and holdings shall remain in their hands, saying that without the Jew to whom the debt was owed they cannot do anything, and that they know nothing, and thus they continually put off the repayment of the borrowed money so that, by the intervention of death or of some other mischance, evident peril and manifest disherison plainly threaten those to whom the holdings belonged.[33]

Here the barons describe a practice we have seen since the 1230s, which had become more widespread in recent years as increasing fiscal pressure obliged small landholders to take out loans at the same time as Jews were constrained to sell off their debts in order to pay exorbitant tallages. Among the chief beneficiaries of this practice, we have seen, were monasteries and other ecclesiastical institutions, absent from the barons' petition. Their target is on the contrary unnamed "magnates and other persons powerful in the kingdom": clearly, given the context, they have in mind the queen, Henry's brother Richard of Cornwall, and above all Henry's Poitevin half brothers.[34] The reforming barons present themselves as the protectors of small landholders exploited by the rich and powerful who usurp their land. We note a neutral tone toward the Jewish lenders, who are not blamed for the phenomenon: all the more striking as it contrasts with the harsh criticism of Jews' usurious exploitation of Christians in writings surrounding Simon's expulsion of the Jews of Leicester in 1231 and in the anti-Jewish rhetoric and violence that would accompany Simon's rebellion in 1263–1265. In 1258, it is the king and his Lusignan clan who are the targets of baronial ire, not the Jews.

The anti-Lusignan bent of the council was even more blatant in other items in the *Petitio baronum*: article 4 specified that the king's castles should be entrusted only to subjects born in England; article 5 prohibited entrusting castles in port towns to foreign-born subjects.[35] These and the other articles became the basis of the Provisions of Oxford, which were drawn up by 22 June. Among them we find the stipulation "Be it noted to provide such reforms in the Jewry and concerning the keepers of the Jewry as to redeem their oath thereby."[36] On 23 June, the council of barons ordered the keepers of royal castles to hand over the castles to representatives of the councils. They then mandated that all royal castles that had been alienated (i.e., handed over by the king to others) be returned to the king (which in fact meant being put in the hands of the council). The target of a supposedly general measure to ensure the financial well-being of the crown was again Henry's Lusignan half brothers, to whom the king had given substantial gifts of land, including royal castles. William of Valence (Guillaume de Lusignan) swore that he and his brothers would not surrender their castles; Simon de Monfort angrily retorted that William would do so or lose his head.[37] William and his brothers left Oxford and took refuge in Winchester Castle; the barons laid siege. Finally, the Lusignans surrendered, and the barons forced them to leave England.

Revolt and Civil War, 1258–1264

The barons who had imposed the Provisions of Oxford on Henry struggled to enforce them, while the king attempted to undermine or annul them, with the help of loyal barons, the king of France, and the Pope. On 4 December 1259, Henry sealed the Treaty of Paris with Louis IX, as the two sisters, Queens Margaret of France and Eleanor of England, who probably played an instrumental role in achieving it, looked on.[38] Henry gave up claims to Normandy, Anjou, and the Poitou, and did homage to Louis for Gascony. In return, he ended decades of ineffective struggle with France and obtained free reign to pursue his ambitions for his son in Sicily. He also gained a key ally in the fight against his baronial opponents. Henry was still in France in early 1260, when he forbade the planned February parliament to meet in his absence. Simon de Montfort in his turn prohibited the royal justiciar Hugh Bigod from sending any money to the king; yet as Henry had received funds from Louis IX as part of the stipulations of the Treaty of Paris, this probably did not cause significant hardship. Over the course of the following year, Henry and his allies were able to weaken the council, and the king regained control over the royal chancery; he again issued charters in his own name. He returned to England and moved into the Tower of London. On 13 April 1261, Pope Alexander IV issued a bull nullifying the Provisions of Oxford and releasing Henry and his associates from the oaths they had taken to uphold them.[39] When the bull arrived in June, Henry published it and held a celebratory feast. He no doubt felt vindicated and restored to power. In the wake of this defeat, Simon de Montfort left England for France, proclaiming that he "preferred to die without a country than to perjure himself and become a liar."[40]

Yet opposition from both barons and churchmen endured. On 8–13 May 1261, Archbishop Boniface of Savoy presided over a provincial council at Lambeth palace. The assembled bishops sought to rework the provisions of Merton/Westminster of 1258 and to make them into law. The resulting thirty canons, many of which sought to limit lay (and particularly royal) interference into church affairs, provoked opposition from the king. The fifteenth of the thirty canons reiterated the 1258 canon from Westminster, affirming that Jews should be subject to ecclesiastical justice for cases that involve clerics or church property.[41] Henry wrote to the pope to complain of this new affront to royal power, while Boniface in 1262 set off for Rome to defend the council's action (he would not return for four years).[42] Pope Urban IV responded to Henry on 30 January 1263, with a diplomatic reply: at the king's request, he would not confirm the canons, but neither would he rebuke them, for they were "proper and just." He urged Henry to show proper deference to the clerical order.[43]

The baronial council of fifteen continued to try to exercise control over the exchequer of the Jews. In fall 1259, the conciliar parliament issued the provisions

of Westminster, which formally enacted, in a modified form, many of the stipulations of the provisions of Oxford. In many cases the general recommendations
made at Oxford were translated into specific actions. For example, article 23 ruled
that "sound and wise men" should be appointed by the justiciar and the treasurer
to decide on the reforms needed at the great exchequer and the exchequer of the
Jews. The decisions were to be taken during Advent, before the following session
of parliament. Philip Lovel and Simon Passelewe, who had controlled the institution for the past decade, were removed from office and replaced by men close
to the baronial council.[44] But by 1261, when the king had regained control over
royal institutions, he appointed his close associate John Mansell over the head
of the justices of the Jews and bade them to obey him in all things.[45]

At the same time, several towns requested that the Jews not be allowed to
reside in their towns: on 21 May 1261, at St. Paul's in London, the king granted
to the burgesses of Derby, for a fine, the "liberty" of not having Jews dwell in their
town.[46] In other towns, Jews were attacked. A royal document from 28 December 1261 records "a grievous complaint" from the Jews of Canterbury: certain persons, clergy and laymen, came by night to the houses of these Jews, broke the
doors and windows of their houses with axes, brought fire to burn their houses,
and afterward beat some of the Jews. Henry ordered the Sheriff of Kent, Walter
de Bersted, to investigate and to punish the culprits.[47] It is not clear whether the
attack in Canterbury was connected with the struggle between the king and rebel
barons.

On 7 June 1262, Henry granted the Jewry to his son Edward for three years.
Edward was to receive all the "issues, profits, debts and customs" that the king
received from England's Jews. An exception was made if Henry made a pilgrimage to Jerusalem (i.e., a crusade), in which case he had the right to levy a special
tallage on the Jews. In return, Edward granted his father the revenues from a
number of his estates, which are listed. It may well be, as Margaret Howell suggests, that the queen and the king sought to improve their son's financial situation in part to assure his loyalty to his father in the struggle against the rebellious
barons; for Richard Huscroft, it is an indication of "royal displeasure" at the way
Edward had been mismanaging his lands.[48]

In November, 1262, another incident provoked violence against Jews of London, according to the *Chronicles of the Mayors and Sheriffs of London*:

In this year, just after the Feast of Saint Martin [11 November] about
the time of Vespers, a certain Jew having wounded a Christian with a
knife, in Colecherche Street, many Christians, indeed a countless

multitude of people, ran in pursuit of the Jew and broke into many
houses belonging to the Jews; not content with which, afterwards at
nightfall they carried off all the goods of the said Jews, and would have
broken into many more houses, and carried off the goods, had not the
Mayor and Sheriffs repaired to the spot and driven away those offenders by force of arms. For which reason, inquisition was made on
the morrow, and so from day to day, by the Mayor and Sheriffs in the
Guildhall, twelve men from each of the Wards of London, to whom
no suspicion attached in reference to that felony, being sworn there-
unto. And afterwards, all the Aldermen made inquisition upon this
matter, each in his own Wardmote; and those who were indicted or
accused, were taken by the Sheriffs and imprisoned, part of them in
Neugate and part in Crepelgate. But afterwards, those who were free
of the City and who could find pledges were liberated on surety.[49]

The violence attributed to one Jew led to pillaging of Jewish homes; there is no
mention of injury or death in this incident. Civic officials, aldermen, and sheriffs intervened to restore order and punish the culprits. But some of them, it appears, were soon released, and there is no evidence that Jews were able to retrieve
their property. Protection from royal officials was reaffirmed but remained largely
ineffective. Less than two years later, the association between Jews and royal officials would provide a pretext for anti-Jewish violence.

For in the meantime, Henry's position was weakening, both on account of
attacks by Prince Llywelyn of Wales, and by the king's antagonizing of key nobles, including Gilbert de Clare (heir to the earldom of Gloucester) and Henry's
own son Edward. In April 1263, Simon de Montfort returned to England intent
on reimposing the Provisions. Rebel forces raided royal estates and secured channel ports. In late June 1263, Londoners rebelled and allied with the rebel barons.
The king and queen were holed up in the Tower of London. On 13 July, Queen
Eleanor, at odds with her husband's capitulation, tried to leave the Tower of London by boat on the Thames; she was insulted by crowds who called her a prostitute and pelted her with stones, offal, and scraps of mutton, forcing her to turn
back.[50] Simon arrived in London on 15 July and negotiated with the king, who
had little choice but to capitulate. On 16 July 1263, the provisions were reimposed.
Henry was made to issue a statute confining royal benefices in England to native-
born men and expelling foreigners, who were "never to return." The royal couple
left the tower and settled in Westminster. Yet the barons, even those who had
supported the 1258 Provisions of Oxford, were sharply divided. By October, Ed-

ward had bribed several of the rebel barons to come back to the royal party, and Henry had broken free of Simon's control. The country was once again in civil war. The Dover/Canterbury Annals relate that in December 1263, at Southwark, near London, Simon had his men "signed with the mark of the holy cross front and back." In other words, they become *crucesignati*, crusaders.[51] Simon's war against the king had become a holy war, a crusade. And like those in England in 1190 and in western France in 1236, Simon's crusaders would wreak violence on Jews.

The rebels nevertheless came to an agreement with Henry III: both parties would submit their case to the arbitration of King Louis IX and would accept his judgment. The rebel party arrived in Amiens in December, 1263; Simon was not with them, since he had fallen from his horse and broken a leg. The small group of barons and prelates were opposed by Henry himself, who argued that the Provisions of Oxford had been forced on him unwillingly. There was little precedent for what a king could only see as a usurpation of his God-given power, and it should come as no surprise that Louis ruled in favor of Henry, proclaiming on 23 January 1264 that he would rather break clods of earth behind a plow than to accept such limitations on royal power.[52] In other words, Louis was asking the rebels to capitulate unconditionally. While some of the barons accepted this verdict and returned to the king, Montfort and others continued the struggle.

Forces loyal to Henry, led by Roger Mortimer, attacked and pillaged Simon's lands. Simon, allied with Llewellyn, retaliated by invading Roger's lands. On 28 February 1264, Robert de Ferrars, Early of Derby, along with Montfort's sons Simon and Henry, captured Worcester and seized the *archa* containing documents concerning debts to Jewish lenders. They reportedly killed some Jews and imprisoned others. Robert took the *archa* to his castle in Tutbury, where Prince Edward would later recover it.[53] For the rebels, the "king's Jews" posed an easy target, all the more so as they could seize or destroy evidence of their own debt to them. On a number of occasions, Simon forgave or cancelled his followers' debts to Jews.[54] In several places, the rebels burned the *archae* containing documentation of debt to Jews: notably in Bristol and Bedford.[55] David Carpenter and others have stressed the degree to which Simon and his followers used xenophobic rhetoric, blaming the ills of the country on foreigners: royal counselors and vassals born in France (as, ironically, was Simon himself), bishops and other prelates imposed by Rome, and Italian moneylenders.[56] Those who spoke French rather than English were eyed with suspicion. As Robert Stacey has remarked, "by the 1260s, there were only two groups of people in England whose children were still being raised in French. One was the Jews; the other was the royal family, including the king's unpopular French relations. Both groups were perceived as foreigners, and both became targets of the patriotic wrath of the Montfortians."[57] With bigotry whipped up into a powerful propaganda tool, those considered not English enough found themselves objects of hatred and violence. London's Jews in particular would be the victims of the rebels' bile.

The London Jewish community was the largest and wealthiest in England. The main Jewish neighborhood in thirteenth-century London was what is now the Guildhall area, east of St. Paul's Cathedral. As in other English towns, Jews lived not in an isolated ghetto, but intermixed with Christians. We saw that during the massacres of 1189, some Jews took refuge with their Christian neighbors; one Christian was hanged for igniting a blaze that spread from a Jewish house to a neighboring Christian one, another for killing a Christian. Archaeology, too, permits us to see both the extent of the London Jewish district and its mixed nature. Jews lived mixed with Christians, and since they were prohibited from buying lands subject to feudal ties, they invested in urban lands and houses, often renting out to Christians (until this practice was explicitly prohibited in 1271).[58] In 1250, scribes drew up an inventory, in Latin and Hebrew, of the houses owned by the late Jacob Crespin, who had been one of London's wealthiest Jews. He had owned seven houses, some occupied by his family, others rented out to both Jewish and Christian tenants.[59]

While the city was in the hands of the rebels, they wreaked vengeance and sought profit. Royalist chronicler Thomas Wykes tells how crowds attacked and looted a mansion owned by Richard of Cornwall in March 1264. Then they robbed the royal palace at Westminster and dismantled it stone by stone. They plundered a chapel dedicated to Cuthbert, on the property of Walter de Merton, who as we have seen had profited greatly from the exploitation of Jewish loans. Yet here Wykes says, not without satisfaction, that three of the robbers were killed by a falling beam, as divine wrath inflicted a just punishment on those who would pillage church property.

It is in April 1264 that rebels attacked the Jews of London. At least three monastic chronicles mention the massacre briefly. Three other chroniclers, writing in French or in Latin, narrate it at length. There is no contemporary Hebrew account. We will look at what each of the writers says, starting with Thomas Wykes:

> Among other things about which one must not remain silent is the slaughter of the Jews which was perpetrated in London at that time.

Since those who were living in London lacked the means to pay their expenses, and in particular could not sustain their families with their own means, they said it would be glorious to remediate their own penury through the earnings of others. Thus they suddenly burst in upon the Jews, of whom a great and carefree multitude was residing in the city of London. Not moved by zeal for the faith but rather lured by lust for worldly comforts, they cruelly slaughtered as many [Jews] as they could find in the city, with no thought for humanity or piety, with no respect for age or sex. They perpetrated unimaginable murder, killing old men along with those yet older, nursing babes with old men and women, children in the laps of their mothers, nurslings hanging from the breasts of their mothers. They slaughtered them inhumanely, forty Jews of all conditions and sexes vilely murdered. And though the Jews were not of our religion, it seemed base and impious to kill them without cause, when according to the canons we ought to love them on account of their humanity and because they have been created in the image of God, and because, according to the prophet, "at the end of time the relic of Israel shall be saved." Nor could any of them escape this danger, except those who bought life through the steepest payment, or those who feigned willingness to receive the mark of baptism, and who, once this madness had passed, returned to their former infidelity, renouncing Christianity and thus worsening their status, as they then lived in sin and died as apostates.

One of the principal authors of this impiety was John Fitz John, who killed with his own hands the famous London Jew Cok son of Abraham, who seemed to be by far the richest Jew of England; John took all his wealth for himself. Later, though unwillingly, he gave to the Earl of Leicester [Simon de Montfort] a large part of this wealth, so that neither of them was innocent of rapine and murder. It is not simple to estimate to what extent, through such evil events the royal treasury was affected, especially since the Jews paid not only tallages, but also pleas, gifts, escheats, and gifts of money contributed considerably to augment the King's treasury.[60]

Wykes paints the rebels responsible for the massacre as grasping, low, and impious. John Fitz John, son of one of John Fitz Geoffrey (c. 1206–1258), one of the legislative architects of the Oxford Parliament, was a strong supporter of Simon de Montfort, who had appointed him sheriff of Bedfordshire and Buckinghamshire.[61]

He seems in April 1264, with Simon absent from London, to be the leader of the rebel forces in London. It is not clear whether he ordered the slaughter of the Jews, but he clearly participated in it, killing Cok Fitz Abraham and seizing his possessions. Six months later, in October 1264, Simon issued orders in the king's name, canceling the debts that several of his men owed to "Cok, former Jew of London, deceased."[62] A document from 18 February 1265 says that Cok's charters were "in the king's hand by reason of Cok's death": in the king's hand means, of course, in possession of Simon.[63]

Wykes says that forty Jews were killed in London in April 1264, and some escaped death either by accepting baptism or by paying their attackers. The *Waverley Annals*, in a much briefer account, say that up to seven hundred Jews were killed, and others robbed, and that their synagogue was desecrated.[64] The *Annales Cambriae* give an even briefer entry on the massacre, also citing the figure of seven hundred Jews killed.[65] An almost identical notice is included in the *Annales de Wigornia*.[66]

The *Chronicles of the Mayors and Sheriffs of London* give the following account:

> Afterwards, in the week before Palm Sunday, the Jewry in London was destroyed, and all the property of the Jews carried off; as many of them as were found, being stripped naked, despoiled, and afterwards murdered by night, to the number of more than five hundred. And as for those who survived, they were saved by the justiciars and the mayor, having been sent to the tower before the slaughter took place; and then too, the chest of chirographs was sent to the tower for safe custody. Then also, as well as before, much money belonging to the Italians and Cahorsins, which had been deposited in the priories and abbeys about London for safe custody, was dragged forth and carried off to London.[67]

This text, written by London alderman Arnold fitz Thedmar, confirms what we have seen in other accounts. He puts the number of victims at over five hundred, corresponding to the "up to 700" of the three monastic chronicles and far superior to the forty of Wykes. He underlines the brutal nature of this slaughter: people systematically rounded up, robbed, stripped naked, and methodically butchered. The municipal officials, mayor, and sheriff were either unwilling or unable to stop the massacre but did offer shelter in the Tower of London to Jews who took refuge there before the violence began. This is confirmed by later royal documents mentioning the names of Jews who stayed in the tower during this period (as we will see in Chapter 7). The author adds one significant detail, absent from other accounts: the riches of Italian and "Cahorsin" moneylenders were also objects of attack. They had been kept for safekeeping in the treasuries of monasteries in the vicinity of London (a practice, we have seen, which church councils repeatedly prohibited to Jews), and were now plundered and brought to London. Yet it does not seem that these Christian moneylenders were physically attacked; they were not butchered by Londoners or by John Fitz John's troops.

The author of the *Chronicles of the Mayors and Sheriffs of London* shares with Thomas Wykes a royalist perspective: the robbery and bloodshed are appalling and unjustifiable crimes. Mayor and sheriff attempt (if ineffectually) to oppose these crimes for Arnold Fitz Thedmar, while for Wykes God himself punishes their blasphemy. Of the two, it is Wykes who waxes lyrical about the compassion due to the Jewish victims and their common humanity. In neither of these texts (nor in the three brief descriptions in the other monastic chronicles) do we get an idea of how the Londoners who perpetrated these atrocities, or soldiers such as John Fitz John, would have seen and justified their actions.

For this we need to turn to a final source, *The Annals of Dunstable Priory,* which give a quite different version:

> The earl [Simon de Montfort] was informed that the Jews of London had raised a rebellion in the city. At this sudden news, he returned and found that the Jews possessed Greek fire, with which they intended to set fire to the city on the eve of Palm Sunday [12 April]. They had acquired counterfeit keys to all the city gates, and, so it was said, they also had underground passages to every gate. In this situation, the earl had all the Jews killed from the youngest to the oldest except for some elders, whom he wanted to question further, and except for those willing to receive baptism. Gilbert de Clare did the same to the Jews of Canterbury.[68]

According to the Dunstable annalist, the decision to kill London's Jews was Simon's. Not motivated by greed, debt-inspired resentment, bloodlust, or religious animosity, Simon here proves a skillful general and tactician who unearths a vicious plot and swiftly punishes the culprits. Since this text is the only one to mention this version, it is hard to know if any such rumors may have been a spark or catalyst to the violence. Or it may be a justification cooked up long after the fact. The monk of Dunstable offers us a full-blown conspiracy theory, a piece of fake news meant to wash Simon and his men of any accusations of base motivations (the sort of accusations made by the other authors who wrote about the massacre).

This is another a fabricated story of Jewish hostility, spite, and duplicity. Those seemingly docile men and women were in fact plotting to murder their Christian neighbors. We have seen this most powerfully in the accusations of ritual murder, such as that surrounding the story of Little Hugh of Lincoln. But here of course there is an important difference. The Jews of London, who are after all the "king's Jews," are suspected of being loyal to the king (which, given the hostility and violence shown to them by Simon and his men, is not surprising). They are imagined as clever and ruthless enemies, possessing an exotic imported weapon, Greek fire, with which they plan to destroy the city and kill its Christian inhabitants. There are secret underground tunnels, in which the Jewish enemies move under the unwitting Christians' feet: we have seen that secret tunnels and passages played a role in the legend of the ritual murder of the boy Richard in the chronicle of Rigord. And these Jews were skilled in the semimagic art of metallurgy, so they had been able to make copies of keys to the gates of the city, to lock the good citizens of London in and watch them burn. London was saved from this horrifying fate by Earl Simon himself, who showed himself to be even cleverer than the Jews. He exposed their dark and secret plot to the light; he opposed their ignoble foreign weapon with the swords of righteous Englishmen. He had all Jews killed, regardless of age and sex, sparing only a few elderly Jews as witnesses. And the annalist adds, almost as an afterthought, that he spared those who accepted baptism, showing his zeal for the true religion (implicitly contrasted, perhaps, with Henry's willingness to profit from Jewish lucre). No mention is made, of course, of the possessions of the slaughtered Jews, nor of any loan documents destroyed.

The London bloodbath was the most horrific of the massacres perpetrated under Simon de Montfort's rule, but it was not the only one and not the last. We have seen that the Dunstable annalist, after his description of Simon's killing of London Jews, says that the Montfortian Gilbert of Clare, Earl of Gloucester, did the same to the Jews of Canterbury. Probably indeed some Jews died in Canterbury and others fled or were expelled, though a number of prominent Jews, it seems, continued to live there.[69] On 14 May, rebel forces and royal troops met at the Battle of Lewes. Walter of Cantilupe, bishop of Worcester, offered remission of sins (like that given to crusaders) to all who fought on the rebel side, and Simon harangued his troops, urging them to fight "for the state of the kingdom of England and for the honor of God, the Virgin Mary, all the saints, and Mother Church."[70] The battle was a resounding victory for the rebels: Henry, his son Edward, and his brother Richard were taken captive and would be closely guarded. For the *Chronicle of St. Martin of Dover*, St. Thomas Becket himself miraculously intervened, alongside St. George, to assure the rebel victory.[71] The king would be forced to travel everywhere with Simon, and to issue in the royal name the decrees that the Montfortians saw fit to have him proclaim. As Nicholas Vincent has remarked, Henry "lacked the ability to achieve anything other than failure."[72] The struggle between the rebels and royalist forces continued, and so did violence against Jewish communities.

Yet even Simon de Montfort and his men finally realized that if they intended to rule England, they needed to ensure the peace to the kingdom's Jews. Between May 1264 and August 1265, Simon attempted to offer reassurance and protection to Jews. On 11 June 1264, at St. Paul's of London, he had a mandate proclaimed in the king's name, that the Jews who had taken refuge in the tower were under the king's special protection and that no one might molest them. They were free to leave the tower and return to their homes.[73] Three days later, a mandate appointed twenty-four men, citizens of Winchester, as "wardens of the Jews of Winchester, now that the peace has been made." They were publicly to proclaim, in the name of the king and his barons, that the Jews were not to be molested.[74] On 6 May 1265 at Gloucester, a similar mandate is issued concerning the Jews of Lincoln: twenty-four men were appointed as their wardens "to protect the Jews of Lincoln in their persons and goods against all persons, as, after the late disturbance in the realm, the king by the counsel of the barons took under his special protection the said Jews, with the rest of the Jews of England, for the preservation of their bodies and goods, and certain persons threaten mischief against them."[75] Simon and his men, whom the Dunstable annalist had painted as righteous executioners of conniving Jewish rebels, now appeared in the role of sage barons who counsel the king to protect the Jews against those who seek to do them "mischief." In a quitclaim dated 26 November 1264, Abraham ben Jacob of Lincoln acknowledged payment from prior of Bullington, concerning a loan that a certain Alan the weaver had taken a loan from Abraham; to obtain the loan, Alan had mortgaged his land in the town of Wickford, near Lincoln; the priory of Bullington paid the debt and received Alan's land.[76] The priory, which had bought out the debt from Abraham ben Jacob, continued to practice, it seems, the type of land seizure that had so incensed the barons in 1258. Nor did the prior seem to have suffered on account of the destruction of Lincoln's loan records: a 1268 document concerning a dispute between a Jewish lender and his Christian debtor mentions that the Lincoln *archa* had been burned "by the king's enemies."[77]

In February 1265, the justices for the Jews resumed their activities.[78] On 3 May 1265, a mandate issued in the name of the king named Adam of Winchester and Robert de Crepping as justices of the Jews. Henry, Edward, and Simon were all witnesses to the mandate. Simon sought to assert his hegemony over Jews in the king's name, to reactivate the judicial system that assured justice for the Jews, and to control this important source of royal income. Yet rebel violence against Jews did not stop. On 15 July 1265, relate the *Chronicles of the Mayors and Sheriffs of London*, "Simon de Montfort the Younger, with other Barons and their adherents, took and plundered Winchester, and destroyed the Jewry there."[79]

In the meantime, the tide began to turn against the rebels. On 28 May 1265, Prince Edward made a dramatic escape from captivity. He joined the royalist forces and became their leader. Just two days later, on 30 May, Simon issued a mandate in the king's name to the royal treasurer and chamberlain. The king lamented that "our son Edward . . . has joined some rebels who seek to molest us and to disturb the peace of our realm." As a result, the king, who had granted to his son *"Judaismum nostrum"* ("our Jewry") now "takes it back into our own hand." He instructs Chancellor Thomas of Cantilupe to assess the London Jewry for a new tallage.[80] Just a little over a year after the massacre of April 1264, Simon seeks to impose a new financial burden on London's Jews. On 7 June, Simon had the king issue a mandate denouncing the rebels and enjoining them to respect his authority and cease disturbing the peace.[81] Simon was losing ground, both militarily and ideologically, to the royalists led by Edward. He was also out of money. He certainly could not get much from the London Jews whom his troops had brutally attacked and plundered a year before. He borrowed or extorted money from whomever he could.[82]

Edward and his allies quickly turned the tables on Simon, and the royalist forces finally trapped Simon's army at Evesham on 4 August 1265. Both sides considered their fight a crusade: the royalists rode into battle sporting red crosses on both arms; Simon and the rebels wore white crosses on their right shoulders.[83] In the battle that followed, Simon was killed and his body mutilated. Simon had placed King Henry in the middle of the melee, in the armor of a foot soldier. He is said to have shouted out "I am Henry of Winchester! Your King! Do not kill me!" He was taken to safety and joined his son's victorious army. Simon de Montfort, who had expelled the Jews from Leicester thirty-four years earlier and whose troops had massacred and pillaged Jewish communities across England, was now dead. English Jews would not mourn his death. The "king's Jews" had been the victims of a surge of antiroyal violence, the easy and lucrative targets of rebels seeking to strike at the king's power and wealth. Yet the death of Simon did not completely quell the revolt. Henry quickly pronounced the seizure of the rebels' land, provoking a fresh revolt of the "disinherited," who under the leadership of young Simon de Montfort, attacked Lincoln in November 1265 and burned its synagogue. The rebels attacked Cambridge on 12 August 1266, slaughtering Jews and carrying off the *archa*; they also took the *archa* from nearby Bedford. They attacked Norwich, took one of the Christian chirographers captive, and left with 140 cartloads of booty. Under the leadership of Gilbert de Clare, they seized London in April 1267, attacking Jews and destroying several of their homes. Only on 1 July 1267 was peace finally imposed.[84] For now, the storm had passed. Those English Jews who had survived would be able to begin to rebuild their lives. But no doubt with an eye uneasily turned toward the horizon.

CHAPTER 7

A Curse upon Edom

We have no Jewish voices describing the massacres of London Jews in 1264, the fear and relief of those who took refuge in the Tower of London, or the feelings of those who were able to leave the tower and return to what was left of their homes. The only Jewish testimonies that have come down to us with distant echoes of their plight come from Nürnberg, whose Jewish community over the course of the fourteenth century compiled a memory book, remembering Jews throughout Europe and beyond who had given up their lives for God as martyrs. Each year, in Nürnberg, Jews would recall and honor those who had died in London in 1264.[1] This of course has been a problem throughout this book, from the first chapter in which we traced the movements and activities of Isaac of Norwich through a rich variety of Latin sources, mostly from the royal administration, but not a word from Isaac himself. While Latin chroniclers wrote about Jews, English and other European Jews themselves wrote very little autobiography or chronicles of contemporary events. What they did do is commemorate those Jews who had fallen at the hands of infidel persecutors, from biblical times to more recent eras, including the victims of crusaders of 1096 and beyond.[2] Susan Einbinder faced the same problems in recounting the expulsion of Jews decreed by French King Philip IV in 1306: no contemporary Jews wrote about it, but their correligionaries across Europe commemorated their plight in liturgy.[3]

After the Storm

After the victory of the royalist forces at Evesham, Henry strove to reassert his control over the kingdom. And, of course, over his Jews. Numerous royal documents over the following years testify to the crown's efforts to protect Jews, to restore lost property to them, and to allow them to collect the debts due them (with special consideration for the fact that the official documents preserved in the *archae* had in many cases been destroyed). A period of relative calm followed, in which these Jews sought to rebuild their lives among the ruins. But it was a short-lived peace. The same pressures that created resentment against the consequences of Jewish lending were to resurface during the reign of Henry's son Edward I, who would outlaw moneylending at interest in 1275 and finally expel the Jews from England in 1290.

The Canterbury Jewry, as we have seen, had been attacked in 1264 by rebel forces. One of its most prominent members, Salomon ben Josche, or "Salle," owned property in both Canterbury and London. He had fled during the violence and taken refuge in France, losing his lands. He subsequently returned to Canterbury. Henry came to Canterbury, where on 23 October 1265 he granted to Salle his houses in the town. Salle, he says, had fled across the sea "in fear of the disturbance after the battle of Lewes," and the king had subsequently seized his houses. He ordered the sheriff of Kent to restore to Salle the lands, houses, and goods that he had possessed on the date of the battle of Lewes.[4] Yet not all who had benefitted from the seizure of his houses gave them up without a legal fight. A mandate dated 12 November 1265 orders that one of Salle's Canterbury houses be torn down. It impinged on the land of a certain Master Omer and abutted his chapel, which prevented the proper celebration of the Mass. By "special grace," Henry allowed Omer to have Salle's house torn down and to take full possession of the property.[5]

Two days later, 14 November 1265, Henry was back in Westminster, where he issued a mandate to Hugh Fitz Otto, constable of the Tower of London:

> In view of the many damages and injuries done to the Jews of England by our enemies during the rebellion in our kingdom, and on the advice of magnates of our council, we grant to each and every Jew that they may recover their goods and possessions so that they are in the same situation as they were on the day of the battle of Lewes. And some of our enemies during the rebellion occupied houses of Jews in the city of London before or after the aforementioned war, and the Jews in fear of the aforementioned rebellion abandoned their houses in the city and went elsewhere. We, wishing to grant them an exceptional favor, concede and return to each and every one of our Jews in London all the abovementioned houses that were taken and occupied during and after the war during the above-mentioned rebellion, with the exception of the houses of those London Jews which we have already granted to others.

And we therefore order you give the above-mentioned Jews full possession of their homes, as has been mentioned. Witness the king at Westminster, 14 November 1265.[6]

Other documents from the years 1265–1270 show how the king offered protection to Jews and confirmed their right to collect the debts due to them. At
Kenilworth on 16 August 1266, Henry revoked the quittance that Simon de
Montfort had made to his knight Saer de Harecurt concerning a debt to a Jewish lender named Cresse, who was now authorized to collect the money due to
him.[7] On 4 December 1266, the king made a similar grant to a group of Jewish
lenders of Bristol "because their chest of chirographs was burned by the king's
enemies and because of their losses at the hands of the said enemies in the time
of the disturbance in the realm, that the pledges named in the chirographs made
between them and their debtors of sums which they can reasonably show to be
due to them, shall be seized into their hands according to the law and custom of
the Jewry, until they be levied and paid, unless the debtors can show that they
are already paid."[8] Henry made another grant on 26 December to eleven named
Jews of Bristol, where "the king's enemies" had also burned the archa.[9]

By the summer of 1267, it seems, the immediate threat of violence to
England's Jewish communities had receded, and Jews had benefitted from numerous royal engagements to assure their safety and to allow them to resume their
lending activities, in particular to collect money due to them. Yet at the same
time, some towns sought to exclude Jews: on 8 July 1266, the king accorded to
the abbess and nuns of Romsey Abbey that no Jews would henceforth live in their
town.[10] At the same time that he offered renewed protection to Jews, King Henry
himself took over the debts due to London's deceased Jews. For example, an entry in the fine rolls on 30 November 1265 concerns Geoffrey Gacelyn's debts of
forty marks to Cok: Henry forgave twenty marks and ordered that Geoffrey pay
the remaining debt to him in two ten-mark installments, Easter and Michaelmas 1266.[11] In November 1265, he confirmed the annulment of debt to Jews that
Simon (in the king's name) had granted to John de Bokeland and Walter de Wauz
in February.[12] Similar quittances, often of the interest, rarely of the capital, were
given for other debts that men of his entourage owed to Jews over the following
years.[13] The king retained the right to annul all or part of the debts of his followers, such as Nicholas Pessim, whose debt to Maurice fitz Abraham of London was annulled on 16 September 1266.

In other cases, Henry confirmed Jews' rights to collect sums due to them
and rescinded the annulments of debts made by Simon. In some of those cases,

Jewish lenders sold off their debts to prominent Christian members of the king's entourage. On 19 December 1267, Elias fitz Moses sold to Alan La Zouche and his wife Helen the debts incurred to Elias by David of Ashby, overdue by four or five years (the earliest had been due in September, 1263), for a total debt (including interest and arrears) of over £600.[14] David Ashby had been one of Simon de Montfort's knights, and hence "the said fees and debts were withdrawn from the London chirograph chest in the time of the Earl of Leicester and at his instance and command; but afterwards releases of this kind were revoked by writ patent of our Lord the King, so as nought to avail against the Jews or in favour of their debtors, and that the Jews of England might have their recovery against their debtors by those parts which they held of the chirographs." With this sale, Elias gave up any claims on David's heirs and affirmed that any other claims against David by any other Jewish lenders would not impinge on this sale. Alan La Zouche was a knight who had remained faithful to the king throughout the barons' war. This transaction permitted the king to punish Ashby as a rebel, recognize the rights of Elias to pursue his debts, and reward Alan La Zouche as a faithful servant. Alan took possessions of the Ashby estate but was not long to benefit from it. John de Warenne, Earl of Surrey and warden of David Ashby's disinherited granddaughter Isabel of Ashby, attacked and killed him in June 1270.[15] Jewish lenders like Elias were pawns in a high-stakes political game being played out around the king.

An incident in Colchester on 7 December 1267 sheds light on relations between Jews and Christians in the town. On that day, a doe, scared by a dog, came near the southern gate of the town. A group of townsmen, Jews and Christians, gave chase to the doe, who ended up breaking her neck trying to jump over a wall. Hunting was a privilege reserved to the king and nobles, and the townsmen were thus clearly infringing the forest law. Hence the culprits were ordered to appear before the sheriff, and the forest roll document describing the incident gives the fines that the guilty parties had to pay: the five Christians collectively pay 14s. 8d., less than a pound, whereas the six Jews were fined a total of 20 marks (£13 6s. 8d.). The incident shows that Jewish and Christian townsmen could together spontaneously participate in illicit poaching, but that they were in no way equal before the law.[16]

A Cross Toppled

It was no doubt with apprehension that English and other European Jews learned that there were preparations for a new crusade. Louis IX, whose 1248 crusade had ended in defeat, took the cross anew, accompanied by his three sons, in Paris, on 24 March 1267. Louis urged Henry's sons Edward and Edmund to join him: they formally took the cross on 24 June 1268. On Ascension Day 1268 (7 May), Edward was in Oxford. As usual on this holiday, a large group of students, professors, clerics, and others crowded the streets and made a procession to St. Frideswide's churchyard, where they were to hear a sermon pronounced by Nicholas de Ewelme, chancellor of the university. As we have seen, St. Frideswide's was adjacent to the main Jewish quarter of Oxford, and the procession may have wended its way through the narrow Fish Street, the heart of the Jewish neighborhood. In the Jewish calendar, it was the third day of Sivan, first of the limitation days before the feast of Shavuot, the holiday that commemorated the revelation of the Torah to Moses. This was also the day on which, in 1096, crusaders had massacred the Jews of Mainz: a date liturgically commemorated annually by Jews in England and elsewhere in Europe. Talk of a new crusade provoked understandable fear: there would be new tallages to pay for the expedition, and perhaps the new crusaders (*crucesignati,* those marked with the cross) would perpetrate violence against Jews similar to the massacres in the Rhineland in 1096, in England in 1190, and in western France in 1236.

These thoughts may have been on the mind of Oxford Jews as they watched the procession squeeze into Fish Street, led by a priest bearing a large ceremonial cross. According to various sources, one or more Jews knocked the cross down and broke it.[17] The principal sources for this incident are three mandates sent by the king to royal officials at Oxford. On 12 September 1268, Henry wrote to the keeper of the castle of Oxford, informing him that Oxford Jew Jacob fitz Mossey and his sons Mosseus and Benedictus were in London on Ascension Day when a small portable cross carried in a procession was broken by Oxford Jews, "as it is said, in disdain of the cross of Christ and of all Christianity." Since Jacob and his sons had been absent and were hence in no ways responsible, they were to suffer no harm either in their goods or in their persons.[18] Four months after the incident, Oxford Jews feared punishment, financial or physical.

Three months later, Henry imposed a collective punishment on Oxford's Jewish community. On 27 December 1268, he sent a mandate to the sheriff of Oxford, affirming that "our Jews of Oxford" had not yet responded to his inquiries and had refused to name "that Jew" who had knocked down and broken a cross "in insult to the crucifix." The king hence held the entire Jewish community of Oxford as culpable, and in punishment ordered the sheriff to have them pay sufficient funds to make two crosses: a large one in marble, with the sculpted image of the crucified Christ on one side and the Virgin and child on the other.

It should have an inscription describing the incident and it should be placed on the very spot where the affront was made, before the feast of St. Edward the Confessor (13 October 1269). They were also to fund a portable gilded silver cross, to be carried in solemn procession before the students and professors of Oxford.[19]

Yet the placement of the stone cross provoked disagreement among Oxford residents. On 11 February 1269, Henry sent a new mandate to the sheriff of Oxford. He recalled the facts of the case and his earlier mandate concerning the two crosses. He had learned, he said, that some burghers of Oxford felt that the marble cross could not be erected on the spot where the incident took place "without damage and harm to that city." A spot across from the city's main synagogue had been subsequently envisioned but was judged an "indecent and dishonorable place."[20] In consultation with his son Edward and others, the king decided that it should be placed in the square before Merton College, alongside the church of St. John the Baptist. There the cross was subsequently erected, with a brief and cryptic Latin inscription:

Who was my author? The Jews.
How? Through payment.
Who ordered it? The ruler.
Who procured it? The magistrates.
Why? Because of a broken wooden cross.
When? The feast of the Ascension of the Lord.
In what place? Here where I stand.[21]

The *Book of the Chancellors and Proctors of the University of Oxford* conserves a brief narration of the incident probably written in the second half of the fourteenth century, and for the most part based on the three royal mandates we have examined.[22] It describes the solemn procession toward St. Frideswide, in the presence of the chancellor, the clergy, and the people of Oxford: "Some very wicked Jews, possessed by the spirit of the devil, proffered an insult to the Crucifix and a scandal to the Church. For they seized a portable cross that was being solemnly carried in the procession, horribly broke it and contemptibly cast it on the ground." The Oxford chronicler says that Edward was in Oxford at the time, that he related the incident to the king, and that Henry ordered "the fabrication of the two crosses."

What might have actually happened? We have already seen that the proximity of St. Frideswide with Oxford's principal Jewish quarter could produce tensions and at times Jewish outbursts of imprudent hostility toward Christian rites. We saw (in Chapter 4) how Jewish youth Deulecresse mocked Christian devotion to St. Frideswide in 1187 or 1188, and how he earned the rebuke not only of the Christians, but of the Jews (including his father), who feared the consequences of such provocation. Here, some of the sources speak of one Jewish culprit, others use the plural. The person (or persons) reportedly grabbed the processional cross from the hands of its bearer, broke it and cast it to the ground. There is no mention of the immediate reaction of the Christian crowd: no violence against the culprits or other Jews. No one was apprehended, it seems, since over seven months later Henry complained that the Jews would not reveal the name of the perpetrator, preferring it seems to suffer a collective punishment than to give up one of their members to royal justice. Perhaps they had on their minds the fate that met Copin and other Lincoln Jews in 1255.

Why would Jews rashly attack a cross carried in procession by Christians? Christoph Cluse and Elliot Horowitz both place this incident in a tradition of European Jewish hostility toward the cross. Various Hebrew texts concerning the massacres of Rhineland Jews in 1096 during the First Crusade emphasize that the infidel soldiers were marked by the cross. Some of the Jewish martyrs, before dying, insult the cross, and spit or urinate on it. We saw in Chapter 2 how a deacon who had converted to Judaism reportedly urinated on a crucifix. While the cross reminded Christians of the suffering of their Lord and the redemption He obtained for them, for the Oxford Jews it evoked the death of an apostate and the hateful symbol worn by crusaders who murdered Jews. While fantasizing about violence toward this symbol was comprehensible (and apparently fairly common), to rashly act out such fantasies was extremely rare.[23] But this is apparently what one or more Jews did at Oxford on 7 May 1268.

Henry responded to this outrage with a symbolically appropriate punishment: to cleanse the affront to the crucifix, the Jews would pay for two crosses. Moreover, the marble cross would mark the very spot where the insult occurred, transforming it from a place of insult to the crucifix to a place where the cross is venerated and the humiliators humiliated. Yet what followed Henry's mandate of 27 December 1268, it seems, was a period of prevarication and negotiation, notably concerning the site on which the marble cross would be erected. Perhaps Oxford's Jews sought to mitigate the humiliating aspect of the punishment by avoiding the erection of the cross on the spot in the Jewish quarter where the incident had taken place (or, worse, across from their synagogue). In any case, some agreement seems to have been made among Oxford residents, Jews and Christians, and communicated to Edward and the king, allowing the cross to be erected in a more distant, less central, and hence less humiliating location.

Finally, there is the curious inscription. The mandate of 27 December 1268 specified that the cross was to bear an inscription clearly explaining why it had been erected (*cum causa predicta manifesta superscripta*). The inscription explains that the Jews were the "authors" of the cross, that they had paid for it at the behest of the king, that it was "because of a broken wooden cross." The date is given, the feast of the Ascension, but not the year. Nothing in this laconic presentation conveys the indignation apparent in the royal documents or the *Book of the Chancellors and Proctors*. A cross had been broken, and the Jews had to pay for this new cross, but it is not said that Jews broke the cross, much less that they insulted or desecrated it. The final line corresponds to Henry's original mandate but not the subsequent agreement: the inscription affirms that the incident took place "where I stand," in the square before Merton college, which was not true. All this seems to indicate that those Oxford authorities responsible for executing the king's orders did so in a way that they could both respect the royal mandate and at the same time diminish its emotional charge, lessening the humiliation caused toward Oxford Jews and the potential accrued tension between Christians and Jews of the town.

New Burdens and Restrictions

The financial burden continued to weigh on English Jews. On 25 May 1269, Henry acknowledged an agreement whereby the kingdoms' Jews pay £1,000 in order not to have tallage assessed for three years—except in case of crusade by Henry or his sons.[24] The community was instructed to have this sum paid above all by the rich, so as not to overly burden the poor among the Jews.[25] Since Edward had already taken his crusading vow, this guarantee must have been of little comfort to England's Jews. They probably knew that Louis IX (on 15 September 1268) had ordered the seizure of the goods of French Jews in order to extract payments to fund the crusade.[26] Indeed, Henry subsequently granted Edward £6,000 from "his Jewry" to contribute to the financing of the crusade.[27] Edward set sail from Dover on 20 August 1270. On 25 August, Louis IX died before the walls of Tunis, and by the time Edward arrived, Louis's brother Charles of Anjou had signed a peace treaty with Tunisian Amir Muhammad I al-Mustansir. Edward and his English troops continued to Acre, where he spent sixteen months without any significant military accomplishments.

Indeed, the dire financial circumstances of many of the king's subjects (including Jews) in the aftermath of the civil war was aggravated by the push to levy new taxes to finance Edward's crusade. Henry called seven or eight parliaments between June 1268 and August 1270, principally in order to raise money for the crusade. "In these months," explains J. R. Maddicott, "taxation, consent, and popular representation came together."[28] One of the demands of the commons (and in particular those who represented the lesser gentry) was restrictions on Jewish lending activities. Henry continued to send mixed signals to his Jewish subjects, protective measures alongside regulations that restricted lending or imposed new financial burdens on them. On 13 January 1269, Henry issued, under pressure from parliament although ostensibly "by the advice of Lord Edward," "Provisions of the Jewry delivered at the Exchequer by Sir Walter de Merton."[29] The provisions banned the practice of perpetual fee debts, in which Christian debtors agreed to pay fixed annual fees indefinitely to Jewish lenders, on the security of their land. This reduced the debtors to the effective status of renters on their own land: default of the rent fee could and often did result in the loss of their land to the Jewish lender or, more often (as we have seen), to the Christian magnate or religious institution that had bought up the debt. Such debts could no longer be incurred, and existing debts were cancelled unless they had already been sold to a Christian. This significant exception was an implicit acknowledgement that many of the king's close associates had benefitted from purchasing such debts: they would no longer be able to do so, but their previous investments were secure. Such was not the case of the Jewish lenders, who lost considerable future income as well as an important tool in their lending practice. In a further attempt to enforce royal control over the system, the king ruled that no Jewish debts could be sold to Christians without explicit royal license. Edward played an important role in this decision: this was the first of a series of restrictions that culminated in the expulsion of 1290. Popular memories of Simon de Montfort's abolition of such debts may have driven parliament to pressure Henry and Edward to make these restrictions.[30]

Two years later, in July 1271, Henry sent a mandate to his sheriffs imposing further restrictions on Jews' financial activities.[31] It prohibited Jews from having freehold (*liberum tenementum*), in other words from owning land. Exception was made for houses that they already owned, either for their own residence or to rent to other Jews. They were not to buy new properties or rent out to Christians. Christians were prohibited from working for Jews as nurses, bakers, brewers, or cooks. This mandate marked another major blow to England's Jewish community, as the right to seize debtors' land, though infrequently exercised by Jewish lenders, was a key part of their toolbox. And their activity as landlords, particularly in London and Oxford, was an important source of income. In fact, it is hard to know to what extent these new restrictions were enforced. At least one of Oxford's major Jewish landlords, Jacob fitz Moses, continued to rent properties out to students and scholars, no doubt protected by his close acquaintance with Walter de Merton, the royal justiciar, who had obtained via Jacob much of the land that he later used to found Merton College.[32] At the same time, Merton took advantage of these restrictions to buy up Jewish land in Cambridge to establish a college.[33] And as we will see, Jewish employers and their Christian servants continued to ignore the prohibitions well into the reign of Edward.

Edward I and the 1290 Expulsion

Henry died on 16 November 1272. Edward was in Sicily, on his way back from Acre: it was there that he received news of his father's death. Yet he seemed in no hurry to return to England and assume the throne. Edward took a leisurely journey through Italy and France and finally arrived in England almost two years later, on 2 August 1274. He was crowned at Westminster on 19 August.

The tale of Edward's policies toward the Jews between his return to England in 1274 and the edict of expulsion of England's Jews pronounced on 18 July 1290 has been told many times.[34] It is a story of increasing restrictions on Jewish financial activities coupled with periodic tallages that sapped what little wealth was left out of the Jewish community. Edward was less dependent on income from his Jews than was his father Henry, simply because there was less income to be had; he turned increasingly to Italian bankers for financing. Henry had proclaimed as early as 1233 that Jews were allowed to reside in the kingdom only as servants of the king. We have seen how, over the course of his reign, Jews played a key role in assuring revenue to the crown, financing the growth of monasteries or Oxford colleges, and more generally contributing to the growth of the English economy. Yet by the 1280s the Jews' usefulness to the crown was severely diminished. After 1275, they no longer could legally practice lending with interest, the principal source of their wealth (and of the tallages they paid to the crown) for over a century. In 1287, a tallage of £13,333 was assessed, the first since 1278, but not even £4,000 was collected: Edward responded by having prominent Jews throughout the kingdom arrested and imprisoned. They were released after promising further payments of £12,000. The Jews' wealth, and their ability to provide money to the crown, was now dwarfed by that of the Italian banking families active in London, such as the Riccardi of Lucca, who loaned over £200,000 to the crown during the first seven years of Edward's reign.[35] The continued presence of Jews in England brought decreasing financial advantage to the crown.

In 1275 Edward promulgated a new statute of Jewry, which prohibited Jews from lending money on interest, urging them to "live by lawful trade," and reiterating the requirement to wear the *tabulae* and the prohibition to employ Christian servants.[36] In the same year, Edward granted to his mother, Eleanor of Provence, the right to exclude Jews from all towns that she held in dower.[37] As if to justify this by showing that Jews were a threat to Christianity, the anonymous chronicler of Bury relates that in 1275 a Dominican friar named Robert de Reading, "who was a famous preacher and very learned in the Hebrew language, apostatized and embraced the Jewish faith; he even married a Jewess, had himself circumcised and changed his name to Haggai. The king sent for him, and when he held forth brazenly he handed him over to the archbishop of Canterbury."[38] Robert Holcott reports that Robert/Haggai died unrepentant in prison.[39] The Bury chronicler does not mention the punishment received by the apostate, but next relates that on 11 September London was struck by an earthquake; he then explains that Edward prohibited Jews from lending money at interest.[40] But despite the 1275 prohibition of usury, Edward's brother Edmund and his Queen Eleanor were accused of exploiting debt to Jews in the same manner as those close to Henry III in the 1250s. In 1278, for example, when William Leyburn amassed considerable debt to Jewish lenders, the royal couple forgave the debts and obtained Leeds Castle as compensation.[41] "The king desires to get our gold; the queen, our manors fair to hold," quipped a chronicler.[42]

There is another crucial element that explains the expulsion: the active anti-Jewish lobbying of a group of bishops, foremost among them John Peckham, archbishop of Canterbury, who vigorously pursued an anti-Jewish policy designed to limit contact between Jews and Christians. In several telling incidents from Edward's reign, bishops that had been part of Simon de Montfort's entourage, Richard de Gravesend, bishop of Lincoln, and Richard Swinfield, bishop of Hereford, expressed their strong objections to fraternization between Jews and Christians.[43] We have already met Richard de Gravesend, archdeacon of Oxford and close associate of Robert Grosseteste, whom he accompanied to see the pope in Lyon in 1250; in August, 1254 he became dean of Lincoln Cathedral: as we saw, it was he in 1255 who orchestrated the burial of Little Hugh in the cathedral and vigorously promoted the cult of the saint. In September 1258, he was elected bishop; he subsequently became one of the bishops closely allied to Simon de Montfort and hence was excommunicated by Pope Urban IV. Suspended from office after the royal victory at Evesham, he subsequently obtained absolution and was restored to his bishopric.[44] On 4 June 1278 he wrote a letter to King Edward, concerning fourteen people (thirteen women and one man) who were employed as servants in Jewish homes.[45] He named each of them and the Jews for whom they worked, identifying the parishes in which those Jews lived. Gravesend informed the king that he had pronounced a sentence of excommunication against the fourteen, and that they had for forty days persisted in working for the said Jews in defiance of the bishop. Unable to compel them, Richard here turned to the king to ask him to "extend the right hand of your majesty," in other words to use royal coercive power to punish the excommunicates. Yet Gravesend failed to include a standard clause asking the king to order that the sheriff imprison the malefactors. We have no record of any response and thus cannot know whether any of the fourteen was punished or if they continued to live and work in the homes of Jews. We know that Swinfield, for his part, bombarded the king with ninety-eight such letters of request to punish excommunicates.[46]

Church authorities frequently prohibited Christians from working as servants in Jewish homes, but to little avail; rabbinical sources from Ashkenaz show that this was a common practice throughout northern Europe.[47] Earlier English bishops' attempts to end this practice by forbidding Christians to sell food to Jews, as we have seen, provoked swift rebukes from Henry III. Gravesend is trying something new, or at least something not documented before this: naming specific Christians working for specific Jews and excommunicating them nominally. He perhaps believed that Edward I, who had after all prohibited Christians from working in Jewish homes just three years earlier, would be more supportive of his efforts than had his father. Yet there is no evidence that Edward did anything to enforce this decision, and without royal enforcement excommunication seems to have borne little sting for these servants. Hence it seems that in spite of the 1275 *Statute of Jewry*, Gravesend was frustrated in his attempts to enforce the prohibition of Christians working in Jewish homes and that his excommunication of these Christian servants had little effect on their behavior.

Between 1273 and 1278, Edward imposed five tallages on the kingdom's Jews, with sharply reduced yields, showing the financial decline of the Jewish community.[48] In 1278–1279, Jews and Christians were accused of coin clipping, clipping or shaving silver from the edges of coins. Hundreds were accused, tried, and imprisoned, both Christians and Jews, though Jews faced much harsher punishments: over two hundred were put to death (and only about thirty Christians).[49] In order to gather evidence against the coin clippers, the crown had employed convert Henry of Winchester, whose godfather had been King Henry himself, as "agent provocateur," infiltrating the network of coin clippers in order to inform the crown about their activities. His testimony provided the evidence used to convict and punish Jewish offenders. When Edward suggested that he bear witness against Christian culprits, however, bishop Thomas Cantilupe, Simon de Montfort's former chancellor and a close advisor to Edward, reportedly objected, and added moreover that the remaining Jews, as "enemies of God and rebels against the faith," should either convert or be expelled from the kingdom; he burst into tears and the king relented.[50] This might be an embellished version, as it comes from Justice Ralph de Hengham's deposition in Cantilupe's fourteenth-century canonization dossier: perhaps Hengham sought to posthumously credit Cantilupe with the idea of the expulsion. But in any case, as Paul Brand has shown, it may explain why many Christian money clippers escaped the fate of their Jewish accomplices.

On 2 January 1280, Edward ordered his sheriffs and bailiffs to compel Jews to attend missionary sermons preached by Dominican friars. In May 1280 (as we saw in Chapter 3), the king undertook major reforms of the *Domus conversorum,* giving it a more solid financial base. He also abolished the previous royal practice of seizing the possessions of Jews who converted to Christianity: henceforth converts would be able to keep half of their goods; the other half would go to the crown but would specifically be used to for the maintenance of converts and the upkeep of the *domus.* Edward, unlike his father, was serious about trying to convert the remnant of English Jews. And given the hardships and dangers they faced, it is no surprise that they were increasingly ready to convert. A certain Yom Tov, son of the renowned scholar Moses of London (d. 1268) is said to have committed suicide to avoid following the "demon" that was urging him to accept baptism. As Paola Tartakoff has shown, this story is to be understood in the context of a number of contemporary texts about how Jews attempted to prevent family members from apostasy. True or not, the story of Yom Tov serves as a model urging Jews to resist pressures to abandon their community, to prefer death to apostasy. As Susan Einbinder notes, Yom Tov frees himself from demonic temptation through recuperative martyrdom.[51]

John Peckham, archbishop of Canterbury from 1279 to 1292, vigorously pursued an anti-Jewish agenda. He sought to enforce traditional prohibitions of fraternizing between Jews and Christians, to eradicate the practice of usury, and to prevent converts from Judaism to Christianity from backsliding. On 30 July 1281, Peckham wrote to Richard Gravesend, bishop of London (not to be confused with Richard de Gravesend, bishop of Lincoln), complaining that the Jews of London had erected a new synagogue, "to the confusion of the Christian religion." He bade him to do all in his power to stop the project.[52] On 19

August 1282, in another letter to the bishop, Peckham observed that the Jews had seven synagogues in London, "cheating the Christian religion and causing scandal to many." He ordered Richard to compel the Jews of London, using every instrument of ecclesiastical censure, to destroy all their synagogues except one within a brief time period to be determined by the bishop.[53] He subsequently sent another letter to the bishop affirming that it was legitimate for the Jews to build one synagogue in the place assigned to them by the king for the use of London's Jews.[54]

Peckham was particularly incensed about reports of Jewish converts to Christianity returning to Judaism. On 2 November 1281 he wrote to Edward, saying that he had heard, "not without pain and anguish in my heart," that some men and women of London, "who had converted from the Jewish perfidy to the Christian religion have returned to their vomit, the Jewish superstition."[55] The following year, he sent a list of seventeen apostates to the king, asking that they be arrested; he obtained a royal writ from Edward the following year, ordering that thirteen of them be imprisoned. But the apostates took refuge in the London Jewry under the protection of the constabulary of the Tower of London. Peckham wrote in complaint to Chancellor Robert Burnell, who responded that if he were to issue a writ to the constable, this would compromise the latter's relation with the London Jewish community. Peckham's efforts to have them arrested came to naught.[56] On 27 July 1267, Pope Clement IV had written to Franciscan and Dominican inquisitors saying that he had learned with a heavy heart that Jews were converting Christians to Judaism and to have such Jews tried and put to death; in many cases, the "corrupted" Christians were probably converts from Judaism who were convinced to return to their religion.[57] The Franciscan Peckham would have been well aware of these concerns and sought to take action against such apostasy.

The archbishop was also critical of those among the elite who profited financially from Jewish lending, including Queen Eleanor. On 23 September 1283, he warned the queen, "when you receive land or a manor through Jewish usury, beware that usury is a mortal sin." He told her that it was not legitimate to retain lands and goods obtained in this manner and advised her to restore to their proper Christian owners all that was accountable to usury, which, he explained, is any interest beyond the capital.[58]

These subjects still rankled in 1285, when at the Easter parliament the clergy of the province of Canterbury drew up a list of seventeen grievances against the crown.[59] The final two of these complaints involved Jews. The prelates asked that the king conduct inquiries concerning these apostates and persecute them. They also demanded "that the Jews' fraud and malice be vigorously opposed," to which the king lamented, "one cannot know how to do so, because of their evilness."[60] In June, the prelates offered their replies to these royal responses. In particular, they affirmed that there was much that the king could and should do to act against the Jews.

> The prelates were amazed that the royal curia did not know how to reign in the Jewish evil. Indeed, it will not be possible to do so as long as it permits Jews to ensnare Christians through usurious contracts and to acquire the manors of nobles through the sink of usury. For this is aiding Jews in their crimes against Christians. The royal clemency should, to the extent it is possible, oblige Jews to restore to Christians all things that they have usurped through the perversity of usury and which they damnably retain from all Christians. Let him compel the Jews to live by the labor of their hands or by dint of trade, and in no way communicate through contracts or secret discussions with Christians, but only in public before reliable witnesses. And through the threat of horrible punishments which our lips will not name, he may strive to punish all usurers, as a manifest sign before and after. And in this way they can easily be restrained.[61]

Ten years after Edward's statute for the Jewry, which in theory abolished usury, John Peckham and his prelates bitterly complained that Jews continued to "ensnare" Christians with usurious contracts, and that the king and queen were largely responsible for this. As Hannah Meyer has noted, this is the first and only time that English conciliar decrees addressed the question of usury and sought its abolition.[62] From the bishops' point of view, the 1275 prohibition of usury was not being respected, despite the fact that former Jewish lenders were now making money by providing "commodity bonds," in particular buying and selling grain. Historians have seen this practice as simply a disguised form of interest loans, though Robin Mundill argued that this marked a fundamental change of Jewish financial activity from lending to investing.[63] Clearly the bishops felt that usurious activity continued; as Paul Brand has shown, even if these bond transactions were bona fide, they still could be considered usurious to canonists.[64]

Questions of fraternization between Jews and Christians continued to trouble English bishops, as we see in an incident concerning a Jewish wedding in Hereford in August 1286. The bishop, Richard de Swinfield, was also a Montfortian: in 1264 he was in the household of Thomas of Cantilupe, chancellor of

Oxford and close ally of Montfort (Thomas was to serve under Simon as royal chancellor from February to May 1265, where as we have seen he was responsible for levying tallages on London Jews). Swinfield probably accompanied Thomas into exile after Evesham and on his return after reconciliation with King Henry. He was at his side when Thomas became bishop of Hereford in 1275. When Thomas died in 1282, Swinfield was chosen to replace him; he presided over his predecessor's burial in the Hereford cathedral and lobbied for his canonization. Thomas was finally canonized in 1320: one of his proofs of sanctity was his harsh opposition to Jews: as we have seen, he purportedly called for their expulsion during the coin clipping crisis of 1278–1279. His protégé and successor Richard de Swinfield would emulate his hostility toward Jews.

On 26 August 1286 Swinfield wrote a letter to the dean of Hereford Cathedral, instructing him strictly to forbid his parishioners from attending the wedding of a prominent Jew of the town, under pain of ecclesiastical censure.[65] Roman and canon law had frequently forbidden Christians from sharing meals with Jews: both because Jews refused the food of Christians and because sharing meals brought potentially dangerous fraternization, possibly leading to interfaith sexual relations and apostasy. Swinfield was thus well within the traditions of canon law when he prohibited Christians from attending the Jewish wedding. He presented Jews as blasphemers who "spew insults to their Creator," and (in the rhetorical tradition of Innocent III, Robert Grosseteste, and many others) as ingrates who ought to humbly accept their status of perpetual servitude, but instead deceived Christians. The bishop clearly wanted to nip this in the bud, as he ordered his chancellor to publish this prohibition not only in all the churches but also in the streets of the city. Given that he issued his orders from his estate at Bosbury (twenty-three kilometers east of Hereford) two days before the wedding (indeed, the festivities would begin on the night of Tuesday, the 27th), time was of the essence. While the bishop did not name either the bride or the groom, Joe Hillaby has speculated that the only Jew in Hereford with sufficient wealth and social prominence to throw such a wedding party was Aaron le Blund, leader of the Hereford Jewish community, and that the groom may have been his grandson Bonenfaunt.[66]

The bishop's harsh assessment of Jews was not shared by a significant number of his flock, who were prepared (he feared) to attend this Jewish wedding. What shocked him most, it seems, is the openness of the invitation, as neither Jews nor Christians seemed to see any need to dissimulate what was for the bishop a baleful fraternization. The threat of ecclesiastical censure did not dissuade Hereford's Christians from attending the wedding. On 9 September, Swinfield sent a second letter to the dean. The bishop had learned that many Christians had attended the wedding party, and he wrote in anger to condemn them and chastise his chancellor. Besides the dangers of frequenting of the "enemies of Christ"—eating, drinking, and dancing with them, and (worse, for the bishop) showing them honor—the bishop was angry at what he saw as a clear challenge to his authority: the Christians townsmen had flouted his mandate, and he clearly suspected his chancellor of not having obeyed his orders. He wanted a show of force and ordered the Christians who attended the wedding to confess and reconcile themselves with the Church or to face excommunication. The bishop himself affirmed his sole authority for granting absolution. His chancellor was to draw up by 29 September a list of those to be excommunicated. Swinfield's financial records show that he had in his employ a certain Thomas de Brugg, his *pugilarius* (boxer); we do not know if he sought to employ his services in this conflict.[67]

This incident occurred in 1286, only four years before the expulsion of the Jews from England. The image of Jews openly inviting Christians to a wedding, where all drink, eat, and dance together suggests an easy affinity across confessional lines, and belies the image of an inexorably and increasingly hostile Christian England at the eve of the expulsion. It is impossible to know how frequent such fraternization was: here it is recorded only because it provoked a hostile reaction from the bishop. Is this in fact (as Swinfield affirms) a rare affront to the normal order of things? Or is this on the contrary a common occurrence, which we know about only because of the hostile reaction of a zealous and bigoted bishop? A roughly contemporary Hebrew source, Jacob ben Judah of London's *'Etz Hayyim,* reassures its Jewish readers, telling them that it is permissible to buy pastries from Christian bakers and to share a beer with Christians in their homes.[68]

What clearly irks the bishop is that all involved, Jews and Christians, seemed to think that such interaction was normal and acceptable, that they did not even attempt to dissimulate it: this may suggest that Hereford's Christians and Jews were normally more discreet about their socialization. What's more, as Joe Hillaby has shown, the bishop had been in frequent conflict with many of the prominent burgers: as Hillaby concludes, "Many of the city oligarchy would have found it difficult to forgo such an opportunity—not merely for display, but as a heaven-sent opportunity to humiliate their bishop."[69] It is impossible to know what the effects were of this second letter. Did it have as little impact as the first? Were these the impotent rantings of a cantankerous bishop, to be ignored as much as possible? Or was there in fact a list of excommunicates drawn up in September 1286? Did some of the partiers have to make amends to their bishop and obtain his absolution? And if so, at what price? And what, if any, were the consequences for the Jewish community of the city, and for its relations with its Christian neighbors? Cecil Roth has speculated that Swinfield may have written to Pope Honorius IV about this affair, and that this provoked a bull addressed to the archbishop of Canterbury, John Peckham, in November the same year, as the bull is copied in Swinfield's episcopal register. Or it may be Peckham himself who solicited the bull, as Solomon Grayzel conjectured.[70]

In any case, Honorius addressed a bull, *Nimis in partibus Anglie*, dated 19 November 1286, to Archbishops John Peckham of Canterbury and John le Romeyn of York and to their suffragan bishops, which is to say to the whole of the Church of England.[71] The pope echoes many of the issues that popes and bishops had been raising throughout the thirteenth century. "Jewish perfidy" in England, he complains, is perpetrating horrendous acts in insult to the Creator and to the detriment of the Catholic faith. They have in "malignant fraud" composed a book called the Talmud, full of lies and abominations: he reiterates the charges against the Talmud made by Gregory IX over forty years earlier. In their daily prayers, Jews curse Christians. Yet not content to blaspheme against Christianity, they lure Christians to work and live in their homes, have them break the Sabbath by working on Sundays, and induce them to participate in their rites in their synagogues. Jews and Christians invite each other into their homes, eating and drinking together. Jewish men mix with Christian women, and Christian men with Jewish women. The situation is a "dangerous disease," a "pestilence" that the good bishops need to eradicate. He orders the bishops to combat the pestilence through prohibitions and spiritual punishments: in other words, through the standard battery of ecclesiastical punishments that English bishops such as Swinfield had been vainly deploying for decades. He does not mention the possibility of expulsion, but clearly Swinfield and other bishops could use the pope's missive as a strong argument in favor of expelling Jews from England.

The bishops' continuing preoccupation with Jewish-Christian contact is seen in the statutes of the synod that Bishop Peter Quinil called at Exeter on 16 April 1287. In continuity with Lateran IV, Oxford, and other councils, the synod's fifty-six statutes attempt to establish standard rules and procedures for the sacraments, offices, management of church lands and buildings, church revenues, accepted behavior of clerics, and clerical exemption from secular justice. Statute 49 concerns "Jews and their servants (*mancipiis*)."[72] The statute opens by affirming that God justly took his kingdom away from the Jews and gave it to the Gentiles. Hence Christians are free and Jews are in perpetual servitude. Echoing Innocent III, Peter Quinil writes that "it is absurd that the son of a free woman serve the son of a servant." Citing the precedent of Lateran III, he prohibits Jews from having Christian servants in their homes, "lest through familiarity with them the souls of these simple women succumb to their perfidy." Christians who contravene this prohibition are excommunicated; Jews are to suffer unspecified "harsh punishment" (*gravi ultioni*). Jews are prohibited from holding public office and from sharing meals with Christians. Christians may not accept medication from Jews. Jews "on Good Friday should keep their doors and windows closed so that they may avoid Christians who are in mourning that day." Jews may not build new synagogues, but may repair old ones, as long as they are not made larger or more elaborate. Finally, the synod reiterates the requirement to wear "woolen tablets."

Evidence from elsewhere in England shows attempts by royal officials to restrict Jewish-Christian fraternization. In Norwich in 1287–1288, among a long list of petty offences committed by residents of the parish of Berstrete, we find Roger de Lakenham accused of selling Jewish meat, or *trepha:* in other words, parts of the animal unfit for consumption under kosher regulations.[73] The following year, "John the pastry-maker" is charged with the same offense.[74] Churchmen since Pope Innocent III had attempted to prohibit this practice, a lucrative and common collaboration between Jewish and Christian butchers: for Innocent, it was insulting to Christians who were to consume what the Jews considered not good enough for their own consumption.[75] The prosecution of this offence in the years leading up to the expulsion both attests to the persistence of such collaboration and to the increasing will of the crown and local officials to put an end to it.

We have seen that the supposed hostility of Jews to Christians and Christianity, their desire to hurt and humiliate Christians, was dramatized through the legends of ritual murder. This was driven home, in many cases, by the scenes of everyday contact in these stories: the unwitting Christian child who plays with Jews does so at his own peril; the Christian woman who works in a Jewish home is a potential ally of the enemy. This is seen in the Latin legend of Adam, a Christian boy supposedly martyred in Bristol in the twelfth century, during the reign of Henry II, but in fact first mentioned in a Latin text from around 1280.[76]

According to this text, a Jew named Samuel lures Adam into his house by offering him apples. Samuel tortures Adam with relish, ignoring the boy's pleas and his prayers to the Virgin Mary. He nails the unconscious boy to the cross. But from boy's throat a loud voice booms out in Hebrew, affirming "I am the God of Abraham, Isaac and Jacob" and telling him to desist from persecuting God. Unfazed, Samuel continues his torture, liberally spiced with blasphemies against Christ and against his mother (whom he calls "a whore"). Divine voices (this time in Latin) issue from the wounds that Samuel continues to inflict on his victim: this leads to the conversion of Samuel's wife and son, whom he murders on the spot. There is no point going into the lurid details of this tale: the disposal of Adam's body in a latrine, the miraculous interventions of an angel bearing a flaming sword, the many parallels to the passion of Christ. Harvey Hames suggests that the text may have been written for use in a liturgical setting, to be either read or enacted either during holy week or one of the Marian feast days; Robert Stacey goes further, suggesting that both form and content of the text suggest that this is a "parish drama" meant to be performed at the Church of St. Mary in Redcliff (mentioned in the text) on the feast of the Assumption of the Blessed Virgin Mary (15 August).

If this is the case, Christians of Bristol celebrating the principal holiday associated with the Virgin Mary would be shown the spectacle of Jewish enmity and violence against Christianity. Jews like Samuel, inspired by the devil, supposedly regularly reenacted the crucifixion of Jesus (Adam was Samuel's fourth victim, we are told), ritually proffering blasphemies against Christ and his mother. The unwitting Christians (Samuel's neighbors, Adam himself) who ignore this do so at their own peril. This crude and inept drama seems, among other things, meant to emphasize the message various bishops had been trying to convey: that fraternization with Jews by Christians who work for them as servants, who share meals with them or do them the honor of attending their wedding parties, was dangerous collusion with the enemies of Christ and his mother. This message is driven home by the image at the opening of the text: the boy Adam is indistinguishable from the crucified Christ, while the man who punctures his side is not a spear-bearing Roman soldier, but a knife-wielding Jew with twisted posture, deformed features, and a huge bulbous nose: a figure of diabolical enmity.

Meanwhile Edward, heavily in debt to his Italian bankers, involved in expensive campaigns of building fortifications in Wales and Gascony, in 1287 again imposed a major tallage on his Jews. Five different accounts (in Latin, French, and Hebrew) describe how royal officials arrested Jews across England on 2 May 1287 and imprisoned them. According to one of the accounts, a number of them were brought to London "in carts." They were released when the agreed to pay a tallage of £12,000, though in the end only about £4,000–£5,000 was collected.[77]

Edward was also Duke of Aquitaine. On 13 May 1286 he left England for three years, most of which he spent in the duchy. In May, 1287, he proclaimed the expulsion of the Jews from Gascony.[78] It has been suggested that the 1287 expulsion was a sort of "test run" for the expulsion from England. Be that as it may, the situation was different: in England Jews depended directly on the crown, and there was an elaborate royal bureaucracy devoted to their affairs (exchequer of the Jews, justices of the Jews) and to keeping track of debts to Jews (the *archa* system). None of this existed in Gascony. For these reasons and others, the two expulsions were different and the consequences were very different.

Edward had become duke in 1252, at the age of thirteen, twenty years before ascending the throne of England. The substantial Jewish community of Gascony was an important source of revenue for the duchy. Yet the regular and excessive taxation caused some of his Jewish subjects to complain in 1281 of the "many and huge tallages" imposed on them and obtain from him writs to his seneschal instructing him not to impose excessive tallages.[79] In a number of charters, he issued privileges granting exemption from tallages to individual Jews in return for annual payments: no doubt a system that provided more reliable and regular income for the duke—and less arbitrary and more manageable payments for the Jews concerned. This revenue became all the more important as Edward amassed heavy debts to pay for his military and diplomatic adventures on the Continent, particularly through his role in the negotiations with the Aragonese in his attempts to secure the freedom of Charles II of Anjou.

On Easter Sunday (7 April) 1287, Edward was standing in a tower in Bordeaux when the floor collapsed: he and his entourage tumbled down eighty feet. Several knights were killed; Edward suffered a broken collarbone and other injuries and was in convalescence for months. In May, he took a crusading vow; soon thereafter, it seems, he decided to expel the Jews from the duchy. In autumn Jews were arrested and their goods seized; by November they were expelled. The expulsion order is not extant, but a number of documents referring to Jews, their debtors, and their finances are extant in the "Gascon Rolls," administrative registers recording revenues, fines, and various other transactions. While Gerald Richardson (and after him Robert Chazan) had affirmed that financial need was the principal motor for the Gascon expulsion, Jean-Paul Trabut-Crussac has shown that Edward profited little financially from the expulsion: usury was forgiven (debtors could plea abusive rates of usury and get off with paying only half of their debt).[80] Revenues went principally to the mendicant orders.[81] In other words Edward, heavily indebted though he was, chose not to profit financially from the expulsion, preferring to give the money he seized from the Gascon Jews to religious orders, perhaps not wishing to profit from Jewish usury.

If the Gascon expulsion might have been a "test run" for the expulsion from England, a closer model was perhaps the expulsion from Anjou pronounced by

Charles II, Count of Anjou on 8 December 1289.[82] In his decree of expulsion, Charles presents himself as "king of Jerusalem and Sicily, prince of the duchy of Apulia and the principality of Capua, count of Achea, Anjou and Forcalquier." As these titles indicate, he laid claim to far-flung domains, over many of which his rights were contested: hence his policies in Anjou were in part subservient to his broader political and military ambitions. His father, Charles I of Anjou (brother of French King Louis IX) had purchased in 1277 the title of king of Jerusalem from Mary of Antioch; hence Charles's claim to the title. Charles I had been crowned king of Sicily in 1265 by Pope Clement IV and subsequently conquered the kingdom from Manfred, son of Frederick II Hohenstaufen. In 1282, Sicilians rose up against Angevin rule in what historians call the Sicilian Vespers: Charles II was taken prisoner by the Catalans in 1284; in 1285, Charles I died. In 1288, Charles II was set free: as a condition of his release, he had relinquished his claim to Sicily (accepting to be called only king of Naples), yet shortly after gaining freedom, Pope Nicholas IV released him from his vow and crowned him king of Sicily. Charles was to pursue this claim until 1302, when he finally renounced it in the Peace of Caltabellotta. His other titles reflect lands over which he had real power (Apulia and Capua in Southern Italy, Forcalquier in Provence) as well as ones in which his overlordship was recognized in theory but brought him little real power or benefit (Achaea, a crusader duchy in the Peloponnese).

In 1289, when Charles arrived in Anjou for the first time as count, he sought to affirm his authority over the county. He was also preoccupied with making good his claim to the throne of Sicily, a preoccupation shared by his French and papal allies. And he was deeply in debt, not least to King Edward I of England, who had played a key role in mediating to obtain his release from prison—and who had advanced considerable sums of money to obtain it. Charles of course knew of Edward's Gascon expulsion. Whether or not he knew that Edward had not profited financially from that expulsion, Charles, in need of money to pursue his claim to Sicily through war with Aragon, would use the expulsion to obtain new taxes from his subjects.

In the expulsion order of 1289, Charles affirmed that the Jews of Anjou and Maine were guilty of "many enormities and crimes." He cites "sacred authority," in fact a bull of Innocent III, which had applied to the Jews an adage warning against trusting those who were "like the mouse in a pocket, like the snake around one's loin, like the fire in one's bosom."[83] In particular, he accuses them of "subverting" Christians and "despoiling" them through the practice of usury and of cohabiting with Christian women. Charles presents the expulsion as his own initiative, the result of his "compassion" for the Christian victims of Jewish perfidy. He says that he consulted with bishops and vassals, implying that the decision to expel was based on a broad consensus. The edict orders expulsion of all Jews from Anjou and Maine. The expulsion is permanent, obliging both the count and his successors. Any of the count's men who exercised authority in his name were allowed (and indeed required) to arrest, despoil, and beat any Jew who did not respect the expulsion order; they were then to expel them. Any other subject could arrest and despoil them and bring them to a judge. Yet the Jews are not the only objects of the expulsion order, which was aimed at usurers more generally: he orders that "the aforesaid expulsion be extended to all Lombards, Cahorsins, and other foreigners who engage in public usury without public contracts and who are properly considered usurers." This is also a permanent expulsion; their goods are to be seized and handed over to "the lords of those places" (which had not been specified for the Jews).

Like John the Red of Brittany, and unlike the kings of France or England, Charles emphasized the permanent nature of this expulsion, which place penalties on himself or any of his successors in the event that they allow Jews (or other foreign usurers) to return to the county: the count's domain was to be put under interdict and he would forfeit the special tax that was authorized in the expulsion order. It is this tax that is the real innovation in this edict: a one-time imposition of three shillings (*solidi*) per hearth and six pennies per worker is accorded to the count to recompense his loss of income (or what is presented as such). In 1182, Philip II profited from the expulsion primarily through seizure of Jews' land and houses (since they were allowed to take moveable property with them); in 1240, John the Red and his barons profited through the canceling of their debt and the reclaiming of items (and land) in pawn; and (as we have seen), Edward I made little if any financial gain from the expulsion from Gascony. Charles took advantage of the expulsion to obtain this exceptional levy, which suggests that the expulsion was a popular move for which his subjects were prepared to pay.

Like his father, Edward sought to exploit the "royal milch cow" through tallages. Yet Jews' capacity to pay such tallages depended on their activity as moneylenders, an activity that Henry's administration had carefully proctored, protected, and exploited. Edward had banned the practice in 1275, but clearly he not only knew full well that it continued, he and those close to him (including his queen) continued to profit from it. Despite repeated royal legislation, and despite the efforts of English bishops, in particular those who had been close to Simon de Montfort and who now had the ear of King Edward, the restrictions against Jewish lending activities, and against Jewish-Christian fraternization, were not being respected—at least not sufficiently to the tastes of Swinfield, Gravesend, Pecham, and their ilk. Thomas of Cantilupe may have already floated the idea of a general expulsion in 1278: it may well be that Swinfield, Pecham and other bishops were pressuring Edward to expel the Jews from England. And perhaps pressuring parliament to insist on this, even at the cost of a massive new tax.

Nothing indicates that Edward was planning to expel the Jews when he returned to England on 12 August 1289.[84] The Barons had in 1288 refused Edward's plea for new taxation, affirming that the king must make the request to them in person. The mood was not propitious: bishops resented what they saw as royal encroachment on episcopal justice; Londoners reproached the king for the heavy hand of royal bailiffs who did not respect organs of city self-government. Edward needed to repay over £100,000 to the Riccardi, but parliament saw little reason to pay for debts Edward had amassed in Gascony. As late as June 1290, Edward was contemplating a new major tallage on Jews to help pay his debts, despite the fact that they had been unable to come up with £13,333 just three years earlier.

Finally, Edward found a more lucrative way of exploiting his Jews: by selling their expulsion. On 18 July 1290, Edward proclaimed the expulsion of England's Jews. The pretext was their failure to abide by the 1275 statute prohibiting them from making loans at interest. "We," Edward proclaims, "in requital for their crimes and for the honour of the Crucified, have banished them from our realm as traitors."[85] The expulsion was a concession to the commons in order to have them agree to a massive new tax of 1/15 of all moveable lay property.[86] Paul Brand has shown that a series of scandals involving forged documents in which Jewish lenders were implicated may have contributed to the decision.[87] Parliament invoked the interests of knights of the shire indebted to Jews, the same dynamic denounced in the 1258 provisions. In return for the expulsion, Parliament conceded the largest single grant of taxation given to any English medieval king. The decision to expel, it seems, was a consequence of the king's cold political and financial calculation. Yet the pressure from bishops of his entourage and the scandal provoked by the failure of the 1275 restrictions no doubt contributed to the decision.

A Curse upon Edom

Once again, we can only regret the lack of Jewish voices narrating these events, describing the episodes that led to the expulsion and the exodus that followed.

A few English Jews evoked their tribulations, but principally in the form of po-
etic complaints directed to God. A poem preserved in Jacob ben Judah of London's *Etz Hayyim*, probably from 1280s, lamented:

> Those who meditate on Your Torah have become fewer and the syna-
> gogues are abolished
> Be zealous for Your Awesome Name, be zealous for the Sanctuary and
> for the Torah
> See how her students have grown fewer, for want of bread and silver
> Have pity on the people who walk in darkness with no teacher.[88]

The "seed of Edom, contender and foe" is responsible for the decimation. The
tribulations seem above all economic, as it is "want of bread and silver" that has
depleted the synagogues of their students.

It is perhaps then fitting to end this book with the poem by one eloquent
English Jewish poet, Meir ben Elijah of Norwich, "Put a Curse on My Enemy."[89]
His description of the tribulations of England's Jews, of the violence, extortion,
and persecution visited upon them, has been thought by various historians to refer to the events of 1255, to the civil war of 1263–1265, to the coin clipping crisis
of 1278–1279, or to the expulsion of 1290. Indeed, it could refer to any of those,
or to any of a number of tribulations of English Jews in the thirteenth century.

As is often the case in such commemorative poetry in medieval Hebrew, the
descriptions of violence and persecution are general and anonymous: no single
person, either Jew or Christian, is named; no information is given about specific
dates or localities. Meir says that the Jews, "the house of Jacob," have been mocked,
insulted, despoiled, put into prison, almost annihilated. His poem is a curse
hurled against the Jews' enemies, and a reproach to God. "Let their victory
spatter Your garment," he writes, hoping that God will then avenge the insult to
Him. Yet in his dark prison Israel awaits the light. Hope, it seems, is not extin-
guished, but it is a bitter hope. The poet calls not for release from prison or a
return to his former life, but the coming of the messianic age. Whether Meir
was writing before the expulsion edict or after, he seems to realize that he is
witnessing the tragic end of an era. Here is his poem, in the translation by Susan
Einbinder:

> Put a curse on my enemy, for every man supplants his brother.
> When will You say to the house of Jacob, come let us walk in the light?
> *You are mighty and full of light, You turn the darkness into light.*

Tear out their hearts—they who brought harm to those who come in
  Your Name
When I hoped for good, evil arrived, yet I will wait for the light.
You are mighty and full of light, You turn the darkness into light.
The words of the seer are garbled, for the foe has mocked Your
  children
Until they don't know which path is the one that gives off light.
You are mighty and full of light, You turn the darkness into light.
The land exhausts us by demanding payments, and the people's
  disgust is heard
While we are silent and wait for the light.
You are mighty and full of light, You turn the darkness into light.
They make our yoke heavier, they are finishing us off.
They continually say of us, let us despoil them until the morning
  light.
You are mighty and full of light, You turn the darkness into light.
Let their victory spatter Your garment/for Your beloved's heart is
  distressed
But she will be consoled for this; her lord will remain until light.
You are mighty and full of light, You turn the darkness into light.
Have You forgotten to be gracious, My God? When will You gather
  in the camps
Scattered to the corners [of the earth], like infants that have not seen
  the light
You are mighty and full of light, You turn the darkness into light.
Let the King bring home His banished one, let Him smell his savory
  offering.
The foes who make his savor stink will never see the light.
You are mighty and full of light, You turn the darkness into light.
And if You have continued to afflict him [Israel], be abundantly
  merciful, be gracious to him.
For he has despaired of [returning to] his dwelling, and of Your ways
  of radiant light.
You are mighty and full of light, You turn the darkness into light.
The vision of His intimates tarries; the predicted time has passed.
Let their [the enemies'] hold on us weaken, one and all, until the light
  [dawns].
You are mighty and full of light, You turn the darkness into light.

If his vision shall be hidden, with no interpreter for his dreams
Why should the glory of the crown remain with the filthy one until
     the light [comes]
You are mighty and full of light, You turn the darkness into light.
Even if his [Israel's] sins have really enraged [You], why should his
     foes wage war [against him]?
They whose mouths have spoken arrogantly, they are rebels against
     the light.
You are mighty and full of light, You turn the darkness into light.
They scattered him with their horns, but he hoped in hidden
     prophecies
For the men of visions have sealed [themselves] up and do not know
     the light.
You are mighty and full of light, You turn the darkness into light.
Malicious men have cast down his crown, and presumed to annihilate
     him.
They put him in prison, where in twilight he hoped for the light.
You are mighty and full of light, You turn the darkness into light.
Bring near his End to raise him up, before he is lost in his exile,
For they have boasted to annihilate him; they mistake the darkness
     for light.
You are mighty and full of light, You turn the darkness into light.
All his days, he [Israel] has surely hoped; day after day [he awaits]
     consolation.
O Awesome and Mighty One in Heaven, who brings His justice into
     the light
You are mighty and full of light, You turn the darkness into light.
If You have given me unto my enemy, rise up to plead my cause.
Establish the Messiah's reign, [so that] light will be seen in Your light.
You are mighty and full of light, You turn the darkness into light.[90]

CONCLUSION

King Edward I, as we have seen, banished the Jews as "traitors" guilty of "crimes" (*scelera*) against "the Crucified one."[1] Whereas popes, church councils, kings, and princes had often used the words "tamquam servi" ("as servants") to describe the proper relation of Jews toward Christian society, Edward expels them "tamquam perfidos," "as traitors" who have abused their position and refused to respect proper hierarchies.[2]

Yet even in their absence, Jews continued to be useful to Edward to affirm the righteousness and piety of his kingship. We see this in his veneration of Little Hugh of Lincoln. Little Hugh's story may have ended up being an embarrassment for Henry, but it proved useful, it seems, to his son Edward. It is probably in the years following his expulsion of Jews from England in 1290 that Edward had an elaborate shrine built, with finishing touches (including the royal coat of arms) added in the years between 1303 and 1307. This suggests that Little Hugh still attracted pilgrims and was deemed worthy of royal patronage. Perhaps, as David Stocker suggests, Hugh's story was useful to Edward in order to justify and celebrate his expulsion of the Jews, who put Christian children in danger.[3] The story and the cult, as we have seen, were still known to Chaucer at the end of the fourteenth century. Seventeenth-century jurist John Selden affirmed that every year at Easter Jews would "steal a young boy, circumcise him, and, after a solemn judgment, making one of their own nation a Pilate, . . . crucify him out of their devilish malice to Christ and Christians."[4] Little Hugh was never canonized, though the Bollandists in the eighteenth century proclaimed 27 July the feast day of "blessed Hugh" and provided a hagiographical narrative derived from Matthew Paris.[5] In 1641, future bishop Robert Sanderson mentioned the shrine, but mistakenly associated it with St. Hugh the Great (who, as we have seen, was bishop of Lincoln from 1186 to 1200, and who was canonized in 1220). In 1644, during the civil war, Cromwell besieged Lincoln, and parts of the cathedral, apparently including Little Hugh's shrine, were damaged or destroyed. In 1790, during renovation work, the skeleton of a young child was discovered underneath the floor pavement in a lead coffin. A guide book to Lincolnshire published in 1880 mentions Little Hugh's shrine and describes his "barbarous murder" as a sort of vengeance for the persecution Jews suffered.[6] Nineteenth-century anti-Semitic writers, in England as on the Continent, relied on Christian medieval writers' stories of Jewish perfidy and murderous hostility in forging their anti-Semitic tracts, in what Ulrich Wyrwa has described as an "invention of tradition."[7] In the early twentieth century, a brochure directed tourists to the very well into which the boy's body had been thrown—until it was revealed in 1928 that the current owner had himself dug the well in order to attract tourists.[8] In the late nineteenth century, folklorist Francis James Child recorded twenty-one different versions of Little Hugh's story. According to the most prevalent version, Hugh was at play when his ball went over the wall into the yard of his Jewish neighbors. A Jewish girl invited him in to retrieve his ball, enticed him with sweets and "a cherry red as blood"; she then stabbed him and disposed of his body in a well or privy.[9] Lincolnshire philanthropists Ronnie and Joan Forbes founded in 1925 St. Hugh's school, named in honor of the supposed martyr: the school's logo showed a ball going over a brick wall. The story of Little Hugh's martyrdom, the founders insisted, was useful to boys to teach them self-control: one has to be careful of how, where, and with whom one plays. The school finally removed the ball from its logo in 2020, but the wall and the name, in honor of the boy martyr, remain.[10] The Anglican Church removed Hugh's shrine from Lincoln Cathedral in 1955, replacing it with a framed text that reads:

> Trumped up stories of "ritual murders" of Christian boys by Jewish communities were common throughout Europe during the Middle Ages and even much later. These fictions cost many innocent Jews their lives. Lincoln had its own legend and the alleged victim was buried in the Cathedral in the year 1255.

> Such stories do not redound to the credit of Christendom, and so we pray:

> Lord, forgive what we have been,
> amend what we are,
> and direct what we shall be.

In May 2015, members of the British Movement, a white supremacist group, came to Lincoln Cathedral to "revive a tradition of the English Middle Ages." They wanted to venerate Little Hugh at his tomb. A priest met them and explained that Hugh was not a saint and that Jews had not killed him. They retorted that his words and the 1955 plaque were "an abomination and an insult to the memory of Little Saint Hugh."[11] While the body of this imagined victim of Jewish murderers was preserved and venerated, those of the real Jewish victims of Christian murderers were lost and forgotten, absent from English historical consciousness. Hence the surprise and shock, as we saw in the introduction to this book, that Norwich residents expressed when bodies of seventeen of those victims were brought to light in 2004.

By All Saints' Day (1 November) 1290, England was exclusively Christian. Those Jews who had not accepted baptism had left, never to return; there would be no Jews permitted in the kingdom until they were readmitted by Cromwell in 1655. But in many ways Jews remained to haunt English culture, from Chaucer's *Prioress' Tale*, to Shylock in Shakespeare's *The Merchant of Venice*, to Fagin in Dickens's *Oliver Twist*, and beyond.[12] Anti-Semitism has been an all too frequent part of genteel English culture, and a handy explanation for what was wrong with the world, well into the twentieth century—if not the twenty-first. Afraid of communism? It's a plot by Jewish Bolshevists to take control the world. Appalled by capitalist oppression of workers? It's the fault of a clique of Jewish bankers who already control the world. England of course is anything but unique in this: English attitudes and policies toward Jews and Judaism are inexorably intertwined with those of the Continent, in the thirteenth century or the twenty-first.

The history we forget or choose to ignore comes back to haunt us. Which is why it is important for me to show that English Jews, though few in number, were an integral part of English society in the thirteenth century, and that they played a key role in its politics and finance. Yet they were objects of suspicion and jealous control both by the king, who sought to retain exclusive jurisdiction over them, and by the Church who saw the easy, day-to-day interactions between Jews and Christians as potential sources of sexual intimacy, religious doubt, and even apostasy. Anti-Semitism became, in the thirteenth century, an integral part of English culture and English character. And the deliberate exclusion of Jews from English history was a key element of this anti-Semitism. The only way to expunge this anti-Semitism from English culture is to pull it up by the roots, to restore the history of Jews to national English history.

Fortunately, much recent work on English history has done just that. The casual anti-Semitism found in the works of respected English historians as recently as the mid-twentieth century is unimaginable today. The best recent academic work on English history of the twelfth and thirteenth century takes into account the presence of Jews in England, their role in English society, and the exclusionary policies of Church and crown. The footnotes of this book are a testimony to the work of these scholars, without which the current book would not have been possible. A plaque now marks the spot of the Jewish cemetery in Oxford's botanical garden; another marks the place where Deacon Robert was put to death for apostasy in 1222. Visitors to Oxford may now take a Jewish heritage tour, where they will see these sites and visit Merton College, financed through Jewish lending activities.

Yet it is less certain that the average English man's or woman's perception of English history has changed in fundamental ways: knowledge of medieval history is scant and vague, and of the Jews' role in it mostly nonexistent. This was made clear, as we saw in the introduction, in the BBC program about the bodies found in Norwich: few were aware that Jews had lived in their city in the Middle Ages, had played an integral role in its trade and commerce, and had been on various occasions victims of brutal violence. This matters today in England, where anti-Semitism has by no means been fully eradicated, as the controversies in recent years in the Labour Party make clear.

Recent decades have seen lively debates on the links between history, memory, and identity in the United Kingdom, in its former empire, and beyond. Mainstream historical narratives have until recently tended to downplay the key role of empire in the politics, culture, and economy of colonial powers like Britain or France, portraying slavery and colonization as nonessential elements of national historical narratives. Paul Gilroy, in *The Black Atlantic* and other works, has insisted on the central role that slavery played in the making of modern European culture, a role often ignored or minimized in the narration of European achievements of an "age of discoveries" encompassing the Renaissance, Reformation, and Enlightenment.[13] The denizens of Gilroy's *Black Atlantic* are not only victims of slavery and racism; they also are actors in the economies and cultures of empire, through complex combinations of participation and resistance. They also played a key role in active opposition to slavery and in its eventual abolition, which was not merely the gift of enlightened (white) English legislators.

Analogously, medieval England's Jews should be remembered not only as victims of prejudice and violence, but as key actors in the construction of English society. The rich range of sources we have examined show Jews participating fully in English society: traveling across the country, helping finance Oxford colleges or monastic institutions, sending gifts to the king and his advisors, appearing in court to press charges against delinquent debtors, drinking beer with their Christian neighbors, and inviting them to their weddings. Yet at the same time as they fully participate in English society, they do not do so as equals. The merry band of poachers in Colchester in 1267 provides a telling example: Christians and Jews participated together in this illegal romp, but when it came to retribution the Jews' punishment was much more severe.

There has been considerable debate among historians on the origins and nature of medieval anti-Judaism or anti-Semitism: is it an expression of "popular" prejudices, or on the contrary is it the product of Christian elites who seek to marginalize Jews within English (and European) Christian society, to impose and enforce their servile status? Robert Chazan, in describing the anti-Jewish violence in the Rhineland in 1096, during the First Crusade, affirmed that the "element in Northern Europe that was most hostile to the newly arriving Jews was the populace at large." He speaks of the "hostility of the general populace" without giving any evidence.[14] In fact, the massacres of 1096 were not carried out by "the general populace" but by crusaders. The same is true of much of the violence we have seen in these pages, with murders committed principally, it seems, by knights (crusaders during the massacres of 1189–1190, rebels against the king in 1264–1267). Richard Southern attributes Grosseteste's anti-Jewish positions to his "peasant's violence and passion," but it in fact is rather the product of his learned clerical education.[15] We have seen that William Jordan's study of restrictions on Jews selling meat at the market in Béziers suggests that this aspect of medieval religious hatred like so many others was an elitist imposition on popular culture.[16] Throughout this book, we have seen bishops, popes, and other churchmen attempting to restrict Jewish-Christian fraternization and on the whole failing, as English Christians continue to conduct commerce with Jews, to work in their houses as servants, to share meals and festivities with them, and on occasion (and more dangerously) to have sexual relations with them. Simple prohibition failed, and some clerical authors penned lurid stories of Jewish enmity and violence toward Christians, supposedly taught to them in the Talmud, that leads them to trick, lure, cheat, and kill Christians. Crude stories about the supposed ritual murders of William of Norwich, Little Hugh of Lincoln, or Adam of Bristol were insufficient, it seems, to quell such fraternization, and some English bishops pushed Edward to expel the Jews from England, and in the end succeeded.

We live in an age in which, in the United Kingdom, Europe, the United States, and elsewhere, new forms of nationalist demagoguery, based on racist propaganda, rear their ugly heads. These ideologies rely on simplified, sanitized versions of national histories, in which minority groups (such as England's Jews) are deliberately ignored, and the brutal crimes of the state and other actors (such as the violence against English Jews and their expulsion) are consigned to the dustbin of history. For these reasons, it has seemed all the more urgent to me to recount the story told in these pages, so that the Jewish men and women who lived in medieval England can make their voices heard.

NOTES

Principal collections of royal and ecclesiastical sources (with abbreviations used in the notes) are listed at the beginning of the bibliography.

INTRODUCTION

1. BBC, *History Cold Case*, "The Bodies in the Well." https://www.youtube.com/watch?v =nhaEgoKva5g. DNA as a criteria for identifying supposed ethnic or religious groups has been met with some healthy skepticism; see for example Michael Toch, "The Emergence of the Medieval Jewish Diaspora(s) of Europe from the Ninth to the Twelfth Centuries, with Some Thoughts on Historical DNA Studies."

2. Vivian Lipman, *The Jews of Medieval Norwich*; Elizabeth Rutledge, "The Medieval Jews of Norwich and Their Legacy."

3. This at least was true as recently as 2008; see Elisa Narin van Court, "Invisible in Oxford: Medieval Jewish History in Modern England."

4. Robert C. Stacey, "Jewish Lending and the Medieval English Economy"; Rutledge, "The Medieval Jews of Norwich and Their Legacy," 121.

5. Joe Hillaby and Caroline Hillaby, *The Palgrave Dictionary of Medieval Anglo-Jewish History*, 311–12.

6. Stacey, "Jewish Lending and the Medieval English Economy." These amounts in fact varied significantly, as the crown assessed tallages irregularly based on needs and opportunities. Hence (to give a few examples) the crown raised through these tallages: £654 in 1221, £1690 in 1223, and £450 in 1226 (David Carpenter, *The Minority of Henry III*, 414.). These amounts increase significantly in the 1240s (see below, and Robert Stacey, *Politics, Policy, and Finance Under Henry III, 1216–1245*, 206–208.)

7. Cecil Roth, *A History of the Jews in England*, 38–67.

8. Robert C. Stacey, "Jews and Christians in Twelfth-Century England: Some Dynamics of a Changing Relationship," 342; Geraldine Heng, *The Invention of Race in the European Middle Ages*, 64. On the broader use of "tallage" to refer to taxes imposed by kings or lords in medieval England, see Mark Bailey, "Tallage-at-Will in Later Medieval England."

9. F. Powicke, *King Henry III and Lord Edward: The Community of the Realm in the Thirteenth Century*, 310–13.

10. "L'état s'avance masqué, sous le masque de la sainteté," Jacques Le Goff, *Saint Louis*, 701.

11. Jean de Joinville, *Vie de saint Louis*, 30–31.

12. William Chester Jordan, *The Apple of His Eye: Converts from Islam in the Reign of Louis IX.*

13. Cited by Le Goff, *Saint Louis*, 802.

14. Joinville, *Vie de saint Louis*, 26–28.

15. Stacey, "Jewish Lending and the Medieval English Economy," 100. Cited by Heng, *The Invention of Race*, 62.

16. William Chester Jordan, *Ideology and Royal Power in Medieval France*, art. XII, 48.

17. R. I. Moore, *The Formation of a Persecuting Society.*

18. Moore, *The Formation of a Persecuting Society*, 153.

19. *Commentarius cantabrigiensis*, passage translated by Beryl Smalley, *The Study of the Bible in the Middle Ages*, 78. See Moore, *The Formation of a Persecuting Society*, 149–50. Moore, "Anti-Semitism and the Birth of Europe.".

20. Hannah Arendt, *The Origins of Totalitarianism*, 5–8, 29. For a collection of essays on the continuities and discontinuities between medieval and modern European hostility to Jews and Judaism, see Jonathan Adams and Cordelia Hess, eds., *The Medieval Roots of Antisemitism: Continuities and Discontinuities from the Middle Ages to the Present Day.*

21. Cord J. Whitaker, *Black Metaphors: How Modern Racism Emerged from Medieval Race-Thinking*, 181.

22. Whitaker, *Black Metaphors*, 195.

23. Gavin Langmuir, *History, Religion, and Antisemitism*, 276.

24. François Soyer, *Medieval Antisemitism?*

25. Paula Fredriksen, *Augustine and the Jews: A Christian Defense of Jews and Judaism.*

26. Bernhard Blumenkranz, *Juifs et Chrétiens dans le monde occidental 430–1096.*

27. Jeremy Cohen, *The Friars and the Jews: The Evolution of Medieval anti-Judaism.*

28. Anna Sapir Abulafia, "Notions of Jewish Service in Twelfth- and Thirteenth-Century England"; Anna Sapir Abulafia, *Christian-Jewish Relations, 1000–1300: Jews in the Service of Medieval Christendom*; M. Lindsay Kaplan, *Figuring Racism in Medieval Christianity.*

29. Most of these sources are available online: see http://www.medievalgenealogy.org.uk /sources/rolls.shtml. For the fine rolls, see https://finerollshenry3.org.uk/.

30. Michael Clanchy has measured this increase by looking at the consumption of sealing wax. In the early years of Henry's majority (1226–1231), his chancery used an average of 3.63 pounds of wax per week to seal royal documents; by the end of his reign (1265–1271), it was 31.9 pounds per week (Michael Clanchy, *From Memory to Written Record: England 1066–1307*, 59.)

31. Jonathan Ray, "The Jew in the Text: What Christian Charters Tell Us About Medieval Jewish Society," 245.

32. See Paul Brand, introduction to BPR; Hillaby and Hillaby, *The Palgrave Dictionary of Medieval Anglo-Jewish History*, 133–35.

33. Judith Olszowy-Schlanger, ed., *Hebrew and Hebrew-Latin Documents from Medieval England: A Diplomatic and Palaeographical Study*; Ann Causton, ed., *Medieval Jewish Documents in Westminster Abbey.*

34. Lauren Fogle, *The King's Converts: Jewish Conversion in Medieval London*, xi.

35. David Carpenter, *Henry III, 1207–1258*, 170–72; Sophia Menache, "Matthew Paris's Attitudes Toward Anglo-Jewry,"

36. Ruth Nisse, *Jacob's Shipwreck: Diaspora, Translation, and Jewish-Christian Relations in Medieval England*; Hillaby and Hillaby, *The Palgrave Dictionary of Medieval Anglo-Jewish History*, 246–57; Judith Olszowy-Schlanger, *Learning Hebrew in Medieval England: Christian He-*

braists and the Longleat House Grammar; Olszowy-Schlanger, *Hebrew and Hebrew-Latin Documents*.

37. See, for example, the *responsa* of Rabbi Elias Menahem of London, in Hans-Georg von Mutius, ed., *Rechtsentscheide mittelalterlicher englischer Rabbinen*, 67–73. On Rabbi Elias Menahem, see Pinchas Roth and Ethan Zadoff, "The Talmudic Community of Thirteenth-Century England."

38. Susan L. Einbinder, *No Place of Rest: Jewish Literature, Expulsion, and the Memory of Medieval France*, 10. On the historiographical works written in Hebrew in medieval Europe, see Eva Haverkamp, "Historiography."

39. For an overview of this poetry in medieval Europe and its liturgical use, see Elisabeth Hollender, "Piyut."

40. For a survey of Hebrew chronicles in medieval Europe, see Haverkamp, "Historiography."

41. Salo W. Baron, *A Social and Religious History of the Jews*.

42. Salo W. Baron, "Newer Emphases in Jewish History."

43. Elisheva Baumgarten, *Mothers and Children: Jewish Family Life in Medieval Europe*, 193–94.

44. On the absence of such sources for England, see Baumgarten, *Mothers and Children*, 6.

45. Charlotte Newman Goldy, "Teaching Jewish and Christian Daily Interaction in medieval England," 306.

46. Paola Tartakoff, *Conversion, Circumcision, and Ritual Murder in Medieval Europe*, 51.

CHAPTER I

1. Emily Rose, "Royal Power and Ritual Murder: Notes on the Expulsion of the Jews from the Royal Domain of France, 1182"; William Chester Jordan, "Princely Identity and the Jews in Medieval France."

2. Robert Stacey, "Crusades, Martyrdoms, and the Jews of Norman England, 1096–1190"; Rose, "Royal Power and Ritual Murder: Notes on the Expulsion of the Jews from the Royal Domain of France, 1182."

3. Jean Flori, *Richard Cœur de Lion: le roi-chevalier*, 76.

4. "Propter magicas incantationes," Roger of Wendover, *Chronica*, vol. 3, p. 7.

5. "Etas auri reditur | Mundus renovatur | Dives nunc deprimitur | Pauper exaltatur." Christopher Page, *Music for the Lion-Hearted King Music to Commemorate the 800th Anniversary of the Coronation of King Richard I of England in Westminster Abbey, 3 September 1189*. Quotation and translation from the liner notes of the CD, 11.

6. Roger of Wendover says that many Jews came into the church "contra regiam prohibitionem" and that subsequently the royal officers (*curiales*) forcibly expelled them from the church (Roger of Wendover, *Flores historiarum*, vol. 3, 7.). This same version is reproduced by Matthew Paris, *Historia Anglorum*.

7. Roger of Howden, *Gesta Regis Henrici Secundi*, 83–84; idem, *The Annals of Roger of Hoveden*, 119. The *Annales de Margan* briefly mention the massacres in London and in "other cities of England" (RS 36, vol. 1, 20). Brief mention of the London massacres is made in other monastic chronicles: *Annales de Wintonia* (RS 36, vol. 2, 63), *Annales de Dunstapalia* (RS 36, vol. 3, 25), *Annales de Oseneia* and the *Chronicle* of Thomas Wykes (RS 36, vol. 4, 42–3) *Annales de Wigornia*

(RS 36, vol. 4, 387), *Annales de Waverleia* (RS 36 vol. 2, 246; the brief description concludes with "per Omnia benedictus Dominus, qui tradidit impios.")

8. Ralph of Diceto, *Opera Historica*, 69.

9. Robert Chazan, *Church, State, and Jew in the Middle Ages*, 161.

10. Stacey, "Crusades, Martyrdoms, and the Jews of Norman England, 1096–1190," 246.

11. Chazan, *Church, State, and Jew in the Middle Ages*, 161.

12. In fact, Palm Sunday was the following Sunday, 25 March.

13. Ralph of Diceto, *Opera Historica*, 75–76.

14. £1 8s. 7.5d., according to PR 2 Richard I, 1; see Joe Hillaby, "Prelude and Postscript to the York Massacre: Attacks in East Anglia and Lincolnshire, 1190," 45.

15. Hillaby, "Prelude and Postscript to the York Massacre," 45–6, citing PR 5 Henry II, 12.

16. Roger of Howden, *Gesta Regis Henrici* 107–9; Roger of Howden, *Chronica*, 33–34; Roger of Howden, *The Annals of Roger of Hoveden*, 137–38. Cf. Roger of Wendover, who says that after the massacre the "cives et milites" burned the homes of the Jews "cum cartis debitorum, thesaurum eorum sibi retinuerunt" (Roger of Wendover, *Flores historiarum*, 19–20.)

17. Ralph of Coggeshall, *Chronicon Anglicanum*, 27–28.

18. R. B. Dobson, *The Jews of Medieval York and the Massacre of March 1190*; Sarah Rees Jones, "Neighbors and Victims in Twelfth-Century York: A Rayal Citadel, the Citizens, and the Jews of York"; Hugh M. Thomas, *Vassals, Heiresses, Crusaders, and Thugs: The Gentry of Angevin Yorkshire, 1154–1216*, 65–67, 165–67, 181–83.

19. Anna Sapir Abulafia, "The Jews."

20. This is the reading of Heather Blurton, "Egyptian Days: From Passion to Exodus in the Representation of Twelfth-Century Jewish-Christian Relations." See also Michael Kennedy, "'Faith in One God Flowed over You from the Jews, the Sons of the Patriarchs and the Prophets': William of Newburgh's Writings on Anti-Jewish Violence"; John Hosler, "William of Newburgh, Henry II, and the Development of English Anti-Judaism"; Ruth Nisse, *Jacob's Shipwreck*, 25.

21. Nisse, *Jacob's Shipwreck*.

22. Translation by Susan Einbinder, *Beautiful Death*, 165.

23. Nisse, *Jacob's Shipwreck*, 91–92; Moses Hadas, *Fables of Jewish Aesop*, 3–4.

24. Thomas, *Vassals, Heiresses, Crusaders, and Thugs*, 156–67.

25. Hillaby, "Prelude and Postscript to the York Massacre," 49–51.

26. For the Latin edition with facing English translation, see Jocelin of Brakelond, *The Chronicle of Jocelin of Brakelond, Concerning the Acts of Samson, Abbot of the Monastery of St. Edmund*. For a more recent translation with introduction and detailed explicative notes, see Jocelin of Brakelond, *Chronicle of the Abbey of Bury St Edmunds*, trans. Diana Greenway and Jane Sayers.

27. Dobson, *The Jews of Medieval York and the Massacre of March 1190*, 9. Dobson cites Jocelin of Brakelond, *The Chronicle of Jocelin of Brakelond, Concerning the Acts of Samson, Abbot of the Monastery of St. Edmund*, 2.

28. Dobson, *The Jews of Medieval York and the Massacre of March 1190*, 9; Henry Gerald. Richardson, *The English Jewry Under Angevin Kings*, 50–61.

29. Translation from Jocelin of Brakelond, *Chronicle of the Abbey of Bury St Edmunds*, 10.

30. Hillaby and Hillaby, *The Palgrave Dictionary of Medieval Anglo-Jewish History*, 373–74.

31. Dobson, *The Jews of Medieval York and the Massacre of March 1190*.

32. Michael Clanchy explains that cathedrals and monasteries often served as repositories for the safe-keeping of treasure and documents and speculates that Jewish bonds were often kept in churches prior to the 1190 massacre of Jews in York (Clanchy, *From Memory to Written Record*, 166–67).

33. Beryl Smalley, *Hebrew Scholarship Among Christians in XIIIth Century England, as Illustrated by Some Hebrew-Latin Psalters*. Smalley cites M. R. James, *The Abbey of S. Edmund at Bury*, 87. The MS is Bodleian, MS Laud. Orient, 174.

34. Jocelin of Brakelond, *The Chronicle of Jocelin of Brakelond, Concerning the Acts of Samson, Abbot of the Monastery of St. Edmund*, 16; Emily Rose, *The Murder of William of Norwich: The Origins of the Blood Libel in Medieval Europe*, 187–206.

35. Jocelin of Brakelond, *Chronicle of the Abbey of Bury St Edmunds*, 41–42.

36. See Robert Stacey, "The Massacres of 1189–90 and the Origins of the Jewish Exchequer, 1186–1226," =111.

37. Adam of Eynsham, *Magna vita Sancti Hugonis = The Life of St. Hugh of Lincoln*, ed. Decima Douie and David Farmer, vol. 2, 17; Jeffrey Cohen, "The Future of the Jews of York"; Hillaby, "Prelude and Postscript to the York Massacre: Attacks in East Anglia and Lincolnshire, 1190," 48; Blurton, "Egyptian Days," 225–27. The incident is not mentioned by Gerald of Wales, *The Life of St. Hugh of Avalon, Bishop of Lincoln 1186–1200*.

38. Hillaby and Hillaby, *The Palgrave Dictionary of Medieval Anglo-Jewish History*, 204–5.

39. Heng, *The Invention of Race in the European Middle Ages*, 67.

40. Lipman, *The Jews of Medieval Norwich*, 103.

41. HRC, 93; HROF, 133.

42. HLP, 33; Sidney Painter, *The Reign of King John*, 143.

43. H. Summerson, "The 1215 Magna Carta: Clause 10, Academic commentary," *Magna Carta Project*, http://magnacartaresearch.org/read/magna_carta_1215/Clause_10?com=aca accessed 06 April 2020.

44. *Annales de Margan* (RS 36, vol. 1, 29), *Annales de Wintonia* (RS 36, vol. 2, 81), *Annales de Waverleia* (RS 36, vol. 2, 264), *Annales de Dunstapalia* (RS 36, vol. 3, 32), *Annalees de Bermundeseia* (RS 36, vol. 3, 451), *Annales de Oseneia* (RS 36, vol. 4, 54).

45. PR57 129, 233; Sydney Knox Mitchell, *Studies in Taxation Under John and Henry III*, 105.

46. Roger of Wendover, *Flores historiarum*, vol. 3, 231–32; *Lowers of History*, vol. 2, 252–53; Matthew Paris, *Historia Anglorum*, vol. 2, 528.

47. Lipman, *The Jews of Medieval Norwich*, 104.

48. Matthew Paris, *Historia Anglorum*, vol. 2, 531.

49. PR57, 104–5; Lipman, *The Jews of Medieval Norwich*, 104.

50. HRLP, 102.

51. 1 September 1213: *The Charters of Norwich Cathedral Priory*, 25. (no. 39): John grants a house and property in King's Lynn (Lenna/Lynna, in diff MSS) "que fuit Isaac Judei de Norwico" to Radulpho de Karleolo, nuntio romano.

52. David Carpenter, *Magna Carta*, 169.

53. Ralph of Coggeshall, *Chronicon Anglicanum*, 171–72. Latin text and English translation by Nicholas Vincent, Feature of the Month: May 2015—The Rebel Seizure of London, 17 May 1215," *Magna Carta Project*, https://magnacarta.cmp.uea.ac.uk/read/feature_of_the_month/May_2015.

54. PR HIII 1216–25, 59–60; Nicholas Vincent, *Peter Des Roches: An Alien in English Politics, 1205–1238*, 130.

55. Walter of Coventry, *Memoriale Fratris Walteri de Coventria*, 219. On John's vow, see Christopher Tyerman, *England and the Crusades, 1095–1588*, 134; Christopher R. Cheney, "The Eve of Magna Carta," in *The Papacy and England, 12th-14th Centuries. Historical and Legal Studies*, ed. Christopher R. Cheney, vol. 154, Collected Studies, 313.

56. Latin text and English translation in "The 1215 Magna Carta: Clause 10," *Magna Carta Project*, trans. H. Summerson et al., http://magnacartaresearch.org/read/magna_carta_1215

/Clause_10 accessed 06 April 2020; "The 1215 Magna Carta: Clause 11," *Magna Carta Project*, trans. H. Summerson et al., http://magnacarta.cmp.uea.ac.uk/read/magna_carta_1215/Clause_11 accessed 05 April 2020. Latin text and English translation are also found in Carpenter, *Magna Carta*, 42–43. See also Carpenter, *Magna Carta*, 115–17.

57. Carpenter, *Magna Carta*, 207, 211–12.

58. H. Summerson, "The 1215 Magna Carta: Clause 10, Academic commentary," *Magna Carta Project*, http://magnacartaresearch.org/read/magna_carta_1215/Clause_10?com=aca accessed 06 April 2020.

59. Simon D. Lloyd, "'Political Crusades' in England, c. 1215–17 and c. 1263–5," 115.

60. Lloyd, "'Political Crusades' in England"; Gaufridus de Vinsauf, *Poetria Nova*, ll. 2090–1; Jennifer Jahner, *Literature and Law in the Era of Magna Carta*, 62–63, 79.

61. Clanchy, *From Memory to Written Record*, 315.

62. Roger of Wendover, *Flores historiarum*, vol. 3, 301.

63. See Carpenter, *The Minority of Henry III*; Carpenter, *Henry III, 1207–1258*.

64. Lloyd, "'Political Crusades' in England."

65. David Carpenter, "Historical Introduction" to *Magna Carta Project*, https://magnacartaresearch.org/about/historical_intro. See Stacey, *Politics, Policy, and Finance under Henry III, 1216–1245*, 1987, 3–9; Carpenter, *Magna Carta*.

66. "Litteras habet de conductu sine termino," *PR HIII 1216–1225*, 95.

67. *PR HIII 1216–1225*, 98.

68. HRLC, vol. 1, p. 342.

69. HRLC, vol. 1, 180. According to Nicholas Vincent, "As late as December 1221, des Roches was still supervising the collection of Isaac's fine at the Exchequer. Subsequently, he was to authorize the first of several writs by which Isaac's liabilities were reduced from 365 marks a year to 250 marks, 200 marks and eventually by 1226 to £100." Vincent, *Peter Des Roches*, 179.

70. Latin text, English translation and commentary at Notice n°254389, RELMIN project, http://www.cn-telma.fr/relmin/extrait254389/.

71. Latin text in ERF vol. 1, 12; English summary at Henry III, Fine Rolls 2/104 (31 May 1218), http://www.finerollshenry3.org.uk/home.html.

72. Lloyd, "'Political Crusades' in England, c. 1215–17 and c. 1263–5."

73. Tyerman, *England and the Crusades*, 97–99.

74. HRLC vol. 1, 354.

75. HRLC vol. 1, 357, 359.

76. *The Annals of Dunstable Priory*, 31.

77. On this sense of the word *communa*, see R. E. Latham, D. R. Howlett, and Richard Ashdowne, *Dictionary of Medieval Latin from British Sources*, 397–98. (esp. definition 5).

78. PR HIII 1216–25, 157. See D'Blossiers Tovey, *Anglia Judaica*, 78–79. Reedition with translation of documents: D'Blossiers Tovey and Elizabeth Pearl, *Anglia Judaica or a History of the Jews in England*. Joe and Caroline Hillaby see this mandate as evidence that English bishops were trying to limit Jewish lending activities in accordance with Lateran IV, canon 67 (which is discussed in Chapter 2); see Hillaby and Hillaby, *The Palgrave Dictionary of Medieval Anglo-Jewish History*, 334.

79. Joe Hillaby, "Hereford Gold: Irish, Welsh and English Land, Part 2. The Clients of the Jewish Community of Hereford, 1179–1253: Four Case Studies." Hillaby's article is the second of a three-part series on the Jews of medieval Hereford. See Joe Hillaby, "Hereford Gold: Irish, Welsh and English Land. The Jewish Community at Hereford and Its Clients, 1179–1253. Part I"; Joe Hil-

laby, "The Hereford Jewry, 1179–1290 (Third and Final Part). Aaron Le Blund and the Last Decades of the Hereford Jewry, 1253–90."

80. Ian Blair et al., "The Discovery of Two Medieval *Mikva'ot* in London and a Reinterpretation of the Bristol *'Mikveh,'*" 16.

81. Richardson, *The English Jewry Under Angevin Kings*, 285–92; Olszowy-Schlanger, *Hebrew and Hebrew-Latin Documents*, 630–31.

82. For a description of the Day Book, see Lipman, *The Jews of Medieval Norwich*, 84–86. For the edition of the Latin text, see 187–225.

83. *The Charters of Norwich Cathedral Priory*, 241 (no. 381).

84. The best recent introduction to the subject is Paul Brand's introduction to BPR.

85. Rigg, ed., *Calendar of the Plea Rolls of the Exchequer of the Jews*, 2. Latin text in Henry Cole, *Documents Illustrative of English History in the Thirteenth and Fourteenth Centuries*, 286.

86. Rigg, *Calendar of the Plea Rolls*, vol. 1, 7. Latin text in Cole, *Documents*, 294.

87. Rigg, *Calendar of the Plea Rolls*, vol. 1, 18. Latin text in Cole, *Documents*, 301.

88. Walter Shirley, *Royal and Other Historical Letters Illustrative of the Reign of Henry III*, 35–36. On this letter see Richardson, *The English Jewry under Angevin Kings*, 183–84; Vincent, *Peter Des Roches*, 178.

89. Latin text and English translation in James Rigg, *Select Pleas, Starrs, and Other Records from the Rolls of the Exchequer of the Jews 1220–1284*. Cf. Rigg, *Calendar of the Plea Rolls*, vol. 1, 22, 26. Latin text in Cole, *Documents*, 304–5, 307–8.

90. Rigg, *Calendar of the Plea Rolls*, vol. 1, 40. Latin text in Cole, *Documents*, 320.

91. Rigg, *Calendar of the Plea Rolls*, vol. 1, 18, 23–24, 26. Latin text in Cole, *Documents*, 301, 306–7.

92. Rigg, *Calendar of the Plea Rolls*, vol. 1, 13; 15–16; Cole, *Documents*, 286.

93. Hillaby and Hillaby, *The Palgrave Dictionary of Medieval Anglo-Jewish History*, 214.

94. Rigg, *Calendar of the Plea Rolls*, vol. 1, 35–47; Cole, *Documents*, 317–26.

95. Many of these documents, in Latin and Hebrew, are edited in Olszowy-Schlanger, *Hebrew and Hebrew-Latin Documents*.

96. Lipman, *The Jews of Medieval Norwich*, 187–225.

97. The house now lacks its original turret and is probably smaller than it once was. See Hillaby and Hillaby, *The Palgrave Dictionary of Medieval Anglo-Jewish History*, 170–72, 402–403.

98. Rigg, *Calendar of the Plea Rolls*, vol. 1, 42–43, 45, 50–51, 55; Cole, *Documents*, 322, 324, 328–29.

99. Rigg, *Calendar of the Plea Rolls*, vol. 1, 39; Cole, *Documents*, 320.

100. I have been unable to identify the other two. Alexander of Dorset appears in two other documents in the plea rolls for 1220; see Rigg, *Calendar of the Plea Rolls*, vol. 1, 36, 43; Cole, *Documents*, 317, 323.

101. PR HIII 1216–25, 498.

102. On the standard procedure for assessing and levying tallages, see the introduction to BPR.

103. There are 1,032 days between 21 June 1218 and 18 April 1221, whereas the payment of £604 equals 906 marks. The receipt is recorded in PR 64, 59.

104. Entry 6/49, https://finerollshenry3.org.uk/content/calendar/roll_016.html#ito49_008.

105. See RR, entry 5156 (6 Henry III, Easter 1222): "De Isaac de Norewich' lx (li) s. viij d. de fine suo."

106. Vincent, *Peter Des Roches*, 179, citing Winchester, Hampshire Record Office ms. Eccl. II 159278 pipe roll for the year 19 Des Roches, Michaelmas 1223–4, m. 12.

107. An entry dated 1 May 1225 in the fine rolls reads: "Norfolk. The king has granted to Isaac of Norwich, Jew, that, of the 200 m. he used to render each year of the fine that he made with King John, he may render £100 to the king each year for as long as it pleases the king. Order to the justices assigned to the custody of the Jews to cause this to be done and enrolled thus." Fine Rolls 9/181, https://finerollshenry3.org.uk/content/calendar/roll_022.html#it181_001.

108. Lipman, *The Jews of Medieval Norwich*, 107. For documents dealing with the transfer of debts from Isaac to his sons in the 1230s, see Olszowy-Schlanger, *Hebrew and Hebrew-Latin Documents*, esp. documents 114, 133, 135, 137.

109. Hannah Meyer, "Female Moneylending and Wet-Nursing in Jewish-Christian Relations in Thirteenth-Century England," 66–72.

CHAPTER 2

1. Tartakoff, *Conversion, Circumcision, and Ritual Murder in Medieval Europe*, 24–28. Conversion from Christianity to Judaism was rare but not unheard of: Tartakoff records about forty cases in Christian Europe during the thirteenth and fourteenth centuries (Tartakoff, *Conversion, Circumcision, and Ritual Murder in Medieval Europe*, 70–71).

2. Alexander III, *Non sine multa admiratione*, text, translation, commentary and bibliography at http://www.cn-telma.fr/relmin/extrait252637/, text from *Sacrosancta Concilia Ad Regiam Editionem Exacta: Quae Nunc Quarta Parte Prodit Auctior. Ab anno MLXXIII. ad annum MCX-CVII*, 1641.

3. *Docs. English Church*, 965–993. Pamela Patton, "Blackness, Whiteness, and the Idea of Race in Medieval European Art." On this council, see the entries from the RELMIN database: http://www.cn-telma.fr/relmin/auteur8701/ and http://www.cn-telma.fr/relmin/extrait252631/.

4. Mary Cheney, "The Council of Westminster 1175: New Light on an Old Source.".

5. Jesse Sherwood, "Alexander III, *Sicut Iudeis*," Notice n° 103877, RELMIN project, http://www.cn-telma.fr/relmin/extrait103877/.

6. Jesse Sherwood, "Alexander III: Qui super his," Notice n°103881, RELMIN project, http://www.cn-telma.fr/relmin/extrait103881/.

7. Luca Fois, "Alexander III, *Consuluit nos*," Notice n°272745, RELMIN project, http://www.cn-telma.fr/relmin/extrait272745/.

8. Jesse Sherwood, "Concilium Lateranense III [c. 26: Iudaei sive Sarraceni]," Notice n°1097, RELMIN project, http://www.cn-telma.fr/relmin/extrait1097/.

9. John Tolan, "Of Milk and Blood: Innocent III and the Jews, Revisited."

10. Translated by Synan, *The Popes and the Jews in the Middle Ages*, 230.

11. Translated by Synan, *The Popes and the Jews in the Middle Ages*, 232.

12. For the full Latin text of the bull, with English and French translations, commentary and bibliography, see John Tolan, "Etsi non displiceat Domino," Notice n° 30385, RELMIN project, http://www.cn-telma.fr/relmin/extrait30385/.

13. Tolan, "Of Milk and Blood: Innocent III and the Jews, Revisited." Jordan, *Ideology and Royal Power in Medieval France: Kingship, Crusades and the Jews*, article XII. The evidence concerning Norwich is from the reign of Edward I, but concerns a practice that seems in context to have been common. See Rutledge, "The Medieval Jews of Norwich and Their Legacy," 123; William Hudson, ed., *Leet Jurisdiction in the City of Norwich: During the 13th and 14th Centuries*, xcv, 6, 28.

14. See John Tolan, "Etsi Iudeos," Notice n° 30352, RELMIN project, http://www.cn-telma.fr/relmin/extrait30352/. See also Kaplan, *Figuring Racism in Medieval Christianity*, 35–50.

15. See John Tolan, "Ut esset Cain," Notice n° 30493, RELMIN project, http://www.cn-telma.fr/relmin/extrait30493/.

16. Fredriksen, *Augustine and the Jews*, 260–89.

17. Jack Watt, "Parisian Theologians and the Jews: Peter Lombard and Peter Cantor."

18. Tolan, "Of Milk and Blood."

19. Baumgarten, *Mothers and Children*, chap. 4.

20. For an excellent introduction to Langton and his career, see Nicholas Vincent, "Stephen Langton, Archbishop of Canterbury." For a fuller biography see Daniel Baumann, *Stephen Langton Erzbischof von Canterbury im England der Magna Carta (1207–1228)*.

21. John Baldwin, "Master Stephen Langton, Future Archbishop of Canterbury: The Paris Schools and *Magna Carta*."

22. Gilbert Dahan, "Exégèse et polémique dans les commentaires de Genèse d'Etienne Langton." On the figure of Hagar, see Deeana Copeland Klepper, "Historicizing Allegory: The Jew as Hagar in Medieval Christian Text and Image."

23. See Chapter 4, and Beryl Smalley, *The Study of the Bible in the Middle Ages*.

24. Dahan, "Exégèse et polémique."

25. Translation slightly modified from that of Watt, "Parisian Theologians and the Jews: Peter Lombard and Peter Cantor." Latin text in Gilbert Dahan, "L'exégèse de l'histoire de Caïn et Abel du XIIe au XIVe siècle en Occident: Textes."

26. Gilbert Dahan, "L'article Iudei de la Summa Abel de Pierre le Chantre"; Watt, "Parisian Theologians and the Jews: Peter Lombard and Peter Cantor," 72.

27. Eton college MS 130, f 92ff; analysis and edition of prologue in Richard Hunt, "The Disputation of Peter of Cornwall Against Symon the Jew"; M. R. James, *A Descriptive Catalogue of the Manuscripts in the Library of Eton College*, 60. On this text, see Alex J. Novikoff, *The Medieval Culture of Disputation: Pedagogy, Practice, and Performance*, 188–90; Peter of Cornwall, *Peter of Cornwall's Book of Revelations*, 16–18.

28. David D'Avray, "Magna Carta: Its Background in Stephen Langton's Academic Biblical Exegesis and Its Episcopal Reception"; Natalie Fryde, "The Roots of the Magna Carta: Opposition to the Plantagenets"; Carpenter, *Magna Carta*.

29. Matthew Paris, *Historia Anglorum*, vol. 2, 550–54; Jahner, *Literature and Law in the Era of Magna Carta*, 104–7.

30. F. Powicke, "The Bull *Miramur Plurimum* and a Letter to Archbishop Stephen Langton"; Vincent, *Peter Des Roches*, 88,125.

31. Philippa Hoskin, *Robert Grosseteste and the 13th-Century Diocese of Lincoln: An English Bishop's Pastoral Vision*, 36.

32. Lateran IV, canon 67, translation by Jessie Sherwood, Notice n°30315, RELMIN project, http://www.cn-telma.fr/relmin/extrait30315/.

33. Translation revised from that of Jessie Sherwood, http://www.cn-telma.fr/relmin/extrait30326/. See also the Latin text and English translation in the appendix to Marie-Thérèse Champagne and Irven M. Resnick, eds., *Jews and Muslims under the Fourth Lateran Council.*.

34. Its sole predecessor was a canon issued at the Council of Nablus in 1120, which forbade Muslims from dressing like "Franks" in the Crusader kingdom. See Concilium Neapolitanum (Capitulum XVI), ed. Adam Bishop, http://www.cn-telma.fr/relmin/extrait40871/. See Ryan Szpiech, "Saracens and Church Councils, from Nablus (1120) to Vienne (1313–14)."

35. King Henry III of England, "Mandate Imposing the Badge on Jews," in HRLC, vol. 1, 378. For text, translation and analysis, see http://www.cn-telma.fr/relmin/extrait252108/.

36. Guala Bicchieri, *The Letters and Charters of Cardinal Guala Bicchieri.*

37. Carpenter, *The Minority of Henry III*, 13.

38. Although, as Nicholas Vincent notes, "there is no direct evidence that Guala played any part in this decision," Guala Bicchieri, *Letters and Charters.*

39. *Councils & Synods*, vol. 2, 52–57. For text, translation and commentary see John Tolan, "Statutes of Bishop William de Blois for the diocese of Worcester," http://www.cn-telma.fr/relmin /extrait252636/.

40. Vincent, *Peter Des Roches*, 172–77.

41. Sophie Thérèse Ambler, *Bishops in the Political Community of England, 1213–1272*, 20; Carpenter, *Henry III, 1207–1258*, 17–19.

42. Carpenter, *The Minority of Henry III*, 228, 254.

43. For the Latin text, translation and commentary on these receipt roll entries, see John Tolan, "De tabula non portanda," http://www.cn-telma.fr/relmin/extrait268769/. Latin text from RR.

44. Henry Richardson, *The English Jewry Under the Angevin Kings*, 178–92.

45. Cecil Roth, *The Jews of Medieval Oxford.*

46. Text and translation from John Tolan, "Cum in generali consilio," http://www.cn-telma .fr/relmin/extrait251655/.

47. Nicholas Vincent, "Two Papal Letters on the Wearing of the Jewish Badge, 1221 and 1229."

48. The royal mandate, dated 25 March 1222, says that these Jews had been arrested "propter ludum quem fecerunt in opprobrium fidis Christiane," HRLC, vol. 1, 491. Robert Stacey suggests that this may have been part of Purim celebration, but in 1222 Purim (14 Adar) fell on 27 March, according to http://www.cgsf.org/dbeattie/calendar/?hebrew=4982. Easter Sunday was 3 April. Robert C. Stacey, "The Conversion of Jews to Christianity in Thirteenth-Century England."

49. On the Oxford Council, see Baumann, *Stephen Langton Erzbischof von Canterbury*, 304–12; Christopher Cheney, "Legislation of the Medieval English Church"; Jane E. Sayers, *Papal Government and England During the Pontificate of Honorius III (1216–1227).*

50. Matthew Paris, *Historia Anglorum*, vol. 2, 254. Translation slightly modified from that given by F. Maitland, "The Deacon and the Jewess; or, Apostasy at Common Law," 269. See Elliot Horowitz, "The Jews and the Cross in the Middle Ages: Towards a Reappraisal."

51. See Maitland, "The Deacon and the Jewess." For the chronicles that mention this, see Ralph of Coggeshall, *Chronicon Anglicanum*, 191; *The Annals of Dunstable Priory*, 46.

52. Tartakoff, *Conversion, Circumcision, and Ritual Murder in Medieval Europe*, 33.

53. *Concilium Oxoniensis*, canon 46, text and translation online (http://www.cn-telma.fr /relmin/extrait246618/); Latin text from *Councils & Synods*, vol. 2, 118–19.

54. *Concilium Oxoniensis*, canon 47, text and translation online (http://www.cn-telma.fr /relmin/extrait246619/); text *Councils & Synods*, vol. 2, 121.

55. The badge was not a "yellow star" as claimed by van Court, "Invisible in Oxford," 6.

56. Carpenter, *The Minority of Henry III*, 279–97; Carpenter, *Henry III*, 25–29.

57. Text and translation from: Ostenderunt nobis Judaei nostri Lincolniae, ed. John Tolan, http://www.cn-telma.fr/relmin/extrait254390/.

58. For text, translation and commentary, see John Tolan, "Ex parte venerabilis fratris nostri Wigorniensis episcopi," http://www.cn-telma.fr/relmin/extrait251656/. Latin text from Vincent, "Two Papal Letters on the Wearing of the Jewish Badge, 1221 and 1229," 220–21.

59. "Pro Judeis. Mandatum est vicecomitibus London' quod, non obstante aliqua inhibicione quam London' episcopus vel aliquis ordinaries fecerit in civitate London' ne victualia vendantur Judeis regis, vendi faciant per totam civitatem predictam eisdem Judeis victualia quibus opus habuerint, sicut prius fieri solet. Teste rege apud Westm' xvij die Decembris [1245]." Latin text from CR 1242–47, 378.

60. See R. Franklin, "Basset, Fulk (d. 1259)," in *Oxford Dictionary of National Biography Online*.

CHAPTER 3

1. Matthew Paris, *Chronica Majora*, vol. 3, 194; Roger of Wendover, *Flowers of History*, 534.

2. Robert C. Stacey, "1240–60: A Watershed in Anglo-Jewish Relations?," 136.

3. William Chester Jordan, "Princely Identity and the Jews in Medieval France."

4. There are numerous studies on Simon, most recently Sophie Thérèse Ambler, *The Song of Simon de Montfort: England's First Revolutionary and the Death of Chivalry.*

5. Dominique Paladilhe, *Simon de Montfort et le drame cathare*, 26–27; G. E. M. Lippiatt, *Simon V of Montfort and Baronial Government, 1195–1218*, 19–25.

6. Monique Zerner, "L'épouse de Simon de Montfort et la croisade albigeoise," 461–62; Lippiatt, *Simon V of Montfort and Baronial Government, 1195–1218*, 90–91, 201–2.

7. Léonce de Bellesrives, *Une Famille de héros, ou Histoire des personnages qui ont illustré le nom de Montmorenci*, 24.

8. Latin text, English translation and commentary by J. Tolan at Notice n°251645, RELMIN project, http://www.cn-telma.fr/relmin/extrait251645/.

9. Hillaby and Hillaby, *The Palgrave Dictionary of Medieval Anglo-Jewish History*, 197.

10. HRLC vol. 2, 123.

11. Robert Grosseteste, *The Letters of Robert Grosseteste,* letter 5. On this letter, see John A. Watt, "The Jews, the Law, and the Church: The Concept of Jewish Serfdom in Thirteenth-Century England"; John Watt, "Grosseteste and the Jews: A Commentary on Letter V"; Joseph Goering, "Robert Grosseteste and the Jews of Leicester"; Oliver Harris, "Jews, Jurats and the Jewry Wall: A Name in Context"; Nicholas Vincent, "Jews, Poitevins and the Bishop of Winchester, 1231–34"; Jahner, *Literature and Law in the Era of Magna Carta*, 153–61.

12. On the basis of no evidence, Mark Elliot affirms "There is some evidence from the year 1231 that Grosseteste managed to assuage de Montfort's fury so that the Leicester decree of that year was not vigorously enforced," Mark Elliott, "Robert Grosseteste, the Jews, and the *De Cessatione Legalium*," 318. Richard Southern on the contrary suggests that Grosseteste was favorable to Simon's expulsion and castigated Margaret for accepting the expelled Jews; Richard Southern, *Robert Grosseteste: The Growth of an English Mind in Medieval Europe*, 246. Ruth Nisse follows Southern and hence misreads Grosseteste's letter (Ruth Nisse, *Jacob's Shipwreck*, 112.)

13. William Chester Jordan, *The French Monarchy and the Jews*, 94–98.

14. Robert Chazan, *Medieval Jewry in Northern France*, 104–8; Gavin Langmuir, "'Judei Nostri' and the Beginning of Capetian Legislation."

15. Joseph Avril, *Les conciles de la province de Tours = Concilia provinciae turonensis: (saec. XIII-XV)*, 130–31; Tartakoff, *Conversion, Circumcision, and Ritual Murder in Medieval Europe*, 24–25, 32.

16. Alexandre Teulet, ed., *Layettes du trésor des chartes: de l'année 1224 à l'année 1246*, 192–93; Jordan, *The French Monarchy and the Jews*, 1989, 131–34.

17. CR 1231–34, 18–19, 79, 122; CRR 14, sec. 1974. See John Maddicott, *Simon de Montfort*, 15–16; Nicholas Vincent, "Simon de Montfort's First Quarrel with King Henry III."

18. See Chapters 4 and 6, and Maddicott, *Simon de Montfort*, 1994, 33; 56–58.

19. See Fogle, *The King's Converts*. For the full Latin text of the foundation charter, see Tolan, "Royal Policy and Conversion of Jews to Christianity in Thirteenth-Century Europe," 108–9.

20. CR 1231–34, 37.

21. CR 1231–34, 77, 346, 380, 383, 415, 440, 441, 469, 494, 499; Michael Adler, *Jews of Medieval England*, 283.

22. Cal Ch R 1, 199; Fogle, *The King's Converts*, 83–84.

23. Fogle, *The King's Converts*, 86.

24. Cal Ch R 1, 283, 336; Fogle, *The King's Converts*, 90.

25. The king's writ orders that the money shall be used to buy lands for the maintenance of the Conversi. CR 27 Hen. III, m. 9, quoted by Tovey, *Anglia Judaica*, 115.

26. CR 41 H III.

27. Carpenter, *Henry III, 1207–1258*, 110.

28. "Circa idem tempus rex Angliae Henricus quandam decentem ecclesiam et congregationi conventuali sufficientem, cum quibusdam aedificiis adjacentibus, propriis sumptibus fabricavit in loco ubi domum Conversorum, pro redemptione animae suae et regis Johannis patris sui et omnium antecessorum suorum, constituit anno regni sui decimo septimo, videlicet Londoniis, haud procul a Veteri Templo; Ad quam domum confugientes Judaei conversi, relicta Judaismi caecitate, sub quadam honesta vivendi regula certum haberent in tota vita sua domicilium, tutum refugium, et sufficiens vitae sustentamentum, sine servili labore et foenoris emolumento. Unde factum est, quod in brevi congregates est ibidem conversorum numerus copiosus; et ibidem baptizati et Christianorum lege instructi, vivent laudabiliter, period rectore ad hoc specialiter deputato gubernati." Matthew Paris, *Chronica Majora*, vol. 3, 362. Translation by C. Trice Martin, "The Domus Conversorum," 16–17.

29. Nicolas Vincent, "Mauclerk, Walter (d. 1248), Bishop of Carlisle," in *Oxford Dictionary of National Biography Online*.

30. CR 1231–34, 415, 503.

31. Fogle, *The King's Converts*, 102.

32. Adler, *Jews of Medieval England*, 299.

33. Joan G. Greatrex, "Monastic Charity for Jewish Converts: The Requisition of Corrodies by Henry III"; David Carpenter, "Crucifixion and Conversion: King Henry III and the Jews in 1255," 140–42; Fogle, *The King's Converts*, 132–34.

34. Cal PR 1272–81, 371–72. Text given in extenso in Tolan, "Royal Policy and Conversion of Jews to Christianity in Thirteenth-Century Europe," 109–10. See Fogle, *The King's Converts*, 99–101.

35. See Tolan, "Royal Policy and Conversion of Jews to Christianity in Thirteenth-Century Europe."

36. Latin text, English translation and commentary by Jessie Sherwood, Notice n°1097, RELMIN project, http://www.cn-telma.fr/relmin/extrait1097/. John A. Watt, "Jews and Christians in the Gregorian Decretals," 98.

37. CR 1234–37, 264, 358; Stacey, "The Conversion of Jews to Christianity in Thirteenth-Century England," 279–80; Tartakoff, *Conversion, Circumcision, and Ritual Murder in Medieval Europe*, 131, 135.

38. Tartakoff, *Conversion, Circumcision, and Ritual Murder in Medieval Europe*, 136.

39. Robert C. Stacey, "The Conversion of Jews to Christianity in Thirteenth-Century England," 269.

40. In this I concur with the assessment of with Robert Dales and Edward King: "Upon closer scrutiny, then, Henry's policies with regard to Jews are seen to have been essentially contradictory. It is highly dubious, on pragmatic grounds, that the king would have initiated a wide-ranging programme to convert the Jews of England. His foundation of the *domus conversorum* may more reasonably be seen as a matter of necessity on the one hand and of a defensive Christian mentality on the other, both served by a public act of traditional piety which, at the same time, may have eased his conscience." Dales and King, introduction to Robert Grosseteste, *De Cessatione Legalium*, xi–xii.

41. On this text, see Hillaby and Hillaby, *The Palgrave Dictionary of Medieval Anglo-Jewish History*, 26; Causton, *Medieval Jewish Documents in Westminster Abbey*, secs. 81, 197.

42. On the increasing use of chirographs in thirteenth-century England, see Clanchy, *From Memory to Written Record*, 87–88.

43. Hillaby and Hillaby, *The Palgrave Dictionary of Medieval Anglo-Jewish History*, 179–80.

44. Carpenter, *Henry III, 1207–1258*, chap. 3.

45. N. Vincent, "Jews, Poitevins, and the Bishop of Winchester, 1231–34"; Vincent, *Peter des Roches*, 363–65.

46. Carpenter, *Henry III, 1207–1258*, 148.

47. For England, see Cal Ch R 1, 163. For Ireland, see Anna Matheson, Notice n°254588, RELMIN project, http://www.cn-telma.fr/relmin/extrait254588/.

48. "Ad computandum impiger / Piger ad Evangelium . . . Sic lucrum Lucam superat, / Marco marcam praeponderat," says the anonymous poet of the *Planctus super episcopis* in Thomas Wright, *The Political Songs of England: From the Reign of John to that of Edward II*, 6–9. Translation by Jahner, *Literature and Law in the Era of Magna Carta*, 92n.

49. PR HIII 1225–32, 453; Lipman, *The Jews of Medieval Norwich*, 105.

50. CFR 18/157 (10 February 1234), https://finerollshenry3.org.uk/content/calendar/roll_033 .html.

51. CR 1231–34, 571; Lipman, *The Jews of Medieval Norwich*, 105.

52. Sara Lipton, "Isaac and Antichrist in the Archives."

53. See John Tolan, "Henry III: Receipt rolls," Notice n°268769, RELMIN project, http://www.cn-telma.fr//relmin/extrait268769/.

54. Tartakoff, *Conversion, Circumcision, and Ritual Murder in Medieval Europe*, 3–4, 141–42.

55. See for example the crowned three-face Antichrist in the *Bible Moralisée*, British Library Harley MS 1527, fol. 127r (mid-thirteenth century). See Bernard McGinn, *Antichrist: Two Thousand Years of the Human Fascination with Evil*, 147–48 (fig. 9); Debra Higgs Strickland, *Saracens, Demons, & Jews: Making Monsters in Medieval Art*, 218.

56. Lipton, "Isaac and Antichrist in the Archives," 25–26.

57. Vincent, "Jews, Poitevins and the Bishop of Winchester, 1231–34." CRR 15, 257–58; Michael Adler, "The Testimony of the London Jewry Against the Ministers of Henry III."

58. Roth, *A History of the Jews in England*, 58.

59. CR 1231–34, 466.

60. CR 1231–34, 515–16.

61. CR 1234–37, 20.

62. CR 1234–37, 13–14. See John A. Watt, "The English Episcopate, the State and the Jews: The Evidence of the Thirteenth-Century Conciliar Decrees," 142.

63. CR 1234–37, 13.

64. CFR, https://finerollshenry3.org.uk/content/calendar/roll_034.html#it007_016.

65. Lipman, *The Jews of Medieval Norwich*, 59–64.

66. Matthew Paris, *Chronica Majora*, vol. 3, 305–6; Roger of Wendover, *Flowers of History*, 602. See Tartakoff, *Conversion, Circumcision, and Ritual Murder in Medieval Europe*, 58–67.

67. Robert C. Stacey, *Politics, Policy, and Finance under Henry III*, 42–43; Nicholas Vincent, *Peter Des Roches*, 474–75; Carpenter, *Henry III, 1207–1258*, 172–75.

68. CFR, http://www.finerollshenry3.org.uk/content/calendar/roll_005E.html#ito90_001. Lipman, *The Jews of Medieval Norwich*, 104–5.

69. Latin text and English translation in Solomon Grayzel, ed., *The Church and the Jews in the XIIIth Century: A Study of Their Relations During the Years 1198–1254*, vol. 1, 200–203.

70. Matthew Paris, *Chronica Majora*, vol. 3, 309; Roger of Wendover, *Flowers of History*, 603.

71. Hillaby and Hillaby, *The Palgrave Dictionary of Medieval Anglo-Jewish History*, 226.

72. Avril, *Les conciles de la province de Tours*, 158–59. J. Tolan, "Concilium turonensis [canon 2]," Notice n°137043, RELMIN project, http://www.cn-telma.fr/relmin/extrait137043/.

73. J. Tolan, "Lachrymabilem Judeorum," Notice n°238137, RELMIN project, http://www.cn-telma.fr/relmin/extrait238137/. See John Tolan, "Lachrymabilem judeorum questionem: la brève histoire de la communauté juive de Bretagne au XIIIe siècle."

74. The poem, which may refer to the 1236 events, is edited and translated into German by Siegmund Salfeld, *Das Martyrologium Des Nürnberger Memorbuches*, 352–58. See Einbinder, *Beautiful Death*, 73.

75. Tolan, "Lachrymabilem judeorum questionem."

76. Matthew says that the massacres happened "in partibus transmarinis, præcipue in Hispania," but in fact the massacres of Jews in 1236 were principally in Brittany, the Poitou and Anjou. Matthew Paris, *Chronica Majora*, vol. 3, 369; Matthew Paris, *English History*, 34.

CHAPTER 4

1. Roth, *The Jews of Medieval Oxford*, 86.

2. Roth, *The Jews of Medieval Oxford*, 64–65.

3. We may contrast Roth's bleak picture with the way that Charlotte Goldy imagines the daily errands of Muriel, a Jewish woman in thirteenth-century Oxford: Charlotte Newman Goldy, "A Thirteenth-Century Anglo-Jewish Woman Crossing Boundaries: Visible and Invisible"; Goldy, "Muriel, a Jew of Oxford: Using the Dramatic to Understand the Mundane in Anglo-Norman Towns."

4. Rainer Berndt, *André de Saint-Victor (mort en 1175): exégète et théologien*; Raphael Loewe, "The Mediaeval Christian Hebraists of England: Herbert of Bosham and Earlier Scholars"; Frans van Liere, "Andrew of St. Victor, Jerome, and the Jews: Biblical Scholarship in the Twelfth-Century Renaissance."

5. Louis Isaac Rabinowitz, "Peshat."

6. Eva De Visscher, *Reading the Rabbis: Christian Hebraism in the Works of Herbert of Bosham*; Deborah Goodwin, *Take Hold of the Robe of a Jew: Herbert of Bosham's Christian Hebraism*; Loewe, "The Mediaeval Christian Hebraists of England"; Smalley, *The Study of the Bible in the Middle Ages*.

7. For the chronology of Herbert's life and works, I am following Visscher, *Reading the Rabbis*, 20. On the possible connection between Andrew and Herbert, see Berndt, *André de Saint-Victor*, 29, 92.

8. See Visscher, *Reading the Rabbis*, 77–78. The manuscript, discussed below, is Judith Olszowy-Schlanger and Anne Grondeux, eds., *Dictionnaire hébreu-latin-français de la Bible hébraïque de l'Abbaye de Ramsey: XIIIe s.*

9. Hadas, *Fables of Jewish Aesop*, 118; Nisse, *Jacob's Shipwreck*, 93–94. On Petrus Alfonsi, see John Tolan, *Petrus Alfonsi and His Medieval Readers*.

10. Gilbert Dahan, "Deux Psautiers Hébraïques Glosés En Latin." One of the manuscripts, Paris BNF Hébreux 113, is online at http://gallica.bnf.fr/ark:/12148/btv1b60004143/f70 .planchecontact. On this manuscript see Judith Olszowy-Schlanger, *Les manuscrits hébreux dans l'Angleterre médiévale: étude historique et paléographique*, 181–87; Judith Olszowy-Schlanger, "The Knowledge and Practice of Hebrew Grammar Among Christian Scholars in Pre-Expulsion England: The Evidence of 'Bilingual' Hebrew-Latin Manuscripts."

11. On this manuscript, see Olszowy-Schlanger, *Manuscrits hébreux*, 220–23.

12. Judith Olszowy-Schlanger, "A School of Christian Hebraists in Thirteenth Century England: A Unique Hebrew-Latin-French and English Dictionary and Its Sources"; Olszowy-Schlanger and Grondeux, *Dictionnaire hébreu-latin-français*.

13. Olszowy-Schlanger and Grondeux, *Dictionnaire hébreu-latin-français*, vii.

14. Olszowy-Schlanger, *Learning Hebrew in Medieval England: Christian Hebraists and the Longleat House Grammar*.

15. Robert Chazan, Jean Hoff, and John Friedman, eds., *The Trial of the Talmud, Paris, 1240*, 18, 92–95.

16. Shlomo Simonsohn, *The Apostolic See and the Jews*, 171–74.

17. Talya Fishman, *Becoming the People of the Talmud: Oral Torah as Written Tradition in Medieval Jewish Cultures*.

18. Tolan, *Petrus Alfonsi and His Medieval Readers*; Petrus Venerabilis, *Petri Venerabilis Adversus Iudeorum Inveteratam Duritiem*.

19. Chazan, Hoff, and Friedman, *The Trial of the Talmud, Paris, 1240*; Gilbert Dahan and Elie Nicolas, eds., *Le brûlement du Talmud à Paris, 1242–1244*; William Chester Jordan, "Marian Devotion and the Talmud Trial of 1240"; Alexander Fidora, "Textual Rearrangements and Thwarted Intentions: The Two Versions of the Latin Talmud"; Einbinder, *Beautiful Death*, 70–90; Alexander Fidora and Görge K. Hasselhoff, *The Talmud in Dispute During the High Middle Ages*; Piero Capelli, "Nicolas Donin, the Talmud Trial of 1240, and the Struggles Between Church and State in Medieval Europe," 159–78.

20. Chazan, Hoff, and Friedman, *The Trial of the Talmud, Paris, 1240*, 152.

21. On Theobald's *Pharetra fidei contra Iudaeos*, see Tolan, *Petrus Alfonsi and His Medieval Readers*, 117–18.

22. Extract from Meir's lament, which is translated in Einbinder, *Beautiful Death*, 76–78.

23. Soyer, *Medieval Antisemitism?*, 33–35.

24. Roth, *The Jews of Medieval Oxford*; Pam Manix, "Oxford: Mapping the Medieval Jewry." Manix's detailed maps of the Oxford Jewry are available online: see http://www.oxfordjewish heritage.co.uk/oxford-jewish-heritage/medieval-period/maps.

25. Richard Southern, "From Schools to University"; Hastings Rashdall, *The Universities of Europe in the Middle Ages, Volume 3: English Universities-Student Life*, 1–273; Alan Cobban, *The Medieval English Universities: Oxford and Cambridge to c. 1500*.

26. Southern, "From Schools to University," 10.

27. Gerald of Wales, *The Autobiography of Gerald of Wales*, 97; Robert Bartlett, *Gerald of Wales, 1146–1223*, 103; Southern, "From Schools to University," 13.

28. Gerald of Wales, *The Jewel of the Church*, 118.

29. AASS October, vol. 8, cols. 576–77; see Adolf Neubauer, "Notes on the Jews of Oxford"; Ephraim Shoham-Steiner, "'Vitam finivit infelilcem': Madness, Conversion and Adolescent Suicide Among Jews in Late Twelfth-Century England"; Roth, *The Jews of Medieval Oxford*; Simon Yarrow, *Saints and Their Communities: Miracle Stories in Twelfth Century England*, 169–89. On the conversion of adolescent Jews to Christianity, see Einbinder, *Beautiful Death*, 25; William Chester Jordan, "Adolescence and Conversion in the Middle Ages: A Research Agenda."

30. Roth, *The Jews of Medieval Oxford*, 6n1.

31. CR 1234–37, 20. See discussion below.

32. Yarrow, *Saints and Their Communities*, 177–78.

33. October, vol. 8, col. 568, translated by Bartlett, *Gerald of Wales, 1146–1223*, 120.

34. Gerald of Wales, *Speculum ecclesie, in Giraldi Cambrensis Opera*, 138–43. See Tartakoff, *Conversion, Circumcision, and Ritual Murder in Medieval Europe*, 25.

35. Gerald of Wales, *Giraldi Cambrensis Opera*, vol. 8, 65–66; H. P. Stokes, "Records of Mss. and Documents Possessed by the Jews in England Before the Expulsion," 84.

36. Ruth Nisse speculates that Jews may have expunged anti-Christian passages from their version of Josephus, the Hebrew *Yosippon,* so as not to provoke Robert, who then suspected them of expunging predictions concerning Jesus. See Nisse, *Jacob's Shipwreck*, 20–22, 32; Irven Resnick, "The Falsification of Scriptures and Medieval Christian and Jewish Polemics."

37. Kati Ihnat, *Mother of Mercy, Bane of the Jews: Devotion to the Virgin Mary in Anglo-Norman England.*

38. Claire Donovan, *The de Brailes Hours: Shaping the Book of Hours in Thirteenth-Century Oxford.* The following description is based on 96–103, 128–29, 78–80.

39. Kaplan, *Figuring Racism in Medieval Christianity*, 98–99.

40. Kaplan, *Figuring Racism in Medieval Christianity*, 94–102.

41. Manix, "Oxford: Mapping the Medieval Jewry."

42. T. Aston and Rosamond Faith, "The Endowments of the University to *circa* 1348," 274–75.

43. On this incident and its aftermath, see Southern, "From Schools to University," 26.

44. While the final charter is no longer extant, a draft exists. See H. E. Salter, ed., *Mediaeval Archives of the University of Oxford*, 8–10.

45. Roth, *The Jews of Medieval Oxford.*

46. HRLC, vol. 1, 359.

47. Conflicts would come later, in the late thirteenth and early fourteenth centuries; see Rashdall, *The Universities of Europe in the Middle Ages, Volume 3: English Universities-Student Life*, 66–74.

48. Vincent, *Peter Des Roches*, 207; Nicholas de Triveti, *Annales sex regum Angliæ, qui a comitibus Andegavensibus originem taxerunt*, 209.

49. Bede Jarrett, *The English Dominican Province*; Hinnebusch, "The Pre-Reformation Sites of the Oxford Blackfriars."

50. The primary narrative source for the early history of the Franciscan order in England is Thomas of Eccleston, *Tractatus de Adventu Fratrum Minorum in Angliam.* See Jim Knowles, "Great Houses Make Not Men Holy: A Study of the Franciscan and Dominican Foundations in Medieval Oxford"; Andrew George Little, *The Grey Friars in Oxford.*

51. Manix, "Oxford: Mapping the Medieval Jewry," 410 (see map, 17); Roth, *The Jews of Medieval Oxford*, 98–100; Thomas of Eccleston, *Tractatus de Adventu Fratrum Minorum in Angliam.*

52. On David of Oxford, see Roth, *The Jews of Medieval Oxford*, 46–57; Reva Berman Brown and Sean McCartney, "David of Oxford and Licoricia of Winchester: Glimpses into a Jewish Family in Thirteenth-Century England," 1–34; Goldy, "A Thirteenth-Century Anglo-Jewish Woman Crossing Boundaries: Visible and Invisible"; Goldy, "Muriel, a Jew of Oxford: Using the Dramatic to Understand the Mundane in Anglo-Norman Towns"; Suzanne Bartlet, *Licoricia of Winchester: Marriage, Motherhood and Murder in the Medieval Anglo-Jewish Community*. Simon de Montfort's was in debt to him for £110: see Roth, *The Jews of Medieval Oxford*, 54–56; Maddicott, *Simon de Montfort*, 1994, 33.

53. CR 1234–37, 20. Roth misunderstood this document, which he presents as a cancellation of the debt: Roth, *The Jews of Medieval Oxford*, 48.

54. *Report on Manuscripts in Various Collections*, vol. 4, 160; Roth, *The Jews of Medieval Oxford*, 49.

55. Cal PR 32–47, 99.

56. Robert Stacey, "Royal Taxation and the Social Structure of Medieval Anglo-Jewry: The Tallages of 1239–1242," 175, 201.

57. CR 1234–37, 323, 83; Roth, *The Jews of Medieval Oxford*, 24–25; Fogle, *The King's Converts*, 140. On Robert Bacon, see Jean Dunbabin, "Bacon [Bacun], Robert (d. 1248)"; Smalley, *The Study of the Bible in the Middle Ages*.

58. CR 1242–47, 298. Tartakoff misidentifies Robert Bacon as Robert Grosseteste, Tartakoff, *Conversion, Circumcision, and Ritual Murder in Medieval Europe*, 105.

59. Tartakoff, *Conversion, Circumcision, and Ritual Murder in Medieval Europe*, 134–35.

60. Bartlet, *Licoricia of Winchester*; Brown and McCartney, "David of Oxford and Licoricia of Winchester"; Goldy, "A Thirteenth-Century Anglo-Jewish Woman Crossing Boundaries"; Pinchas Roth, "Jewish Courts in Medieval England." On infertility as grounds for divorce in Jewish law, see Baumgarten, *Mothers and Children*, 32–38. One of the three English rabbis of the *bet din*, Moses of London, wrote a responsa about divorce law: see Mutius, *Rechtsentscheide*, 14–18.

61. Cal LR, 223.

62. CFR, http://www.finerollshenry3.org.uk/content/calendar/roll_041.html#it307_005. See also the undated letter concerning Licoricia's release and David's estate in SRHL, vol. 2, 46.

63. Roth, *The Jews of Medieval Oxford*, 131–33; Victoria Hoyle, "The Bonds That Bind: Money Lending Between Anglo-Jewish and Christian Women in the Plea Rolls of the Exchequer of the Jews, 1218–1280," 127.

64. Cal Ch R 1, 283.

65. Vincent, *Peter Des Roches*, 289; *A Cartulary of the Hospital of St. John the Baptist*, vol. 3, xiv–xviii.

66. Olszowy-Schlanger, *Hebrew and Hebrew-Latin Documents*, 660–62.

67. Olszowy-Schlanger, *Hebrew and Hebrew-Latin Documents*, 665–84; John Roger Loxdale Highfield, *The Early Rolls of Merton College, Oxford with an Appendix of Thirteenth-Century Oxford Charters*, 12–13, 17, 34–36; Stacey, "1240–60: A Watershed in Anglo-Jewish Relations?," 142.

68. David Wasserstein, "Grosseteste, the Jews, and Medieval Christian Hebraism," 357.

69. For an introduction to Grosseteste, his life and his thought, see Hoskin, *Robert Grosseteste and the 13th-Century Diocese of Lincoln*.

70. Southern, *Robert Grosseteste*, 141–69.

71. Grosseteste, *Letters*, 75–80 (letters 8 and 9). See James R. Ginther, *Master of the Sacred Page: A Study of the Theology of Robert Grosseteste, ca. 1229/30–1235*, 163–64.

72. CR 1231–34, 568; Southern, *Robert Grosseteste*, 71.

73. On the complex nature of this text and the different versions in extant manuscripts, see James R. Ginther, "The *Super Psalterium* in Context," 34. For a partial electronic edition of the text, see http://www.grosseteste.com/cgi-bin/textdisplay.cgi?text=super-psalterium.xml.

74. John Chrysostom's *Homilies on Matthew*, trans. Philip Schaff.

75. Robert Grosseteste, *De Decem Mandatis*, 2; James McEvoy, "Robert Grosseteste on the Ten Commandments"; Lesley Smith, "The *De Decem Mandatis* of Robert Grosseteste"; James McEvoy, "The Text and Sources of the Treatise De Decem Mandatis of Robert Grosseteste." Most Grosseteste scholars consider the *De decem mandatis* to be one of his earlier theological works, written c. 1229–1231, before the *De cessatione*, though Smith argues for a later date, in the 1240s.

76. Robert Grosseteste, *De Cessatione Legalium*; Robert Grosseteste, *On the Cessation of the Laws*. On the theological and legal problem of the supercession of the Old Law, with particular attention paid to Grosseteste's *De Cessatione Legalium,* see Elsa Marmursztejn, "Loi ancienne, loi nouvelle et normes chrétiennes dans la théologie scolastique du XIIIe siècle."

77. Robert Grosseteste, *De Cessatione Legalium*, 7; *On the Cessation of the Laws*, 27.

78. Robert Grosseteste, *De Cessatione Legalium*, 57; *On the Cessation of the Laws*, 87.

79. Robert Grosseteste, *De Cessatione Legalium*, 72; *On the Cessation of the Laws*, 105.

80. Robert Grosseteste, *De Cessatione Legalium*, 168, 177–79; *On the Cessation of the Laws*, 208, 218–20.

81. Robert Grosseteste, *De Cessatione Legalium*, 194–95; *On the Cessation of the Laws*, 238.

82. Southern, *Robert Grosseteste*, 244–49. On Innocent's attitudes toward the Jews, see Tolan, "Of Milk and Blood: Innocent III and the Jews, Revisited"; Gilbert Dahan, *Les intellectuels chrétiens et les juifs au Moyen Age*, 571, 577.

83. Grosseteste, *Letters*, 67 (letter 5).

84. "Prohibemus etiam sub interminatione anathematis ne mulieres christiane nutriant pueros iudeorum, nec habeant iudea famulas christianas in eorum hospitiis pernoctantes. Prohibemus etiam ne christiani recipiant pecuniam iudeorum quasi res proprias, ut magis salvo custodiantur, in ecclesiis deponendas. Quia vero parum refert an quis per se vel per alium in crimen inpecuniam committat, ut eam iudeus simulate suo nomine proprio nutuet ad usuram. In aliis autem statuta conciliorum circa iudeos volumus et precipimus firmiter observari." *Councils & Synods*, vol. 2, 318.

85. *Councils & Synods*, vol. 2, 265–78; Watt, "The English Episcopate, the State and the Jews: The Evidence of the Thirteenth-Century Conciliar Decrees," 138.

86. "Et cohabitationem Christianorum cum Judaeis quantum vobis possibile est, impedire curetis," letter 107 (RS, vol. 25, 317–18), translation Grosseteste, *Letters*, 334–36. The Latin text is also available in *Councils & Synods*, vol. 2, 479–80. See Hoskin, *Robert Grosseteste*, 156–57. The earlier prohibitions of clerical participation in festivals and miracle plays are found in letters 22 and 52.

87. Roth, *A History of the Jews in England*, 59; Roth, *The Jews of Medieval Oxford*, 25–26; 127–28.

88. *Annales monasterii de Oseneia (A.D. 1016–1347). Chronicon vulgo dictum Chronicon Thomae Wykes (A.D. 1066–1289). Annales Prioratus de Wigornia (A.D. 1–1377)*, 91; *The Chronicle of the Monastery of Abingdon from A.D. 1218–1304*, 5; Rashdall, *The Universities of Europe in the Middle Ages, volume 3: English Universities-Student Life*, 86–6; Roth, *The Jews of Medieval Oxford*, 127–8; Cobban, *The Medieval English Universities: Oxford and Cambridge to c. 1500*, 38–9.

89. Grosseteste, *Letters*, 447–49.

90. CFR: http://www.finerollshenry3.org.uk/content/calendar/roll_045.html.

91. CR 1247–51, 114.

92. Salter, *Mediaeval Archives of the University of Oxford*, 18–19.

93. Matthew Paris, *Chronica Majora*, vol. 5, 405.

94. Aston and Faith, "The Endowments of the University to *circa* 1348," 266–68.

95. Tiziano Dorandi and Michele Trizio, "Editio Princeps Del *Libro Qui Vocatur Suda* Di Roberto Grossatesta." For a partial English translation, see Wasserstein, "Grosseteste, the Jews, and Medieval Christian Hebraism." On the thirteenth-century French translation perhaps done by Grosseteste himself, see Ruth J. Dean, "An Anglo-Norman Version of Grosseteste: Part of His Suidas and Testamenta XII Patriarcharum."

96. M. de Jonge, "Robert Grosseteste and the Testaments of the Twelve Patriarchs"; Nisse, *Jacob's Shipwreck,* 127–47; Nisse, "A Romance of the Jewish East: The Ten Lost Tribes and The Testaments of the Twelve Patriarchs in Medieval Europe." On the thirteenth-century French translation, see Dean, "An Anglo-Norman Version of Grosseteste: Part of His Suidas and Testamenta XII Patriarcharum."

97. Matthew Paris, *Chronica majora*, vol. 4, 232–33.

98. For an English translation, see R. H. Charles, *The Apocrypha and Pseudepigrapha of the Old Testament in English: With Introductions and Critical and Explanatory Notes to the Several Books.*

99. "Ad majorem Judaeorum confusionem," Matthew Paris, *Chronica majora*, vol. 4, 232–3.

100. Nicholas de Triveti, *Annales,* 243; Roger Bacon, *Opera Quaedam Hactenus Inedita,* 472; D. A. Callus, "Robert Grosseteste as Scholar," 33–36; Dahan, *Les intellectuels chrétiens et les juifs au Moyen Age,* 265–67.

101. Smalley, *Hebrew Scholarship Among Christians in XIIIth Century England,* 5; Smalley, *The Study of the Bible in the Middle Ages,* 343–47; Raphael Loewe, "The Mediaeval Christian Hebraists of England: The Superscriptio Lincolniensis," 212–14. Judith Olszowy-Schlanger carefully weighs the pros and cons of the attribution to Grosseteste, which for her remains plausible (Olszowy-Schlanger, *Manuscrits hébreux,* 53–57, 157–61.)

102. Smalley, *Hebrew Scholarship Among Christians in XIIIth Century England,* 8. This is Smalley's translation of the conclusion to the preface. See Olszowy-Schlanger, *Les manuscrits hébreux,* 157–61.

103. *Decrees of the Ecumenical Councils,* vol. 1.

104. Joseph Goering, "Robert Grosseteste at the Papal Curia"; Hoskin, *Robert Grosseteste,* 79–80.

105. Philippa Hoskin, "Robert Grosseteste, Natural Law and Magna Carta: National and Universal Law in 1253"; *Councils & Synods*; Ambler, *Bishops in the Political Community of England, 1213–1272,* 92–93, 156–57; *Annales monastici,* vol. 1, 422–25.

CHAPTER 5

1. CR 1251–53, 312–13. http://www.cn-telma.fr//relmin/extrait252152/. The Latin text is also found in *Councils & Synods*, vol. 2, 472–74.The translation has been adapted from RSPS, xlix. On this text, see John Edwards, "The Church and the Jews in Medieval England"; Zefira Entin Rokéah, "The State, the Church and the Jews in Medieval England," 112–14.

2. Stacey, "1240–60: A Watershed in Anglo-Jewish Relations?"

3. Stacey, "1240–60: A Watershed in Anglo-Jewish Relations?"; Stacey, "Royal Taxation and the Social Structure of Medieval Anglo-Jewry."

4. Carpenter, *Henry III, 1207–1258,* chap. 5.

5. Bernart de Rovenac, Ja no vuelh do ni esmenda, text and translation from http://www .rialto.unina.it/BnRov/66.3/66.3%28Paterson%29.htm. See Jahner, *Literature and Law in the Era of Magna Carta*, 222.

6. Carpenter, *Henry III*, 433.

7. Carpenter, *Henry III*, 199.

8. Carpenter, *Henry III*, 239–244; Michael Clanchy, "Did Henry III Have a Policy?"

9. Matthew Paris, *Chronica Majora*, vol. 4, 260; Matthew Paris, *English History*, vol. 1, 459.

10. Stacey, *Politics, Policy and Finance Under Henry III*, 154.

11. Stacey, *Politics, Policy and Finance Under Henry III*, 154.

12. Matthew Paris, *Chronica Majora*, vol. 4, 373.

13. CR 1242–47, 275. (Text, translation and analysis at http://www.cn-telma.fr//relmin /extrait252612/).

14. CR 1242–47, 133; Cal LR, 133; Tartakoff, *Conversion, Circumcision, and Ritual Murder*, 105.

15. CR 1242–47, 247–52; Carpenter, *Henry III*, 452–63; Christopher Cheney, "The 'Paper Constitution' Preserved by Matthew Paris."

16. Matthew Paris, *Chronica Majora*, vol. 4, 608. See Carpenter, *Henry III*, 464–67.

17. Matthew Paris, *Chronica Majora*, vol. 5, 15–16.

18. Matthew Paris, vol. 5, 114.

19. Matthew Paris, vol. 5, 136. CR 1251–53, 49, 60, 100. Stacey, "1240–60: A Watershed in Anglo-Jewish Relations?," 141.

20. CR 1254–56, 140. Stacey, "1240–60: A Watershed in Anglo-Jewish Relations?," 141.

21. Carpenter, *Henry III*, 474–78; Nicholas Vincent, *The Holy Blood: King Henry III and the Westminster Blood Relic*.

22. This was all to little avail, as the relic never attracted much devotion or many pilgrims. See Vincent, *The Holy Blood*.

23. Carpenter, *Henry III*, 515–17.

24. Goering, "Robert Grosseteste at the Papal Curia."

25. Hoskin, "Robert Grosseteste, Natural Law and Magna Carta: National and Universal Law in 1253," 122. On Henry's crusading plans, see Tyerman, *England and the Crusades, 1095–1588*, 111–23.

26. Hoskin, *Robert Grosseteste*, 201.

27. *Councils & Synods*, vol. 2, 447–51; Hoskin, "Robert Grosseteste, Natural Law and Magna Carta"; Carpenter, *Henry III*, 525–26.

28. Matthew Paris, *Chronica Majora*, vol. 5, 274; Menache, "Matthew Paris's Attitudes Toward Anglo-Jewry," 160. The *Chronica maiorum et Vicecomitum Londoniarum*, 19 affirms: "Eodem tempore cepit Rex a Judeis universis totam partem omnium mobilium suorum, credendo eis per starrios suos; et assignatis, ut siquis Judeus non satisfecisset de tallagio suo infra decimum diem post visum dicti brevis, quod ipse utlagaretur, et portus ei assignaretur et omni domui sue apud Dovre quod postea non stetit."

29. *Councils & Synods*, vol. 2, 467–72.

30. On the mandate, see Watt, "The English Episcopate, the State and the Jews: The Evidence of the Thirteenth-Century Conciliar Decrees," 143–44; David Carpenter, "Magna Carta 1253: The Ambitions of the Church and the Divisions Within the Realm."

31. Carpenter, "Magna Carta 1253," 186–87.

32. Carpenter, "Magna Carta 1253"; Hoskin, "Robert Grosseteste, Natural Law and Magna Carta"; Hoskin, *Robert Grosseteste*, 189–98.

33. David Carpenter, "King Henry III and the Sicilian Affair," *Henry III Fine Rolls Project*, n.d., https://finerollshenry3.org.uk/redist/pdf/fm-02-2012.pdf.

34. William Chester Jordan, "Archbishop Eudes Rigaud and the Jews of Normandy, 1248–1275," 46; Juliette Sibon, *Chasser les Juifs pour régner: les expulsions par les rois de France au Moyen Âge*, 65–66.

35. Matthew Paris, *Chronica Majora*, vol. 5, 361–62; Juliette Sibon, *Les juifs au temps de saint Louis*, 42–43; William Chester Jordan, *The French Monarchy and the Jews: From Philip Augustus to the Last Capetians*, 148–49; Robert Chazan, *Medieval Jewry in Northern France: A Social and Political History*, 121–22. The text of the ordinance is in Eusèbe Jacob de Laurière and Denis F. Secousse, eds., *Ordonnances Des Roys de France de La Troisième Race*, 75.

36. Matthew Paris, *Chronica Majora*, vol. 5, 441. See Hillaby and Hillaby, *The Palgrave Dictionary of Medieval Anglo-Jewish History*, 244–45.

37. Matthew Paris, *Chronica Majora*, vol. 5, 487; Matthew Paris, *English History*, vol. 3, 114.

38. Matthew Paris, *Chronica Majora*, vol. 5, 488; Matthew Paris, *English History*, vol. 3, 114–15. On the grant of the Jewry to Richard, see Hillaby and Hillaby, *The Palgrave Dictionary of Medieval Anglo-Jewish History*, 9–10, 187–88.

39. Menache, "Matthew Paris's Attitudes toward Anglo-Jewry," 145.

40. Joan G. Greatrex, "Monastic Charity for Jewish Converts: The Requisition of Corrodies by Henry III."

41. *The Prioress' Tale*, v. 1874–80, in Chaucer, *A Variorum Edition of the Works of Geoffrey Chaucer. The Prioress' Tale*, 165–68. For an introduction to the significant bibliography on the prioress' tale, see Heather Blurton and Hannah R. Johnson, *The Critics and the Prioress: Antisemitism, Criticism, and Chaucer's Prioress's Tale*.

42. David A. Stocker, "The Shrine of Little St. Hugh."

43. David Carpenter, "Crucifixion and Conversion: King Henry III and the Jews in 1255"; Kate McGrath, "English Jews as Outlaws or Outcasts: The Ritual Murder of Little St. Hugh of Lincoln in Matthew Paris's *Chronica Majora*"; Roger Dahood, "English Historical Narratives of Jewish Child-Murder, Chaucer's Prioress's Tale, and the Date of Chaucer's Unknown Source"; Dahood, "The Punishment of the Jews, Hugh of Lincoln, and the Question of Satire in the Prioress's Tale"; Richard J. Utz, "Der Heilige Hugh von Lincoln: Hugh von Lincoln Und Der Mythos Vom Jüdischen Ritualmord"; Gavin Langmuir, "The Knight's Tale of Young Hugh of Lincoln"; Barbara Hanawalt, "Narratives of a Nurturing Culture: Parents and Neighbors in Medieval England"; Francis Hill, *Medieval Lincoln*, 224–32; Heng, *The Invention of Race*, 81–96.

44. *Annales monastici*, vol. 1, 340–48; Roger Dahood, "The Anglo-Norman 'Hugo de Lincolnia'"; Matthew Paris, *Chronica Majora*, 516–19. Dahood gives an English translation of the Anglo-Norman text; another translation is found in Maureen Boulton, *Piety and Persecution in the French Texts of England*, 135–40.

45. Matthew Paris, *Chronica Majora*, vol. 5, 516–17; Matthew Paris, *English History*, vol. 3, 138–39.

46. Rose, *The Murder of William of Norwich*, 89. Some of the more conjectural elements of Rose's analysis are called into question by Eamon Duffy, *Royal Books and Holy Bones: Essays in Medieval Christianity*, 125–35.

47. See Miri Rubin's translation (and her introduction) of Thomas of Monmouth, *The Life and Passion of William of Norwich*, 70–71. For the Latin text (and another English translation), see Thomas of Monmouth, *The Life and Miracles of St William of Norwich*, 109–10. On this text, see also Kathy Lavezzo, *The Accommodated Jew: English Antisemitism from Bede to Milton*, chap. 2.

48. Rose, *The Murder of William of Norwich*, 100.

49. Yuval, *Two Nations in Your Womb*, 163–73.

50. Rose, *The Murder of William of Norwich*. On the Blois incident, and its commemoration by Jewish poets, see Einbinder, *Beautiful Death*, chap. 2; Yuval, *Two Nations in Your Womb*, 170–96; Tolan, "Il y a 850 ans, à Blois, 32 juifs furent envoyés au bûcher,"

51. CR 1231–34, 80; Vincent, *Peter Des Roches*, 288–89.

52. See Andrea Sommerlechner, "Das Judenmassaker von Fulda 1235 in Der Geschichtess-chreiben Um Kaiser Friedrich II." For the broader context of Frederick's policies toward Jews and Muslims, see David Abulafia, "Ethnic Variety and Its Implications: Frederick II's Relations with Jews and Muslims."

53. On the blood libel, see Hannah Johnson, *Blood Libel: The Ritual Murder Accusation at the Limit of Jewish History*; Joanna Tokarska-Bakir, *Légendes du sang: pour une anthropologie de l'antisémitisme chrétien*; Magda Teter, *Blood Libel: On the Trail of an Antisemitic Myth*.

54. SHRL, vol. 2, 8–9; *Historia diplomatica Friderici II, sive Constitutiones, privilegia istius imperatoris et filiorum ejus*, vol. 4, 809–10.

55. Yuval, *Two Nations in Your Womb*, 280–83.

56. Frederick II, *Constitutiones*. English translation in Chazan, *Church, State, and Jew in the Middle Ages*, 124–26.

57. *Councils & Synods*, vol. 2, 216. Translation by Grayzel, *The Church and the Jews*, vol. 1, 328.

58. Matthew Paris, *Chronica Majora*, vol. 4, 377; Matthew Paris, *English History*, vol. 2, 21.

59. Matthew Paris, *Chronica Majora*, vol. 5, 114–15. See Hillaby and Hillaby, *The Palgrave Dictionary of Medieval Anglo-Jewish History*, 50–52.

60. Ihnat, *Mother of Mercy*, 157–62.

61. Yuval, *Two Nations in Your Womb*, 258–66, 284–88.

62. Sibon, *Chasser les Juifs pour régner*, 72.

63. Matthew Paris, *Chronica Majora*, vol. 4, 77–78; Menache, "Matthew Paris's Attitudes Toward Anglo-Jewry," 143; Sophia Menache, "Tartars, Jews, Saracens and the Jewish–Mongol 'Plot' of 1241"; Nisse, *Jacob's Shipwreck*, 134–39.

64. Bernard McGinn, *Antichrist: Two Thousand Years of the Human Fascination with Evil*, 74–75.

65. Suzanne Lewis, "Tractatus Adversus Judaeos in the Gulbenkian Apocalypse"; Lewis, *Reading Images Narrative Discourse and Reception in the Thirteenth-Century Illuminated Apocalypse*, 40–43, 215–21; Richard Kenneth Emmerson, *Apocalypse Illuminated the Visual Exegesis of Revelation in Medieval Illustrated Manuscripts*, 112–27; Emmerson, "Apocalypse and/as History."

66. Nina Rowe, *The Jew, the Cathedral and the Medieval City: Synagoga and Ecclesia in the Thirteenth Century*.

67. Nigel J. Morgan, *Stained Glass of Lincoln Cathedral*; Morgan, *The Medieval Painted Glass of Lincoln Cathedral*, 11, 30.

68. Pamela A. Patton, "The Little Jewish Boy: Afterlife of a Byzantine Legend in Thirteenth-Century Spain"; Miri Rubin, *Gentile Tales*, 17; Ihnat, *Mother of Mercy*, 148–54.

69. Gautier de Coinci, *Les miracles de notre dame*, vol. 2, 95–100. See Gilbert Dahan, "Les Juifs Dans Les Miracles de Gautier de Coincy."

70. Dahan, *Les juifs en France médiévale dix études*, 204, 207.

71. Langmuir, "The Knight's Tale of Young Hugh of Lincoln.," 477.

72. Cal PR 1247–58, 451–52.

73. Cal PR 1247–58, 453; Hillaby and Hillaby, *The Palgrave Dictionary of Medieval Anglo-Jewish History*, 215–16.

74. SRHL, vol. 2, 110.

75. Cal PR 1247–58, 457.

76. Cal PR 1247–58, 510.

77. Cal PR 1247–58, 493.

78. CR 1256–59, 236–37.

79. Langmuir, *History, Religion, and Antisemitism*, 276.

80. Robert C. Stacey, "From Ritual Crucifixion to Host Desecration: Jews and the Body of Christ."

81. Moore, "Anti-Semitism and the Birth of Europe," 50.

82. Watt, "Jews and Christians in the Gregorian Decretals," 97.

CHAPTER 6

1. Thomas Walsingham and Matthew Paris, *Gesta abbatum monasterii Sancti Albani*, 193–94.

2. EEAW, lv, 38–40, 62–63.

3. Robert Génestal, *Rôle des monastères comme établissements de crédit, étudié en Normandie du XIe à la fin du XIIIe siècle*; Stacey, "Crusades, Martyrdoms, and the Jews of Norman England, 1096–1190," 238.

4. Olszowy-Schlanger, *Hebrew and Hebrew-Latin Documents*, 188–89.

5. Olszowy-Schlanger, *Hebrew and Hebrew-Latin Documents*, 536–56.

6. Olszowy-Schlanger, *Hebrew and Hebrew-Latin Documents*, 599–601.

7. Olszowy-Schlanger, *Hebrew and Hebrew-Latin Documents*, 515–17.

8. Olszowy-Schlanger, *Hebrew and Hebrew-Latin Documents*, 593–95.

9. Olszowy-Schlanger, *Hebrew and Hebrew-Latin Documents*, 596–98.

10. Olszowy-Schlanger, *Hebrew and Hebrew-Latin Documents*, 531–32, 557–58.

11. Olszowy-Schlanger, *Hebrew and Hebrew-Latin Documents*, 561–62.

12. Olszowy-Schlanger, *Hebrew and Hebrew-Latin Documents*, 693–98.

13. *The Annals of Dunstable Priory*, 137; Cal PR 1247–58, 393, 396, 403; CR 1254–56, 170–72, 203–4; N. Denholm-Young, *Richard of Cornwall*, 70; Robert C. Stacey, "1240–60: A Watershed in Anglo-Jewish Relations?," 142–43.

14. Hillaby and Hillaby, *The Palgrave Dictionary of Medieval Anglo-Jewish History*, 414–16; Joe Hillaby, "The Worcester Jewry, 1158–1290: Portrait of a Lost Community."

15. What follows is based on Stacey, "1240–60: A Watershed in Anglo-Jewish Relations?," 143.

16. Margaret Howell, *Eleanor of Provence: Queenship in Thirteenth-Century England*, 275–76.

17. Cal PR 1247–58, 635; Stacey, "1240–60: A Watershed in Anglo-Jewish Relations?," 143.

18. See Howell, *Eleanor of Provence*, 116, 263–64, 266, 277–78; H. P. Stokes, "The Relationship Between the Jews and the Royal Family of England in the Thirteenth Century."

19. Matthew Paris, *Chronica Majora*, vol. 4, 367; Roth, *A History of the Jews in England*, 59.

20. *Councils & Synods*, vol. 2, 549–67.

21. Philippa Hoskin, "Cantilupe's Crusade? Walter de Cantilupe Bishop of Worcester and the Baronial Rebellion," 96; Hoskin, *Robert Grosseteste and the 13th-Century Diocese of Lincoln*, 193–94.

22. *Councils & Synods*, vol. 2, 545.

23. Cal PR 1247–58, 532.

24. On the famine, see Carpenter, *Henry III, 1207–1258*, 678–79.

25. Tyerman, *England and the Crusades, 1095–1588*, 123.

26. Matthew Paris, *Chronica Majora*, vol. 5, pp. 524–26; Ambler, *Bishops in the Political Community of England*, 96, 120. On Walter, see Hoskin, "Cantilupe's Crusade."

27. Matthew Paris, *Chronica Majora*, vol. 5, 637–38; Ambler, *Bishops in the Political Community of England, 1213–1272*, 98.

28. The anonymous French "Song of the Church" edition, translation and commentary in Fiona Somerset, "Complaining About the King in French in Thomas Wright's Political Songs of England," 95. See Jahner, *Literature and Law in the Era of Magna Carta*, 196.

29. David Carpenter, *The Reign of Henry III*, 187–90; Carpenter, *Henry III, 1207–1258*, 691–99.

30. Ambler, *Bishops in the Political Community of England, 1213–1272*, 105–24.

31. *Councils & Synods*, vol. 2, 568–85: Council of Merton and Westminster (6–8 June 1258).

32. Ambler, *The Song of Simon de Montfort*, 179–205.

33. John Tolan, "Petitio baronum 25," Notice n°252151, RELMIN project, http://www.cn-telma.fr/relmin/extrait252151/; *Docs. Bar.*, 86–87.

34. For Robert Stacey, this provision "was specifically directed against the Lusignans and their agents" (Stacey, "1240–60: A Watershed in Anglo-Jewish Relations?," 143–44.)

35. *Docs. Bar.*, 80–81.

36. "A remembrer fet ke lem mette tel amendement a la Guuerie et as gardeins de la Gyuerie, ke lem i sauue le serement," French text and English translation from *Docs. Bar.*, 108–9.

37. Matthew Paris, *Chronica Majora*, vol. 5, 697–98; Ambler, *The Song of Simon de Montfort*, 199–200.

38. Howell, *Eleanor of Provence*, 155–65.

39. *Docs. Bar.*, 238–41.

40. *The Annals of Dunstable Priory*, 150.

41. *Councils & Synods*, vol. 1, 679.

42. Hoskin, "Cantilupe's Crusade," 97.

43. *Councils & Synods*, vol. 1, 659–94.

44. Roth, *A History of the Jews in England*, 60.

45. Cal PR 1258–66, 156; Roth, *A History of the Jews in England*, 60.

46. Cal PR 1258–66, 153.

47. Cal PR 1258–66, 229; Dan Cohn-Sherbok, "Medieval Jewish Persecution in England: The Canterbury Pogroms in Perspective," 23–37; Robin Mundill, *The King's Jews: Money, Massacre and Exodus in Medieval England*, 88.

48. Cal PR 1258–66, 1971, 233; Howell, *Eleanor of Provence* 189; Richard Huscroft, *Expulsion: England's Jewish Solution*, 113–14.

49. *Cronica maiorum et vicecomitum Londoniarum*, 50–51; *Chronicles of the Mayors and Sheriffs of London 1188–1274*, 54–61. British History Online, http://www.british-history.ac.uk/no-series/london-mayors-sheriffs/1188-1274/pp54–61.

50. *Annales Monastici*, vol. 4, 136. *Annales monastici*, vol. 3, 223; *The Annals of Dunstable Priory*, 154; Howell, *Eleanor of Provence*, 196.

51. Gervase of Canterbury, *The Historical Works*, vol. 2, 231; John Maddicott, *Simon de Montfort*, 247; Ambler, *The Song of Simon de Montfort: England's First Revolutionary and the Death of Chivalry*, 251; Ambler, *Bishops in the Political Community of England, 1213–1272*, 134–35; Jahner,

Literature and Law in the Era of Magna Carta, 198–99; Lloyd, "'Political Crusades' in England, c. 1215–17 and c. 1263–5."

52. Ambler, *Bishops in the Political Community of England, 1213–1272*, 147–69. For the documents concerning the Mise of Amiens, see *Docs. Bar.*, 252–91.

53. *Annales de Wigornia* in *Annales Monastici*, vol. 4, 448–9. *Flores Historiarum*, vol. 2, 486–87; Hillaby, "The Worcester Jewry, 1158–1290: Portrait of a Lost Community"; CR 1264–68, 83; Mundill, *The King's Jews*, 89; Ambler, *The Song of Simon de Montfort*, 261.

54. Various documents in the fine rolls, issued by Simon in the king's name, annul in full or partially debts of his knights to Jews: Stephen Cheyndut (18 December 1264), Walter de Wau (17 February 1265), Henry de Cramarvill (26 February), John de Bokeland (27 February), Frarius de Burnham and Baldwin Filole (3 March), John de Eyvill, Walter Maureward, John Daiville and Thomas de Clare (5 March), Fulk de Lucy (7 March), Robert de Grendon and Adam Despenser (8 March), Gervase de Bestenour and William de Tracy of Toddington (11 March), and Richard de La Hyde (19 June). For these entries, see CFR.

55. Cal PR 1266–72, 13–14, 21; Mundill, *The King's Jews*, 88.

56. David Carpenter, *The Struggle for Mastery: Britain 1066–1284*, 375–76.

57. Stacey, "Jews and Christians in Twelfth-Century England: Some Dynamics of a Changing Relationship.," 343–44.

58. See Joe Hillaby, "London: The 13th-Century Jewry Revisited"; Hillaby, "The London Jewry: William I to John"; Ian Blair et al., "The Discovery of Two Medieval Mikva'ot in London and a Reinterpretation of the Bristol 'Mikveh.'"

59. Olszowy-Schlanger, *Hebrew and Hebrew-Latin Documents*, 604–5.

60. Thomas Wykes in *Annales Monastici*, vol. 4, 141–43.

61. David Carpenter, "John, Sir, Fitz John (c. 1240–1275), Baronial Leader."

62. See entries for 30 October 1264 in CFR.

63. CFR. Debts to Cok are also mentioned in entries dated 19 October 1264 and 24 February 1265.

64. *Annales Monastici*, vol. 2, 101.

65. John Williams, ed., *Annales Cambriae* (London: Longman, Green, Roberts, 1860), 102.

66. *Annales Monastici*, vol. 4, 450.

67. *Cronica maiorum et vicecomitum Londoniarum*, 62; *Chronicles of the Mayors and Sheriffs of London 1188–1274*, ed. H. T. Riley, 61–74. *British History Online*, http://www.british-history .ac.uk/no-series/london-mayors-sheriffs/1188-1274/pp61-74. Translation slightly modified.

68. *Annales monastici*, vol. 3, 230; *The Annals of Dunstable Priory*, 159.

69. *Annales monastici*, vol. 3, 230; *The Annals of Dunstable Priory*. The massacre is mentioned Gervase of Canterbury, *Historical works*, vol. 2, 235. A 1270 case before the exchequer of the Jews concerns the seized Canterbury chirography chest: see RSPS, 51; Michael Adler, "The Jews of Canterbury"; Mundill, *The King's Jews*, 88.

70. Johannes de Oxenedes, *Chronica*, 222. Translation from Jahner, *Literature and Law in the Era of Magna Carta*, 175. See also Hoskin, "Cantilupe's Crusade."

71. *The Song of Lewes*, 85; Anne Duggan, "The Cult of St. Thomas Beckett in the Thirteenth Century," 32n74.

72. Vincent, *The Holy Blood*, 189.

73. Cal PR 1258–66, 322.

74. Cal PR 1258–66, 323.

75. Cal PR 1258–66, 421–22.

76. Olszowy-Schlanger, *Hebrew and Hebrew-Latin Documents*, 557–58.

77. RSPS, 41. Patent Roll entries from 18 July 1266 and 28 July 1267 also mention the losses of Lincoln's Jews during the civil war: Cal PR 1258–66, 1971, 617; Cal PR 1266–72, 95. See Francis Hill, *Medieval Lincoln*, 209.

78. CR 1264–68, 32.

79. *Cronica maiorum et vicecomitum Londoniarum*, 74; *Chronicles of the Mayors and Sheriffs of London 1188–1274*, 61–74. The massacre is briefly mentioned in the Waverley annals, *Annales Monastici*, vol. 2, 363.

80. CR 1264–68, 62.

81. CR 1264–68, 125.

82. Ambler, *The Song of Simon de Montfort*, 314.

83. Lloyd, "'Political Crusades' in England, c. 1215–17 and c. 1263–5," 116.

84. Hillaby and Hillaby, *The Palgrave Dictionary of Medieval Anglo-Jewish History*, 128–29. Hillaby, "London: The 13th-Century Jewry Revisited." For Norwich, see Rutledge, "The Medieval Jews of Norwich and Their Legacy," 124.

CHAPTER 7

1. Roth, *A History of the Jews in England*, 62. Roth cites Salfeld, *Das Martyrologium Des Nürnberger Memorbuches*, 153 On this text, see Rainer Barzen, "Das Nürnberger Memorbuch. Eine Einführung." On the Ahkenazi Memorbücher, including that of Nürnberg, see Yuval, *Two Nations in Your Womb*, 136–38. As Susan Einbinder has remarked, "the prominent role played by martyrological literature among the Jewish communities of northern France makes the absence of such writing from England striking, all the more given the close relationship between the two communities" (Susan L. Einbinder, "Meir b. Elijah of Norwich: Persecution and Poetry among Medieval English Jews.")

2. Eva Haverkamp, *Hebräische Berichte über die Judenverfolgungen während des Ersten Kreuzzugs*.

3. Einbinder, *No Place of Rest*.

4. CR 1264–68, 77. See Adler, "The Jews of Canterbury."

5. CR 1264–68, 146. This "Sille" is the same person as Salle, according to Adler, *Jews of Medieval England*, 80. On Magister Omer, see Robert and Janet Wolfe, *Janet and Robert Wolfe Genealogy*, "Notes for Magister Omer," www.umich.edu/~bobwolfe/gen/pn/p20439.htm.

6. CR 1264–68, 147.

7. Cal PR 1258–66, 628.

8. Cal PR 1266–72, 13–14.

9. Cal PR 1266–72, 21.

10. Cal PR 1258–66, 1910, 613.

11. CFR.

12. CFR.

13. Pardon of John Carbonel concerning his debt to Diaye son of Bonetti in December 1266 (CFR, entry 120, https://finerollshenry3.org.uk/content/calendar/roll_064.html); to Anastasia de Byrton for her debt to Copin of Oxford, pardon dated 19 May 1267 (CFR, entry 413), pardon to Alan la Zouche for his debt to Manasser son of Aaron (4 June 1267, CFR, entry 419), pardon to Stephen of Edworth for his debt to Gamaliel of Oxford (21 June 1267, CFR, entry 425), pardon to

Nicholas de Barmeflet for his debt to Copin son of Salomon, Jew of Worcester (10 September 1267, CFR, entry 607). In the following regnal year (1267–1268), see similar pardons of debts to Jews (https://finerollshenry3.org.uk/content/calendar/roll_065.html, CFR, entries 270, 463).

14. RSPS, 43–46.

15. John de Warenne on 22 June 1271 pays 350 marks to the crown to obtain a pardon Cal PR 1266–72, 545.

16. The incident is described by Joseph Jacobs, *Jewish Ideals and Other Essays*, 225–33.

17. Robert Stacey, "The Conversion of Jews to Christianity in Thirteenth-Century England"; Christoph Cluse, "Stories of Breaking and Taking the Cross. A Possible Context for the Oxford Incident of 1268," 396; Horowitz, "The Jews and the Cross in the Middle Ages: Towards a Reappraisal"; Roth, *The Jews of Medieval Oxford*, 151–54.

18. CR 1264–68, 553.

19. CR 1268–72, 14–15.

20. CR 1268–72, 22–23.

21. "Quis meus author erat? Judaei.
Quomodo? Sumptu.
Quis jussit? Regnans.
Quo procurante? Magistris.
Cur? Cruce pro fracta ligni.
Quo tempore? Festo ascensus Domini.
Quis erat locus? Hic ubi sisto."

Tovey says that antiquarian John Ross had seen the cross and gives Ross's transcription of the inscription; Ross affirmed that the cross "fell to the ground" during the reign of Henry VI (1422–1471), Tovey, *Anglia Judaica.*, 174–75. The same inscription is added in a seventeenth-century annotation to the fourteenth-century *Libri cancelarii et procuratorum* of the University of Oxford, where it is identified as the inscription of the portable gilt silver cross in St. Frideswide's (*Munimenta Academica, or Documents Illustrative of Academical Life and Studies at Oxford*, vol. 1, 37).

22. *Munimenta Academica*, 36–37.

23. Cluse, "Stories of Breaking and Taking the Cross"; Horowitz, "The Jews and the Cross in the Middle Ages"; Harvey Hames, "Urinating on the Cross." Susan Einbinder shows how, according to Hebrew narratives of Jews' martyrdom at the hands of Christians, Jews defiantly insult Christianity and its symbols, including the cross (Einbinder, *Beautiful Death*, 106, 145.)

24. The "grant" is dated 25 May 1269 in Cal PR 1266–72, 345. It is confirmed in another text the following day, as a "fine": CR 1268–72, 53–54. See Huscroft, *Expulsion: England's Jewish Solution*, 108.

25. Zefira Entin Rokéah, *Medieval English Jews and Royal Officials: Entries of Jewish Interest in the English Memoranda Rolls, 1266–1293*, 42–43.

26. Chazan, *Medieval Jewry in Northern France*, 148.

27. Cal PR 1266–72, 545–46.

28. John Maddicott, "The Crusade Taxation of 1268–1270 and the Development of Parliament," 93.

29. The French text is in Cal PR 1266–72, 376. The Latin text, dated 14 May 1270, referring to the previous issue of the provisions on 13 January 1269, is in CR 1268–72, 268. Latin text and English translation in RSPS, xlviii–li. On this text, see Huscroft, *Expulsion*, 109–10; Shael Herman, *Medieval Usury and the Commercialization of Feudal Bonds*, 55–56; Stacey, "1240–60: A Watershed in Anglo-Jewish Relations?," 145; Maddicott, "The Crusade Taxation of 1268–1270."

30. Maddicott, "The Crusade Taxation of 1268–1270," 116.

31. Two mandates, dated 7 and 25 July 1271, are preserved in *Cronica maiorum et vicecomitum Londoniarum*, 234–37; *Chronicles of the Mayors and Sheriffs of London 1188–1274*, ed. H. T. Riley (London: Trübner, 1863), 194–201. The text of 25 July 1271 is also given in RSPS, l–lv. See Joe Hillaby, "London: The 13th-Century Jewry Revisited."

32. Hillaby and Hillaby, *The Palgrave Dictionary of Medieval Anglo-Jewish History*, 31–32; 303–5.

33. Hillaby and Hillaby, *The Palgrave Dictionary of Medieval Anglo-Jewish History*, 76.

34. Most recently by Robin Mundill, *England's Jewish Solution*; Huscroft, *Expulsion*.

35. Huscroft, *Expulsion*, 142–43.

36. *Statutes of the Realm*, vol. 1, 221. On the statute, see Paul Brand, "Jews and the Law in England, 1275–90"; Mundill, *England's Jewish Solution*, 119–21.

37. CPR 1272–81, 76; Howell, *Eleanor of Provence*, 299.

38. *The Chronicle of Bury St. Edmunds, 1212–1301*, 58.

39. Tartakoff, *Conversion, Circumcision, and Ritual Murder in Medieval Europe*, 85.

40. The 11 September 1275 earthquake, perhaps one of the most powerful ever to strike England, destroyed the church of St Michael on Glastonbury Tor and is recorded by several chroniclers. See R. Musson, "Fatalities in British Earthquakes," 14–16.

41. Michael Prestwich, *Edward I*, 155.

42. *The Chronicle of Guisbourough*, cited by Prestwich, 124.

43. Jennifer Jahner and John Tolan, "Violence, Letters, and the Law: Jewish-Christian Interaction and Episcopal Sanction in Thirteenth-Century England."

44. Hoskin, *Robert Grosseteste*, 207–8.

45. National Archive, Kew, file C 85/99, Latin text, translation and commentary by John Tolan in Notice n°252635, RELMIN project, http://www.cn-telma.fr/relmin/extrait252635/.

46. Burger, *Bishops, Clerks, and Diocesan Governance in Thirteenth-Century England*, 145.

47. Baumgarten, *Mothers and children*, chap. 4.

48. Huscroft, *Expulsion*, 122–23.

49. Brand, "Jews and the Law in England, 1275–90," 1147–50; Zefira Entkin-Rokéah, "Money and the Hangman in Late-13th-Century England."

50. AASS, October, vol. 1, 547–48. See Stacey, "The Conversion of Jews to Christianity in Thirteenth-Century England," 1992, 277–78; Debra Strickland, "Edward I, Exodus, and England on the Hereford World Map," 463–64; Irven Resnick, *Marks of Distinction: Christian Perceptions of Jews in the High Middle Ages*, 286–91; Fogle, *The King's Converts*, 55–58; Brand, "Jews and the Law in England, 1275–90," 1152–53.

51. Einbinder, *Beautiful Death*, 25; Mutius, *Rechtsentscheide*, 32–35; Tartakoff, *Conversion, Circumcision, and Ritual Murder in Medieval Europe*, 109. On the literary topos of the teenage convert, see Jordan, "Adolescence and Conversion in the Middle Ages."

52. John Peckham, *Registrum epistolarum*, vol. 1, 212–13.

53. John Peckham, *Registrum epistolarum*, vol. 2, 407; Mundill, *The King's Jews*, 139–40; Huscroft, *Expulsion*, 135–37.

54. John Peckham, *Registrum epistolarum*, vol. 2, 410–11.

55. John Peckham, *Registrum epistolarum*, vol. 1, 239; Fogle, *The King's Converts*, 30. Most of the cases of apostasy to Judaism in thirteenth- and fourteenth-century Christian Europe involved Jewish converts to Christianity returning (or attempting to return) to Judaism. See Tartakoff, *Conversion, Circumcision, and Ritual Murder in Medieval Europe*, 99–124.

56. Fogle, *The King's Converts*, 30–33.

57. Luca Fois, "Turbato corde," Notice n°268771, RELMIN project, http://www.cn-telma .fr/relmin/extrait268771/. See Cohen, *The Friars and the Jews*, 48–49; Tartakoff, *Conversion, Circumcision, and Ritual Murder in Medieval Europe*, 40, 105.

58. "Quaunt vuz recevez terre ou manoir, encuru par usure de Juis, pernez vus garde ke usure est peche mortel . . . Vous ne poez choses issi encurrues retenir, si vous ne fetes le assez a ceus qui les unt perdues de autre taunt come eles valent plus ke la dette principal. Ou il convient ke vous rendez les choses encurues as Crestiens, qui les unt perdue, sauve a vous taunt come la dette principal amunta, kar plus ne pout doner li usurier," John Peckham, *Registrum*, vol. 2, 619. For an analysis of this letter and a comparison with Grossetestes's letter to Margaret of Winchester and Thomas Aquinas's letter to Duchess Margaret of Brabant, see Meyer, "Female Moneylending and Wet-Nursing in Jewish-Christian Relations in Thirteenth-Century England," 215–21.

59. *Councils & Synods*, vol. 2, 955–63; Solomon Grayzel and Kenneth R. Stow, *The Church and the Jews in the XIIIth Century*, vol. 2, 294–97. See Decima L. Douie, *Archbishop Pecham*, 302–16; Donald Logan, "Thirteen London Jews and Conversion to Christianity: Problems of Apostasy in the 1280s"; Fogle, *The King's Converts*, 33–34.

60. *Councils & Synods*, vol. 2, 959.

61. *Councils & Synods*, vol. 2, 961–62.

62. Meyer, "Female Moneylending and Wet-Nursing," 224–28.

63. Mundill, *England's Jewish Solution*, 146–209.

64. Brand, "Jews and the Law in England, 1275–90"; Meyer, "Female Moneylending and Wet-Nursing," 248–49.

65. Richard Swinfield, *Registrum*, 120–21. Latin text, English translation and commentary in John Tolan, Notice n°252629, RELMIN project, http://www.cn-telma.fr/relmin/extrait 252629/.

66. Joe Hillaby, "The Hereford Jewry, 1179–1290 (Third and Final Part): Aaron Le Blund and the Last Decades of the Hereford Jewry, 1253–90," 463–64.

67. Richard Swinfield, *A Roll of the Household Expenses*, 125–26; Burger, *Bishops, Clerks, and Diocesan*, 87, 94.

68. Abulafia, "Notions of Jewish Service in Twelfth- and Thirteenth-Century England," 214–15. Rabbi Moses of London (d. 1268) also declared that it was permissible to drink Christians' beer: Mutius, *Rechtsentscheide*, 27–28.

69. Hillaby, "The Hereford Jewry, 1179–1290 (Third and Final Part)," 464.

70. Richard Swinfield, *Registrum*, 77; Grayzel and Stow, *The Church and the Jews in the XIIIth Century*, vol. 2, 160.

71. CPR 491; Shlomo Simonsohn, *The Apostolic See and the Jews: Documents*, 262–64; Richard Swinfield, *Registrum*, 139–40; Fogle, *The King's Converts*, 26–28; Grayzel and Stow, *The Church and the Jews in the XIIIth Century*, vol. 2, 157–62.

72. *Councils & Synods*, vol. 2, 1044–45. See Meyer, "Female Moneylending and Wet-Nursing," 222.

73. *Leet Jurisdiction in the City of Norwich: During the 13th and 14th Centuries*, 6.

74. *Leet Jurisdiction in the City of Norwich*, 28.

75. Tolan, "Of Milk and Blood."

76. The text is edited by Christoph Cluse, "'Fabula Ineptissima': Die Ritualmordlegende Um Adam von Bristol Nach Der Handschrift London, British Library, Harley 957." Harvey Hames dates the text and manuscript to c. 1280; see Hames, "The Limits of Conversion: Ritual Murder and the Virgin Mary in the Account of Adam of Bristol." For Robert Stacey, the text was probably written in the mid-thirteenth century and the manuscript probably dates between 1310 and

1320: Stacey, "'Adam of Bristol' and Tales of Ritual Crucifixion in Medieval England"; Stacey, "From Ritual Crucifixion to Host Desecration: Jews and the Body of Christ."

77. For a full discussion of this incident, see Zefira Entin Rokéah, "An Anglo-Jewish Assembly or 'Mini-Parliament' in 1287."

78. For an introduction to the subject, see Mundill, *England's Jewish Solution*, 64–67, 276–82.

79. *Rôles gascons*, vol. 2, 139–41, 167; Jean-Paul Trabut-Cussac, *L'Administration anglaise en Gascogne sous Henry III et Édouard I de 1254 à 1307*, 312–13.

80. Richardson, *English Jewry*, 225–227; Chazan, *Medieval Jewry of Northern France*, 184; Trabut-Cussac, 85–86.

81. See, for example, *Records of the Wardrobe and the Household, 1286–1289*, no. 2578.

82. Notice n° 252866, RELMIN project, Orléans http://www.cn-telma.fr/relmin /extrait252866/ (accessed 11/3/2015). For background on the Jews of Anjou and their expulsion, see William Chester Jordan, "Anciens Maîtres/Nouveaux Maîtres: Les Juifs de La France de l'Ouest et La Transition Des Angevins Aux Capétiens"; Joseph Shatzmiller, "Les Angevins et Les Juifs de Leurs États: Anjou, Naples et Provence."

83. "Mus in pera, serpens in gremio et ignis in sinu," Innocent III, Etsi Iudeos, http://www .cn-telma.fr/relmin/extrait30352/.

84. This paragraph is based principally on Stacey, "Parliamentary Negotiation and the Expulsion of the Jews from England."

85. RSPS, xli.

86. Stacey, "Parliamentary Negotiation and the Expulsion of the Jews from England."

87. Brand, "New Light on the Expulsion of the Jewish Community from England in 1290."

88. Translation in Einbinder, "Meir b. Elijah of Norwich," 154–55. See Nisse, *Jacob's Shipwreck*, 49–50.

89. Einbinder, "Meir b. Elijah of Norwich"; Abulafia, "Notions of Jewish Service in Twelfth- and Thirteenth-Century England"; Miriamne Ara Krummel, "Bringing Meir b. Elijah of Norwich into the Classroom: Discovering a Medieval Minority Poet."

90. Einbinder, "Meir b. Elijah of Norwich."

CONCLUSION

1. RSPS, xl–xlii.

2. Abulafia, "Notions of Jewish Service," 220–21.

3. Stocker, "The Shrine of Little St. Hugh," 115–16; Hill, *Medieval Lincoln*, 1965, 228–30; Hillaby and Hillaby, *The Palgrave Dictionary of Medieval Anglo-Jewish History*, 327–30.

4. John Selden, "Of the Iewes Somtime Living in England, Colleced out of Ancient Records." See Tartakoff, *Conversion, Circumcision, and Ritual Murder in Medieval Europe*, 67.

5. AASS, vol. 33, 494–95.

6. Charles Anderson, *The Lincoln Pocket Guide*, 116–17.

7. Ulrich Wyrwa, "The Making of Antisemitism in Nineteenth-Century Europe as an Invention of Tradition."

8. Langmuir, "The Knight's Tale of Young Hugh of Lincoln," 460–61.

9. Langmuir, "The Knight's Tale of Young Hugh of Lincoln," 460. For an early twentieth-century version, a folk ballad called "Little Sir Hugh," see Cecil James Sharp, *One Hundred English Folksongs*, xx, 22–23.

10. Orlando Radice, "School to Drop Antisemitic Blood Libel Logo," *The Jewish Chronicle*, 29 January 2020, https://www.thejc.com/news/uk-news/lincolnshire-school-is-to-drop-95-year -old-logo-after-jc-points-out-it-symbolised-an-antisemitic-blo-1.496174.

11. Teter, *Blood Libel*, 1–2; Teter, "Blood Libel, a Lie and Its Legacies."

12. Lavezzo, *The Accommodated Jew: English Antisemitism from Bede to Milton*; Anthony Bale, *The Jew in the Medieval Book English Antisemitisms, 1350–1500*. On Shakespeare, see David Nirenberg, *Anti-Judaism: The Western Tradition*, chap. 8.

13. Paul Gilroy, *The Black Atlantic: Modernity and Double Consciousness*.

14. Robert Chazan, "The Role of Medieval Northern Europe in Generating Virulent Anti-Jewish Imagery," 103.

15. Southern, *Robert Grosseteste*, 248.

16. Jordan, *Ideology and Royal Power*, art. XII, 48.

BIBLIOGRAPHY

PRINCIPAL COLLECTIONS OF ROYAL AND ECCLESIASTICAL SOURCES (WITH ABBREVIATIONS)

AASS *Acta Sanctorum*. 68 vols. Brussels and Antwerp: Société des Bollandistes, 1643–1940.

BPR Paul Brand, ed. *Plea Rolls of the Exchequer of the Jews Preserved in the National Archives (Formerly the Public Record Office): Volume 6: Edward I, 1279–81*. London: Jewish Historical Society of England, 2005.

Cal Ch R 1 *Calendar of the Charter Rolls Preserved in the Public Records Office*. Vol. 1. London: HMSO, 1903.

Cal LR *Calendar of the Liberate Rolls Preserved in the Public Record Office. Henry III, Vol. III: A.D. 1245–1251*. London: HMSO, 1937.

Cal PR 1232–47 *Calendar of the Patent Rolls. Henry III. Vol. 3, 1232–1247*. London: HMSO, 1906.

Cal PR 1247–58 *Calendar of the Patent Rolls. Henry III. Vol. 4, 1247–1258*. London: HMSO, 1908.

Cal PR 1258–66 *Calendar of the Patent Rolls. Henry III. Vol. 5, 1258–1266*. London: HMSO, 1910.

Cal PR 1266–72 *Calendar of the Patent Rolls. Henry III. Vol. 6, 1266–1272*. London: HMSO, 1913.

Cal PR 1272–81 *Calendar of the Patent Rolls. Edward I. Vol. 1, 1272–1281*. London: HMSO, 1971.

CFR *Calendar of the Fine Rolls of the Reign of Henry III 1223–24*, online (http://www.finerollshenry3.org.uk).

The Charters of Norwich Cathedral Priory. London: Pipe Roll Society, 1974.

Councils & Synods. Edited by Friedrich Maurice Powicke and Christopher Robert Cheney. *Councils and Synods with Other Documents Relating to the English Church*. 2 vols. Oxford: Clarendon, 1964.

CPR *Calendar of Entries in the Papal Registers Relating to Great Britain and Ireland 1, Vol. 1*. Dublin: Stationary Office for Irish Manuscripts Comm., 1893.

CR 1227–31. *Close Rolls of the Reign of Henry III, Preserved in the Public Record Office. Vol. 1, A.D. 1227–1231*. London: HMSO, 1902.

CR 1231–34. *Close Rolls of the Reign of Henry III, Preserved in the Public Record Office. Vol. 2, A.D. 1231–1234*. London: HMSO, 1905.

CR 1234–37. *Close Rolls of the Reign of Henry III, Preserved in the Public Record Office. Vol. 3, A.D. 1234–1237*. London: HMSO, 1908.

CR 1237–42. *Close Rolls of the Reign of Henry III, Preserved in the Public Record Office. Vol. 4. A.D. 1237–1242*. London: HMSO, 1911.

CR 1242–47. *Close Rolls of the Reign of Henry III Preserved in the Public Record Office. Vol. 5, 1242–1247*. London: Public Record Office, 1916.

CR 1247–51. *Close Rolls of the Reign of Henry III Preserved in the Public Record Office,* Vol. 6, *A.D. 1247–1251.* London: HMSO, 1922.

CR 1251–53. *Close Rolls of the Reign of Henry III Preserved in the Public Record Office.* Vol. 7, A.D. 1251–1253. London: Public Record Office, 1927.

CR 1253–54. *Close Rolls of the Reign of Henry III. Preserved in the Public Record Office.* Vol. 8, A.D. 1253–1254. London: Public Record Office, 1929.

CR 1254–56. *Close Rolls of the Reign of Henry III. Preserved in the Public Record Office.* Vol. 9, A.D. 1254–1256. London: Public Record Office, 1928.

CR 1256–59. *Close Rolls of the Reign of Henry III, Preserved in the Public Record Office.* Vol. 10, A.D. 1256–1259. London: HMSO, 1932.

CR 1259–61. *Close Rolls of the Reign of Henry III Preserved in the Public Record Office.* Vol. 11, A.D. 1259–1261. London: HMSO, 1934.

CR 1261–64. *Close Rolls of the Reign of Henry III Preserved in the Public Record Office.* Vol. 12, 1261–1264. London: HMSO, 1936.

CR 1264–68. *Close Rolls of the Reign of Henry III Preserved in the Public Record Office.* Vol. 13, 1264–1268. London: HMSO, 1937.

CR 1268–72. *Close Rolls of the Reign of Henry III Preserved in the Public Record Office.* Vol. 14, 1268–1272. London: HMSO, 1938.

CRR 14 *Curia regis Rolls 14: The Reign of Henry III, 14.* London: HMSO, 1961.

CRR 15 *Curia regis Rolls 15: 17 to 21 Henry III (1233–1237).* London: HMSO, 1972.

Decrees of the Ecumenical Councils. Edited by Norman Tanner. Vol. 1. Washington, DC: Georgetown University Press, 1990.

Docs. Bar. Edited by Reginald Treharne and Ivor Sanders. *Documents of the Baronial Movement of Reform and Rebellion, 1258–1267.* Oxford: Clarendon Press, 1973.

Docs. English Church. Edited by D. Whitelock, M. Brett, and C. Brooke, *Councils and Synods with other Documents Relating to the English Church.* Vol. 1, AD 871–1204, part 2: 1066–1204. Oxford: Clarendon Press, 1981.

Documents Illustrative of English History in the Thirteenth and Fourteenth Centuries, Selected from the Records of the Department of the Queen's Remembrancer of the Exchequer. Edited by Henry Cole. London: Eyre and Spottiswoode, 1844.

EEAW Vincent, Nicholas, ed. *English Episcopal Acta. IX: Winchester 1205–1238.* Oxford: British Academy/Oxford University Press, 1994.

ERF *Excerpta e rotulis finium in Turri Londinensi.* Carol Roberts, et al. 2 vols. London: Public Records Office, 1835–1836.

HRC Hardy, Thomas Duffus, ed. *Rotuli Chartarum in Turri Londinensi Asservati.* London, 1837.

HRLC Hardy, Thomas Duffus, ed. *Rotuli litterarum clausarum in Turri Londinensi asservati.* 2 vols. London: G. Eyre and A. Spottiswoode, 1833–1844.

HRLP Hardy, Thomas Duffus, ed. *Rotuli Litterarum Patentium in Turri Londinensi Asservati.* London, 1835.

HROF Hardy, Thomas Duffus, ed. *Rotuli de Oblatis et Finibus in Turri Londinensi Asservati.* London, 1835.

PR 57 *The Great Roll of the Pipe for the Thirteenth Year of the Reign of King John, Michaelmas 1211. (Pipe Roll 57).* London: Pipe Roll Society, 1953.

PR 64. Harris, Brian, ed. *The Great Roll of the Pipe for the Fourth Year of the Reign of King Henry III, Michaelmas 1220: (Pipe Roll 64); Now First Printed from the Original in the Public Record Office.* London: Pipe Roll Society, 1987.

PR HIII 1216–25. *Patent Rolls of the Reign of Henry III, AD 1216–1225*. London: Public Record Office, 1901.

PR HIII 1225–32. *Patent Rolls of the Reign of Henry III, AD 1225–1232*. London: Public Record Office, 1903.

RCPR. Rigg, James, ed. *Calendar of the Plea Rolls of the Exchequer of the Jews Preserved in the Public Record Office*. Vol. 1. London: Macmillan, 1905.

RR Barratt, Nicholas, and Laura Napran, eds. *Receipt Rolls for the Fourth, Fifth and Sixth Years of the Reign of King Henry III, Easter 1220, 1221, 1222: (Receipt Rolls 3B, 4 and 5): Now First Printed from the Originals in the National Archives Public Record Office*. London: Pipe Roll Society, 2003.

RS: Rolls Series. *Rerum Britannicarum Medii Ævi Scriptores, or Chronicles and Memorials of Great Britain and Ireland During the Middle Ages*. 70 volumes. London: Longman, 1858–1911.

RSPS: Rolls Series. *Select Pleas, Starrs, and Other Records from the Rolls of the Exchequer of the Jews 1220–1284*. London: Selden Society, 1902.

SRHL Shirley, Walter, ed. *Royal and Other Historical Letters Illustrative of the Reign of Henry III: From the Originals in the Public Record Office*. London: Rolls Series, 1862.

OTHER PRIMARY SOURCES

Adam of Eynsham. *Magna vita Sancti Hugonis. The Life of St. Hugh of Lincoln*. Edited by Decima Douie and David Farmer. Oxford: Clarendon Press, 1985.

Annales monastici. Edited by Henry Richards Luard. 4 vols. London: Longman, Green, Longman, Roberts, and Green, 1864–1869.

The Annals of Dunstable Priory. Edited by Harriett Webster. Translated by David Preest. Rochester: Boydell Press, 2018.

Cartulary of the Hospital of St. John the Baptist. Vol. 3. Oxford: Clarendon Press, 1917.

Chaucer, Geoffrey. *A Variorum Edition of the Works of Geoffrey Chaucer. The Prioress' Tale*. Edited by Paul G. Ruggiers. Vol. 20. Norman: University of Oklahoma Press, 1987.

The Chronicle of Bury St. Edmunds, 1212–1301. Translated by Antonia Gransden. London: Nelson, 1964.

Les conciles de la province de Tours = Concilia provinciae turonensis: (saec. XIII–XV). Joseph Avril, ed. Paris: Centre national de la recherche scientifique, 1987.

Cronica maiorum et vicecomitum Londoniarum: et quedam, que contingebant temporibus illis ab anno 1178 A.D. annum 1274; cum appendice = De antiquis legibus liber. Edited by Thomas Stapleton. London: Camden Society, 1846.

———. Translated by Henry Riley. *Chronicles of the Mayors and Sheriffs of London—1188–1274*. London: Trübner, 1863. http://www.british-history.ac.uk/source.aspx?pubid=560.

Flores Historiarum. 2 vols. London: Eyre and Spottiswoode, 1890.

Frederick II. *Constitutiones, Monumenta Germaniae historica*, col. Constitutiones et acta publica imperatorum et regum, vol. 2. Edited by L. Weiland. Hannover: MGH, 1896.

Gaufridus de Vinsauf. *Poetria Nova*. Edited by Martin Camargo. Translated by Margaret Frances Nims. Toronto: Pontifical Institute of Mediaeval Studies, 2010.

Gautier de Coinci. *Les miracles de notre dame*. 4 vols. Edited by Victor Frederic Koenig. Genève: Droz, 1961.

Gerald of Wales. *The Autobiography of Gerald of Wales*. Rochester: Boydell Press, 2005.

———. *Giraldi Cambrensis Opera*, vol. 4. Edited by J. S. Brewer. London: Longman, 1873.

———. *The Jewel of the Church.* Translated by John J. Hagen. Lugduni Batavorum: Brill, 1979.

———. *The Life of St. Hugh of Avalon, Bishop of Lincoln 1186–1200.* Edited by Richard Morgan Loomis. New York: Garland, 1985.

Gervase of Canterbury. *The Historical Works of Gervase of Canterbury,* 2 vols. Edited by William Stubbs. London: Longman, 1880.

Guala Bicchieri. *The Letters and Charters of Cardinal Guala Bicchieri, Papal Legate in England, 1216–1218.* Edited by Nicholas Vincent. Woodbridge: Boydell, 1996.

Historia diplomatica Friderici II, sive Constitutiones, privilegia istius imperatoris et filiorum ejus. Edited by J. Huillard-Bréholles. Paris: H. Plon, 1852.

Jean de Joinville. *Vie de saint Louis.* Edited by Jacques Monfrin. Paris: Garnier, 1997.

Jocelin of Brakelond. *The Chronicle of Jocelin of Brakelond, Concerning the Acts of Samson, Abbot of the Monastery of St. Edmund.* London: T. Nelson, 1949.

———. *Chronicle of the Abbey of Bury St Edmunds.* Translated by Diana Greenway and Jane Sayers. Oxford: Oxford University Press, 1989.

Johannes de Oxenedes. *Chronica Johannis de Oxenedes.* London: Longman, 1859.

John Chrysostom. *Homilies on Matthew.* Vol. 10. *A Select Library of the Nicene and Post-Nicene Fathers of the Christian Church.* Translated by Philip Schaff. New York: Christian Literature Company, 1888.

John Peckham. *Registrum epistolarum fratris Johannis Peckham, Archiepiscopus Cantuariensis.* 3 vols. Edited by Charles Trice Martin. London: Longman, 1884.

Leet Jurisdiction in the City of Norwich: During the 13th and 14th Centuries. With a Short Notice of Its Later History and Decline from Rolls in the Possession of the Corporation. Edited by William Hudson. Norwich: Selden Society, 1892.

Matthew Paris. *Chronica Majora.* Edited by Henry Richards Luard. Nendeln: Kraus Reprint, 1964.

———. *Chronica Majora.* Translated by J. A. Giles. *English History: From the Year 1235 to 1273.* 3 vols. London: Bohn, 1852.

———. *Historia Anglorum, sive, ut vulgo dicitur, Historia minor: Item, ejusdem Abbreviatio chronicorum Angliæ.* Edited by Frederic Madden. London: Longmans, 1866.

Munimenta Academica, or Documents Illustrative of Academical Life and Studies at Oxford. London: Longman, Brown, Green, Londmans, and Roberts, 1868.

Nicholas de Triveti. *Annales sex regum Angliæ, qui a comitibus Andegavensibus originem taxerunt.* Edited by Thomas Hog. London: Sumptibus Societatis, 1845.

Ordonnances Des Roys de France de La Troisième Race Recueillies Par Ordre Chronologique Avec Des Renvoys Des Unes Aux Autres, Des Sommaires, et Des Observations Sur Le Texte. Vol. 1. Edited by Eusèbe Jacob de Laurière and Denis F. Secousse. Paris: Imprimerie Royale, 1723.

Peter of Cornwall. *Peter of Cornwall's Book of Revelations.* Edited by Robert Easting and Richard Sharpe. Toronto: Pontifical Institute of Mediaeval Studies, 2013.

Petrus Venerabilis. *Petri Venerabilis Adversus Iudeorum Inveteratam Duritiem.* Edited by Yvonne Friedman. Turnholti: Brepols, 1985.

Ralph of Coggeshall. *Chronicon Anglicanum.* Edited by Joseph Stevenson. London: Longman, 1875.

Ralph of Diceto. *Opera Historica.* Edited by William Stubbs. London: Rolls Series, 1876.

Records of the Wardrobe and Household 1286–1289. Edited by Benjamin Byerly. London: HMSO, 1986.

Richard Swinfield. *Registrum Ricardi de Swinfield, Episcopi Herefordensis, A.D. 1283–1317.* Edited by William Wolfe Capes. London: Canterbury and York Society, 1909.

————. *A Roll of the Household Expenses of Richard de Swinfield, Bishop of Hereford, During Part of the Years 1289 and 1290. Abstracts, Illustrations, Glossary and Index Abstracts, Illustrations, Glossary and Index.* Edited by John Webb. London: Camden Society, 1855.

Robert Grosseteste. *De Cessatione Legalium.* Édité par Richard Dales and Edward King. London: British Academy/Oxford University Press, 1986.

————. *De Cessatione Legalium. On the Cessation of the Laws.* Translated by Stephen Hildebrand. Washington, DC: Catholic University of America Press, 2012.

————. *De Decem Mandatis.* Edited by Richard C. Dales. Oxford: British Academy/Oxford University Press, 1987.

————. *The Letters of Robert Grosseteste, Bishop of Lincoln.* Translated by Frank Mantello and Joseph Goering. Toronto: University of Toronto Press, 2010.

Roger Bacon. *Opera Quaedam Hactenus Inedita.* Edited by J. S. Brewer. London: Longman, Green, Longman, and Roberts, 1859.

Roger of Howden. *Chronica.* 3 vols. Edited by William Stubbs. London: Longman, 1868.

————. *Chronica. The Annals of Roger of Hoveden.* Translated by Henry Riley. London: H. G. Bohn, 1853.

————. *Gesta Regis Henrici Secundi Benedicti Abbatis: The Chronicle of the Reigns of Henry II and Richard I, A.D. 1169–1192.* Edited by William Stubbs. RS 49, 1867.

Roger of Wendover. *Chronica, sive, Flores historiarum.* 4 vols. Edited by H. Coxe. London: Sumptibus Societatis, 1841.

————. *Chronica, sive, Flores historiarum. Roger of Wendover's Flowers of History: Comprising the History of England from the Descent of the Saxons to A.D. 1235: Formerly Ascribed to Matthew Paris.* Translated by J. A. Giles. London: Henry G. Bohn, 1849.

Rôles gascons: transcrits et publiés. Edited by Charles Bémont. Paris: Imprimerie Nationale, 1900.

Royal and Other Historical Letters Illustrative of the Reign of Henry III. Nendeln: Kraus Reprints, 1965.

The Song of Lewes. Edited by Charles Lethbridge Kingsford. Oxford: Clarendon Press, 1890.

Statutes of the Realm. 11 vols. Edited by A. Luders. London: Eyre and Strahan, 1810.

Thomas of Eccleston. *Tractatus de Adventu Fratrum Minorum in Angliam.* Edited by A. Little. Manchester: Manchester University Press, 1951.

Thomas of Monmouth. *The Life and Miracles of St William of Norwich.* Edited by A. Jessopp and M. R. James. Cambridge: Cambridge University Press, 1896.

————. *The Life and Passion of William of Norwich.* Translated by Miri Rubin. London: Penguin, 2014.

Thomas Walsingham, and Matthew Paris. *Gesta abbatum monasterii Sancti Albani, a Thoma Walsingham, regnante Ricardo Secundo, ejusdem ecclesiæ præcentore, compilata.* Edited by Henry Riley. London: Longmans, Green, 1867.

Walter of Coventry. *Memoriale Fratris Walteri de Coventria: The Historical Collections of Walter of Coventry.* Vol. 2. Edited by William Stubbs. London: Longman, 1873.

SECONDARY WORKS

Abulafia, Anna Sapir. *Christian-Jewish Relations, 1000–1300: Jews in the Service of Medieval Christendom.* New York: Pearson Longman, 2011.

————. "The Jews." In *A Social History of England, 900–1200,* edited by Julia Crick and Elisabeth van Houts, 256–64. Cambridge: Cambridge University Press, 2011.

————. "Notions of Jewish Service in Twelfth- and Thirteenth-Century England." In Rees Jones and Watson, *Christians and Jews in Angevin England*, 204–21.

Abulafia, David. "Ethnic Variety and Its Implications: Frederick II's Relations with Jews and Muslims." *Studies in the History of Art* 44 (1994): 213–24.

Adams, Jonathan, and Cordelia Hess, eds. *The Medieval Roots of Antisemitism: Continuities and Discontinuities from the Middle Ages to the Present Day*. London: Routledge, 2018.

Adler, Michael. "The Jews of Canterbury." *Transactions (Jewish Historical Society of England)* 7 (1911): 19–96.

————. *Jews of Medieval England*. London: Jewish Historical Society of England/E. Goldston, 1939.

————. *The Song of Simon de Montfort: England's First Revolutionary and the Death of Chivalry*. Oxford: Oxford University Press, 2019.

————. "The Testimony of the London Jewry Against the Ministers of Henry III." *Transactions (Jewish Historical Society of England)* 14 (1935): 141–85.

Ambler, Sophie Thérèse. *Bishops in the Political Community of England, 1213–1272*. Oxford: Oxford University Press, 2017.

Anderson, Charles Henry John. *The Lincoln Pocket Guide, Being a Short Account of the Churches and Antiquities of the County and of the Cathedral . . . of Lincoln . . .* London: E. Stanford, 1880.

Arendt, Hannah. *The Origins of Totalitarianism*. New York: Harcourt Brace Jovanovich, 1951.

Aston, T., and Rosamond Faith. "The Endowments of the University to *circa* 1348." In *The History of the University of Oxford. The Early Oxford Schools*, Vol. 1, edited by J. I. Catto, 265–309. Oxford: Clarendon Press, 1984.

Bailey, Mark. "Tallage-at-Will in Later Medieval England." *English Historical Review* 134, no. 566 (2019): 25–58.

Baldwin, John. "Master Stephen Langton, Future Archbishop of Canterbury: The Paris Schools and *Magna Carta*." *English Historical Review* 123 (2008): 811–46.

Bale, Anthony. *The Jew in the Medieval Book English Antisemitisms, 1350–1500*. Cambridge: Cambridge University Press, 2008.

Baron, Salo W. "Newer Emphases in Jewish History." *Jewish Social Studies* 25 (1963): 235–48.

————. *A Social and Religious History of the Jews*. 18 vols. New York: Columbia University Press, 1952.

Bartlet, Suzanne. *Licoricia of Winchester: Marriage, Motherhood and Murder in the Medieval Anglo-Jewish Community*. London: Vallentine Mitchell, 2009.

Bartlett, Robert. *Gerald of Wales, 1146–1223*. Oxford: Clarendon Press, 1982.

Barzen, Rainer. "Das Nürnberger Memorbuch. Eine Einführung." In *Corpus der Quellen zur Geschichte der Juden im spätmittelalterlichen Reich*, http://www.medieval-ashkenaz.org /quellen/1273-1347/nm01/einleitung.html.

Baumann, Daniel. *Stephen Langton Erzbischof von Canterbury im England der Magna Carta (1207–1228)*. Leiden: Brill, 2009.

Baumgarten, Elisheva. *Mothers and Children: Jewish Family Life in Medieval Europe*. Princeton: Princeton University Press, 2004.

Bellesrives, Léonce de. *Une Famille de héros, ou Histoire des personnages qui ont illustré le nom de Montmorenci*. Limoges: Babou Frères, 1860.

Berndt, Rainer. *André de Saint-Victor (mort en 1175): exégète et théologien*. Turnhoult: Brépols, 1991.

Blair, Ian, Joe Hillaby, I. Howell, R. Sermon, and B. Watson. "The Discovery of Two Medieval Mikva'ot in London and a Reinterpretation of the Bristol 'Mikveh'." *Jewish Historical Studies* 37 (2002): 15–40.

Blumenkranz, Bernhard. *Juifs et Chrétiens dans le monde occidental 430–1096*. Paris: Imprimerie Nationale, 1960.

Blurton, Heather, "Egyptian Days: From Passion to Exodus in the Representation of Twelfth-Century Jewish-Christian Relations." In Rees Jones and Watson, *Christians and Jews in Angevin England*, 222–37.

Blurton, Heather, and Hannah R Johnson. *The Critics and the Prioress: Antisemitism, Criticism, and Chaucer's Prioress's Tale*. Ann Arbor: University of Michigan Press, 2017.

Boulton, Maureen. *Piety and Persecution in the French Texts of England*. Tempe: Arizona Center for Medieval and Renaissance Studies, 2013.

Brand, Paul. "Jews and the Law in England, 1275–90." *English Historical Review* 115, no. 464 (2000): 1138–58.

———. "New Light on the Expulsion of the Jewish Community from England in 1290." *Reading Medieval Studies* 40 (2014): 101–16.

Brown, Reva Berman, and Sean McCartney. "David of Oxford and Licoricia of Winchester: Glimpses into a Jewish Family in Thirteenth-Century England." *Jewish Historical Studies* 39 (2004): 1–34.

Burger, Michael. *Bishops, Clerks, and Diocesan Governance in Thirteenth-Century England: Reward and Punishment*. Cambridge: Cambridge University Press, 2012.

Callus, D. A. "Robert Grosseteste as Scholar." In *Robert Grosseteste, Scholar and Bishop; Essays in Commemoration of the Seventh Centenary of His Death*, edited by D. A. Callus, 1–69. Oxford: Clarendon, 1955.

Capelli, Piero. "Nicolas Donin, the Talmud Trial of 1240, and the Struggles Between Church and State in Medieval Europe." In *Entangled Histories: Knowledge, Authority, and Jewish Culture in the Thirteenth Century*, edited by Elisheva Baumgarten, Ruth Mazo Karras, and Katelyn Mesler, 159–78. Philadelphia: University of Pennsylvania Press, 2016.

Carpenter, David. "Crucifixion and Conversion: King Henry III and the Jews in 1255." In *Laws, Lawyers and Texts: Studies in Medieval Legal History in Honour of Paul Brand*, edited by Susanne Jenks, Jonathan Rose, and Christopher Whittick, 130–48. Leiden: Brill, 2012.

———. *Henry III, 1207–1258*. New Haven: Yale University Press, 2020.

———. "John, Sir, Fitz John (c. 1240–1275), Baronial Leader." *Oxford Dictionary of National Biography*. September 23, 2004. https://www.oxforddnb.com/view/10.1093/ref:odnb /9780198614128.001.0001/odnb-9780198614128-e-38272.

———. "King Henry III and the Sicilian Affair." Henry III Fine Rolls Project, n.d. https:// finerollshenry3.org.uk/redist/pdf/fm-02-2012.pdf.

———. *Magna Carta*. London: Penguin Books, 2015.

———. "Magna Carta 1253: The Ambitions of the Church and the Divisions within the Realm." *Historical Research* 86, no. 232 (May 1, 2013): 179–90.

———. *The Minority of Henry III*. Berkeley: University of California Press, 1990.

———. *The Reign of Henry III*. London: Hambledon Press, 1996.

———. *The Struggle for Mastery: Britain 1066–1284*. London: Allen Lane, 2003.

Causton, Ann, ed. *Medieval Jewish Documents in Westminster Abbey*. London: Jewish Historical Society of England, 2007.

Champagne, Marie-Thérèse, and Irven M. Resnick, eds. *Jews and Muslims under the Fourth Lateran Council. Papers Commemorating the Octocentenary of the Fourth Lateran Council (1215).* Turnhout: Brepols, 2019.

Charles, R. H. *The Apocrypha and Pseudepigrapha of the Old Testament in English: With Introductions and Critical and Explanatory Notes to the Several Books.* Oxford: Clarendon Press, 1913.

Chazan, Robert. *Church, State, and Jew in the Middle Ages.* New York: Behrman House, 1980.

———. *Medieval Jewry in Northern France: A Social and Political History.* Baltimore: Johns Hopkins University Press, 1973.

———. "The Role of Medieval Northern Europe in Generating Virulent Anti-Jewish Imagery." In *The Medieval Roots of Antisemitism: Continuities and Discontinuities from the Middle Ages to the Present Day,* edited by Jonathan Adams and Cordelia Hess, 97–106. London: Routledge, 2018.

Chazan, Robert, Jean Hoff, and John Friedman, eds. *The Trial of the Talmud, Paris, 1240.* Toronto: Pontifical Institute of Mediaeval Studies, 2012.

Cheney, Christopher. "The Eve of Magna Carta." In *The Papacy and England, 12th–14th Centuries. Historical and Legal Studies,* article XIII. London: Variorum Reprints, 1982.

———. "Legislation of the Medieval English Church." *English Historical Review* 50 (1935): 193–224.

———. "The 'Paper Constitution' Preserved by Matthew Paris." *English Historical Review* 65 (1950): 213–21.

Cheney, Mary. "The Council of Westminster 1175: New Light on an Old Source." *Studies in Church History* 11 (1975): 61–68.

Clanchy, Michael. "Did Henry III Have a Policy?" *History* 54 (1968): 203–216.

———. *From Memory to Written Record: England 1066–1307.* Oxford: Blackwell, 1994.

Cluse, Christoph. "'Fabula Ineptissima': Die Ritualmordlegende Um Adam von Bristol Nach Der Handschrift London, British Library, Harley 957." *Aschkenas: Zeitschrift Für Geschichte Und Kultur der Juden* 5 (1995): 293–330.

———. "Stories of Breaking and Taking the Cross. A Possible Context for the Oxford Incident of 1268." *Revue d'Histoire Ecclésiastique* 90 (1995): 396–442.

Cobban, Alan. *The Medieval English Universities: Oxford and Cambridge to c. 1500.* Berkeley: University of California Press, 1988.

Cohen, Jeffrey. "The Future of the Jews of York." In Rees Jones and Watson, eds. *Christians and Jews in Angevin England,* 278–93.

Cohen, Jeremy. *The Friars and the Jews: The Evolution of Medieval Anti-Judaism.* Ithaca: Cornell University Press, 1982.

Cohn-Sherbok, Dan. "Medieval Jewish Persecution in England: The Canterbury Pogroms in Perspective." *Southern History: A Review of the History of Southern England* 3 (1981): 23–37.

Court, Elisa Narin van. "Invisible in Oxford: Medieval Jewish History in Modern England." *Shofar: An Interdisciplinary Journal of Jewish Studies* 26 (2008): 1–20.

Dahan, Gilbert. "Deux Psautiers Hébraïques Glosés En Latin." *Revue d'Etudes Juives* 158 (1999): 61–87.

———. "Exégèse et polémique dans les commentaires de Genèse d'Etienne Langton." In *Les Juifs au regard de l'histoire: mélanges en l'honneur de Bernhard Blumenkranz,* edited by Gilbert Dahan, 130–48. Paris: Picard, 1985.

———. "L'article Iudei de La Summa Abel de Pierre Le Chantre." *Revue Des Études Augustiniennes* 27, no. 1–2 (1981): 105–26.

———. *Les intellectuels chrétiens et les juifs au Moyen Age*. Paris: Cerf, 1990.

———. "Les Juifs Dans Les Miracles de Gautier de Coincy." *Archives Juives* 16 (1980): 41–49, 59–68.

———. *Les juifs en France médiévale dix études*. Paris: Cerf, 2017.

———. "L'exégèse de l'histoire de Caïn et Abel Du XIIe Au XIVe Siècle En Occident: Textes." *Recherches de Théologie Ancienne et Médiévale*, resnick, 50 (1983): 5–68.

Dahan, Gilbert, and Elie Nicolas, eds. *Le brûlement du Talmud à Paris, 1242–1244*. Paris: Cerf, 1999.

Dahood, Roger. "The Anglo-Norman 'Hugo de Lincolnia'." *Chaucer Review* 49, no. 1 (2014): 1–38.

———. "English Historical Narratives of Jewish Child-Murder, Chaucer's Prioress's Tale, and the Date of Chaucer's Unknown Source." *Studies in the Age of Chaucer: Yearbook of the New Chaucer Society* 31 (2009): 125–40.

———. "The Punishment of the Jews, Hugh of Lincoln, and the Question of Satire in the Prioress's Tale." *Viator: Medieval and Renaissance Studies* 36 (2005): 465–91.

D'Avray, David. "Magna Carta: Its Background in Stephen Langton's Academic Biblical Exegesis and Its Episcopal Reception." *Studi Medievali* 38 (1997): 423–38.

Dean, Ruth J. "An Anglo-Norman Version of Grosseteste: Part of His Suidas and Testamenta XII Patriarcharum." *PMLA* 51, no. 3 (1936): 607–20.

Denholm-Young, N. *Richard of Cornwall*. Oxford: Basil Blackwell, 1947.

Dobson, R. B. *The Jews of Medieval York and the Massacre of March 1190*. York: St. Anthony's Press, 1974.

Donovan, Claire. *The de Brailes Hours: Shaping the Book of Hours in Thirteenth-Century Oxford*. London: British Library, 1991.

Douie, Decima. *Archbishop Pecham*. Oxford: Clarendon Press, 1952.

Duffy, Eamon. *Royal Books and Holy Bones: Essays in Medieval Christianity*. London: Bloomsbury Continuum, 2018.

Duggan, Anne. "The Cult of St. Thomas Beckett in the Thirteenth Century." In *St. Thomas Cantilupe, Bishop of Hereford: Essays in His Honour*, edited by E. Jancey, 21–44. Hereford: Friends of Hereford Cathedral Publications Committee for the Dean and Chapter, 1982.

Edwards, John. "The Church and the Jews in Medieval England." In *The Jews in Medieval Britain: Historical, Literary and Archaeological Perspectives*, edited by Patricia Skinner, 85–95. Woodbridge: Boydell Press, 2003.

Einbinder, Susan. *Beautiful Death: Jewish Poetry and Martyrdom in Medieval France*. Princeton: Princeton University Press, 2008.

———. "Meir b. Elijah of Norwich: Persecution and Poetry among Medieval English Jews." *Journal of Medieval History* 26 (2000): 145–62.

———. *No Place of Rest: Jewish Literature, Expulsion, and the Memory of Medieval France*. Philadelphia: University of Pennsylvania Press, 2008.

Elliott, Mark. "Robert Grosseteste, the Jews, and the *De Cessatione Legalium*." In *Robert Grosseteste: His Thought and Its Impact*, edited by Jack Cunningham, 314–26. Toronto: Pontifical Institute of Medieval Studies, 2012.

Emmerson, Richard. "Apocalypse and/as History." In *Medieval Historical Writing: Britain and Ireland, 500–1500*, edited by Elizabeth M. Tyler, Emily Steiner, and Jennifer Jahner, 51–66. Cambridge: Cambridge University Press, 2019.

———. *Apocalypse Illuminated the Visual Exegesis of Revelation in Medieval Illustrated Manuscripts*. University Park: Pennsylvania State University Press, 2018.

Entkin-Rokéah, Zefira. "Money and the Hangman in Late-13th-Century England: Jews, Christians and Coinage Offences Alleged and Real (Part I)." *Jewish Historical Studies* 31 (1990): 83–109.

———. "Money and the Hangman in Late 13th-Century England: Jews, Christians and Coinage Offences Alleged and Real (Part II)." *Jewish Historical Studies* 32 (1993): 159–218.

Fidora, Alexander. "Textual Rearrangements and Thwarted Intentions: The Two Versions of the Latin Talmud." *Journal of Transcultural Medieval Studies* 2 (2015): 63–78.

Fidora, Alexander, and Görge K. Hasselhoff. *The Talmud in Dispute During the High Middle Ages.* Bellaterra: Universitat Autonoma de Barcelona, 2019.

Fishman, Talya. *Becoming the People of the Talmud: Oral Torah as Written Tradition in Medieval Jewish Cultures.* Philadelphia: University of Pennsylvania Press, 2013.

Flori, Jean. *Richard Cœur de Lion: le roi-chevalier.* Paris: Payot and Rivages, 1999.

Fogle, Lauren. *The King's Converts: Jewish Conversion in Medieval London.* Lanham: Lexington Books, 2019.

Fredriksen, Paula. *Augustine and the Jews: A Christian Defense of Jews and Judaism.* New York: Doubleday, 2008.

Fryde, Natalie. "The Roots of the Magna Carta: Opposition to the Plantagenets." In *Political Thought and the Realities of Power in the Middle Ages,* 53–65. Göttingen: Vandenhoeck and Ruprecht, 1998.

Génestal, Robert. *Rôle des monastères comme établissements de crédit, étudié en Normandie du XIe à la fin du XIIIe siècle.* Paris: A. Rousseau, 1901.

Gilroy, Paul. *The Black Atlantic: Modernity and Double Consciousness.* Cambridge: Harvard University Press, 1993.

Ginther, James R. *Master of the Sacred Page: A Study of the Theology of Robert Grosseteste, ca. 1229/30–1235.* Aldershot: Ashgate, 2004.

———. "The *Super Psalterium* in Context." In *Editing Robert Grosseteste Papers Given at the Thirty-Sixth Annual Conference on Editorial Problems, University of Toronto, 3–4 November 2000,* edited by Joseph Goering and Evelyn Mackie, 31–60. Toronto: University of Toronto Press, 2003.

Goering, Joseph. "Robert Grosseteste and the Jews of Leicester." In *Robert Grosseteste and the Beginnings of a British Theological Tradition,* edited by Maura O'Carroll, 181–200. Rome: Istituto Storico dei Cappuccini, 2003.

———. "Robert Grosseteste at the Papal Curia." In *A Distinct Voice: Medieval Studies in Honor of Leonard E. Boyle,* edited by Jacqueline Brown and William Stoneman, 253–76. South Bend: University of Notre Dame Press, 1997.

Goldy, Charlotte Newman. "Muriel, a Jew of Oxford: Using the Dramatic to Understand the Mundane in Anglo-Norman Towns." In *Writing Medieval Women's Lives,* edited by Goldy Charlotte Newman and Livingstone Amy, 227–45. New York: Palgrave Macmillan, 2012.

———. "Teaching Jewish and Christian Daily Interaction in Medieval England." In *Jews in Medieval England: Teaching Representations of the Other,* edited by Miriamne Ara Krummel and Tison Pugh, 295–309. Cham: Palgrave Macmillan, 2017.

———. "A Thirteenth-Century Anglo-Jewish Woman Crossing Boundaries: Visible and Invisible." *Journal of Medieval History* 34 (2008): 130–45.

Goodwin, Deborah L. *Take Hold of the Robe of a Jew: Herbert of Bosham's Christian Hebraism.* Leiden: Brill, 2006.

Grayzel, Solomon. *The Church and the Jews in the XIIIth Century: A Study of Their Relations During the Years 1198–1254 Based on the Papal Letters and the Conciliar Decrees of the Periods.* Philadelphia: Dropsie College for Hebrew and Cognate Learning, 1933.

Grayzel, Solomon, and Kenneth R. Stow. *The Church and the Jews in the XIIIth Century*. Vol. 2. Detroit: Wayne State University Press, 1989.

Greatrex, Joan G. "Monastic Charity for Jewish Converts: The Requisition of Corrodies by Henry III." *Studies in Church History* 29 (1992): 133–43.

Hadas, Moses. *Fables of Jewish Aesop*. New York: Columbia University Press, 1967.

Hames, Harvey. "The Limits of Conversion: Ritual Murder and the Virgin Mary in the Account of Adam of Bristol." *Journal of Medieval History* 33, no. 1 (2007): 43–59.

———. "Urinating on the Cross: Christianity as Seen in the Sefer Yoseph Ha-Mekaneh (ca. 1260) and in Light of Paris 1240." In *Ritus Infidelium: Miradas Interconfesionales Sobre Las Prácticas Religiosas En La Edad Media*, edited by John Tolan and José Martínez Gázquez, 209–20. Madrid: Casa de Velázquez, 2013.

Hanawalt, Barbara A. "Narratives of a Nurturing Culture: Parents and Neighbors in Medieval England." *Essays in Medieval Studies* 12 (1995): 1–21.

Harris, Oliver. "Jews, Jurats and the Jewry Wall: A Name in Context." *Transactions of the Leicestershire Archaeological and Historical Society* 82 (2008): 113–33.

Haverkamp, Eva. *Hebräische Berichte über die Judenverfolgungen während des Ersten Kreuzzugs*. Hannover: Hahn, 2005.

———. "Historiography." In *The Cambridge History of Judaism, 6: The Middle Ages—The Christian World*, edited by Robert Chazan, 835–59. Cambridge: Cambridge University Press, 2018.

Heng, Geraldine. *The Invention of Race in the European Middle Ages*. Cambridge: Cambridge University Press, 2018.

Herman, Shael. *Medieval Usury and the Commercialization of Feudal Bonds*. Berlin: Duncker and Humblot, 1993.

Highfield, John Roger Loxdale. *The Early Rolls of Merton College, Oxford with an Appendix of Thirteenth-Century Oxford Charters*. Oxford: Clarendon Press, 1964.

Hill, Francis. *Medieval Lincoln*. Cambridge: Cambridge University Press, 1948.

Hillaby, Joe. "Hereford Gold: Irish, Welsh and English Land, Part I. The Jewish Community at Hereford and Its Clients, 1179–1253." *Transactions of the Woolhope Naturalists' Field Club* 44 (1983): 358–419.

———. "Hereford Gold: Irish, Welsh and English Land, Part 2. The Clients of the Jewish Community of Hereford, 1179–1253: Four Case Studies." *Transactions of the Woolhope Naturalists' Field Club* 45 (1987): 193–270.

———. "The Hereford Jewry, 1179–1290 (Third and Final Part): Aaron Le Blund and the Last Decades of the Hereford Jewry, 1253–90." *Transactions of the Woolhope Naturalists' Field Club* 46 (1990): 432–87.

———. "The London Jewry: William I to John," *Jewish Historical Studies* 33 (1992–1994): 1–44.

———. "London: The 13th-Century Jewry Revisited," *Jewish Historical Studies* 32 (1990–1992): 89–158.

———. "The Worcester Jewry, 1158–1290: Portrait of a Lost Community." *Transactions of the Worcester Archaeological Society* ser. 3, 12 (1990): 73–122.

Hillaby, Joe, and Caroline Hillaby. *The Palgrave Dictionary of Medieval Anglo-Jewish History*. Basingstoke: Palgrave Macmillan, 2013.

Hinnebusch, William. "The Pre-Reformation Sites of the Oxford Blackfriars." *Oxoniensia* 3 (1938), 57–82.

Hollender, Elisabeth. "Piyut." In *The Cambridge History of Judaism, 6: The Middle Ages—The Christian World*, edited by Robert Chazan, 664–77. Cambridge: Cambridge University Press, 2018.

Horowitz, Elliot. "The Jews and the Cross in the Middle Ages: Towards a Reappraisal." In *Philosemitism, Antisemitism, and 'the Jews': Perspectives from the Middle Ages to the Twentieth Century*, edited by Tony Kushner and Nadia Valman, 114–31. Aldershot: Ashgate, 2004,.

Hoskin, Philippa. "Cantilupe's Crusade? Walter de Cantilupe Bishop of Worcester and the Baronial Rebellion." *Transactions of the Worcestershire Historical Society* 23 (2012): 91–102.

———. *Robert Grosseteste and the 13th-Century Diocese of Lincoln: An English Bishop's Pastoral Vision*. Leiden: Brill, 2019.

———. "Robert Grosseteste, Natural Law and Magna Carta: National and Universal Law in 1253." *International Journal of Regional and Local History* 10 (2015): 120–32.

Hosler, John. "William of Newburgh, Henry II, and the Development of English Anti-Judaism." In *Christian Attitudes towards the Jews in the Middle Ages: A Casebook*, edited by Michael Frassetto, 167–82. New York: Routledge, 2013.

Howell, Margaret. *Eleanor of Provence: Queenship in Thirteenth-Century England*. Oxford: Blackwell, 2001.

Hoyle, Victoria. "The Bonds That Bind: Money Lending between Anglo-Jewish and Christian Women in the Plea Rolls of the Exchequer of the Jews, 1218–1280." *Journal of Medieval History* 34 (2008): 119–29.

Hunt, Richard. "The Disputation of Peter of Cornwall against Symon the Jew." In *Studies in History Presented to Frederick Maurice Powicke*, edited by Richard Hunt, Richard Southern, and W. Pantin, 143–56. Oxford: Clarendon Press, 1948.

Huscroft, Richard. *Expulsion: England's Jewish Solution*. Stroud: Tempus, 2005.

Ihnat, Kati. *Mother of Mercy, Bane of the Jews: Devotion to the Virgin Mary in Anglo-Norman England*. Princeton: Princeton University Press, 2016.

Jacobs, Joseph. *Jewish Ideals and Other Essays*. London: D. Nutt, 1896.

Jahner, Jennifer. *Literature and Law in the Era of Magna Carta*. Oxford: Oxford University Press, 2019.

Jahner, Jennifer, and John Tolan. "Violence, Letters, and the Law: Jewish-Christian Interaction and Episcopal Sanction in Thirteenth-Century England." *Global Intellectual History* 7 (2022).

James, M. R. *The Abbey of S. Edmund at Bury*. Cambridge: Cambridge Antiquarian Society, 1895.

———. *A Descriptive Catalogue of the Manuscripts in the Library of Eton College*. Cambridge: Cambridge University Press, 1895.

Jarrett, Bede. *The English Dominican Province (1221–1921)*. London: Catholic Truth Society, 1921.

Johnson, Hannah. *Blood Libel: The Ritual Murder Accusation at the Limit of Jewish History*. Ann Arbor: University of Michigan Press, 2012.

Jonge, M. de. "Robert Grosseteste and the Testaments of the Twelve Patriarchs." *Journal of Theological Studies* 42, no. 1 (1991): 115–25.

Jordan, William Chester. "Adolescence and Conversion in the Middle Ages: A Research Agenda." In *Jews and Christians in Twelfth-Century Europe*, edited by Michael Signer and John Van Engen, 77–93. South Bend: University of Notre Dame Press, 2001.

———. "Anciens Maîtres/Nouveaux Maîtres: Les Juifs de La France de l'Ouest et La Transition Des Angevins Aux Capétiens." In *Plantagenêts et Capétiens: Confrontations et Héritages*, edited by Martin Aurell and Noël-Yves Tonnerre, 387–94. Turnhout: Brepols, 2006.

———. *The Apple of His Eye: Converts from Islam in the Reign of Louis IX*. Princeton: Princeton University Press, 2019.

———. "Archbishop Eudes Rigaud and the Jews of Normandy, 1248–1275." In *Friars and Jews in the Middle Ages and the Renaissance*, edited by Steven Michael and Susan Myers, 39–52. Leiden: Brill, 2004.

———. *The French Monarchy and the Jews: From Philip Augustus to the Last Capetians*. Philadelphia: University of Pennsylvania Press, 1989.

———. *Ideology and Royal Power in Medieval France: Kingship, Crusades and the Jews*. Aldershot: Ashgate, 2001.

———. "Marian Devotion and the Talmud Trial of 1240." *Wolfenbütteler Mittelalter-Studien* 4 (1992): 61–76.

———. "Princely Identity and the Jews in Medieval France." *Wolfenbütteler Mittelalter-Studien* 11 (1996): 27–45. Reprinted in Jordan, *Ideology and Royal Power*.

Kaplan, M. Lindsay. *Figuring Racism in Medieval Christianity*. Oxford: Oxford University Press, 2019.

Kennedy, Michael. "'Faith in One God Flowed over You from the Jews, the Sons of the Patriarchs and the Prophets': William of Newburgh's Writings on Anti-Jewish Violence." *Anglo-Norman Studies* 25 (2003): 139–52.

Klepper, Deeana Copeland. "Historicizing Allegory: The Jew as Hagar in Medieval Christian Text and Image." *Church History: Studies in Christianity and Culture* 84, no. 2 (2015): 308–44.

Knowles, Jim. "Great Houses Make Not Men Holy: A Study of the Franciscan and Dominican Foundations in Medieval Oxford." https://nesolicitisitis.wordpress.com/mendicants-in-medieval-oxford/.

Krummel, Miriamne Ara. "Bringing Meir b. Elijah of Norwich into the Classroom: Discovering a Medieval Minority Poet." In *Jews in Medieval England: Teaching Representations of the Other*, edited by Miriamne Ara Krummel and Tison Pugh, 279–94. Cham: Palgrave Macmillan, 2017.

Langmuir, Gavin. *History, Religion, and Antisemitism*. Berkeley: University of California Press, 1990.

———. "'Judei Nostri' and the Beginning of Capetian Legislation." *Traditio* 16 (1960): 203–39.

———. "The Knight's Tale of Young Hugh of Lincoln." *Speculum* 47 (1972): 459–82.

Latham, R. E., D. R. Howlett, and Richard Ashdowne. *Dictionary of Medieval Latin from British Sources*. 17 vols. London: Oxford University Press for the British Academy, 1975.

Lavezzo, Kathy. *The Accommodated Jew: English Antisemitism from Bede to Milton*. Ithaca: Cornell University Press, 2016.

Le Goff, Jacques. *Saint Louis*. Paris: Gallimard, 1996.

Lewis, Suzanne. *Reading Images Narrative Discourse and Reception in the Thirteenth-Century Illuminated Apocalypse*. Cambridge: Cambridge University Press, 1995.

———. "*Tractatus Adversus Judaeos* in the Gulbenkian Apocalypse." *Art Bulletin* 68 (1986): 543–66.

Lipman, Vivian. *The Jews of Medieval Norwich*. London : Jewish historical Society of England, 1967.

Lippiatt, G. E. M. *Simon V of Montfort and Baronial Government, 1195–1218*. Oxford: Oxford University Press, 2017.

Lipton, Sara. "Isaac and Antichrist in the Archives." *Past & Present* 232 (2016): 3–44.

Little, Andrew George. *The Grey Friars in Oxford*. Oxford: Clarendon Press, 1892.

Lloyd, Simon D. "'Political Crusades' in England, c. 1215–17 and c. 1263–5." In *Crusade and Settlement: Papers Read at the First Conference of the Society for the Study of the Crusades and the Latin East and Presented to R.C. Smail*, edited by Peter W. Edbury, 113–20. Cardiff: University College Cardiff Press, 1985.

Loewe, Raphael. "The Mediaeval Christian Hebraists of England: Herbert of Bosham and Earlier Scholars." *Transactions (Jewish Historical Society of England)* 17 (1951): 225–49.

———. "The Mediaeval Christian Hebraists of England: The Superscriptio Lincolniensis." *Hebrew Union College Annual* 28 (1957): 205–52.

Logan, Donald. "Thirteen London Jews and Conversion to Christianity: Problems of Apostasy in the 1280s." *Bulletin of the Institute of Historical Research* 45, no. 112 (1972): 214–29.

Maddicott, John. "The Crusade Taxation of 1268–1270 and the Development of Parliament." In *Thirteenth Century England, II: Proceedings of the Newcastle upon Tyne Conference 198*, edited by Peter R. Coss and S. D. Lloyd, 93–117. Woodbridge: Boydell and Brewer, 1988.

———. *Simon de Montfort*. Cambridge: Cambridge University Press, 1994.

Maitland, F. "The Deacon and the Jewess; or, Apostasy at Common Law." *Transactions (Jewish Historical Society of England)* 6 (1908): 260–76.

Manix, Pam. "Oxford: Mapping the Medieval Jewry." In *The Jews of Europe in the Middle Ages (Tenth to Fifteenth Centuries)*, edited by Christoph Cluse, 405–20. Turnhout: Brepols, 2004.

Marmursztejn, Elsa. "Loi ancienne, loi nouvelle et normes chrétiennes dans la théologie scolastique du XIIIe siècle." *Revue de l'histoire des religions* 228 (2011), 509–39.

Martin, C. Trice. "The Domus Conversorum." *Transactions (Jewish Historical Society of England)* 1 (1893): 15–24.

McEvoy, James. "Robert Grosseteste on the Ten Commandments." *Recherches de Théologie Ancienne et Médiévale* 58 (1991): 167–205.

———. "The Text and Sources of the Treatise De Decem Mandatis of Robert Grosseteste." *Recherches de Théologie Ancienne et Médiévale* 58 (1991): 206–12.

McGinn, Bernard. *Antichrist: Two Thousand Years of the Human Fascination with Evil*. New York: Columbia University Press, 2000.

McGrath, Kate. "English Jews as Outlaws or Outcasts: The Ritual Murder of Little St. Hugh of Lincoln in Matthew Paris's Chronica Majora." In *British Outlaws of Literature and History: Essays on Medieval and Early Modern Figures from Robin Hood to Twm Shon Catty*, edited by Alexander L. Kaufman, 11–27. Jefferson: McFarland, 2011.

Menache, Sophia. "Matthew Paris's Attitudes Toward Anglo-Jewry." *Journal of Medieval History* 23 (1997): 139–62.

———. "Tartars, Jews, Saracens and the Jewish–Mongol 'Plot' of 1241." *History* 81 (1996): 319–42.

Meyer, Hannah. "Female Moneylending and Wet-Nursing in Jewish-Christian Relations in Thirteenth-Century England." PhD dissertation, University of Cambridge, 2009.

Mitchell, Sydney Knox. *Studies in Taxation Under John and Henry III*. New Haven: Yale University Press, 1914.

Moore, R.I. "Anti-Semitism and the Birth of Europe." *Studies in Church History* 29 (1992): 33–57.

———. *The Formation of a Persecuting Society: Power and Deviance in Western Europe: 950–1250*. Oxford: Blackwell, 1987.

Morgan, Nigel J. *The Medieval Painted Glass of Lincoln Cathedral*. London: British Academy/ Oxford University Press, 1983.

———. *Stained Glass of Lincoln Cathedral*. London: Scala, 2012.

Mundill, Robin. *England's Jewish Solution: Experiment and Expulsion, 1262–1290*. Cambridge: Cambridge University Press, 1998.

———. *The King's Jews: Money, Massacre and Exodus in Medieval England*. London: Continuum, 2010.

Musson, R. M. W. "Fatalities in British Earthquakes." *Astronomy & Geophysics* 44 (2003): 14–16.

Mutius, Hans-Georg von, ed. *Rechtsentscheide mittelalterlicher englischer Rabbinen*. Frankfurt am Main: P. Lang, 1995.

Neubauer, Adolf. "Notes on the Jews of Oxford." *Oxford Historical Society Collectanea* 2, no. 4 (1890): 277–318.

Nirenberg, David. *Anti-Judaism: The Western Tradition.* New York: W.W. Norton, 2013.

Nisse, Ruth. *Jacob's Shipwreck: Diaspora, Translation, and Jewish-Christian Relations in Medieval England.* Ithaca: Cornell University Press, 2017.

———. "A Romance of the Jewish East: The Ten Lost Tribes and The Testaments of the Twelve Patriarchs in Medieval Europe." *Medieval Encounters* 13 (2007): 499–523.

Novikoff, Alex J. *The Medieval Culture of Disputation: Pedagogy, Practice, and Performance.* Philadelphia: University of Pennsylvania Press, 2013.

Olszowy-Schlanger, Judith, ed. *Hebrew and Hebrew-Latin Documents from Medieval England: A Diplomatic and Palaeographical Study.* Turnhout: Brepols, 2015.

———. "The Knowledge and Practice of Hebrew Grammar among Christian Scholars in Pre-Expulsion England: The Evidence of «bilingual» Hebrew-Latin Manuscripts." In *Hebrew Scholarship in the Medieval World,* edited by Nicholas De Lange, 107–28. Cambridge: Cambridge University Press, 2001.

———. *Learning Hebrew in Medieval England: Christian Hebraists and the Longleat House Grammar.* Toronto: University of Toronto Press, 2021.

———. *Les manuscrits hébreux dans l'Angleterre médievale: étude historique et paléographique.* Leuven: Peeters, 2003.

———. "A School of Christian Hebraists in Thirteenth Century England: A Unique Hebrew-Latin-French and English Dictionary and Its Sources." *European Journal of Jewish Studies* 1 (2007): 249–77.

Olszowy-Schlanger, Judith, and Anne Grondeux, eds. *Dictionnaire hébreu-latin-français de la Bible hébraïque de l'Abbaye de Ramsey: XIIIe s.* Turnhout: Brepols, 2008.

Page, Christopher. *Music for the Lion-Hearted King Music to Commemorate the 800th Anniversary of the Coronation of King Richard I of England in Westminster Abbey, 3 September 1189.* London: Hyperion, 1989.

Patton, Pamela. "Blackness, Whiteness, and the Idea of Race in Medieval European Art." In *Whose Middle Ages? Teachable Moments for an Ill-Used Past,* edited by Andrew Albin, Mary C. Erler, Thomas O'Donnell, Nicholas L. Paul, and Nina Rowe, 131–39. New York: Fordham University Press, 2019.

———. "The Little Jewish Boy: Afterlife of a Byzantine Legend in Thirteenth-Century Spain." In *Byzantine Images and Their Afterlives: Essays in Honour of Annemarie Weyl Carr,* edited by Lynn Jones, 61–80. Farnham: Ashgate, 2014.

Powicke, F. "The Bull *Miramur Plurimum* and a Letter to Archbishop Stephen Langton." *English Historical Review* 44 (1929): 90–93.

———. *King Henry III and Lord Edward: The Community of the Realm in the Thirteenth Century.* 2 vols. Oxford: Oxford University Press, 1947.

Prestwich, Michael. *Edward I.* New Haven: Yale University Press, 1997.

Rabinowitz, Louis Isaac. "Peshat." In *Encyclopaedia Judaica.* 2nd. ed. Edited by Michael Berenbaum and Fred Skolnik, vol. 16, 8–9. Detroit: Macmillan Reference USA, 2007.

Rashdall, Hastings. *The Universities of Europe in the Middle Ages, Volume 3: English Universities-Student Life.* Oxford: Oxford University Press, 1936.

Ray, Jonathan. "The Jew in the Text: What Christian Charters Tell Us about Medieval Jewish Society." *Medieval Encounters* 16 (2010): 243–67.

Rees Jones, Sarah. "Neighbors and Victims in Twelfth-Century York: A Rayal Citadel, the Citizens, and the Jews of York." In Rees Jones and Watson, *Christians and Jews in Angevin England,* 15–42

Rees Jones, Sarah, and Sethina Watson, eds. *Christians and Jews in Angevin England: The York Massacre of 1190, Narratives and Contexts.* York: York Medieval Press, 2013.

Report on Manuscripts in Various Collections. Vol. 4. London: Mackie, 1907.

Resnick, Irven. "The Falsification of Scriptures and Medieval Christian and Jewish Polemics." *Medieval Encounters* 2 (1996): 344–80.

———. *Marks of Distinction: Christian Perceptions of Jews in the High Middle Ages.* Washington: Catholic University of America Press, 2012.

Richardson, Henry. *The English Jewry Under the Angevin Kings.* London: Methuen, 1960.

Rokéah, Zefira Entin. "An Anglo-Jewish Assembly or 'Mini-Parliament' in 1287." In *Thirteenth Century England, VIII: Proceedings of the Durham Conference, 1999,* edited by Michael Prestwich, Richard H. Britnell, and Robin Frame, 71–95. Woodbridge, Suffolk: Boydell and Brewer, 2001.

———. *Medieval English Jews and Royal Officials: Entries of Jewish Interest in the English Memoranda Rolls, 1266–1293.* Jerusalem: Hebrew University Magnes Press, 2000.

———. "The State, the Church and the Jews in Medieval England." In *Antisemitism Through the Ages,* edited by Shmuel Almog, 99–125. Oxford: Pergamon Press, 1988.

Rose, Emily. *The Murder of William of Norwich: The Origins of the Blood Libel in Medieval Europe.* Oxford: Oxford University Press, 2015.

———. "Royal Power and Ritual Murder: Notes on the Expulsion of the Jews from the Royal Domain of France, 1182." In *Center and Periphery: Studies on Power in the Medieval World in Honor of William Chester Jordan,* edited by Katherine L. Jansen, Guy Geltner and Anne E. Lester, 51–63. Leiden: Brill, 2013.

Roth, Cecil. *A History of the Jews in England.* 3rd edition. Oxford: Clarendon Press, 1964.

———. *The Jews of Medieval Oxford.* Oxford: Clarendon Press, 1951.

Roth, Pinchas. "Jewish Courts in Medieval England." *Jewish History* 31 (2017): 67–82.

Rowe, Nina. *The Jew, the Cathedral and the Medieval City: Synagoga and Ecclesia in the Thirteenth Century.* Cambridge: Cambridge University Press, 2014.

Rubin, Miri. *Gentile Tales: The Narrative Assault on Late Medieval Jews.* Philadelphia: University of Pennsylvania Press, 2004.

Rutledge, Elizabeth. "The Medieval Jews of Norwich and Their Legacy." In *Art, Faith and Place in East Anglia: From Prehistory to the Present,* edited by T. A. Heslop, Elizabeth Mellings and Margit Thøfner, 117–29. Woodbridge: Boydell, 2012.

Salfeld, Siegmund. *Das Martyrologium des Nürnberger Memorbuches.* Berlin: Leonhard Simeon, 1898.

Salter, H. E., ed. *Mediaeval Archives of the University of Oxford.* Oxford: Clarendon Press, 1920.

Sayers, Jane E. *Papal Government and England during the Pontificate of Honorius III (1216–1227).* Cambridge: Cambridge University Press, 1984.

Selden, John. "Of the Iewes Somtime Living in England, Colleced out of Ancient Records." In *Purchas, His Pilgrimage,* 151–63. London: William Stansby, 1626.

Sharp, Cecil James. *One Hundred English Folksongs.* Boston: Oliver Ditson, 1916.

Shatzmiller, Joseph. "Les Angevins et Les Juifs de Leurs États: Anjou, Naples et Provence." In *L'Etat angevin: pouvoir, culture et société entre XIIIe et XIVe siècle,* edited by André Vauchez, 289–300. Rome: Ecole française de Rome, 1998.

Shoham-Steiner, Ephraim. "'Vitam finivit infelilcem': Madness, Conversion and Adolescent Suicide Among Jews in Late Twelfth-Century England." In *Jews in Medieval Christendom: "Slay Them Not,"* edited by Kristine T. Utterback and Merrall Llewelyn Price, 71–90. Leiden: Brill, 2013.

Sibon, Juliette. *Chasser les Juifs pour régner: les expulsions par les rois de France au Moyen Âge*. Paris: Perrin, 2016.

———. *Les juifs au temps de saint Louis*. Paris: Albin Michel, 2017.

Simonsohn, Shlomo. *The Apostolic See and the Jews*. Toronto: Pontifical Institute of Mediaeval Studies, 1988.

Smalley, Beryl. *Hebrew Scholarship Among Christians in XIIIth Century England, as Illustrated by Some Hebrew-Latin Psalters*. London: Shapiro, Vallentine and Company, 1939.

———. *The Study of the Bible in the Middle Ages*. South Bend: Notre Dame University Press, 1964.

Smith, Lesley. "The *De Decem Mandatis* of Robert Grosseteste." In *Robert Grosseteste and the Beginnings of a British Theological Tradition*, edited by Maura O'Carroll, 265–88. Rome: Istituto storico dei Cappuccini, 2003.

Somerset, Fiona. "Complaining about the King in French in Thomas Wright's Political Songs of England." In *The French of Medieval England: Essays in Honour of Jocelyn Wogan-Browne*, edited by Thelma S. Fenster, and Carolyn P. Collette, 82–99. Cambridge: D. S. Brewer, 2017.

Sommerlechner, Andrea. "Das Judenmassaker von Fulda 1235 in Der Geschichtesschreiben Um Kaiser Friedrich II." *Römische Historische Mitteilungen* 44 (2002): 121–50.

Southern, Richard. "From Schools to University." In *The History of the University of Oxford. The Early Oxford Schools*, vol. 1, edited by J. I. Catto, 1–36. Oxford: Clarendon Press, 1984.

———. *Robert Grosseteste: The Growth of an English Mind in Medieval Europe*. Oxford: Clarendon Press, 1986.

Soyer, François. *Medieval Antisemitism?* Leeds: Arc Humanities Press, 2019.

Stacey, Robert C. "'Adam of Bristol' and Tales of Ritual Crucifixion in Medieval England." In *Thirteenth Century England XI: Proceedings of the Gregynog Conference, 2005*, edited by Bjorn Weiler, Janet Burton, and Philipp Schofield, 1–15. London: Boydell and Brewer, 2007.

———. "The Conversion of Jews to Christianity in Thirteenth-Century England." *Speculum* 67 (1992): 263–83.

———. "Crusades, Martyrdoms, and the Jews of Norman England, 1096–1190." In *Juden Und Christen Zur Zeit Der Kreuzzüge*, edited by Alfred Haverkamp, 233–51. Simarigen: Jan Thorbecke Verlag, 1999.

———. "From Ritual Crucifixion to Host Desecration: Jews and the Body of Christ." *Jewish History* 12, no. 1 (1998): 11–28.

———. "Jewish Lending and the Medieval English Economy." In *A Commercialising Economy: England 1086 to c. 1300*, edited by Richard H. Britnell and Bruce M.S. Campbell, 78–101. Manchester: Manchester University Press, 1995.

———. "Jews and Christians in Twelfth-Century England: Some Dynamics of a Changing Relationship." In *Jews and Christians in Twelfth-Century Europe*, edited by Michael A. Signer and John Van Engen, 340–54. Notre Dame: University of Notre Dame Press, 2001.

———. "The Massacres of 1189–90 and the Origins of the Jewish Exchequer, 1186–1226." In Rees Jones and Watson, *Christians and Jews in Angevin England*, 106–24.

———. "Parliamentary Negotiation and the Expulsion of the Jews from England." In *Thirteenth Century England, VI: Proceedings of the Durham Conference, 1995.*, edited by Michael Prestwich, R.H. Britnell, and Robin Frame, 77–101. Woodbridge, Suffolk: Boydell and Brewer, 1997.

———. *Politics, Policy, and Finance under Henry III, 1216–1245*. Oxford: Clarendon Press, 1987.

———. "Royal Taxation and the Social Structure of Medieval Anglo-Jewry: The Tallages of 1239–1242." *Hebrew Union College Annual* 56 (1985): 175–249.

———. "1240–60: A Watershed in Anglo-Jewish Relations?" *Historical Research* 61 (1988): 135–50.

Stocker, David A. "The Shrine of Little St. Hugh." In *Medieval Art and Architecture at Lincoln Cathedral*, edited by T. A. Heslop and V.A. Sekules, 109–17. London: British Archaeological Association, 1986.

Stokes, H. P. "Records of Mss. and Documents Possessed by the Jews in England Before the Expulsion." *Transactions (Jewish Historical Society of England)* 8 (1915): 78–97.

———. "The Relationship Between the Jews and the Royal Family of England in the Thirteenth Century." *Transactions (Jewish Historical Society of England)* 8 (1915): 153–70.

Strickland, Debra Higgs. "Edward I, Exodus, and England on the Hereford World Map." *Speculum: A Journal of Medieval Studies* 93, no. 2 (2018): 420–69.

———. *Saracens, Demons, & Jews: Making Monsters in Medieval Art*. Princeton: Princeton University Press, 2003.

Stubbs, William, ed. *Chronicles of the Reigns of Edward I and Edward II*. London: Longman, 1882.

Szpiech, Ryan. "Saracens and Church Councils, from Nablus (1120) to Vienne (1313–14)." In *Jews and Muslims Under the Fourth Lateran Council. Papers Commemorating the Octocentenary of the Fourth Lateran Council (1215)*, edited by Marie-Thérèse Champagne and Irven M. Resnick, 115–37. Turnhout: Brepols, 2019.

Tartakoff, Paola. *Conversion, Circumcision, and Ritual Murder in Medieval Europe*. Philadelphia: University of Pennsylvania Press, 2020.

Teter, Magda. "Blood Libel, a Lie and Its Legacies." In *Whose Middle Ages? Teachable Moments for an Ill-Used Past*, edited by Andrew Albin, Mary C. Erler, Thomas O'Donnell, Nicholas L. Paul, and Nina Rowe , 44–57. New York: Fordham University Press, 2019.

———. *Blood Libel: On the Trail of an Antisemitic Myth*. Cambridge: Harvard University Press, 2020.

Teulet, Alexandre, ed. *Layettes du trésor des chartes: de l'année 1224 à l'année 1246*. Paris: H. Plon, 1866.

Thomas, Hugh M. *Vassals, Heiresses, Crusaders, and Thugs: The Gentry of Angevin Yorkshire, 1154–1216*. Philadelphia: University of Pennsylvania Press, 1993.

Tiziano Dorandi, and Michele Trizio. "Editio Princeps Del *Libro Qui Vocatur Suda* Di Roberto Grossatesta." *Studio Graeco-Arabica* 4 (2014): 145–90.

Toch, Michael. "The Emergence of the Medieval Jewish Diaspora(s) of Europe from the Ninth to the Twelfth Centuries, with Some Thoughts on Historical DNA Studies." In *Regional Identities and Cultures of Medieval Jews*, edited by Javier Castaño González, Talya Fishman, and Ephraim Kanarfogel, 21–35. London: Littman Library of Jewish Civilization, 2018.

Tokarska-Bakir, Joanna. *Légendes du sang: pour une anthropologie de l'antisémitisme chrétien*. Paris: Albin Michel, 2015.

Tolan, John. "Il y a 850 ans, à Blois, 32 juifs furent envoyés au bûcher." *Le Monde*. May 26, 2021. https://www.lemonde.fr/le-monde-des-religions/article/2021/05/26/il-y-a-850-ans-a-blois -32-juifs-furent-envoyes-au-bucher_6081483_6038514.html.

———. "Lachrymabilem judeorum questionem: la brève histoire de la communauté juive de Bretagne au XIIIe siècle." In *Hommes, cultures et paysages de l'Antiquité à la période moderne*, edited by Monique Clavel-Lévêque, Fatima Ouachour, and Isabelle Pimouguet-Pédarros, 417–32. Rennes: Presses universitaires de Rennes, 2012.

———. "Of Milk and Blood: Innocent III and the Jews, Revisited." In *Jews & Christians in Thirteenth-Century France*, edited by Elisheva Baumgarten and Judah Galinksy, 139–49. London: Routledge, 2015.

———. *Petrus Alfonsi and His Medieval Readers*. Gainesville: University Press of Florida, 1993.

———. "Royal Policy and Conversion of Jews to Christianity in Thirteenth-Century Europe." In *Contesting Inter-Religious Conversion in the Medieval World*, edited by Yaniv Fox and Yosi Yisraeli, 96–111. London: Routledge, 2017.

Tovey, D'Blossiers. *Anglia Judaica*. Oxford: Fletcher, 1738.

Tovey, D'Blossiers, and Elizabeth Pearl. *Anglia Judaica or a History of the Jews in England*. London: G. Weidenfeld and Nicolson, 1990.

Trabut-Cussac, Jean-Paul. *L'Administration anglaise en Gascogne sous Henry III et Édouard I de 1254 à 1307*. Genève: Droz, 1972.

Tyerman, Christopher. *England and the Crusades, 1095–1588*. Chicago: University of Chicago Press, 1988.

Utz, Richard J. "Der Heilige Hugh von Lincoln: Hugh von Lincoln Und der Mythos Vom Jüdischen Ritualmord." In *Herrscher, Helden, Heilige*, edited by Ulrich Müller and Werner Wunderlich, 681–92. St. Gallen: Universitätsverlag Konstanz, 1996.

Van Liere, Frans. "Andrew of St. Victor, Jerome, and the Jews: Biblical Scholarship in the Twelfth-Century Renaissance." In *Scripture and Pluralism: Reading the Bible in the Religiously Plural Worlds of the Middle Ages and Renaissance*, edited by Thomas Heffernan and Thomas Burman, 59–75. Leiden: Brill, 2005.

Vincent, Nicholas. *The Holy Blood: King Henry III and the Westminster Blood Relic*. Cambridge: Cambridge University Press, 2001.

———. "Jews, Poitevins and the Bishop of Winchester, 1231–34." *Studies in Church History* 29 (1992): 119–32.

———. *Peter Des Roches: An Alien in English Politics, 1205–1238*. Cambridge: Cambridge University Press, 1996.

———. "Simon de Montfort's First Quarrel with King Henry III." In *Thirteenth Century England IV: Proceedings of the Newcastle upon Tyne Conference 1991*, edited by P. Coss and S. Lloyd, 167–77. London: Boydell and Brewer, 1992.

———. "Two Papal Letters on the Wearing of the Jewish Badge, 1221 and 1229." *Jewish Historical Studies* 34 (1997): 209–24.

Visscher, Eva De. *Reading the Rabbis: Christian Hebraism in the Works of Herbert of Bosham*. Leiden: Brill, 2014.

Wasserstein, David. "Grosseteste, the Jews, and Medieval Christian Hebraism." In *Robert Grosseteste: New Perspectives on His Thought and Scholarship*, edited by James McEvoy, 357–76. Turnhout: Brepols, 1995.

Watt, Jack. "Parisian Theologians and the Jews: Peter Lombard and Peter Cantor." In *The Medieval Church: Universities, Heresy, and Christian Life: Essays in Honour of Gordon Leff*, edited by Peter Biller and Barrie Dobson, 55–76. Woodbridge: Boydell and Brewer, 1999.

Watt, John. "The English Episcopate, the State and the Jews: The Evidence of the Thirteenth-Century Conciliar Decrees." In *Thirteenth Century England, II: Proceedings of the Newcastle upon Tyne Conference 1987*, edited by Peter R. Coss and S. D. Lloyd, 137–47. Woodbridge, Suffolk: Boydell and Brewer, 1988.

———. "Grosseteste and the Jews: A Commentary on Letter V." In *Robert Grosseteste and the Beginnings of a British Theological Tradition*, edited by Maura O'Carroll, 201–16. Roma: Istituto Storico dei Cappuccini, 2003.

———. "Jews and Christians in the Gregorian Decretals." *Studies in Church History* 29 (1992): 93–105.

————. "The Jews, the Law, and the Church: The Concept of Jewish Serfdom in Thirteenth-Century England." In *The Church and Sovereignty, c.590–1918: Essays in Honour of Michael Wilks*, vol. 9, edited by Diana Wood, 153–72. Studies in Church History, Subsidia. Oxford: Blackwell, 1991.

Whitaker, Cord. *Black Metaphors: How Modern Racism Emerged from Medieval Race-Thinking*. Philadelphia: University of Pennsylvania Press, 2019.

Williams, John, ed. *Annales Cambriae*. London: Longman, Green, Roberts, 1860.

Wolfe, Robert, and Janet Wolfe. "Notes for Magister Omer," *Janet and Robert Wolfe Genealogy*. www.umich.edu/~bobwolfe/gen/pn/p20439.htm.

Wright, Thomas. *The Political Songs of England: From the Reign of John to That of Edward II*. London: Camden Society, 1839.

Wyrwa, Ulrich. "The Making of Antisemitism in Nineteenth-Century Europe as an Invention of Tradition." In *The Medieval Roots of Antisemitism: Continuities and Discontinuities from the Middle Ages to the Present Day*, edited by Jonathan Adams and Cordelia Hess, 30–41. London: Routledge, 2018.

Yarrow, Simon. *Saints and Their Communities: Miracle Stories in Twelfth Century England*. Oxford: Clarendon Press, 2010.

Yuval, Israel Jacob. *Two Nations in Your Womb: Perceptions of Jews and Christians in Late Antiquity and the Middle Ages*. Berkeley: University of California Press, 2008.

Zerner, Monique. "L'épouse de Simon de Montfort et la croisade albigeoise." In *Femmes. Mariages–Lignages, XIIe-XIVe Siècles: Melanges Offert à Georges Duby*, edited by Jean Dufournet, 449–70. Bruxelles: De Boeck-Wesmael, 1992.

INDEX

Aaron ben Isaac, 90–91
Aaron le Blund, 175
Aaron of Lincoln, 19, 37, 140
Aaron of York, 101, 119, 121
Abelard, Peter, 11
Abraham Crespin, 104
Abraham ben Jacob, 157
Abraham of Berkhamsted, 130
Abulafia, Ana, 13
Adam of Ensham, 26
Adam of Illeg, 36–37
Adam of Winchester, 158
Alan La Zouche, 163
Albigensian crusade, 65–66
Alexander III, 41, 42
Alexander IV, 139, 148
Alexander of Stainsby, 129–130
Alfonsi, Petrus, 85–86, 88
Alice de Montmorency, 66–67
Amaury V of Montfort, 67, 70
Ambler, Sophie, 145
Andrew of St. Victor, 84–85
Anjou: expulsion of Jews from, 180–182
annulment of debts, 27, 140, 162–163, 217n54
Antichrist, 78, 131
anti-Jewish violence, 9, 20–27, 82, 140;
    accusations of Jewish ritual murder and,
    125, 127–128, 130, 136–138, 156, 188; baronial
    revolts and, 140, 149, 151–155, 159; in Bury
    St. Edmonds, 24–25; in Canterbury,
    155–156, 161; conversion and, 75; coronation
    of Richard I and, 19; Crusades and, 13,
    20–22, 33, 82, 123, 164, 166, 191; destruction
    of synagogues, 154, 159; fines for, 26;
    following Civil War, 158–159; in France,
    81–82; justifications for, 155–156; in
    Lincoln, 26; in London, 28, 149–150,
    152–155, 159; moneylending and, 23–24;

Newburgh on, 22; in Norwich, 1, 22, 81; in
    Oxford, 110–111; Simon de Montfort and,
    66; in Winchester, 158; in York, 22–23.
    See also expulsion of English Jews
anti-Judaism, 12, 138, 191
anti-Semitism, 11–13, 138, 189–190; contrasted
    with anti-Judaism, 11–12, 138, 191; financial
    exploitation of Jews and, 138; as racism,
    11–13. *See also* anti-Jewish violence
apostasy, 57, 63, 86, 93, 172–173, 189–190,
    220n55
Archae system, 26, 38–39, 151, 161
Arendt, Hannah, 11
Aristotle, 105
Arnold fitz Thedmar, 154, 155
Assize of Arms, 19
Augustine, 45, 107, 109
"Augustinian" doctrine, 12, 114
Aymer of Lusignan, 145

Bacon, Robert, 101–102, 105, 113, 120
badges, wearing of by Jews, 4, 8, 40, 52–57,
    60–62, 116–118, 142–143, 202n55;
    enforcement of, 56, 62, 71, 143; in Oxford
    town, 83–84; payments to avoid, 7, 54–57,
    78, 84, 100
Baldwin, John, 46
Baldwin II, 121
Barnabas de Stukeley, 142
Baron, Salo, 16
baronial revolt (1263-1265), 8, 139–140,
    147–154, 157; anti-Jewish violence and, 140,
    149, 151–155, 159; arbitration by Louis IX,
    151; as crusade, 151
"barons' crusade," 82
Basset, Fulk, 144
Battle of Bouvines, 4, 50
Battle of Lewes, 156–157

Baumgarten, Elisheva, 16

Beatrice of Savoy, 82

Becket, Thomas, 41, 46, 50, 85, 145, 157; jubilee of, 54

Berekhia ha-Naqdan, 23, 85–86

Berengaudus, 131

bet din, 38, 102

Bicchieri, Guala, 30, 50, 53–54

Blanche de Castile, 64, 89

blood libel, 4, 128–129, 138

Blund, Elias, 121

Blund, John, 77

Blunville, Thomas, 80

Boniface of Savoy, 114, 143, 145–146, 148

Book of Hours, 93–98

Bouchard V de Montmorency, 67

British Movement, 188–189

Burnell, Robert, 173

Bury St. Edmunds, 24–25, 65, 70

butchers, 9–10, 44, 178

Cain/Abel (biblical story), 13, 44–45, 48–49, 109

Calixtus II, 32

Canterbury city: anti-Jewish violence in, 155–156, 161

Canterbury Tales (Chaucer), 124–125

Carpenter, David, 119

Celestine III, 42

censura ecclesiastica, 60–61

Charles I of Anjou, 167, 181

Charles II of Anjou, 180–181

Chaucer, Geoffrey, 124–125, 189

Chazan, Robert, 180, 191

Child, James, 188

Christian Hebraism, 84–90

Chrysostom, John, 106–107

Clement III, 42

Clement IV, 173, 181

Cluse, Christoph, 166

coin clipping, 101, 121, 171–172, 175, 184

Cok Fitz Abraham, 153–154

Comitissa, 37–38

Constantine Fitz Aluf, 72

Constitution pro Judeis, 43

conversions, 101–102, 205n40; apostasy and, 57, 63, 86, 93, 172–173, 189–190, 220n55; converts' return to Judaism, 102, 120, 172–173; forced conversion of Jews, 42, 66–67, 154; Muslim converts to Christianity, 5; seizure of possessions following, 74,

172; testimony of converts, 125, 171–172. *See also domus conversorum*

Copin, 125

Council of Oxford, 40, 57–58, 118; canons issued by, 57–60; Langton and, 45

Council of Westminster (1175), 41

Cristia, Pablo, 90

Cromwell, Oliver, 187, 189

cross-breaking incident, 164–167

Crusades: Albigensian crusade, 65–66; anti-Jewish violence and, 13, 20–22, 33, 82, 123, 164, 166, 191; baronial revolt as, 151; "barons' crusade," 82; English Civil War as, 158; Fifth Crusade, 32–33; First Crusade, 13, 20, 166, 191; funding of, 8–9, 121–123, 144, 164, 167–168; Henry III and, 9, 121–122, 144; John as crusader, 28–29; Mainz massacre of 1096 and, 13, 20, 160, 164, 166, 191; Second Crusade, 20, 42; Sicily campaign and, 144

Dahan, Gilbert, 86

David of Ashby, 163

David of Oxford, 72, 100–103

De cessatione legalium (Grosseteste, 1230s), 83, 107–108

Deulecresse, 91–92

Deulesalt, 127

Dickens, Charles, 189

Disputation Against Symon the Jew, 49

Dobson, R.B., 24

Dominicans, 99–100

domus conversorum, 7, 14, 64, 71–75, 124, 172, 205n40; funding of, 73–74, 103

Edmund, 123, 144, 170; Crusades and, 164

Edward I: anti-Jewish edicts of, 9; baronial revolt and, 150–151; captured at Lewes, 157; Charles of Anjou and, 181; conversion of Jews and, 172; cross-breaking incident and, 165; Crusades and, 164, 167, 180; defeat of rebels by, 158–159; *Domius conversorum* and, 74, 172; expulsion of English Jews and, 2, 9, 161, 170, 179–180, 183, 187; Hugh of Lincoln and, 187; Italian financing of, 169–170; moneylending and, 168, 182; relationship with English Jews, 149, 169–172, 187

Einbinder, Susan, 15, 160, 184

Eleanor of Provence, 5, 82, 142, 144, 150; expulsion of English Jews and, 170; moneylending and, 173

Elias fitz Moses, 139–142, 146–147, 163
Elias of London, 124
Ephraim of Bonn, 21
Etsi Iudeos, 44–45
Etsi non displiceat Domino, 43–45
Eugenius III, 42
expulsion of English Jews, 2–3, 76–77, 80, 161,
    183; accusations of Jewish ritual murder
    and, 191; aftermath of, 189; Edward I and, 2,
    9, 170, 179–180, 183; expulsion from Bury,
    25; Henry III and, 71, 80; Hugh of Lincoln
    and, 187; Jews prevented from leaving
    England, 32, 120, 124; from Leicester, 7,
    64–71, 75, 80; Statute of the Jews and,
    117–118, 120; usury and, 68–69, 181–182
expulsion of French Jews, 4, 15, 19, 138, 160;
    accusations of Jewish ritual murder and,
    128; expulsion from Anjou, 180–182;
    expulsion from Gascony, 179–180; Jewish
    primary sources and, 161

Fermin of Amiens, 75
Fifth Crusade, 32–33
First Council of Lyon, 114
First Crusade, 13, 20, 166, 191; Mainz
    massacres and, 13, 20, 160, 164, 166, 191
Fitz John, John, 153–154
Fogle, Lauren, 74
Forbes, Ronnie and Joan, 188
Fourth Lateran Council, 4, 40, 42–43, 50–51,
    53–54; badge mandate and, 57, 60;
    moneylending and, 54, 198n78; usury and, 35
Franciscan faith, 105
Frederick II, 81, 122, 128–129, 136
Fulda: accusations of Jewish ritual murder in,
    128–129

Gabbay, Abraham, 38
Gacelyn, Geoffrey, 162
Gascony: expulsion of Jews from, 179–180
Gautier de Coincy, 132–133
Gemma ecclesiastica (Jewel of the Church)
    (Gerald of Wales, c. 1187), 91–92
Geoffrey, John Fitz, 145, 153
Geoffrey de Lusignan, 142
Geoffrey de Mandeville, 28
Geoffrey de Vinsauf, 30
Geoffrey of Lusignan, 142
Gerald of Wales, 91, 93, 104
Gilbert of Clare, 150, 155–156, 159
Giles of Bridport, 142

Gilroy, Paul, 190
Geoffrey V Plantagenet, 4
Graecus, Nicholas, 112
Grant, Richard, 62
Grayzel, Solomon, 177
Gregorian reform movement, 10
Gregory IX, 6, 62, 77; anti-Jewish violence
    and, 81–82; moneylending and, 101;
    Talmud and, 87–89, 103, 177
Gregory X, 138
Grimbaud, Peter, 80
Grosseteste, Robert, 7–8, 68–69, 71, 83,
    104–115, 191, 203n12; Christian Hebraism
    and, 84, 87, 113; Greek translations by,
    112–113; Henry III and, 114–115, 122–123;
    on moneylending, 109–112; pastoral duties
    of, 105; on Paul's letter to the Galatians,
    107–108; Psalms and, 84, 105–107, 113;
    scientific works produced by, 105; taxation
    and, 120, 122
Guillaume de Beaumont, 69
Guillaume de Chartres, 5–6
"Gulbenkian Apocalypse" (c. 1265–1270),
    131–133
Guy de Lusignan, 142

Hagar, 45–48
Hames, Harvey, 179
Hamo, 34, 39
Heng, Geraldine, 11, 26
Henry I, 4, 50, 91
Henry II, 3–4, 19; English Church and, 46;
    moneylending and, 24; relationship with
    English Jews, 41, 42; taxation and, 23
Henry III, 5, 61, 139; actions after Civil War,
    160–162; annulment of debts by, 162;
    anti-Jewish violence and, 81, 138; anti-
    Semitism and, 138; badge mandate and, 8,
    52–53, 56, 116–118; baronial revolt and, 8,
    140, 147–154; captured at Lewes, 157;
    coronation of, 33; cross-breaking incident
    and, 164–167; Crusades and, 9, 121–122,
    144; death of, 169; defeat of rebels by,
    158–159; documentation and, 14; *Domius
    conversorum* and, 14, 64, 71–75, 103,
    205n40; expulsion of English Jews and, 71,
    80; Grosseteste and, 114–115; Hugh of
    Lincoln and, 116, 125–127, 134–135, 137–138;
    Isaac of Norwich and, 17; Jewish-Christian
    relations and, 61–63; Magna Carta and, 9,
    30, 123; moneylending and, 75–76, 168;

Henry III (continued)
   prostitution and, 105; as protector of
      English Jews, 4–5, 8–9, 17, 33–34, 62, 99,
      127, 160–162, 168; Provisions of Oxford
      and, 151; regency of, 5, 30–31, 38, 52–53, 56;
      relationship with English Jews, 17, 64, 77,
      91, 102, 116, 120, 124, 144, 161, 168, 205n40;
      Sicilian campaign and, 122–123, 144–145,
      148; Statute of the Jews and, 117–118,
      122–124; struggle against Louis VIII,
      64–65, 119; tallages and, 3, 34, 65, 78,
      118–121; Treaty of Paris and, 148
Henry of Winchester, 171–172
Herbert of Bosham, 85–87, 107
Hereford, 33–34
Herlicun, John, 72
Hillaby, Joe, 34, 175–176
History Cold Case, 1
Honorius III, 54, 60–61; badge mandate and,
      56–57
Honorius IV, 177
Howell, Margaret, 149
Horowitz, Elliot, 166
Hubert de Burgh, 35, 57, 61, 71, 77
Hugh, Bishop of Lincoln, 26, 104
Hugh de Vivonne, 78
Hugh Fitz Otto, 161
Hugh of Foliot, 104
Hugh of Lincoln, 116, 124–128, 134–137, 156,
      187–189; canonization of, 188–189; Edward
      I and, 187; expulsion of English Jews and,
      187; liminal figures and, 136; shrine to,
      187–188; trial of Lincoln Jews and, 137
Hugh of Lusignan, 119, 139
Hugh of St. Victor, 84–85

Ihnat, Kati, 93
inherited debt, 29, 36–37
Innocent III, 9–10, 13, 43–45, 63, 99, 109;
      Becket and, 46; expulsion of Jews and, 69;
      Fourth Lateran Council and, 50–51; Guala
      and, 53; Langton and, 49; Magna Carta
      and, 29–30
Innocent IV, 114, 123; burning of Jewish
      books and, 89; crusading taxes and, 121–122
intra-Jewish conflict, 102
Isaac of Canterbury, 28
Isaac of Norwich, 6, 17, 18–19, 34–39; arrest
      of, 27–28; Comitissa and, 37–38; death of,
      81; fining of, 28, 198n69, 200n107;
      imprisonment of, 6, 18; as moneylender, 32,

34–37, 78; Peter des Roches and, 38, 78;
      political cartoon about, 78–80; release
      from prison, 31–32; tallages and, 38, 78
Isabella (sister of Henry III), 81
Ishmael 13, 45-48

Jacob ben Judah, 184
Jacob fitz Moses, 169
Jacob fitz Mossey, 164
Jacob of Exeter, 120
Jaume I, 74
Jean de Joinville, 5–6
Jewish boy of Bourges, 132–134
Jewish-Christian relations, 9–10, 16, 61–62,
      174–177, 190–191; accusations of Jewish
      ritual murder, 116, 124–130, 134–138, 154,
      178–179, 188; censura ecclesiastica and,
      60–61; Christian servants in Jewish homes,
      7–8, 39, 40, 42–44, 54, 59, 61–62, 71,
      80–81, 117, 142–143, 170–171, 179, 191;
      conversion of Jews (See conversions);
      differential punishments and, 163, 171, 191;
      fraternization and, 174–179, 190–191;
      Hebrew language and, 87; Hugh of Lincoln
      and, 125–127; Innocent III and, 43–44;
      intermixed neighborhoods, 152; Jewish
      money kept in Christian churches, 25, 54,
      60, 110, 196n32; moneylending and, 25, 51,
      54; Mongol invasion and, 130–131; in
      Oxford town, 83–84; papal bulls regarding,
      41–44, 69, 81–82, 109, 177, 181; purchase of
      Jewish debt by Christians, 139–142;
      religious prohibitions against commerce,
      61; restrictions on Jewish landholding and,
      168–169; selling of food and, 44, 117, 171,
      178, 191; sexual relations, 4, 10, 17, 40,
      57–60, 63, 118, 143–144, 175, 189, 191;
      sharing of meals, 10, 16, 175, 178; Statute of
      Jewry (1275), 170–171; Statute of the Jews
      (1253), 7, 64, 117–120, 122–124; Statute of
      the Jews and, 117–118; Third Lateran
      Council and, 42–43; violence against Jews
      (See anti-Jewish violence); wet nurses, 45,
      63, 110, 117, 137
Jewish ownership of Church property,
      41–42
Jewish primary sources, 15, 160, 183–186
Jocelin of Brakelond, 24–25
John I, 4–5, 27; anti-Jewish activities of, 27, 31,
      34; as crusader, 28–29; death of, 30;
      excommunication of, 99; Innocent III and,

49; Magna Carta and, 29–30; moneylending and, 36; rebellion against, 28–30; tallages and, 17, 18; war with Philip II, 49–50
John de Bokeland, 162
John de Gray, 49
John de Warenne, 163
John de Wincle, 137
John of Basingstroke, 57–58, 112
John of Darlington, 137
John of Lexington, 134–136
Jordan, William, 7–8, 9, 65, 68–69, 71, 83, 104–115, 191
Josche Solomon ben "Salle," 161
Joseph of Chartres, 23
Josephus, 23, 93, 208n36
Judah ben David, 88–89

Kaplan, Lindsay, 13

Lambeth council, 148–149
Langmuir, Gavin, 12, 138
Langton, Stephen, 7, 29, 40, 45–50; as archbishop, 49–50, 54, 56, 99; biblical interpretations of, 46–49; *censura ecclesiastica* and, 60–61; Dominican friars and, 100; royal power and, 61
Lateran Councils. *See* Third Lateran Council; Fourth Lateran Council
Le Goff, Jacques, 5
Leicester: expulsion of Jews from, 7, 64–71, 75, 80
Leo of York, 101
Licoricia (wife of David of Oxford), 102–103
Lincoln: anti-Jewish violence in, 26; Jewish boy of Bourges and, 132–134. *See also* Hugh of Lincoln
Lipton, Sarah, 78
Llewellyn of Wales, 150
Lombard, Peter, 85, 106
London massacre of 1264, 149–150, 152–155, 159, 160; restoration of properties following, 161–162
Louis VIII, 4–5, 30, 64–65; relationship with French Jews, 69
Louis IX, 5–6, 119, 121; anti-Jewish violence and, 82; anti-Semitism of, 5–6, 123–124; as Crusader, 121, 163–164, 167; English baronial revolt and, 151; moneylending and, 70; seizure of Jewish books and, 88–89, 123; Treaty of Paris and, 148
Lovel, Philip, 149

Magna Carta, 29–30, 50, 123
Mainz massacre of 1096, 13, 20, 160, 164, 166, 191
Malebysse, Richard, 22
al-Malik al-Kamil, 33
Manfred, 181
Mansell, John, 149
Margaret de Quincy, 68, 70, 109–110
Margaret of Winchester, 104, 112, 221n58
Marguerite of Provence, 5
Marsh, Adam, 105, 111
Marshal, William, 30–32, 52, 99
Marshall, William, 33
Masada, 22–23
Matthew Paris, 14–15, 57–58, 81, 119, 122, 144; accusations of Jewish ritual murder and, 126, 130; Mongol invasion and, 131
Mauclerck, Walter, 71–73, 100
Maurice fitz Abraham, 162
Meir ben Elijah, 15, 184–186
Meir of Rothenburg, 90
Merton College, 104, 165
moneylending, 3, 31, 140, 168; annulment of debts, 27, 140, 162–163, 217n54; anti-Jewish violence and, 23–24, 162; *Archae* system and, 26; Church payment of debts and, 104; collateral for, 19, 103, 140; Crusades and, 114; David of Oxford and, 100–101; Edward's banning of, 182; Eleanor of Provence and, 173; following Civil War, 157–158; Fourth Lateran Council and, 51; in France, 70; Grosseteste on, 109–112; Henry III and, 104, 109; inherited debt and, 29, 36–37; Isaac of Norwich as moneylender, 6, 32, 34–37, 78; Jewish-Christian cooperation and, 24–25, 51, 54; Lateran IV and, 54, 198n78; Magna Carta and, 29; monastic financial activities and, 140–141; Papal bulls and, 43–44; perpetual fee debts and, 168; *Petitio baronum* and, 146; purchase of Jewish debt by Christians, 139–142, 146–147, 163, 168; selling of debts and, 139; tallages and, 182; use of churches in, 60; usury and, 44, 69–70, 75–77, 101, 111, 169–170, 172–174; violence and, 37; women as moneylenders, 39
Mongol invasion, 130–131
Monmouth, Thomas, 127
Moore, R. I., 10, 12, 138
Mortimer, Roger, 151
Moses of Wallingford, 91–92

"Mosse Mokke," 78
Muhammad I al-Mustansir, 167

Nachmanides of Gerona, 90
Nicholas de Ewelme, 164
Nicholas de Triveti, 100, 113
Nicholas de Turri, 137
Nicholas IV, 181
Nicholas of Donin, 88–89, 114, 129
Nicolò of Tusculum, 50, 99
Nimis in partibus Anglie (Honorius IV, 1286),
    177
Norman conquest, 2
Norwich: anti-Jewish violence in, 1, 22, 81.
    See also Isaac of Norwich
Norwich Day Book, 34

Odo of Chateauroux, 89
Olszowy-Schlanger, Judith, 87, 140–141
Ordonnances de Melun, 75, 77
Otto IV, 28
Oxford, Provisions of. See Provisions of
    Oxford
Oxford city, 7–8, 99–100; anti-Jewish
    violence in, 110–111; cross-breaking
    incident in, 164–167; Dominicans in, 100;
    intra-Jewish conflict in, 102; Jewish
    cemetery in, 91–92, 190; Jewish population
    of, 83–84, 91, 98–100; preparations for
    Crusade in, 164; town/university conflict,
    111
Oxford Council, 40, 62, 142–143
Oxford University, 7–8, 99; Grosseteste and,
    104; Jewish money and, 2, 90, 190; town/
    university conflict, 111

Pandulf Verraccio, 35–36, 50, 53–54, 56
Parhon, Ibn, 86
Parliament of Oxford, 145–147
Passelewe, Robert, 80
Passelewe, Simon, 137, 149
Peace of Caltabellotta, 181
Peckham, John, 170, 172–173, 177
Pessim, Nicholas, 162
Peter de Rivallis, 77–78, 80
Peter des Roches, 6, 30, 32, 35, 50, 80; as
    crusader, 33; Domus conversorum and,
    71–72; expulsion of English Jews and,
    77–78; Isaac of Norwich and, 38, 78;
    purchase of Jewish loans by, 140
Peter of Blois, 23

Peter of Brittany, 64–65
Peter of Cluny, 88
Peter of Cornwall, 49
Peter of Nereford, 37
Peter the Chanter, 45, 46
Petitio baronum, 139, 146–147
Philip II, 4, 19, 27; expulsion of French Jews
    and, 19, 65, 67, 128, 138, 182; military
    victories of, 28; war with John, 49–50, 66
Philip IV, 15, 160
Philip of St. Frideswide, 91–92
Pinche, Abraham, 128
plea rolls of the exchequer, 14, 35, 37
political cartoons, 78–80
Provisions of Oxford, 139, 142, 144, 147–150;
    Canterbury council and, 143–144
Psalms: Book of Hours and, 94–95; Christian
    Hebraism and, 85–87; Grosseteste on, 84,
    105–107, 113
Psalterium cum commento (Herbert, 1190s), 85
"Put a Curse on My Enemy" (Meir ben
    Elijah), 15, 184–186

racism, 190–192; anti-Semitism and, 11–13
Ralph de Hengham, 172
Ralph of Carlisle, 28
Ralph of Coggeshall, 22, 28
Ralph of Diceto, 21–22
Ramsey Abbey, 86–87
Ranulf de Blundeville, 67
Rashi of Troyes, 88
Ray, Jonathan, 14
Raymond Berenger, count of Provence, 82
Rhineland massacres of 1096, 13, 20, 160, 164,
    166, 191
Riccardi of Lucca, 169
Richard de Clare, 128
Richard de Gravesend, 114, 125, 170–171
Richard I, 4, 19–20, 66, 124; anti-Jewish
    violence and, 20–21, 26; captured at Lewes,
    157; coronation of, 20–21; Crusades and, 19,
    21; Hugh of Lincoln trial and, 125–126
Richard of Canterbury, 24, 41, 92
Richard of Cornwall, 130, 147, 152
Richardson, Gerald, 77, 180
Rigord, 128, 138, 156
ritual murder, accusations of, 116, 124–130,
    134–138, 154, 178–179, 188–189, 191; liminal
    figures and, 136; trials of Jews for, 116,
    125–126, 137. See also Hugh of Lincoln
Robert de Beaumont IV, 64

Robert de Cokfeld, 35
Robert de Crepping, 158
Robert de Cricklade, 93
Robert de Ferrars, 151
Robert de Reading "Haggai," 170
Robert Fitz Walter, 18, 30
Roger de Lakenham, 178
Roger de Parten, 72
Roger de Thirkelby, 137
Roger of Howden, 20–22
Roger of Wendover, 14–15, 20, 27–28, 30, 50, 65, 81
Rose, Emily, 127
Roth, Cecil, 56, 83–84, 142, 177
Rubin, Miri, 12
Russell, Abraham, 144

Saer de Harecurt, 162
St. Frideswide, 91–93, 110–111, 164–165; cross toppling incident and, 164–166
Saladin (Salah ad-Din) 20
Sampson, Abbot, 24–25, 70
Sanderson, Robert, 187
Sarah/Hagar (biblical story), 46–48
Second Crusade, 20, 42
Selden, John, 187
servitus Iudeorum, 13
Shakespeare, William, 189
Sicilian campaign, 122–123, 144–145, 148
Sicilian Vespers, 181
Sicut Judaeis, 42
Simon de Montfort, 7–8, 66, 148; ancestry of, 66–67; anti-Jewish violence and, 8, 153, 155–156, 158–159; conflict with Henry III, 148, 150–151, 156–159; as crusader, 151; death of, 158; expulsion of Leicester Jews and, 64–66, 68–71; as protector of Jews, 157–158; taxation and, 120, 158
Simon de Novers, 127
slavery, 2, 190; Jewish ownership of Christian slaves, 59; as punishment for Jews, 13, 44–45; servitus Iudeorum and, 13
Smalley, Beryl, 113–114
Solomon ben Joseph, 82
Southern, Richard, 109, 191
Soyer, François, 12–13
Stacey, Robert, 9, 21, 75, 119, 179
Statute of Jewry (1275), 170–171
Statute of the Jews (1253), 7, 64, 117–120, 122–124
Stephen, 2–3, 90–91

Stocker, David, 187
Suda, 112
Swinfield, Richard, 170, 174–177
synagogues, 22, 44, 177; construction of in London, 172–173; destruction of, 154, 159; in Oxford, 100, 165–166; prohibitions on building, 42–43, 59, 117–118, 173, 178

tallages, 3, 6, 18, 101; Civil War and, 158; conversion and, 75; under Edward I, 169, 171, 179, 182–183; fines in lieu of, 167–168; funding of Crusades and, 121–123, 144, 149, 167–168; in Gascony, 180; under Henry III, 34, 65, 118–121; Isaac of Norwich and, 38, 78; raising of money for, 139–140; Sicilian campaign and, 144–145
Talmud, 13, 86–90, 114, 129, 177, 191; burning of, 6, 89–90, 103, 123, 129
Tartakoff, Paola, 81, 172
taxes. See tallages
Testaments of the Twelve Patriarchs (trans. Grosseteste, 1242), 112–113
Theobald of Saxony, 90
Thibaut V, 128, 138–139
Third Lateran Council, 74
Thomas, Hugh, 23
Thomas de Brugg, 176
Thomas de Burgo, 24
Thomas de Heningham, 80–81
Thomas de Neville, 32
Thomas of Cantilupe, 158, 172, 174–175, 183
Thomas of Monmouth, 127
treaty of Lambeth, 18, 30
Treaty of Paris, 148
Turbe, Solomon, 38
Turbe, William, 127

Urban IV, 148
usury, 44, 69–70, 101, 172–174; Edward I opposition to, 170, 174, 180; expulsion of Jews and, 68–69, 181–182; Henry III opposition to, 104, 109; Louis IX opposition to, 75, 123–124; religious prohibition of, 35, 82. See also moneylending
Ut esset Cain, 44–45

Vincent, Nicholas, 157

Walter de Bersted, 149
Walter de Cantilupe, 110, 144–145
Walter de Lacy, 33–34, 39

Walter de Merton, 8, 104, 140
Walter de Wauz, 162
Walter of Thorpe, 36
Westminster Abbey, 122; moneylending and, 35–36
Whitaker, Cord, 11–12
William de Beauchamp, 141–142
William de Beaumont, 31
William de Blois, 53, 62
William de Brailes, 93–98, 132
William de la Barre, 104
William de Lergton, 137
William de Longchamp, 85
William de Vere, 104

William de Walsham, 35
William fitz Isabelle, 24
William of Newburgh, 22
William of Norwich, 116, 127, 191
William of Valence, 142, 147
William of Warblington, 101
William the Conqueror, 4
Wykes, Thomas, 152–155
Wyrwa, Ulrich, 188

Yehiel ben Joseph, 88–89
Yom Tov, 172
Yom Tov of Joigny, 23
York: anti-Jewish violence in, 22–23